PRESERVING YOUR AMERICAN HERITAGE

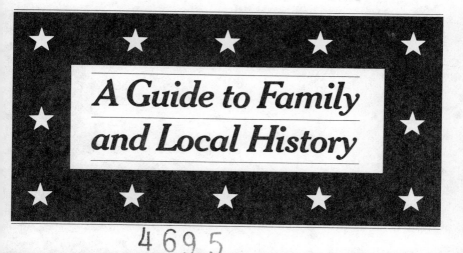

A Guide to Family and Local History

PRESERVING YOUR AMERICAN HERITAGE

Norman E. Wright

A Guide to Family and Local History

Brigham Young University Press

Library of Congress Cataloging in Publication Data

Wright, Norman Edgar.
Preserving your American heritage.

Edition for 1974 published under title: Building an American pedigree.
Bibliography: p. 253
Includes index.
1. United States—Genealogy. 2. United States—History—Sources—Bibliography. I. Title.
CS47.W68 1981 929'.1'072073 80-27934
ISBN 0-8425-1863-0

Library of Congress Catalog Card Number: 80-27934
International Standard Book Number: 0-8425-1863-0
Brigham Young University Press, Provo, Utah 84602

Printed in the United States of America
7/81 48006

Contents

Preface and Acknowledgments

This book has been written for those who want to learn more about their personal heritage and who want to record that information in an acceptable manner for historical preservation. A practical guide, it is based upon my own training and experience, with emphasis on source materials and their use. Although directed to the American researcher, these principles may be used successfully by others if applied correctly.

I have included illustrations of documents to make the book more helpful to the beginner and the teacher in the classroom. Both the amateur and the professional will find the book useful because of its step-by-step approach and its in-depth coverage of the subject.

The present work is an extensive revision of *Building an American Pedigree* published by Brigham Young University Press in 1974. I have rearranged much of the earlier information for better effect, added new chapters, and placed genealogy and family history in proper perspective. I also have included a chapter on the genealogy and family history of the North American Indian. For seven years I instructed a course in this subject at Brigham Young University that was a pioneer work in the field. The information included in this book evolved from my close work with Indian students during that time and is, so far as I know, found in no other publication.

I would like to take this opportunity to express appreciation to the many people who made use of my earlier book, and especially those who offered helpful suggestions for its improvement. My colleagues at Brigham Young University—V. Ben Bloxham, David H. Pratt, and Carl-Erick Johansson in particular—should be given special thanks for their encouragement. Special thanks are also due Phyllis Colonna of Brigham Young University Press for her excellent editorial assistance.

My lovely wife, Daniele, and our twelve children—Preston Dean, Craig Jeromy, Joel Kirk, Marie-Agnes, Jerry Bevan, Dianne Lucille, Suzanne Marie, Kathryn Ann, Nathan Mark, Don-Paul, Mark Sebastian, and Soroya

Rachelle—have been kind in allowing me time to bring the project to completion. It is really because of them that I am engaged in this work of gathering and recording family history.

Introduction

The study of family and local history is receiving a great deal of attention today, with increasing numbers of ordinary people getting involved in genealogical and historical research. They are gaining new insights into their personal identity, origins, and heritage, and learning more about the importance of family and community. By studying the past they gain a greater understanding of the present and find themselves better able to cope with many of life's perplexing problems.

This new interest does not seem to be a passing fad but rather a genuine awakening to the importance of the individual and family in society. Several recent social phenomena—including the civil rights movements of the 1960s and the general disruption of the 1970s—might well evidence a deep-running current of human unrest that demands answers to difficult questions. What is the place of the ordinary person and his children in today's society and in the world of the future? The great interest shown in Alex Haley's publication *Roots* demonstrates this awakening. Haley is riding the crest of a great tide of human concern for the individual and family—particularly the disadvantaged and the oppressed.

Modern microfilming techniques and expanded programs of record acquisition by libraries and genealogical and historical societies have opened an entirely new world of source materials to the interested searcher. Many original records and manuscripts previously restricted to a few are now available for investigation by almost anyone. An increasing amount of published family and local history is appearing in local libraries, and record custodians seem to be more empathetic and cooperative with researchers.

Local genealogical and historical societies continue to increase in number and importance, providing motivation, education, and physical facilities for those interested. Some universities, colleges, and public schools now offer formal courses in family and local history or in genealogy. Texts, manuals, and guide books appear in print at an increasing rate. Prior to 1950 fewer than a half-dozen printed texts related to American genealogical research; since that time more than thirty have been published, half of them since 1970.

Not least among those fostering involvement in the family and community are Brigham Young University in Provo, Utah, and the Genealogical Society of Utah in Salt Lake City—both organizations of The Church of Jesus Christ of Latter-day Saints. Brigham Young University offers undergraduate and graduate degrees in family and local history studies. In addition, qualified genealogists and family historians from the university conduct regional seminars throughout the United States and Canada. The Genealogical Society of Utah, its library already known throughout the world, continues to microfilm and gather source materials from many parts of the globe. It now has embarked on a massive indexing project, using the most modern computer technology.

Individual and group programs to gather and record oral history also are on the increase. Through pen and tape recorder, ordinary people are making real contributions, capturing priceless historical information that otherwise would be lost. Special projects for the preservation of family and local history are carried out in primary and secondary schools; courses in the social sciences are infused with new life through such projects, and students find purpose in studying the past when they feel they are a real part of it.

Academic historians have traditionally disdained genealogy and shown little interest in family and local history, but a new social and economic history seems to be emerging that draws the historian, genealogist, antiquarian, and sociologist closer together. In this new field, importance is placed on the day-to-day experiences of ordinary people rather than the careers of the noble, the wealthy, the educated, or the politically prominent. Much of the information used is coming from work done by nonacademic historians.

Join in one of the most interesting quests you will ever undertake—that of discovering and preserving your heritage through a study of family and local history. You will not be able to complete it in a day, but you can begin the project, then work as time and resources permit. Start with the present, then study the past little by little until you have accomplished what you desire.

You will hold your head higher because of your new-found heritage, and society as well as your family will benefit.

1 Family and Local History in Perspective

Family is more than a name; it is an institution with many important responsibilities and functions. It is the primary and most fundamental unit of society and exerts a great force for good in the world. It is responsible for the continuation of the human race and the transmitting of culture from one generation to the next. It strengthens the community and influences the actions of local, state, and national governments, and it cares for the physical, spiritual, and emotional needs of the individual.

Why Family History

Each of us has a yearning to know who we are and where we came from—to understand our place in the family, the community, and the world. Family and local history research provides answers to important questions.

Why do I live in the western states rather than the southern states? Why did my ancestors live in Canada, Great Britain, Denmark, or Switzerland? What motivated my people to come from the many countries they lived in and settle where they did? Why did some leave in the sixteenth and seventeenth centuries and others during the nineteenth and twentieth centuries? Through which ports did they enter the United States, and what were conditions like on ships and in seaport towns in those days? Did they travel "steerage" or "cabin class," and how long did it take them to cross the Atlantic in 1649? In 1849? Were they wealthy and educated, or were they poor with little chance for formal education? Did they have large families and live to be old, or did many of them die young? One of my ancestors supposedly lived 114 years! Could that be true? Another in the same family was documented as living to age 106, so it is possible.

What were the occupations or trades of my ancestors? One was a butcher in England but a woolgrower in America; that is not a major shift. But another was a tenant farmer in Europe and a publisher in America;

what conditions and motivating factors caused this major change? Why did the children of one ancestor move to the western United States and raise livestock, while those of another ancestor migrated to the eastern states and specialized in education and the arts? A hundred such questions may be asked and the answers sought through the study of family and local history.

One person may engage in family history research hoping to find an unclaimed legacy, while another wants to join a patriotic society by proving descent from a soldier of the Revolution. Others are motivated by simple curiosity or special concern about a hereditary disease. Mormons engage in this work for religious reasons, believing that the family is eternal and certain proxy ordinances may effectively be performed for deceased relatives.

Whatever the reasons, family and local history can be a satisfying and rewarding study. The information gathered not only helps preserve our heritage, but also aids in solving complex and threatening problems. It augments professional studies relating to mobility, fertility, longevity, heredity, and health care in general.

A team of professionals using modern computer technology has investigated the family group records of thousands of Mormon families, plotting some very interesting hereditary patterns regarding cancer. Other similar studies from records of selected parishes and communities make it possible to determine the probability of inheriting certain illnesses. Problems relating to urban renewal, ecology, and industrial expansion or relocation are also being studied through local history projects; when these are coupled with family history studies, the possibilities for worthwhile contributions seem endless.

Family History Versus Genealogy

Genealogy and family history are very closely related, but there are subtle differences. The word *genealogy* is Greek in origin and means "the study of family or race." Usually it is limited in scope to the identification of one or more ancestral lines and collateral relatives. The genealogist investigates source materials, as does the historian, but he concentrates on facts of birth, marriage, and death; his concern is primarily with kinship and matters of descent, not with social, economic, or political development.

He uses techniques in source analysis and evaluation of evidence to reach his conclusions, but he does not engage in reasoned argument to show why certain events happened. His work is directed to a limited audience, usually interested relatives of the families included in his study, and his results are most often published in family-descent form. Because of lack of source materials or other resources, his work is often incomplete, and he does not attempt to influence thought as does the general historian.

Family history is an extension of genealogy but with more depth; it might be referred to as genealogy with a historical touch. It can be further classified as either personal family history or general family history. The personal family historian attempts to locate *all facts* relating to *selected families* while the general family historian attempts to locate *selected facts* relating to *all families.* Personal family history is a term currently used to distinguish between history that is genealogy related and history that is more general in nature.

Personal family history attempts to put meat on the bones of genealogy by including historical information in the narrative. The personal historian concentrates on particular ancestral lines and collateral relatives—as does the genealogist—but he is also interested in every aspect of time and place that affected his subjects. He not only attempts to identify the immigrant ancestor, he also tries to learn why he immigrated, which routes he followed, and who accompanied him. He is interested in the social, economic, and political conditions of the time and tries to show how his families reacted to the stimuli they encountered. By locating and preserving all possible information relating to the family's heritage, he uses the work of genealogists, historians, antiquarians, and sociologists to accomplish his objectives.

Family history is sometimes general in nature, not concerning itself with a particular family or individual. Most academic historians prefer this kind of family history, which is not genealogical in makeup or intent. Such studies concern themselves with families in a particular population, with no attempt made to identify or distinguish between them by name, date, place or kinship. This approach is designed to show such general trends and patterns as mobility, fertility, longevity, and heredity.

The general family historian uses the work of personal family historians to accomplish his purposes, but his work is much broader in scope. Although the two approaches seem to be coming closer together, much distance still remains between them as far as academic respectability is concerned. Dialogue and cooperation between the two could accomplish much and should be encouraged.

Local History

Local history deals with the political, economic, and social development of a community; for different reasons, it is of interest to both the personal and general family historian. H. P. R. Finberg, a respected advocate of local history studies in England, explained that local history attempts to describe "the origin, growth, decline, and fall of a local community" (1973, p. 32). In the mind of the academic historian, family history is one aspect of local history (an aspect that traditionally has not been highly regarded).

People and places are really inseparable, and so also are family and local history. Family history, which deals with people, cannot be properly presented without considering local history, which deals with places. Perhaps some aspects of local history can be studied without regard to family history, but the reverse is less true.

An increased popular interest in local and family history has taken place since the end of World War II. There are many reasons for this. More leisure time has become available to the ordinary individual, and transportation has been economical and widely available. Source materials in libraries, archives, historical societies, and museums have been opened at an increasing rate, and workers seem to be developing more empathy toward family and local history researchers. Local, state and national officials have begun to recognize the importance of more and better records preservation, and in many instances legislatures have appropriated adequate funds to accomplish the task. As a consequence more and better facilities have been provided, and people from all walks of life have become involved.

Often local history—in common with family history and genealogy—has not rated well with traditional historians because the quality of the work varied with the researcher's ability, time, money, and sources investigated. Traditional historians felt that untrained amateurs dominated the field. They felt that too often local history consisted of disorganized collections of unrelated and unverifiable facts, leaving too many whys and wherefores unanswered and neglecting the presentation of reasoned argument. This led them to relegate it to the bottom of the historical studies scale (just above genealogy and antiquarianism).

On the other hand, advocates of family and local history feel that any history is incomplete that fails to give an account of ordinary people and their affairs. They maintain that local history should not be isolated, but rather it should be an integral part of the history of the state and nation where it takes place. If general history is a story of the past and a blueprint for the future, to be accurate it must include ordinary people, events, and places. Indeed good national history cannot be written without reference to local history, they reason.

Others advocate that such studies be used to enliven and enhance general history classes in schools and universities, which have suffered in recent years from disinterest and declining enrollment. A survey of ten thousand students in English schools in 1966 placed history low on the list of "useful and interesting" subjects and high on the list of "useless and boring" subjects (Stephens 1977, p. 1). It was proposed that both teachers and students would profit from the study of local history. Students would get involved in the real world around them, interviewing contemporary people and handling actual source materials; they would thus gain better backgrounds for the study of other subjects and better see their own places in society. Teachers, on the other hand, would be able to avoid the endless repetition of stale lecture materials.

Others not associated with schools and universities may also reap rich rewards from the study of local history. Factory workers, trades people, clerks, accountants, doctors, lawyers, farmers, and wives and mothers can find enjoyment in such work. They can change their daily routines, expand their knowledge, cultivate their intellects, and satisfy an inherent creative urge while contributing something worthwhile to the community.

The history of every community is worth preserving, and although a fair amount of local history has already been published, much still remains to be written. Traditional historians may not give local history much more attention in the future than they have in the past because their primary interest is in larger areas of study; local historians should lead out in the gathering and writing of community history, and now is the time to do it.

The 1876 centennial observance of American independence led to the production of hundreds of books and pamphlets on local history, and our recent bicentennial celebration provided additional stimulus. These volumes serve as rich repositories of information about people, organizations, and communities. They also serve as useful models for new writings.

Many of these earlier histories were the work of commercial businesses that solicited subscriptions from local citizens to finance publication. For a price almost anyone could become prominent, and for additional fees pictures and sketches of farms and outbuildings were included. Biographical sections extolled in extravagant terms the lives of the simplest citizens, for those who could afford the subscription price. Unfortunately many otherwise stalwart citizens were not included.

Following these commercial ventures, local enthusiasts took over the publication of pamphlets and smaller books covering less prominent pioneer settlers still living at the time; they formed societies and prepared and published accounts of the settlers' lives and their memories of the localities where they lived. Many amateur historians and individuals working on a private basis also were involved. The 1880s saw hundreds of volumes come forth, with another surge during the 1920s and yet another in the 1930s. Not much was produced during the 1940s, but a notable increase took place in the next two decades and is still continuing. At least one volume of local history has been published—and sometimes five or six—for the more than three thousand counties throughout the United States.

Every locality is teeming with information just waiting to be revealed by some enterprising researcher or group of researchers. Each community has its public records, its newspaper files, its Fourth of July orations, its old-timers and sages, plus considerable information reposing in the minds of local individuals and families. The records and files of businesses, industries, and social and fraternal organizations also contain valuable local history. A great amount of material is waiting to be discovered in regional and national repositories.

Firsthand observation and personal visits to the community can also yield important local history. Just look around and begin to gather and write. Geography, topographical change, ecology, urban development, architecture, homes and buildings, certain aspects of culture, and many other things are worthy of study.

Before much gathering and writing is done, however, certain goals should be outlined and specific objectives defined. Personal interests should be correlated with local needs, and the proposed project determined. A decision must be made whether to compile a complete history of the community or to cover a single topic. Monographs and papers may be written on such single subjects of local history as agriculture, trade and industry, the church, custom and dress, the military, transportation, education, native inhabitants, politics, labor movements, biography, or family history; these specialized studies can then be made available for others to use in more comprehensive compilations.

Individual talents, abilities, and resources should also be taken into account, and the need for outside financing or other assistance must often be considered before a project is begun. But you should not demur from writing about local history merely because you do not have the time and resources to complete a major project. If you are interested in local history at all, you can use your talents and resources to produce something; then see that your work is made available in some form for others to consider.

Individuals and groups may profitably work together; several people working in cooperation may easily complete a major project that one person alone could never complete. Those involved in adult education might concentrate on this area; projects can be planned in cooperation with local citizens and officials, then carried out by students and teachers over a number of months or years.

A survey should determine what specific local history has already been compiled about the area of interest. The subject then may be enlarged or redefined to meet the established requirements and goals. You should not waste time republishing something already in print, for that is not the local historian's role. It might be all right to republish a rare book or pamphlet that is no longer accessible to the public, but your role will more probably be to gather and present information that previously has not been available.

The real thrill of research is finding many little-known, significant facts in a number of different places, then bringing them together in a coherent and interesting narrative (Cumming 1974).

2 Fundamental Concepts

Family history research is the process of investigating source materials for genealogical and historical information relating to particular families and individuals. This is usually done with the intent of gathering and publishing information in narrative form for the benefit of family members and society in general.

Kinship or Relationship

The primary factors to consider in individual and family identification are names, dates, places, and kinship. In addition to names, the dates and places of birth or christening, marriage, and death or burial generally are considered necessary for the identification of individuals, while kinship must be established for family identification.

For two or more people to be related by blood, they must share a common ancestor or progenitor. An ancestor or progenitor may be defined as any person, male or female, from whom someone descends biologically. Parents, grandparents, great-grandparents, and so forth are referred to as ancestors or progenitors. Although the term *direct ancestor* is used popularly throughout western America, in reality all ancestors are direct.

From a legal standpoint adoption transfers an individual to a family as though he were actually born to the adoptive parents, but of course from a genealogical standpoint he is not a blood descendant.

Your immediate family consists of you, your spouse, and any children you might have—or of you, your parents, and any brothers and sisters you might have. An *ancestral* family consists of any ancestor, his parents (who are also your ancestors), and his parents' other children. Brothers and sisters, aunts and uncles, grandaunts and granduncles, and so forth are *collateral* relatives, as are their descendants. They are related to you by blood, because all of you descend from a common progenitor, but they are not your ancestors. People may be related to one another in more than one way or degree, due to intermarriage in their ancestral lines.

An *in-law* relationship exists between you and the spouse of a blood relative. Hence, the wife of your brother is your sister-in-law, and the wife of your first cousin is your first cousin-in-law. The wife of your uncle is actually your aunt-in-law, though you probably (and quite properly) refer to her as your aunt.

Relationship Chart Showing a Common Progenitor

Azariah Doty = Sarah Tucker

Ephriam Doty = S. Cooper	(brother and sister)	Nancy A. Doty = A. Haines
William C. Doty = M. Berry	(1st cousins)	Azariah Haines = P. Newman
William D. B. Doty = R. Kilday	(2nd cousins)	Kindness Haines = J. Badger
Samuel W. Doty = M. Babb	(3rd cousins)	Kindness Badger = J. Wright
Carl W. Doty = H. Reeves	(4th cousins)	Cleeo Wright = M. Musser
John D. Doty = M. Bird	(5th cousins)	Norman Wright = D. Piquee

A *step* relationship exists between you and the spouse of an ancestor when that spouse is not your biological progenitor. Suppose your father dies and your mother marries a second husband; he becomes your stepfather. Or if your grandfather dies and your grandmother marries a second husband, her second husband becomes your stepgrandfather. A stepbrother is a stepparent's child by another marriage. A stepson is a spouse's child by another marriage. Biological offspring of an ancestor and a stepparent are blood relatives to you but only of *half-degree*; that is, children of your father and stepmother are your *half* brothers and sisters.

Relationship Chart Showing Degrees of Removal

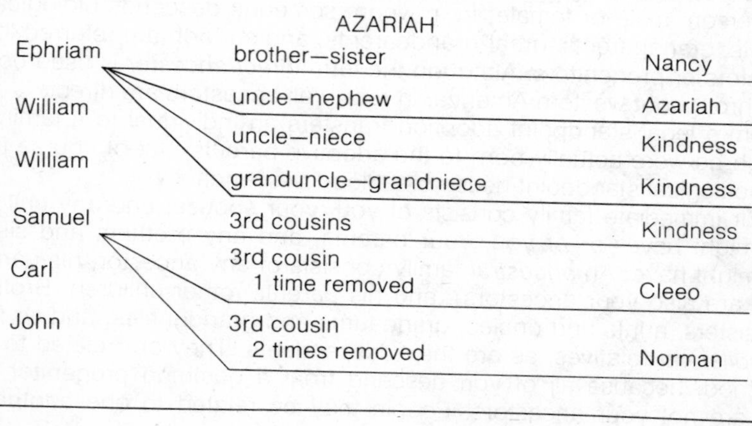

However in most circles it is popular to disregard half-degree terminology.

The biological children of a particular couple are brothers and sisters to each other, and children of brothers and sisters are first cousins to each other. Children of first cousins are second cousins to each other, and children of second cousins are third cousins to each other. Children of third cousins are fourth cousins, and so forth.

Relationship Chart

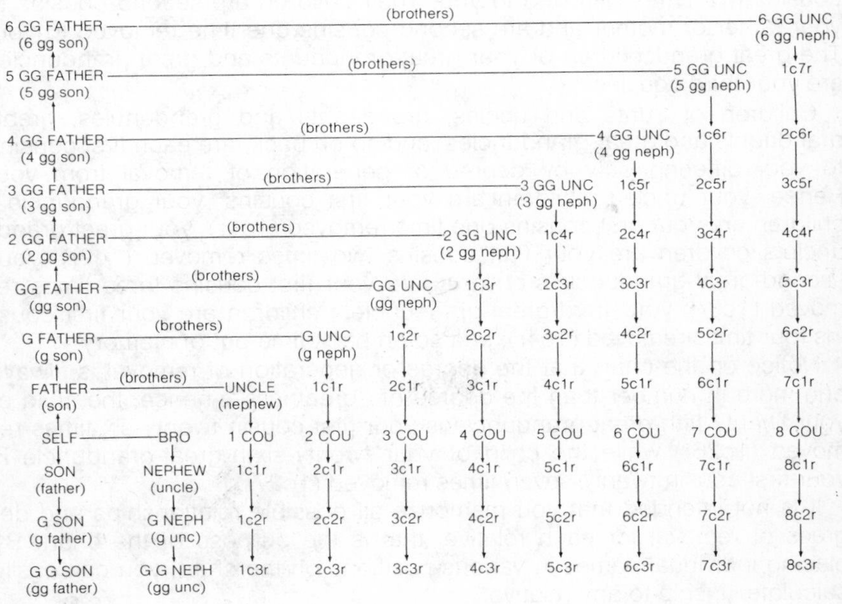

Abbreviations: g father = grandfather; gg father = great grandfather; unc = uncle; bro = brother; c = cousin; neph = nephew; r = generations removed.

Key to Using the Relationship Chart

1. To determine the relationship of the brothers (or sisters) of direct ancestors, follow the horizontal line from the direct ancestor.

Examples:

a. The brother of your 6 gg father is your 6 gg uncle. Your relationship to him is shown in parentheses immediately below the uncle relationship—in this case 6 gg nephew.

b. The sister of your 6 gg father is your 6 gg aunt.

2. To determine your relationship to the children of the brothers (and sisters) of your direct ancestors, follow the vertical line down from the uncle (or aunt) relationship.

Examples:

a. The son of your 4 gg uncle is your 1c5r.

b. The grandson of your gg uncle is your 2c1r.

Your first cousins are children of your parent's brothers and sisters—offspring of your aunts and uncles. Your grandparents may also have had brothers and sisters who had offspring; the children of grandaunts and granduncles are first cousins to your father or mother and first cousins one time removed to you. The grandchildren of your grandaunts and granduncles are first cousins one time removed to your father or mother and are second cousins to you. In a similar manner, your great-grand-aunts and great-granduncles may have had descendants; their children are first cousins to your grandfather or grandmother, but they are first cousins two times removed to you. Their children are second cousins to your father or mother and are second cousins one time removed to you. The great grandchildren of your great-grandaunts and great-granduncles are your third cousins.

Children of aunts and uncles, grandaunts and granduncles, great-grandaunts and great-granduncles, and so on back, are each first cousins to you, differing only by degree or generation of removal from you. Hence, your uncle's children are your first cousins; your granduncle's children are your first cousins one time removed (1c1r); your great-grand-uncle's children are your first cousins two times removed (1c2r); your second-great-granduncle's children are your first cousins three times removed (1c3r); your third-great-granduncle's children are your first cousins four times removed (1c4r); and so on back time out of memory.

Notice on the chart that the degree or generation of removal is always one more in number than the degree of "greatness"; hence, the child of your twenty-fifth-great-granduncle is your first cousin twenty-six times removed (1c26r) while the child of your twenty-sixth-great-granduncle is your first cousin twenty-seven times removed (1c27r).

It is not intended that you memorize all possible relationships and degrees of removal for each relative; that is the purpose of the chart. By placing individual names in various positions on the chart, you can easily calculate kinship to any relative.

Ancestral Numbers

The total number of ancestors any person has in a given generation can be calculated by mathematical formula, but the number of collateral relatives cannot. They must be individually identified to be counted. Ancestral numbers increase geometrically; that is, they double each generation. You have two parents, four grandparents, eight great-grandparents, sixteen second-great-grandparents, thirty-two third-great-grandparents, sixty-four fourth-great-grandparents, and so on. By the tenth generation you technically have 1,024 ancestors. You may not actually have that many different progenitors because of intermarriage, but you do have that number of name places on your pedigree chart. By the twentieth generation, you have name places for 1,048,576 ancestors.

In not many generations you have more direct ancestors by theoretical number than actually lived in the countries in which your ancestors were found. How can this be? Your pedigree is somewhat like the crescendo sign in music—it starts at a certain point then expands, but not in-

Ancestral Numbers Shown by Generation

1st generation	2	
2nd generation	4	(1980–1880)*
3rd generation	8	
4th generation	16	
5th generation	32	(1880–1780)
6th generation	64	
7th generation	128	
8th generation	256	(1780–1680)
9th generation	512	
10th generation	1,024	
11th generation	2,048	(1680–1580)
12th generation	4,096	
13th generation	8,192	
14th generation	16,384	(1580–1480)
15th generation	32,768	
16th generation	65,536	
17th generation	131,072	(1480–1380)
18th generation	262,144	
19th generation	524,288	
20th generation	1,048,576	(1380–1280)
21st generation	2,097,152	

*Dates based on the assumption that there are approximately three generations for every hundred years.

definitely. At some point it reverses, decreasing to a point where two people were your first mortal ancestors.

According to world population estimates, you are one of about four billion persons living on the earth today, and according to the Bible all mankind descends from Adam and Eve (or, more recently, from Noah and his wife). This would make everyone on the earth related in some degree, with all pedigrees interweaving at one point or another. Estimates of total population from the beginning of human history vary from eight billion—twice the present world population—to more than sixty billion. Whatever the facts, you and I are related to a lot of people and descend from a large number of progenitors. Although each of us is closely related to very few of the billions of people living today, the further back we trace our ancestry, the more closely our progenitors were related to the progenitors of others.

For genealogical purposes, a generation averages thirty-three years and represents one link in the succession of descent. This works out to about three generations for every hundred years, thirty for a thousand years, and one hundred and eighty for the last six thousand years. Of course documenting a pedigree that far back is impossible with presently known sources. Pedigrees purporting to extend to Adam and Eve are based upon oral traditions that the royal lines of Europe connect with indi-

Pedigree of Norman E. Wright

1—Norman Edgar Wright; born 9 Jan 1927; md Daniele Y. Piquee
2—Cleeo Datell Wright; born 9 Sept 1893; md Mary Hill Musser
3—Kindness Ann Badger; born 23 Dec 1856; md Joseph Alma Wright
4—John Chamberlain Badger; born 12 Sept 1825; md Kindness Ann Haines
5—John Badger; born 11 Sept 1800; md Lydia Chamberlain
6—Hannah Sawyer; born 19 Mar 1777; md James Badger
7—Elias Sawyer; born 1 Aug 1747; md Hannah Farrar
8—Elisha Sawyer; chr. 17 Aug 1718; md Ruth White
9—Elias Sawyer; born 1692; md Beatrice Houghton
10—Thomas Sawyer; born 2 July 1649; md Hannah Houghton
11—Mary Prescott; chr. 24 Feb 1624; md Thomas Sawyer
12—John Prescott; born 1604; md Mary Platts
13—Ralph Prescott; born 1571; md Ellen; will dated 24 Jan 1609
14—Roger Prescott; born about 1540; md Ellen Shaw; will dated 26 Sept 1594
15—Alice Standish; born about 1520; md James Prescott; buried 10 Mar 1564
16—Roger Standish; born about 1490
17—Alice Harington; born about 1480; md Ralph Standish
18—Isabella Radcliffe; born 1450; md Sir James Harington; died 1497
19—Sir Alexander Radcliffe; born 1401; md Agnes Harington; died 1476
20—Sir John Radcliffe; born 1377; died 26 July 1442
21—Sir John Radcliffe; born 1356; md Margaret Trafford 1375; died 1422
22—Richard Radcliffe; born about 1336; md Maude Legh; died 1380
23—Joan or Jennet Holland; born 1313; md Sir John Radcliffe
24—Maud Zouche; born 1290; md Sir Robert Holland; died 31 May 1341
25—Alan Zouche; born 1267; md Eleanor Seagrave; died 1313
26—Ela Longspee; md Roger Zouche
27—Stephen Longspee; born 1215; died 1260
28—William Longspee; born 1153; died 7 Mar 1225
29—Henry II (King of England 1154–1189) born 1132; died 1189
30—Geoffrey V (Plantagenet); born 24 Aug 1113; died 7 Sept 1151
31—Fulk V (King of Jerusalem); Count of Anjou; born 1092; died 10 Nov 1143
32—Fulk IV (Richin); Count of Anjou; md Bertrade; died 14 Apr 1109
33—Ermengard of Anjou; md Aubri-Geoffry; died 21 Mar 1076
34—Fulk II (the Black); Count of Anjou; md Hildegarde; died 21 June 1040
35—Adelaide of Vermandois; md Geoffrey I (Count of Anjou); died 978
36—Robert; Count of Troyes; md Adelaide; died 967/8
37—Herbert II; Count of Vermandois; md Liegarde; died 943 at Troyes, France
38—Herbert I; Count of Vermandois; born about 840; died about 902
39—Pepin of Peronne; Count of Senlis and Peronne; born 818
40—Barnard; King of Italy 813–817; born 797; died 17 Apr 818 at Milan, Italy
41—Pepin; King of Italy 781–810; born Apr 773; died 8 July 810 at Milan, Italy
42—Charlemagne (Carolus Magnus); King of the Franks; born 2 Apr 742
43—Pepin the Short; King of the Franks; died 24 Sept 768
44—Charles Martel; Ruler of the Franks; died 22 Oct 741
45—Pepin (Le Gros); Duke of the Franks; died 16 Dec 714

Documented

More Conclusive Evidence Needed

viduals mentioned in the Bible.

Soundly documenting an American pedigree earlier than the middle of the seventeenth century is difficult, although some lines have been successfully traced earlier—particularly when they connect with the landed aristocracy in Europe. Sections of many pedigrees can be authenticated in certain periods of time, but documenting our own generation-by-generation descent from these pedigrees is difficult.

To give an example, the pedigree at left is traced to the sixth century, but not every connection has been authenticated. The first twelve generations are fairly well documented, and the last twenty-eight generations are also well documented. The evidence establishing the direct relationship of generations thirteen through seventeen (Ralph Prescott—Alice Harington) is still somewhat questionable. That means further research may prove that additional sections of the pedigree are sound, or it may prove that the entire pedigree beyond John Prescott (born 1604 in Massachusetts) is incorrect. Or it may disclose that researchers mistakenly accepted a brother or an uncle as ancestral, which would negate only a small section of the pedigree.

Methods, Procedures, and Sources

Family history research, then, is the process of investigating genealogical and historical sources for information relating to individuals and families. The family historian is not only interested in all facts that will help him identify family members and relatives, but also wants to learn all he can about the family's actions and circumstances.

A young couple get married and begin family life; they acquire land, build a home, and earn a living. They have children born to them; these children attend school, work, go to church, and become involved in various social, economic, and political activities. Some die young while others reach adulthood and begin families of their own. Family members experience sorrows and hardships as well as successes and happiness. Economic depression comes, but so does prosperity. Parents and grandparents are cared for, die, and are buried; friends are visited and communicated with; interchanges take place with other relatives, family associates, and public officials.

These events and others not named are the fountainhead from which family history is written. An event or circumstance occurs and someone witnesses it; that information (fact, date, evidence) is recorded or passed along in oral form, becoming a source for family history. Such sources may include the following:

Oral history and family tradition. Oral history may be obtained from almost anyone: immediate and distant relatives (especially old-timers), family friends, local public officials, or other individuals. It provides a wealth of information that can sometimes be corroborated by other evidence.

Records, documents, and memorabilia originating with the family and in the home. Such family records as family Bibles, diaries, journals, letters, photographs, clippings, manuscripts, business and employment records, insurance records, land and estate papers, and other miscellaneous personal documents and papers constitute a primary source for family history.

Compiled secondary materials. A rich variety of secondary sources await the family historian: published and manuscript genealogies, family histories, biographies, genealogical dictionaries, compendia, special genealogical indexes, genealogical and historical periodicals, and regional and local histories.

Records, documents, and memorabilia created by private and governmental organizations at the local, state, and national levels. This group presents an almost inexhaustible source for family history: vital records; censuses; court, land, military, and emigration records; and files of schools, universities, hospitals, businesses, fraternal and patriotic organizations, churches, and other private institutions.

Family and local history research methods and procedures are similar to those in other history fields. The family historian sets goals and defines research objectives. He locates and investigates source materials and evaluates and analyzes the information obtained. He reconciles conflicting data and verifies facts, then reaches his conclusions. He publishes his findings for the benefit of others and for review.

While no standard method of research has been accepted by all historians, family history researchers are in general agreement on essential research steps and the use of major source materials. The preliminary steps include gathering and recording basic facts from personal knowledge and memory, checking relevant compiled secondary sources, and carefully analyzing and evaluating all survey findings.

After the preliminary work has been done, research objectives are defined and investigations are launched in original source materials of the localities that influenced the family. These sources include official vital records, church and cemetery records, census records, court and land records, military records, emigration records, newspapers and periodicals, and miscellaneous social/commercial records.

Although the specific steps in research might vary according to individual circumstances or availability of sources, the researcher should begin with known facts (names, dates, places, and kinship information already at hand) then proceed to the unknown. Investigating the more recent records first is also advisable, because they usually include more information and may provide helpful clues for additional research. They also may be more readily available.

As new families and individuals are identified, research often must be repeated in sources already investigated. Often certain facts were unknown when a particular record was searched, so it must be searched again in light of the new information. For instance, perhaps the researcher did not know the maiden surname of an ancestor when he first read a certain census, but after learning the name he may—by rechecking that census—discover many new facts about previously unidentified relatives.

Another point: if your people, like most Americans, moved from place to place, local records may mention them in each locality where they resided. Also, family members tended to follow one another in their migrations across the country. Parents, grandparents, and even great-grandparents are sometimes found buried in the same cemeteries. County marriage registers often include entries for aunts, uncles, nieces, nephews, and cousins in addition to the ancestor you have traced to that source.

Evaluating evidence. From time to time, the researcher finds conflicting or incorrect information that must somehow be reconciled. You will find certain techniques in source analysis and evaluation of evidence useful in such instances. Because it is impossible to prove all genealogical data to absolute certainty without being there and observing them personally, you must collect enough supporting evidence to convince yourself (and others) of the truth.

An original source is the first recording of any particular information in a particular form—any subsequent transcription is a copy. An original record, other things being equal, is more reliable than copies, just as a contemporary record (being recorded at or near the time of the event) is more reliable than records made long afterwards.

If oral history is obtained from a reliable individual having personal knowledge of an event or circumstance—or if it is obtained from someone closely associated in place and time with the event—the information generally is considered primary rather than secondary in nature, and it should receive a high rating in probability of correctness. However, the fact that information is from a primary source does not guarantee its correctness; it only greatly improves the probability.

For example, assume that a death record exists for one of your ancestors, and assume that the record is the original. The date and place of death were entered by the physician in attendance at the time of death. Those particular facts would be considered both primary in nature and contemporary with the event. However, the death record might also include the date and place of the deceased ancestor's birth, this information being supplied by a grandson. The grandson was not present at the birth of his grandfather, and the recording of those facts on the death certificate was not done at the time of the grandfather's birth. Therefore that part of the information is secondary in nature.

Since you must often use secondary and noncontemporary evidence in family history, you must gather and present as much confirming information to support your conclusions as possible. A preponderance of circumstantial evidence can sometimes be more valuable than a small amount of direct evidence. A lack of conflicting information also supports the probability of correctness. Circumstantial evidence provides the answers to questions in an indirect way, while direct evidence answers the questions outright. While neither guarantees correctness, both can be used to arrive at the probability of truth.

Deductive reasoning and theory also have their places in family history research, not only in providing possible approaches, but also in providing possible answers. Some questions may never be answered, because of lack of source materials or because of other good reasons; deduction or theory provides ways to reach probable answers. However, in the latter case you should clearly indicate that conclusions are based upon deduction and probability, not on direct evidence.

Notekeeping and documentation. An effective and simple notetaking system is essential to successful research, and proper documentation is the hallmark of quality work. Research is a continuing process with many variables; locating, investigating, extracting, abstracting, analyzing, evaluating, reconciling, and verifying information without a workable notetaking system is impossible. The complete and accurate recording of all your research activities can help you in several ways. It can help you avoid duplication of effort and unnecessary waste of resources; it can also aid you in the analysis of source materials and evaluation of evidence. And only through adequate and proper documentation can you support your conclusions and gain acceptance as a competent researcher; your published work will not be given much credit by others if it is not well documented.

There are nearly as many different notetaking and filing systems in use today as there are researchers. However, workable systems follow similar methods and procedures. Each researcher is encouraged to consider his own circumstances and develop the system that works best for him.

A variety of charts and forms are in print. Pedigree charts, family group record forms, calendars or logs of research and correspondence, extract/abstract forms, summary forms, and so on are widely available. Many researchers prefer to design and print their own.

Pedigree charts and family group records are used to list basic genealogical facts and to analyze and evaluate that information. They also can help you define research objectives and guide you in applying research. Calendars and log sheets serve as bibliographic lists to show which sources have been searched and which remain to be searched. They also can be used as indexes to your research findings. Special forms for extracting and abstracting source information can be used when facilities for duplicating records are not available. Individual summary forms are used to list all facts that pertain to a particular person.

Whatever system you use, it should be kept simple; if you find yourself spending more time in record keeping than in research, your system should be modified or simplified. An adequate system includes the following information:

- What you did and why you did it.
- When and where you did it.
- What you found or did not find.
- What you further plan to do about it.

You should identify each investigated source in sufficient detail that another person could find the same information without difficulty. If your source was a book or manuscript, include the title, author or compiler, place and name of publisher, date, and the appropriate volume and page number. Documents and individual items should be described in detail and their location noted. When a personal interview is your source, the description should include names, addresses, times, and other essential facts.

In each instance of notetaking, indicate what you were hoping to learn from the source, what you found, and what you concluded. It is also helpful to others who follow you to know that you investigated certain sources even though you did not find what you were looking for. It can be as important to know that an individual was not in a particular place as to know that he was.

You should make a special effort to copy information accurately and neatly. This will make evaluation and analysis easier, and it will also help others who may review your work later. You should not skimp on paper, thinking you will quickly jot down facts on an envelope now then record them in better form later. Later usually never comes, and error may result or the research may have to be done again.

Copy or extract information on separate sheets and on one side only rather than combine information from different sources on the same page. "Different source—different paper!" This allows you to better analyze and evaluate information and also helps you avoid losing certain facts. The answers to many genealogical problems are already in the researcher's notes, but he does not always recognize them or find them because of his defective notetaking system. Proper identification of research findings and the ability to retrieve information for analysis and evaluation are essential for successful research.

Sometimes a brief extract from a genealogical source is not enough. When a document pertains to an ancestor (as opposed to a collateral relative) and when it has special historical significance or has been used as the basis for a genealogical connection, you should make a verbatim copy or a photocopy. All the facts may not apply at the moment, but further research may disclose their relevance. In census searches, for instance, the next-door neighbor may be a brother or the father of an ancestor. Similarly, the plots surrounding an ancestor's grave may belong to other close relatives, even though the surnames are different. A full copy of these records should be made; any abridgment or rearrangement of the facts may destroy or confuse relevant genealogical information.

The most important aspects of the research notetaking process are what you find and what you conclude from your work. The facts you locate are the real substance of research, and your conclusions are the final results. All the various charts, forms, procedures, and techniques are merely aids to help you accomplish these final objectives as conveniently and accurately as possible.

As research continues, your notes will increase in volume to the point where a workable system for filing and retrieving them will become imperative. Your ability to reach correct conclusions through analysis and evaluation will depend heavily on the system you choose.

Many researchers accumulate considerable material before they compile permanent records; some system is necessary for filing this material while continuing research. Regular manila folders are handy—one can be set up for each family unit. Work pedigree charts, family group records, and certificates, clippings, and extracts pertaining to the children of that unit are some of the records that might be filed there. This folder should not be considered the final resting place for such information—merely a convenient place to store it during research. After the search has been completed, documents and files should be mounted or placed in some more permanent form for future reference.

Your system for filing is a matter of personal preference and should permit you to accomplish your final objectives in an efficient and effective manner. If you are writing a biography, perhaps your findings can be filed according to subject or topic heading. But if you are compiling a family history or genealogy, pertinent facts may better be filed according to individual or family name. When several different families are involved, or when you are writing local history, it may be to your advantage to file the facts by source or locality. This approach requires less time and effort than the others. For example, if you file information by name, you must duplicate the extract and file copies for each person shown, or use some other method to cross reference. Even though most family historians file information by name, that does not mean you have to. You should consider individual and family names, places or jurisdictions, sources, or even time periods as factors in your filing system.

Successful genealogical research requires correspondence because not all sources are available for personal investigation. Nor are all pertinent records and sources in a central repository; agents and record searchers must be used from time to time to get desired information. Special forms have already been mentioned that can assist you in genealogical correspondence.

Your correspondence should be kept brief and courteous, but specific. Outlining extensive family history when corresponding with officials is usually a waste of time. Get right to the point and make your request in clear, concise terms. If an index is to be searched, say so; if a statement is needed about official record holdings, indicate that it is, rather than ramble in vague generalities. Librarians and public officials are seldom qualified to evaluate research problems but they can help you gain access to the records. Many cannot or will not make involved genealogical searches because they are too busy with their regular duties or have little interest in the subject. However, most will respond to concise, reasonable requests.

You should give special attention to letters and reports that contain genealogical information from such agents. These letters and reports should be considered in the same light as your own research extracts and abstracts. They should be adequately identified and filed in such a way that pertinent facts can be reviewed and correlated with information already at hand. Frequently facts must be lifted from correspondence and posted to family group records, pedigree charts, and individual summary forms; otherwise the information may be lost in your correspondence files. Some researchers xerox pertinent sections from letters and include them with their regular notes. Where correspondence is filed separately from your regular research notes, some system of cross referencing is essential.

Tape recorders and cameras also have important roles in the note-taking and record-keeping process. Many family historians find them indispensible in research. Through their use important facts can be captured in a very short time and greater accuracy can be assured. Some repositories have adequate copy facilities, but many do not; having your own camera and tape recorder is an advantage. With few exceptions record custodians will allow you to copy genealogical and historical material. (Some have restrictions on flash attachments when originals are fragile.)

The tape recorder is an excellent means of gathering and preserving oral history and family tradition; it also can be used effectively to transcribe information from records and documents. However, the researcher must take care to enunciate words correctly and spell many of them out so the facts can be correctly transcribed from the tape at a later date.

The camera is even better for copywork, whether of the written word, other photographs, physical objects, or landscape. It is surprising what can be accomplished by an amateur photographer with an average camera, a close-up lens, and ordinary black and white film. Documents and other material can be copied economically and effectively with only moderately expensive equipment and limited photographic experience.

Any of the popular 35 millimeter cameras on the market today can be used successfully in family history research. For copying documents you will need a camera with a removable lens and single reflex action. With these you get what you see. Flash attachments, tripods, and other professional equipment are fine if you can afford them but not essential for good work.

Using a 35 mm single lens reflex camera with a macro 50 mm lens, I have successfully copied records and documents, photographs, tombstones, physical objects and scenery, and even film extracts from microfilm readers. I have used my camera and tape recorder for copywork in courthouses, libraries, archives, and historical societies throughout the United States and Canada. An employee in the Hall of Records at Annapolis, Maryland, refused me the right to camera copy any material in the repository, and a surrogate clerk in St. Lawrence County, New York, refused to let me copy probate records in his custody—other than those, I have had few restrictions in gaining access to public and official records for camera copywork.

Excellent results can be obtained through using ordinary black and white film and regular commercial processing. The lighting in most public record repositories is adequate for Kodak Plus-X Panchromatic 125 ASA speed film without flash equipment, but some situations may require the faster Tri-X 400 ASA speed film. The cost is no more expensive than the xerox or other photocopying processes available at most libraries, and you have the advantage of being able to copy at your own speed and pleasure.

3 Getting a Proper Start

An eastern journalist is reported to have asked Joseph Smith, the Mormon prophet, how he was so successful in governing his people—since they were very diverse and came from many different countries and backgrounds. He replied that he taught them correct principles and they governed themselves.

There is a parallel between that and successful family history research. Too many different sources and circumstances exist to explain each one in detail. Also, a certain amount of luck is associated with successful research, particularly in locating and investigating source materials. Therefore, my approach here will be to help you identify the major record groups, outline general research methods and procedures, then encourage you to use your own intellect and apply the principles to your own particular circumstances.

Family and Home Sources

The most logical place to begin compiling a family history is with the family in the home; a variety of primary sources can be found there. You can use your own personal knowledge and memory as well as that of other family members. Family tradition and the testimony of relatives, friends, and family associates are also important. Records and documents originating with the family—including family Bibles, diaries, journals, letters, photographs, clippings, manuscripts, business and employment records, insurance records, land and estate papers—can be useful, as can miscellaneous real and personal items.

Personal knowledge and memory. You can begin writing your personal family history by listing all the important facts you can remember about yourself and your family—your date and place of birth, your parents and facts about them, your brothers and sisters and their vital statistics, and essential information about your spouse. Then proceed to each ancestral family and record all the facts you can remember about them, their children, and other relatives. You can also begin to record important historical events and circumstances that influenced your life and your family's lives, because they will add depth and richness to other genealogical information.

Perhaps you will not be able to remember some important dates and events. Do not get discouraged; they will come to you as research continues. The important thing at this point is recalling and listing all you can remember about yourself and your family. Proceed at a comfortable pace and do not insist on completing everything about a particular topic before moving to another. Let your mind and memory work freely, recording those things you can recall without too much difficulty. As you record certain experiences, others will come to mind—leading you toward your ultimate goal of an acceptable family history. Also, do not be too concerned about literary form or personal writing style at this point; later work can make those refinements. Carry a pencil and paper with you at all times; jot down topic sentences or major subject headings as they pop into your mind and expand them later.

Oral history and family tradition. You should also note and encourage the recollections of other family members as you begin research. Your knowledge coupled with theirs can bring to light things that would otherwise be overlooked. Do not attempt always to set up formal interviews; question people whenever and wherever circumstances permit. You may have to discuss family history with someone several times before you obtain the answers you seek; people experience different moods at different times, and sometimes they recall information better than at other times.

Try to visit and interview older family members first; they may die or become seriously ill, thus taking with them valuable information that cannot be obtained from any other source. During the spring of 1968 I visited Samuel Willard Doty—a third cousin twice removed—at his home in Greene County, Tennessee. He was able to give me information about a certain ancestral family that I could not have obtained anywhere else. He knew the burial place of my fourth-great-grandparents and also was able to tell me the relationship of almost every other person buried in the cemetery. He died the following year.

Allan J. Lichtman gives very excellent pointers on interviewing in his book *Your Family History* (1978).

If possible, take a camera and tape recorder with you when interviewing people, because you can capture information more accurately and efficiently. However, take care not to offend or pressure people; they may not respond to your requests or invite you back. Some individuals object to being recorded, but others welcome the experience, actually becoming more informative. People also must be in the mood to disclose family information—physical as well as mental conditions must be just right for success. Consequently some interviews result in great success while others bring nothing but discouragement; learn to exercise patience and determination. Also remember that information obtained from one interview may lead to interviews with other people, or one successful interview may generate several more with the same person.

Family members are often reluctant to discuss certain confidential information with strangers because they feel it might adversely affect the family name or image. Therefore you should be careful in your questions and not insist on delving into confidential matters unless the information is volunteered. On the other hand, nearly every family has a skeleton or two in its closet; often it does no harm to make the truth known.

Family tradition is another area where you must learn to use discretion. It can't always be taken at face value, but it can result in useful information in some instances. Sometimes a grain of truth is contained in the tradition that can be used to reach other truths; at other times there is nothing more than romantic imagination. Almost every family has a tradition that three brothers came to America during the colonial period and everyone with that surname descends from them. Or they have the tradition that an ancestor was of royal birth, was disowned for marrying a commoner, came to the New World as a stowaway, and changed his name shortly after arrival. Almost every Mormon who had an ancestor living in Nauvoo, Illinois, in the 1840s will insist he was a bodyguard of Joseph Smith or Brigham Young, and every family with a progenitor in the colonies during the revolutionary war will affirm he was a bodyguard of George Washington.

Sometimes the grain of truth in family tradition can provide information needed to solve a difficult research problem. This was the case with an Idaho family who insisted their Montey ancestor came from France with General Lafayette in 1777 to save this country. Research in the records of Illinois, Ohio, New York, and Canada revealed that their Montey family had been in Canada and America since 1640—many years before the American Revolution. However, it also was established that two progenitors—Francois Montey, Jr., and Francois Montey, Sr.—both served in the Revolution, and the senior Francois's mother was named Mary Lafayette. So there was some truth in that family tradition.

Documents and memorabilia originating with the family. Family records, Bibles, diaries, journals, letters, photographs, and other documents are primary sources for family history. They not only provide basic genealogical facts but also contain information that can make the family history live. They are excellent substitutes for the often missing or nonexistent official vital records and also supplement other sources. They are a prime source to establish kinship, and they can produce genealogical facts of the highest quality.

Family letters and photographs make individuals live again, and also contain helpful clues for continued research. To give a rich example, my second-great-grandfather, Azariah Haines, converted to "Mormonism" in Ohio in 1844 and moved to Nauvoo, Illinois; after a few years he became disenchanted with the prospects of a future in the West so he moved to Grant County, Indiana, with most of his large family. However, three of his daughters remained strong in the Mormon faith and migrated to the Great Salt Lake Basin in the early 1850s. They corresponded with their father

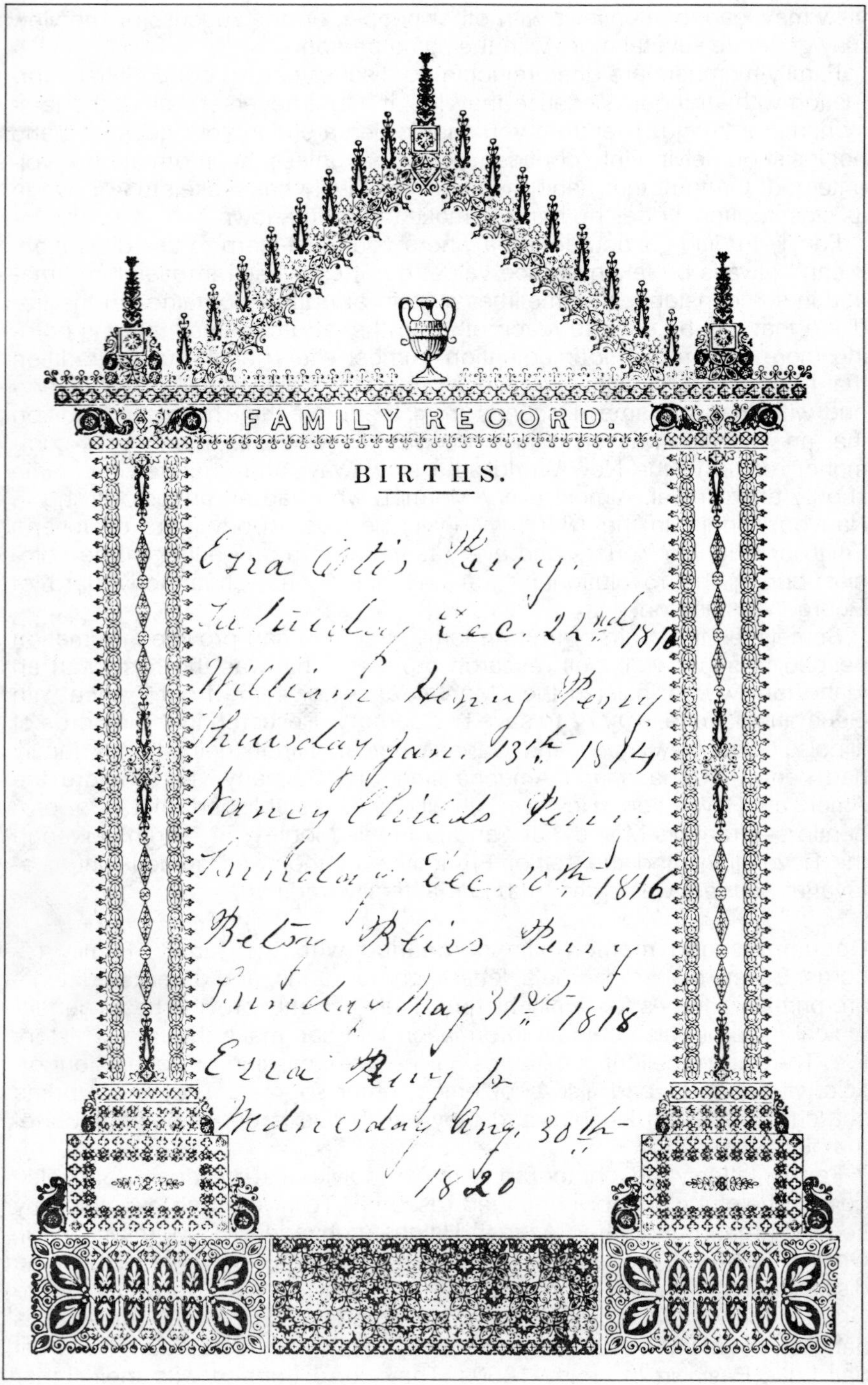

FAMILY RECORD.

BIRTHS.

Ezra Otis Perry
Tuesday Dec. 22nd 1812
William Henry Perry
Thursday Jan. 13th 1814
Nancy Childs Perry
Tuesday Dec. 10th 1816
Betsey Bliss Perry
Sunday May 31st 1818
Ezra Perry Jr
Wednesday Aug. 30th
1820

until his death in 1879, and the letters are filled with genealogical and family history information. They give details of births and deaths of family members, record places of residence of relatives and family associates, express concern about polygamy, explain marriages of family members, and even identify one of Azariah's grandfathers.

Business and employment records, land and estate papers, insurance records, and other documents useful to family history often can be found in the home. Original estate papers and land records usually are with the family and not at the courthouse or town hall; those documents are copies. In some cases families lived on a particular tract or parcel of land for several generations without officially recording a transfer of title at the courthouse or town hall. (Samuel W. Doty, mentioned previously, had the original 1783 deed to land in Greene County, Tennessee, until his death in 1969; his son now has it.)

Military pension records, citizenship and naturalization papers, and various items in the family's possession can be useful. Dishes, furniture, clothing, guns, tools, implements, and other memorabilia can be used to determine family origins or family circumstances. Nearly any record, document, or family possession can be useful to family history.

Compiled Secondary Sources

A considerable amount of genealogy and family history has already been compiled on American families, and most of it is conveniently available for inspection in local, state, and national libraries. It can be found in both published and manuscript form and seems to be increasing at a rapid pace. These compiled works are classified "secondary" because they usually are based on other sources—though many contain well-documented information based on competent research. Unfortunately others are nothing more than hearsay, though any of them might provide clues that cannot be found in other sources. Included in the category of compiled secondary sources are family histories, genealogies, biographical works, genealogical dictionaries and compendia, special genealogical indexes, genealogical and historical periodicals, and regional and local histories.

Guides and bibliographies are in print, but use the surname and locality approach in each library you visit. You should consider each individual's name, each family surname, and each locality of importance to your problem, then look for references in the card catalog or other available guides that might pertain to them. Check each reference carefully because the title may not reveal the actual content of the record; pertinent facts often are buried in the record and may not be identified from the reference card or title. When the surname is common and several references pertaining to it are on file, do selective research and investigate those in your localities of interest first. A lot of time can be spent in these records; you do not want to waste it.

Family history, genealogy, and biography. The first family history published in America is believed to be that of the Samuel Stebbins family of

Connecticut, published at Hartford in 1771. By the end of the Civil War, approximately three hundred family histories had been published; by the end of World War I, an estimated eight thousand were in print. It is estimated that more than thirty thousand volumes of family history and genealogy have been compiled to date, and the number undoubtedly will continue to increase at a rapid rate.

A few good bibliographic guides and indexes to genealogy and family history have been published and are useful in locating information. Complete publishing information for the following volumes may be found in the bibliography at the end of this book.

Marion J. Kaminkow edited *Genealogies in the Library of Congress: A Bibliography* in two volumes and a supplement. This work includes more than twenty-five thousand references. It supersedes the 1954 microcard edition of *American and English Genealogies in the Library of Congress* first published in 1919. The *Library of Congress Catalog of Printed Cards* and its supplement are available at many libraries, and the Library of Congress sells copies of the printed cards to participating libraries.

P. William Filby recently compiled an excellent list of printed materials relating to American genealogy in his *American and British Genealogy and Heraldry* (1970). Filby was the librarian and assistant director of the Maryland Historical Society in Baltimore; he created the book primarily out of his own need for such a reference tool.

In 1862 William H. Whitmore edited works published by Joel Munsell's Sons under the title *The American Genealogist* (not to be confused with the Connecticut quarterly of the same name). It was a bibliography of family histories in print, with editions in 1862, 1868, 1875, and 1900. In 1899 Munsell's Sons also published *A List of Titles of Genealogical Articles in American Periodicals and Kindred Works,* designed to be a companion volume. In 1896 Thomas Allen Glenn compiled *A List of Some American Genealogies Which Have Been Printed in Book Form in 1896* (recently reprinted by the Genealogical Publishing Company in Baltimore) that includes two thousand entries.

In 1895 and 1900 Munsell's Sons published *Index to American Genealogies* and *Supplement to the Index to Genealogies 1900–1908,* both of which are very useful. The title page to the fifth edition indicates that almost fifty thousand references were included, but this refers to names and not titles. The same work discloses that Daniel S. Durrie edited the first and second editions, and Filby says Durrie also edited the third edition under the title *Bibliographica Americana.*

Several thousand names and many family histories have been indexed in Fremont Rider's *American Genealogical Index,* in forty-eight volumes. *The American Genealogical-Biographical Index,* also by Rider, is a second series currently under compilation. Volumes 1–113 are available at this writing, covering A through McAllister of the alphabet. When it is completed, this series will list an estimated twelve million entries. Consolidated "key title indexes" appear in selected volumes, showing the records used in compiling the series.

The Long Island Historical Society in Brooklyn has a very rich collection of American family history in print; it published *A Catalog of American Ge-*

nealogies in the Long Island Historical Society in 1935, compiled under the direction of Emma Toedteberg. This catalog contains titles to more than eight thousand printed books and pamphlets and eight hundred and fifty manuscripts.

Three excellent guides to Virginia genealogies are Stuart E. Brown's *Virginia Genealogies: A Trial List of Printed Books and Pamphlets,* Robert Armistead Stewart's *Index to Printed Virginia Genealogies,* and the *Virginia Historical Index* compiled by Earl G. Swem. Swem's work indexes names from several important Virginia periodicals.

Other states and organizations similarly have published guides and bibliographic works that help the family historian. A good example is *The Genealogical Index of the Newberry Library—Chicago,* in four volumes. This index is widely circulated in public and university libraries and is a photographic reproduction of the analytic index at the Newberry Library. It contains over one million entries arranged by surnames in variant spellings; it also groups surnames under states, counties, and towns, or under surnames allied by intermarriage.

The LDS genealogical library in Salt Lake City, Utah, has cataloged more than one hundred and seventy thousand volumes of family and local history but has not published bibliographies of its collections. However, the MCC (microfilm copy of its card catalog), with supplements, is found in LDS branch libraries of the Genealogical Society throughout the United States, Canada, and Mexico. Selected cards relating to surnames and localities were filmed from the main library's card catalog to make the collection.

The library is now using the technology of the future to help researchers locate records of the past by converting its card catalog to computer-produced microfiche entries, copies of which will be furnished branch libraries as they are produced. Since January 1979 all cataloging of material received has been put into the computer catalog; it is not found in the main catalog. This means that until the catalog is completed (in about ten years), researchers will need to use both the card catalog and the computer-produced microfiche entries to get a full view of the library's holdings. In the meantime, the library continues to add to its family and local history collection and is probably the best repository of its kind in the world.

Do not neglect biographical collections in family history research. Perhaps a direct ancestor is not the main subject of a publication, but he or one of his relatives might be included in group collections. It is hard to estimate how many biographical publications have been compiled, but they must number in the thousands. There are local, state, regional, national, and specialized biographical collections in libraries throughout the country.

Appleton's Cyclopaedia of American Biography, edited by James Grant Wilson and John Fiske, was published in eleven volumes in 1887; and *Who's Who in America* has been published continuously since 1899. Later compilations include the *Dictionary of American Biography* and *The National Cyclopaedia of American Biography,* each containing hundreds of entries. Specialized biographical publications are also in print, such as the *Biographical Directory of the American Congress 1774–1961* and *American Men of Science,* edited by Jaques Cattell.

Andrew Jenson, former assistant historian of the LDS Church, compiled the *Latter-day Saint Biographical Encyclopedia,* four volumes, in 1920. *The Colonial Clergy of Virginia, North Carolina, and South Carolina* by Frederick Lewis Weis is cataloged at Brigham Young University in Provo, Utah, as are biographical works on Baptists, Catholics, Mennonites, and Methodists. The Brigham Young University also has biographical collections relating to alumni of several American universities, some dating back to the seventeenth, eighteenth, and nineteenth centuries. Other libraries undoubtedly have similar collections.

Genealogical dictionaries and compendia. John Farmer's *A Genealogical Register of the First Settlers of New England* was the first real attempt to publish a genealogical dictionary in America and has served the family historian well. His work was followed by James Savage's *Genealogical Dictionary of the First Settlers of New England,* reprinted in four volumes by the Genealogical Publishing Company in Baltimore in 1965. Savage used Farmer as his primary source but did not conduct original research to support his listings. However, his work has been very useful, especially with regard to the earliest families of New England. Many individual family histories and genealogies have been published subsequent to those of Farmer and Savage that perhaps should be given preference over them.

The *Genealogical Dictionary of Maine and New Hampshire* by Sybil Noyes, Charles Thornton Libby, and Walter Goodwin Davis is another example of a good genealogical dictionary. Three generations of Rhode Island settlers who came to America before 1690 are listed in John Osborn Austin's *Genealogical Dictionary of Rhode Island* published in 1887. Corrections and additions by G. Andrews Moriarty have been published in volumes 19, 21, 26, and 30 of the *American Genealogist: The Connecticut Quarterly Magazine*.

Perhaps one of the most popular genealogical compendiums is Frederick A. Virkus's *The Abridged Compendium of American Genealogy* in seven volumes. It includes information on descendants of many of America's first families, based on Savage's work plus circularized requests. This work must be used with caution, as it contains some errors.

Periodical literature. A quantity of material relating to family history has been published in genealogical and historical periodicals, much of it indexed. All kinds of information has been included—not only family and local history, but also valuable source information: Bible records, church records, cemetery and tombstone inscriptions, marriage records, land and court records, census records, and others. Nearly any topic or subject can be found.

State and national organizations—including libraries, archives, and societies—have been responsible for most of the literature, but private and local organizations also have been active. Logically, historical periodicals concentrate more on social, economic, and political topics, while genealogical periodicals cover subjects specializing in family history. Examples are available from every state and many private and local sources.

Kip Sperry, a graduate of the genealogical program at Brigham Young University currently employed by the Genealogical Society of Utah, compiled *Survey of American Genealogical Periodicals and Indexes,* an authoritative work on the subject.

Lester J. Cappon compiled *American Genealogical Periodicals: A Bibliography with a Chronological Finding List,* also very useful for family historians. And the late Donald Lines Jacobus is responsible for an excellent three-volume series that indexes family history in American genealogical periodicals. His first volume was published in 1932 and covered the chief genealogical periodicals through 1931—except those that provided their own complete general indexes, such as the *New England Historical and Genealogical Register.* His second volume was published in 1948 and covered 1932–46, including a few titles that were overlooked in the first volume. His third volume was published in 1952 and covered 1946–52. The foundation for Jacobus's work was a card file made for his own use from complete sets of the *New York Genealogical and Biographical Record* through 1931 and volumes 51 through 85 of the *New England Historical and Genealogical Register;* they were two of the oldest publications of their type and contained masses of important genealogical material. From there Mr. Jacobus expanded his work to include many other valuable periodicals.

Volume three included Jacobus's own index, chiefly concerning families of New England and New York. In his last volume, he wrote that he "now lays down the task, feeling that his efforts have been of great aid to many seekers and that he now deserves a rest from his labors, but with the hope that some altruist may assume the thankless task and continue an index of this type."

Since 1962, the *Genealogical Periodical Annual Index* (GPAI) has attempted to fulfill Mr. Jacobus's wishes. Ellen Stanley Rogers edited volumes 1–4 and George Ely Russel has edited those since.

Regional and local history. A wealth of genealogical and historical information can also be found in regional and local histories. Many towns, cities, and counties have had books and pamphlets published about their inhabitants, and regional histories also include such information. There are more than three thousand counties in the United States, and all of them have had one or more histories published about them. Some town histories for New England are nothing more than genealogies of early inhabitants, and more than half of many regional histories are made up of portraits and biographical references.

United States Local Histories in the Library of Congress, edited by Marion J. Kaminkow, has been published in five volumes (1975). It lists some 90,000 works, arranged on a geographical basis according to the Library of Congress classification system. Many of the works listed provide valuable information about early settlers, churches, schools, industry, and local government, as well as sketches of community leaders. An index to works with biographical content in the Library of Congress local history collection is in print and also on microfilm.

A Consolidated Bibliography of County Histories in Fifty States in 1961 by Clarence Stewart Peterson is a popular guide to local history, but it is not exhaustive. Several of the references cited above, such as the Newberry Index and Munsell's works, can also be used as guides to regional and local history.

Research Publications Incorporated, an organization headquartered in Woodbridge, Connecticut, is providing an excellent service to family and local history through its microfilming of county and regional histories. Its "Reel Index to the Microfilm Edition of New York County and Regional Histories and Atlases" provides bibliographic information on just under five hundred works relating to New York. It is part of an extensive preservation program that makes available local and regional histories and atlases published in the nineteenth and early part of the twentieth centuries.

Special Genealogical Indexes

Many libraries have compiled special indexes and files of genealogical significance, particularly where a strong local interest in family history exists. The work—usually done by local people and library personnel on a volunteer basis—includes the indexing or clipping of newspaper obituaries, births, marriages, deaths, burials, tombstone inscriptions, and census records. Other sources also are included in some instances.

Three special genealogical indexes and files of general significance to family history are the Temple Records Index Bureau, the Family Group Record Archives, and the International Genealogical Index (formerly known as the Computer File Index) at the LDS genealogical library in Salt Lake City, Utah. Nearly one hundred million individuals have been identified in these three collections, and the last two continue to expand at a rapid rate each year. I will explain their origin, content, and availability in more detail in Chapter 4.

You can see from the different record groups and sources identified in this section that a great amount of genealogy and family history is already in print, merely waiting for you to locate and investigate it. You can begin in the nearest local library, then branch out to other jurisdictions and facilities as time and circumstances permit until you have completed your intended project.

4 Vital, Church, and Cemetery Records

The primary sources for family history are records, documents, and memorabilia created by private and governmental organizations at local, state, and national levels. They go hand-in-hand with family and home sources, compiled secondary sources, and special genealogical indexes, and they usually provide the greatest volume of material for research. Included in this category are vital records, church and cemetery records, court and land records, military records, emigration records, and miscellaneous sources.

Vital Records

This record group is comprised of birth, marriage, and death records created and maintained by governmental authority at local, state, or national level. Unlike many foreign countries, the United States and Canada have not enacted national registration programs; responsibility is left to states and provinces. The U.S. Department of Health, Education, and Welfare publishes guides to state and local health statistics and lists addresses and fees for state vital records.

State registration of births and deaths. The registration of births and deaths in the United States began as early as 1841 in Massachusetts and as late as 1920 in New Mexico, with the median year being 1907. In most state offices birth records are confidential and may be obtained only by the individuals to whom they pertain and their descendants. Fees vary from state to state, currently averaging between three and five dollars per certificate. Copies of death records can be obtained from most state offices without restriction, but for a fee. A copy of *DHEW Publication No. HRA 76-1142* (revised) may be obtained from the Superintendent of Documents, U.S. Government Printing Office, Washington, D.C. 20402, giving current fees and addresses by state.

1. PLACE OF BIRTH
STATE OF TEXAS

TEXAS DEPARTMENT OF HEALTH
BUREAU OF VITAL STATISTICS
STANDARD CERTIFICATE OF BIRTH

COUNTY OF Hall

CITY OR PRECINCT NO. Memphis, — GIVE STREET AND NUMBER OR NAME OF INSTITUTION

2. FULL NAME OF CHILD Ronald J.Melton

RESIDENCE OF THE MOTHER STREET AND NO. CITY Memphis COUNTY Hall STATE Texas

3. SEX	4. TWIN, TRIPLET, OTHER (FOR PLURAL BIRTHS ONLY)	5. NUMBER, IN ORDER OF BIRTH (FOR PLURAL BIRTHS ONLY)	6. LEGITIMATE?	7. DATE OF BIRTH
male			yes	March 24th 19 12

FATHER		MOTHER	
8. FULL NAME	John G.Melton	14. FULL MAIDEN NAME	Minnie Pearl Knox
SOCIAL SECURITY NUMBER		SOCIAL SECURITY NUMBER	
9. POSTOFFICE ADDRESS	Memphis, Texas	15. POSTOFFICE ADDRESS	Memphis, Texas.
10. COLOR OR RACE	white	16. COLOR OR RACE	white
11. AGE AT LAST BIRTHDAY (YEARS)	22	17. AGE AT LAST BIRTHDAY (YEARS)	20
12. BIRTHPLACE (STATE OR COUNTRY)	Rockwall, Texas	18. BIRTHPLACE (STATE OR COUNTRY)	Tennessee
OCCUPATION 13A. TRADE, PROFESSION OR KIND OF WORK DONE	Farmer	OCCUPATION 19A. TRADE, PROFESSION OR KIND OF WORK DONE	Housewife
13B. INDUSTRY OR BUSINESS IN WHICH ENGAGED	Farm	19B. INDUSTRY OR BUSINESS IN WHICH ENGAGED	Home
20. NUMBER OF CHILDREN BORN TO THIS MOTHER INCLUDING THIS BIRTH	1	21. NUMBER OF CHILDREN BORN TO THIS MOTHER AND NOW LIVING	1
SIGNATURE OF INFORMANT	John Gordon Melton	ADDRESS OF INFORMANT	Wilmington, Calif

22. MEDICAL ATTENDANCE

I HEREBY CERTIFY THAT I ATTENDED THE BIRTH OF THIS CHILD BORN ALIVE XXXXX AT ______ M. ON THE ABOVE DATE, AND THE PROPHYLACTIC USED TO PREVENT OPHTHALMIA NEONATORUM WAS ______

3-24- 19 12 (DATE) Chas.F.Wilson (SIGNATURE) M. D. XXXX Memphis, (POSTOFFICE ADDRESS) TEXAS

23. FILE NUMBER	FILE DATE	SIGNATURE OF LOCAL REGISTRAR	POSTOFFICE ADDRESS
1212	3-24 19 12	S.G.Alexander	Memphis, TEXAS

MILITARY EX-SERVICE RECORD OF FATHER

(A) IS THE FATHER REPORTED TO HAVE BEEN IN SUCH SERVICE?

(B) NAME OF ORGANIZATION IN WHICH SERVICE WAS RENDERED

(C) SERIAL NUMBER OF DISCHARGE PAPERS OR ADJUSTED SERVICE CERTIFICATE

THE STATE OF TEXAS
County of Hall

I hereby certify that the above certificate is a true and accurate copy of the record of birth of Ronald J.Melton, filed in my office, and is of record on Page 24 Vol. 2 of the Record of Births of Hall County, Texas.

Witness my hand and seal of office this 16th day of November 19 42.

G.M.Dial
County Clerk, Hall County, Texas.

By Gladys Johnson
Deputy

Birth records filed with state offices vary in content but usually contain the name, date, and place of birth for the principle subject; the names of his parents and sometimes their ages and residences or places of birth; the occupation of the father; sometimes the number of other children born alive to the parents; the name of the attending physician or midwife and address or residence; and registration place and date.

Death records also vary in content from state to state but usually are as inclusive as birth records. Generally they list the name of the deceased and his address or residence; the town, county, and state of death; the cause of death; the place and date of birth (often calculated from the age at death); age at death; names of parents and their places of birth (though often just the state or country); the name and address of the informant; the name and address of the undertaker; signature of the attending physician; and registration data.

State birth records usually originate with the attending physician or midwife; they generally are forwarded to the town or county for recording, then the original is sent to the state office where it is registered and filed. Death records usually originate with the mortician or physician—or some other state official when death was due to unusual circumstances—then follow the same recording procedure as birth records.

Vital records are registered and filed with the state where the event occurred. Usually death records of spouses are filed according to the married name at death, not according to the maiden name.

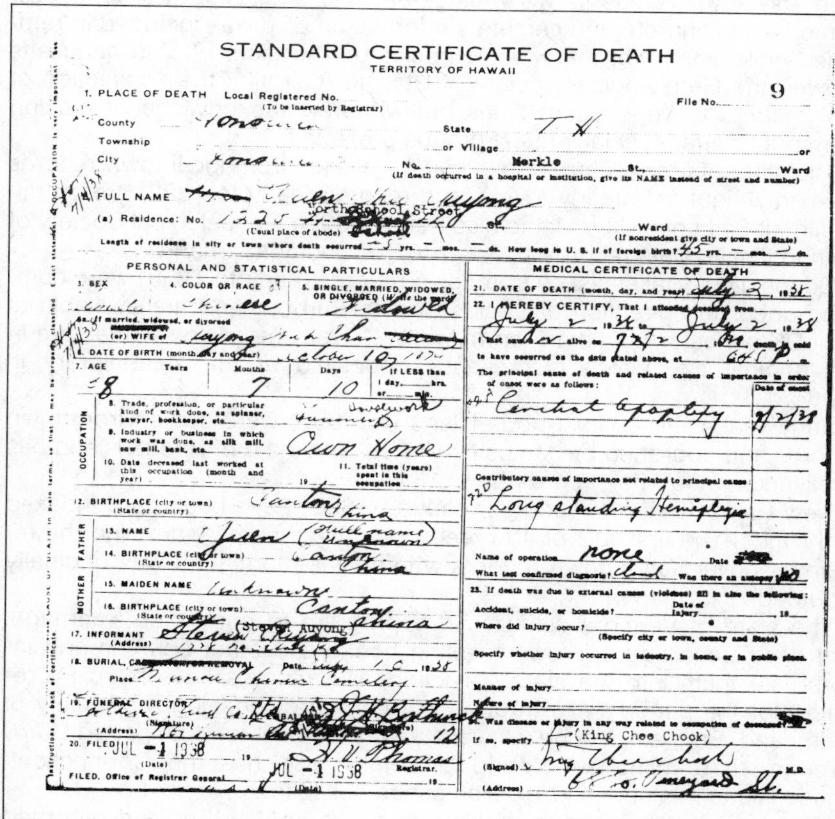

STANDARD CERTIFICATE OF DEATH
TERRITORY OF HAWAII

1. PLACE OF DEATH Local Registered No. (To be inserted by Registrar) File No. 9
County Honolulu State T H
Township or Village
City Honolulu No. Merkle St. Ward
(If death occurred in a hospital or institution, give its NAME instead of street and number)
2. FULL NAME Chun Kee Auyong
(a) Residence: No. 1325 North School Street St. Ward
(Usual place of abode) (If nonresident give city or town and State)
Length of residence in city or town where death occurred 45 yrs. — mos. — ds. How long in U. S. if of foreign birth? 45 yrs. — mos. — ds.

PERSONAL AND STATISTICAL PARTICULARS

3. SEX Female
4. COLOR OR RACE Chinese
5. SINGLE, MARRIED, WIDOWED, OR DIVORCED (write the word) Widowed
5a. If married, widowed, or divorced (or) WIFE of Auyong Hak Chan
6. DATE OF BIRTH (month, day and year) October 10, 1874
7. AGE Years 58 Months 7 Days 10 If LESS than 1 day, ___ hrs. or ___ min.
OCCUPATION
8. Trade, profession, or particular kind of work done, as spinner, sawyer, bookkeeper, etc. Housework
9. Industry or business in which work was done, as silk mill, saw mill, bank, etc. Own Home
10. Date deceased last worked at this occupation (month and year) 19
11. Total time (years) spent in this occupation
12. BIRTHPLACE (city or town) (State or country) Canton China
FATHER
13. NAME Chun (Full name unknown)
14. BIRTHPLACE (city or town) (State or country) Canton China
MOTHER
15. MAIDEN NAME Unknown
16. BIRTHPLACE (city or town) (State or country) Canton China
17. INFORMANT (Stewart Auyong) (Address) 1325 No. School St.
18. BURIAL, CREMATION, OR REMOVAL Date July 10 1938
Place Manoa Chinese Cemetery
19. FUNERAL DIRECTOR EMBALMER (Signature) (Address)
20. FILED JUL -1 1938 (Date) 19 H. V. Thomas Registrar.
FILED, Office of Registrar General JUL -1 1938 (Date) 19

MEDICAL CERTIFICATE OF DEATH

21. DATE OF DEATH (month, day, and year) July 2, 1938
22. I HEREBY CERTIFY, That I attended deceased from July 2 1938 to July 2 1938
I last saw her alive on 7/2 1938, death is said to have occurred on the date stated above, at 6:45 P. m.
The principal cause of death and related causes of importance in order of onset were as follows: Cerebral apoplexy — Date of onset 7/2/38
Contributory causes of importance not related to principal cause: Long standing Hemiplegia
Name of operation none Date of
What test confirmed diagnosis? Clinical Was there an autopsy? no
23. If death was due to external causes (violence) fill in also the following:
Accident, suicide, or homicide? Date of Injury 19
Where did injury occur? (Specify city or town, county and State)
Specify whether injury occurred in industry, in home, or in public place.
Manner of injury
Nature of injury
24. Was disease or injury in any way related to occupation of deceased? no
If so, specify (King Chee Chook)
(Signed) King Chee Chook M.D.
(Address) 68 S. Vineyard St.

Local registration of births and deaths. In many states registration at the county level took place much earlier than registration at the state level, but such programs were rather ineffective and the records somewhat incomplete. Illinois counties began registering as early as 1838, New York in 1847 (but only through 1850), Pennsylvania in 1852 (but only through 1854, then again in 1890), Virginia in 1853, Kentucky in 1862, Michigan in 1867, and Indiana in 1882. Some county programs were aborted after a very few years, but most continued into the late nineteenth century or early twentieth century when state registration was implemented.

Registration at the town level took place in New England from a very early date, and many early town vital statistics have been incorporated into state collections. Details of births, marriages, and deaths were included with historical entries in New England town meeting books, and many have been copied and published or microfilmed and made available to the public.

Over 60 percent of Massachusetts towns have published their early vital statistics (early to 1850) in book form—comprising more than two hundred and fifty volumes at this writing—and the publishing still continues. Some family, church, and cemetery information also was included in published collections that are widely circulated. The state of Massachusetts allowed the Genealogical Society of Utah to microfilm their collection of vital records to very recent times but withdrew the privilege of making them public after special interest groups protested.

The state of Maine card indexed vital statistics from local town records for eighty-eight of its early towns, and records (early to 1892) are on microfilm at Salt Lake City. Maine also permitted the Genealogical Society of Utah to film its state records (1892–1907) including marriages.

Connecticut vital statistics from town records (early to 1850) were compiled under the direction of Lucius Barnes Barbour and are available at the LDS genealogical library on microfilm. Over one million entries are in the original file, which is presently deposited at the state library in Hartford.

Early vital statistics for Rhode Island (to 1850) were copied from town records and published by James N. Arnold. The state of Rhode Island has published annual vital records since 1847.

New Hampshire town records (early to 1890) have been card indexed and filmed. The first 112 of 435 reels comprise a name index and the remainder cover actual town records where vital information was originally recorded.

The state of Vermont established a program to copy birth, marriage, and death records from town meeting books and other sources and incorporate them into the state collection. The records have been microfilmed for the period 1770 through 1971 by the Genealogical Society of Utah, and Brigham Young University has copies for the period 1770 through 1870. (Brigham Young University also has the Connecticut, Rhode Island, Maine, and New Hampshire collections.)

Many towns and cities in addition to those in New England recorded vital statistics independent of the state or county. Some predated state registration by several years, and several continued registration programs after state registration began. For a survey of over one hundred cities in the United States that recorded vital statistics before state registration, see the first edition of *Building an American Pedigree.* Consult it also about state policies and procedures governing public access to official vital records (Wright 1974).

Jurisdictions other than civil have also recorded birth, marriage, and death information; some provide certificates and copies of documents to interested persons. Churches, schools, and hospitals are examples; details concerning their records are discussed in later chapters.

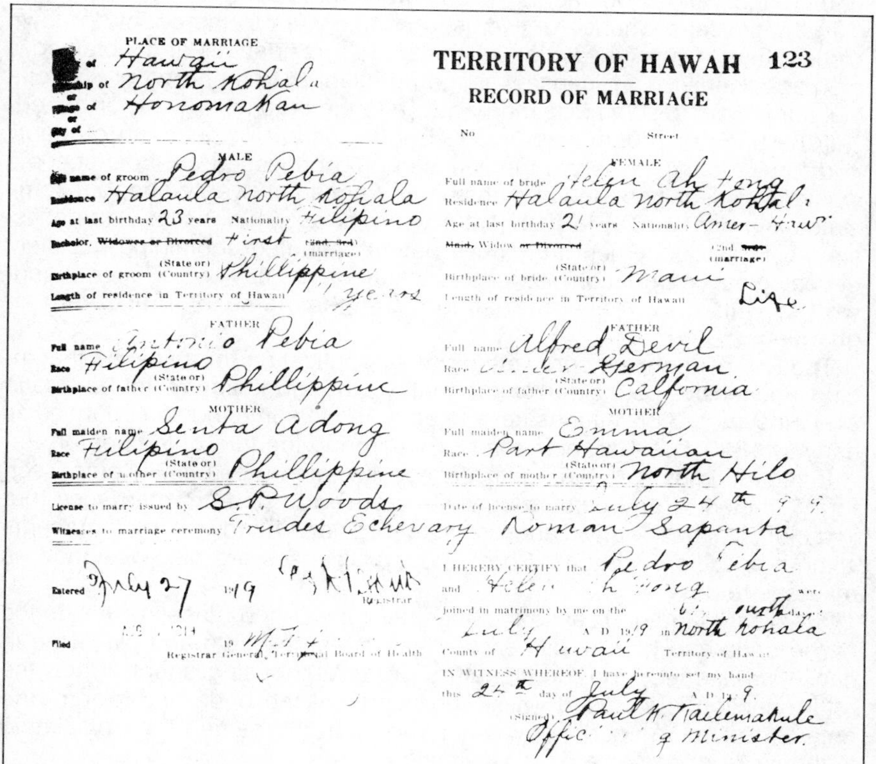

PLACE OF MARRIAGE

of Hawaii
of North Kohala
of Honomakau
of ...

TERRITORY OF HAWAII 123

RECORD OF MARRIAGE

No Street

MALE

Full name of groom Pedro Pebia
Residence Halaula North Kohala
Age at last birthday 23 years Nationality Filipino
Bachelor, ~~Widower or Divorced~~ first (2nd, 3rd) (marriage)
Birthplace of groom (State or) (Country) Phillippine
Length of residence in Territory of Hawaii 1 years

FATHER

Full name Antonio Pebia
Race Filipino
Birthplace of father (State or) (Country) Phillippine

MOTHER

Full maiden name Senta Adong
Race Filipino
Birthplace of mother (State or) (Country) Phillippine

License to marry issued by S. P. Woods
Witnesses to marriage ceremony Trudes Echevary Roman Sapanta

Entered July 27 1919 [illegible] Registrar

Filed AUG 1919 [illegible] Registrar General, Territorial Board of Health

FEMALE

Full name of bride Helen Ah Fong
Residence Halaula North Kohala
Age at last birthday 21 years Nationality Amer-Haw
~~Maid~~, Widow ~~or Divorced~~ 2nd ~~3rd~~ (marriage)
Birthplace of bride (State or) (Country) Maui
Length of residence in Territory of Hawaii Life

FATHER

Full name Alfred Devil
Race [illegible] German
Birthplace of father (State or) (Country) California

MOTHER

Full maiden name Emma
Race Part Hawaiian
Birthplace of mother (State or) (Country) North Hilo

Date of license to marry July 24th 919

I HEREBY CERTIFY that Pedro Pebia and Helen Ah Fong were joined in matrimony by me on the [illegible] day of July A D 1919 in North Kohala County of Hawaii Territory of Hawaii

IN WITNESS WHEREOF, I have hereunto set my hand this 24th day of July A D 1919.

(Signed) Paul K. Kaiewakule
Officiating Minister

Marriage records. The civil registration of marriages has been the responsibility of counties and towns in America since early settlement; only recently have some states assumed this responsibility. Civil marriage records usually date from the organization of the respective county or town, except where records have been destroyed or in the states of New York, Utah, South Carolina, and Pennsylvania. Of course unofficial marriage records have been kept by many ecclesiastical officials and family members in all states, but we are considering only official civil registration at this point.

Marriage records date from the early 1600s in many New England towns, and some county records in the South have been preserved from the early 1700s—but most county records are incomplete until the revolutionary war period. Marriage records in the Midwest, Southwest, and Far West are more complete, usually dating from the organization of the respective counties.

A variety of civil marriage records have been kept in counties and towns: applications for licenses, licenses to marry, consent notices or decrees, marriage intentions, bonds, certificates, returns, and register entries. The genealogical content varies according to the period and jurisdiction, but the record usually includes names, marriage date, and place of marriage. Some documents include much more.

In the typical sequence of events, a couple went to the county or town clerk (often in the jurisdiction of the bride's residence) and obtained a marriage license. The license was then presented to a church or civil official authorized to solemnize marriages, and the ceremony was performed.

If the bride or groom was under age, the parent or guardian probably had to give consent before the license could be issued. In most states a woman was legally of age at eighteen and a man at twenty-one, but some states allowed women to marry at a younger age. If consent was necessary, a formal document may have been completed containing excellent genealogical information, or a short statement may have been handwritten with only the authorization and the name of the parent or guardian.

Today most couples complete a formal application for a license that includes extensive genealogical information, though this may not be true in every instance. Applications have been noted in some Indiana counties as early as 1850, but elsewhere they begin around the turn of the century.

In recent times the marriage license is issued in a beautifully embossed form directed to any person legally authorized to perform marriages, but in colonial times many licenses were ordinary handwritten documents without specific directions. Some modern licenses are also designed as marriage returns.

A typical marriage license includes the names and places of residence of the bride and groom, sometimes their ages, the date and place the license was issued, and the signature of the authorizing agent. When the return section is included it lists the names of the bride and groom, the date and place the ceremony was performed, the name of the officiating authority, and the names of any witnesses.

Obtaining a marriage license has not always been necessary to legally marry in the United States. The publication or proclamation of banns for two or three consecutive sabbath days without objection being voiced authorized a minister to perform the ceremony without the couple obtaining a license. A fee was generally assessed for a license but not necessarily for a church ceremony, and many people availed themselves of that opportunity to save money. Social custom dictated the proper procedure to follow, and it varied from time to time and place to place. The practice of proclaiming banns was still in effect in Ohio as late as 1952.

In New England it was customary to publish the couple's "intention to marry" in the town meeting books; sometimes this is the only available evidence that the marriage took place. On one occasion in Biddeford, Maine, a couple indicated their intention to marry, and the town clerk so entered it in the town meeting books. However, the father of the bride objected to the marriage, and the town clerk also recorded that. Evidently the father's desires were ignored, because numerous descendants of the couple are living in Utah and Wyoming at the present time.

In many southern states, at or near the time the license was obtained the couple also had to post a bond showing eligibility for marriage. In many instances marriage bonds predate other marriage records, and sometimes they have survived where licenses, returns, and register entries have been lost or destroyed. Sometimes the bondsman, surety, or security was a close relative of the bride or groom, and helpful kinship information can therefore be obtained from the bond record.

After the authorized official performed the marriage ceremony, the couple was given a certificate and similar information was sent to the courthouse or town hall for official registration. Sometimes the marriage license and the return were attached, but in other cases a separate form was used for the return. Although the marriage certificate was usually given to the bride and groom, some are found among marriage records in courthouses or town halls.

Marriage registers (books of entry) have been kept in many counties and towns. The entries usually consist of chronological listings compiled when the marriage license was issued or when the marriage return was received from the officiating authority. Early New England marriage entries were often listed chronologically in the town meeting books among other entries of town business, but later special volumes or sections in volumes were reserved for marriage entries.

The registers were generally designed to show the names of the bride and groom, date of marriage, and information relating to the actual performance of the ceremony (information from the marriage return). In some cases the marriage register entry was made and numbered at the time the license was issued—not necessarily after the ceremony was performed or when the return was received—so the date the license was issued might vary from the date the ceremony was performed. Some marriages were performed the same day the licenses were issued while others were performed several days after. It is also possible that some couples never actually married, even though they obtained a license and such information was recorded in the marriage registers.

County and town officials will usually provide copies of marriage entries for a fee. They are often certified copies of the original register entries, but they may be copied from other documents. Where facilities are available, photostats are provided, but generally a certified copy of the original record is made.

Official registration of vital statistics in the United States and territories. The Genealogical Society of Utah has microfilmed extensively in Arkansas, Connecticut, Delaware, District of Columbia, Florida, Georgia, Illinois, Indiana, Iowa, Kentucky, Louisiana, Maine, Maryland, Massachusetts, Michigan, Mississippi, Missouri, New Hampshire, New Jersey, New York, North Carolina, Ohio, Pennsylvania, Rhode Island, South Carolina, Tennessee, Texas, Utah, Vermont, Virginia, Washington, and West Virginia.

Wherever possible they have filmed vital records—including marriages—

at the town, county, and state levels. Some states allowed all records to be filmed, while others were very selective. However, most allowed filming of county records, which include marriage and some early birth and death records.

When the birth, marriage, or death you are looking for occurred in a modern period (1900 or after), you first should approach the state offices for vital statistics registration, then try the county, town, or city. For marriage records, the county or town will usually be more productive. For an interesting article on variations in state vital statistics registration, see *Genealogical Journal* 8:3 (September 1979, pp. 135–58).

The following list shows current locations of state offices for vital statistics registration in the United States and includes their earliest dates for recording. Keep in mind that the earliest date for recording may not necessarily be the date complete records were kept; this may have been several years later—but *some* records are on file as early as the dates listed.

Locality	B	D	M	Address
Alabama	1908	1908	1908	Bureau of Vital Statistics, State Department of Public Health, Montgomery 36104.
Alaska	1913	1913	1913	Bureau of Vital Statistics, Department of Health and Welfare, Pouch "H", Juneau 99801.
Samoa	1900	1900	1900	Territorial Registrar, Government of American Samoa, Pago Pago 96799.
Arizona	1909	1909	1909	Division of Vital Records, State Department of Health, P.O. Box 3887, Phoenix 84030.
Arkansas	1914	1914	1917	Division of Vital Records, Department of Health, 4815 West Markham, Little Rock 72201.
California	1905	1905	1905	Vital Statistics Section, State Department of Health, 410 N Street, Sacramento 95814.
Canal Zone	1905	1905		Vital Statistics Clerk, Health Bureau, Balboa Heights, Canal Zone.
Colorado	1910	1900	1968	Records and Statistics Section, Department of Health, 4210 East 11th Avenue, Denver 80220.
Connecticut	1897	1897		Public Health Statistics Section, State Department of Health, 79 Elm Street, Hartford 06115.
Delaware	1861	1861	1847	Bureau of Vital Statistics, Division of Public Health, J. S. Cooper Memorial Building, Dover 19901.
Washington, D.C.	1871	1855	1811	Department of Human Resources, Vital Records Section, Rm 1022, 300 Indiana Avenue N.W., Washington, D.C. 20001.
Florida	1865	1877	1927	Division of Health, Bureau of Vital Statistics, P.O. Box 210, Jacksonville 32201.

Locality	B	D	M	Address
Georgia	1919	1919	1953	Vital Records Unit, State Department of Human Resources, Rm 217-H, 47 Trinity Avenue S.W., Atlanta 30334.
Guam	1901	1902	1899	Vital Statistics, Department of Public Health and Social Services, P.O. Box 2816, Agana, M.I. 96910.
Hawaii	1850	1861	1849	Research and Statistics Office, State Department of Health, P.O. Box 3378, Honolulu 96801.
Idaho	1911	1911	1911	Bureau of Vital Statistics, Department of Health and Welfare, State House, Boise 83720.
Illinois	1916	1916	1962	Office of Vital Records, Department of Public Health, 535 West Jefferson Street, Springfield 62761.
Indiana	1907	1907		Division of Vital Records, State Board of Health, 1330 West Michigan Street, Indianapolis 46206.
Iowa	1880	1880	1880	Division of Records and Statistics, State Department of Health, Des Moines 50319.
Kansas	1911	1911	1913	Bureau of Registration and Health Statistics, 6700 South Topeka Avenue, Topeka 66620.
Kentucky	1911	1911	1958	Office of Vital Statistics, State Department of Health, 275 East Maine Street, Frankfort 40601.
Louisiana	1914	1914		Office of Vital Records, State Department of Health, P.O. Box 60630, New Orleans 70160.
Maine	1892	1892	1892	Office of Vital Records, State Department of Health and Welfare, State House, Augusta 04333.
Maryland	1898	1898	1951	Division of Vital Records, State Department of Health, 201 W. Preston, P.O. Box 13146, Baltimore 21203.
Massachusetts	1841	1841	1841	Registrar of Vital Statistics, Room 103 McCormack Bldg., 1 Ashburton Place, Boston 02108.
Michigan	1867	1867	1868	Vital and Health Statistics, Department of Public Health, 3600 N. Logan Street, Lansing 48914.
Minnesota	1900	1900	1958	Department of Health, Section of Vital Statistics, 717 Delaware Street S.E., Minneapolis 55440.
Mississippi	1912	1912	1926	Vital Records Registration Unit, State Board of Health, P.O. Box 1700, Jackson 39205.
Missouri	1910	1910	1948	Bureau of Vital Records, Division of Health, State Department of Public Health, Jefferson City 65101.

Locality	B	D	M	Address
Montana	1907	1907	1943	Bureau of Records and Statistics, State Department of Health and Environmental Sciences, Helena 59601.
Nebraska	1904	1904	1909	Bureau of Vital Statistics, State Department of Health, Lincoln Bldg., 1003 "O" Street, Lincoln 68508.
Nevada	1911	1911	1968	Department of Human Resources, Office of Vital Records, Capitol Complex, Carson City 89710.
New Hampshire	1640	1640	1640	Bureau of Vital Statistics, Department of Health and Welfare, 61 South Spring Street, Concord 03301.
New Jersey	1878	1878	1878	Bureau of Vital Statistics, State Department of Health, Box 1540, Trenton 08625.
New Mexico	1920	1920		Vital Records, Health and Social Services Department, PERA Building, Room 118, Santa Fe 87501.
New York	1880	1880	1880	Bureau of Vital Records, State Department of Health, Empire State Plaza, Tower Building, Albany 12237.
North Carolina	1913	1913	1962	Dept. of Human Resources, Div. of Health Services, Vital Records Branch, P.O. Box 2091, Raleigh 27602.
North Dakota	1893	1893	1925	Division of Vital Records, Office of Statistical Services, State Department of Health, Bismarck 58505.
Ohio	1908	1908	1949	Division of Vital Statistics, Department of Health, G-20 Ohio Departments Bldg, 65 Front St., Columbus 43215.
Oklahoma	1908	1908		Vital Records Section, State Department of Health, P.O. Box 53551, Oklahoma City 73105.
Oregon	1903	1903	1907	Vital Statistics Section, State Health Division, P.O. Box 231, Portland 97207.
Pennsylvania	1906	1906		Division of Vital Statistics, State Department of Health, P.O. Box 1528, Newcastle 16103.
Puerto Rico	1931	1931	1931	Division of Demographic Registry and Vital Statistics, Department of Health, San Juan 00908.
Rhode Island	1853	1853	1853	Division of Vital Statistics, State Department of Health, Room 101 Health Bldg., Providence 02908.
South Carolina	1915	1915	1950	Division of Vital Records, Bureau of Health Measurement, 2600 Bull Street, Columbia 29201.
South Dakota	1905	1905	1905	Division of Public Health Statistics, State Department of Health, Pierre 57501.

Locality	B	D	M	Address
Tennessee	1914	1914	1945	Division of Vital Statistics, State Department of Health, Cordell Hull Building, Nashville 37219.
Texas	1903	1903	1966	Bureau of Vital Statistics, Department of Health Resources, 410 East 5th Street, Austin 78701.
Utah	1905	1905	1954	Department of Social Services, Bureau of Health Statistics, 150 West South Temple Street, Salt Lake City 84101.
Vermont	1770	1770	1770	Secretary of State, Vital Records Department, State House, Montpelier 05602.
Virgin Islands	1906	1906	1954	Registrar of Vital Statistics, Charlotte Amalie, St. Thomas 00802.
St. Croix	1893	1893	1890	Registrar of Vital Statistics, Charles Harwood Memorial Hospital, St. Croix, Virgin Islands.
Virginia	1912	1912	1912	Bureau of Vital Records, State Department of Health, James Madison Building, Box 1000, Richmond 23208.
Washington	1907	1907	1968	Bureau of Vital Statistics, Department of Social and Health Services, P.O. Box 709, Olympia 98504.
West Virginia	1917	1917	1921	Division of Vital Statistics, State Department of Health, State Office Building No. 3, Charleston 25305.
Wisconsin	1876	1876	1840	Bureau of Health Statistics, Division of Health, P.O. Box 309, Madison 53701.
Wyoming	1909	1909	1914	Vital Records Services, Division of Health and Medical Services, State Office Building West, Cheyenne 82002.

Official registration of vital statistics in Canada. The registration of births, marriages, and deaths in Canada has been similar to that in the United States. Each province recorded its own vital statistics, and the beginning dates for registration vary from province to province.

The following provincial offices in charge of civil registration in Canada have records covering the periods indicated. Inquiries should be directed to the respective offices:

Alberta: Complete records date from 1898, supplemented by some records of birth as early as 1853 and death from 1893. They are in custody of The Director of Vital Statistics, Department of Public Health, Edmonton.

British Columbia: Although official registration of births, marriages, and deaths date from 1872, records in the early years are incomplete. There are some baptismal records on file as early as 1849, but the effective registration date is 1872. Originals or copies are available from The Division of Vital Statistics, Department of Health Services and Hospital Insurance, Victoria.

Manitoba: The registration of births, marriages, and deaths is complete from 1882; the office also has some incomplete church records in its possession. For the latter, the denomination must be known. Records are in custody of The Recorder of Statistics and Registrar: Births, Marriages, and Deaths, Department of Health, Winnipeg.

New Brunswick: The registration of vital statistics in this province is complete from 1888, with some records of birth on file earlier than that date. Records are in custody of The Registration General, Department of Health, Fredericton.

Newfoundland: Civil registration in this province began in 1892; its records are in custody of The Registrar of Vital Statistics, Department of Health, St. John's.

Nova Scotia: This province has vital statistics on file for the period 1864 through 1876, but from 1876 to 1908 only marriages were recorded. Complete records date from 1909. Records are in custody of The Registrar General, Department of Public Health, Halifax.

Ontario: The registration of births, marriages, and deaths in Ontario province dates from 1 July 1869. The records are in custody of The Deputy Registrar General, 70 Lombard Street, Toronto.

Prince Edward Island: Effective registration began in 1906, but some marriage records are on file dating from 1783. The records are in custody of The Director of Vital Statistics, Department of Health, Charlottetown.

Quebec: Effective provincial registration did not begin until 1926 in Quebec Province; records are in custody of The Department of Health, Demography Branch, Quebec City. Catholic church records exist from a very early period in this province.

The Public Archives at Ottowa has some records not found in provincial offices, including seven linear feet of microfilmed marriage bonds relating to Quebec (1779 and 1818–67) and approximately eleven linear feet relating to Ontario (1803–45). The records are indexed and may be borrowed through interlibrary loan programs. The Public Archives has many other major genealogical sources among its collections as well.

The Genealogical Society of Utah has done extensive microfilming in Canada. At this writing, Canada ranks eleventh among forty-six foreign countries whose records have been copied. Catholic parish registers, Protestant church records, national and local census records, cemetery records, land and probate court records, emigration records, and newspapers are among the Canadian records copied and on file at Salt Lake City. Of special significance are more than two hundred volumes of marriage contracts relating to the province of Quebec (dating from 1636) and more than one hundred and forty reels of microfilm relating to marriages in Quebec that were copied from Catholic parish registers (1640–1959). The latter is popularly known as the "Loiselle" collection.

Church and Cemetery Records

Church and cemetery records are good supplements to civil vital records and may be considered primary sources in their own right. They are excellent sources to fill gaps where official records are missing or were never kept, and they often contain important facts that are not recorded in any other source.

Church affiliation. America has been a mixture of national and ethnic groups since the beginning; consequently Americans have always differed greatly in their philosophies and religious affiliations. No state church has been established as in many foreign countries; rather religious diversity has been the rule.

During the colonial period, settlers in New England were predominantly Congregationalists and Baptists, with a few Quakers (Friends) centered in Rhode Island, and other Protestant groups scattered throughout the region.

Religious affiliation was more diversified in the middle colonies, with Dutch Reformed, Lutheran, Quaker, Presbyterian, and Catholic churches dominant. Mennonites, Amish, Moravians (Brethren), and other Pietist groups were also present, with Baptists, Methodists, and other Christian denominations established by the eighteenth century.

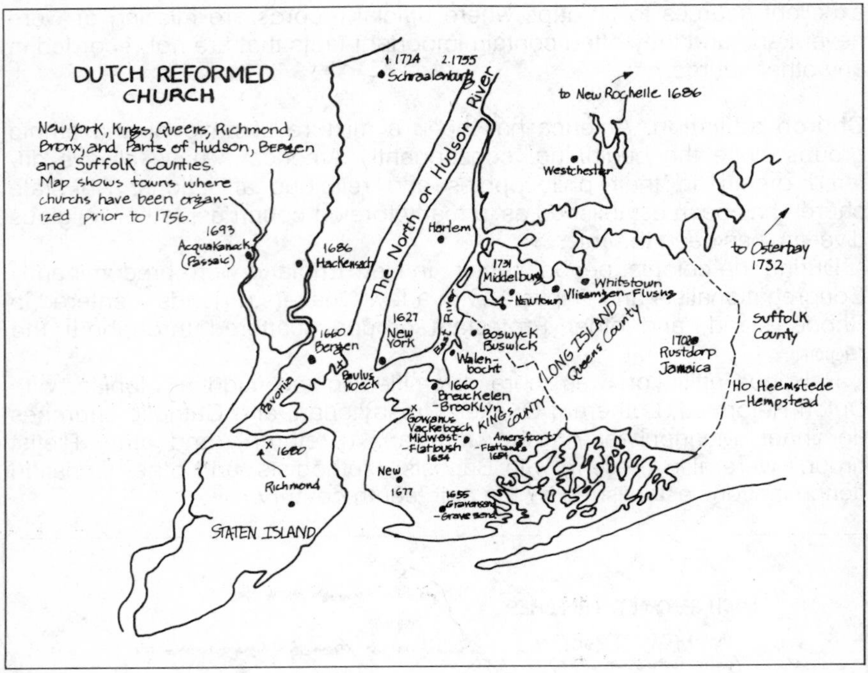

The first English settlers in the southern colonies were primarily Church of England or Anglican (called Protestant Episcopal after the Revolution), but Quakers, Moravians, Baptists, Presbyterians, and other Protestant groups became more numerous during the eighteenth century as migration increased and the population grew.

French Protestants (Huguenots) were early settlers in the southern colonies, with a church established in Charleston, South Carolina, in 1680. They were also among the early settlers along Pamlico Sound in the tidewater region of North Carolina, and they were numerous in Virginia, Maryland, and New York. Perhaps they settled as far north as New England, but if so they were integrated into the mainstream of population and seemingly did not retain exclusive ethnic identity.

Even though the country at the close of the Revolution was quite diversified religiously, it was still based primarily on national origin and ethnic background.

British immigrants belonged to Church of England, Presbyterian, Baptist, Quaker, Congregationalist, and Catholic denominations. Settlers from Flanders and the Netherlands were generally Dutch Reformed or Anabaptist; those from the Scandinavian countries (including Finland) and the northern part of Germany usually were Lutheran or Reformed Lutheran.

Many settlers from Switzerland, the southern part of Germany, the Rhineland, Westphalia, and Holstein were termed "Pietists" or "Anabaptists." Mennonites, Amish, Moravians (Brethren), and many other Protestant denominations in America today trace their origin to these groups.

Immigrants from France included Catholics as well as Protestants; most of those who emigrated from southern Europe after the American Revolution were Catholic. Immigrants from Ireland and central Europe also were predominantly Catholic.

As America's population grew, migration increased to the South and

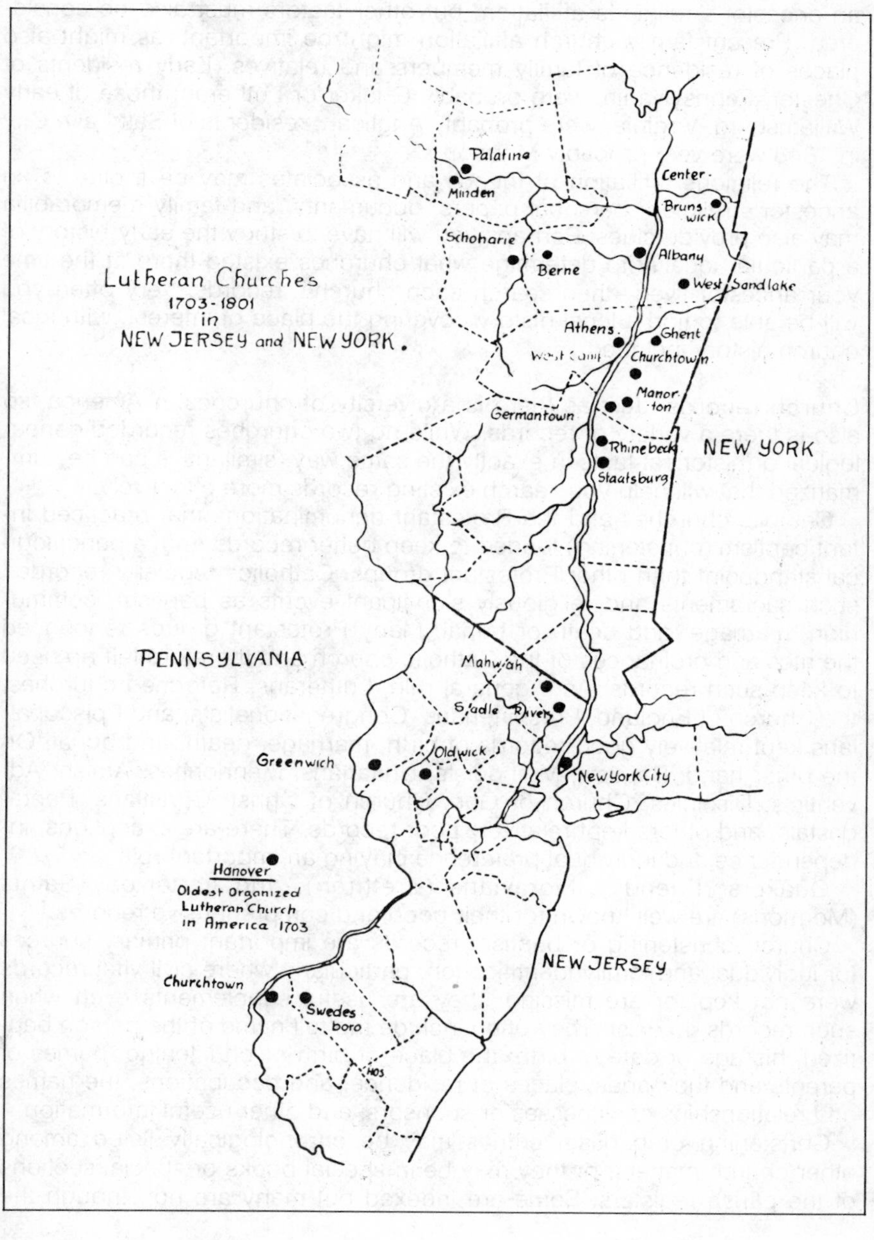

West—mixing settlers with different religious philosophies and backgrounds. Social, economic, and political life also had its effect on the religious life of the settlers; emotional religious revivals and spiritual experiences of individuals and their leaders added to the diversity of religious affiliation in the country.

National origin and ethnic background are still important in determining an ancestor's religious affiliation, but other factors must also be considered. Present family church affiliation might be important, as might also places of residence of family members and relatives. Early residents of Chester, Pennsylvania, were probably Quaker or Lutheran; those of early Williamsburg, Virginia, were probably Anglican; residents of Salt Lake City in 1848 were very probably Mormon.

The religious affiliation of friends and associates may be a clue to an ancestor's religion; personal papers, documents, and family memorabilia may also provide clues. Perhaps you will have to study the early history of a particular locality to determine what churches existed there at the time your ancestor lived—then search each church's records. Very often you will be able to find a local history covering the place of interest, with local church history included.

Church records. Just as there is a diversity of churches in America, so also is there a variety of records. While no two churches recorded genealogical or historical facts in exactly the same way, similarities can be summarized that will help you search existing records more effectively.

Catholic churches and the Protestant denominations that practiced infant baptism (christening) tended to keep better records from a genealogical standpoint than other Protestant groups. Catholics regularly recorded such sacraments and religiously significant events as baptism, communion, marriage, and death or burial. Many Protestant groups renounced the rites and ordinances of the Catholic church and therefore felt no need to keep such records. As a general rule, Lutherans, Reformed churches, the Church of England, Presbyterians, Congregationalists, and Episcopalians kept relatively good records of birth, marriage, death, and burial. On the other hand, Baptists, Methodists, Unitarians, Mennonites, Amish, Adventists, Disciples, Church of God, Church of Christ, Christians, Pentacostals, and others kept relatively poor records. There are exceptions, independence and individual preference playing an important role.

Quakers (Friends), Moravians (Brethren), and Latter-day Saints (Mormons) are well known for their good and comprehensive records.

Church christening or baptism records are important primary sources for individual and family identification, particularly where civil vital records were not kept or are missing; they are useful supplements even when such records do exist. They often include the full name of the person baptized; his age or date of birth; the place of birth or christening; names of parents and their ages, places of residence, and occupations; the names and relationships of witnesses or sponsors; and other useful information.

Christening or baptism entries may be chronologically listed among other church matters, or they may be in special books or special sections of the parish registers. Some are indexed but many are not, though the surname is often written in large captions in the margins of the registers. Most records are in English, but some Catholic registers are in Latin, and Reformed church records are in German, Dutch, or other languages.

Baptism entries may appear in church records where the christening of infants is not an accepted practice; such entries usually result from adult baptisms into church membership. At times the record is merely a single line entry giving the name of the individual and the date of the event, but other times the individual's age and the name of the officiating minister are given.

While some church records do not include birth or baptism entries, they do contain other information about individual members of the church. Admissions, removals, certificates of membership, communicant lists, lists of ministers, and disciplinary proceedings are examples. They seldom provide vital statistics but are still useful for kinship and other historical purposes. Records relating to church business and administration also may be useful, including vestry proceedings, minutes of other meetings, financial accounts, and so on.

Marriage is a matter of importance to church as well as civil authorities, and sometimes church records are the only source of marriage information. Ministers of the established church were the only persons authorized to perform legal marriages for a time in Virginia. But it is doubtful that everyone complied with the authorized procedure. Publication of banns in the church was the equivalent of obtaining a marriage license from the county courthouse or town hall, and many people followed that practice rather than obtaining a license from civil authorities.

Special marriage registers were kept by many churches, but others merely listed marriage information among other entries in church books. Copies of marriage returns—the originals of which were usually forwarded to county or town officials—may also be found in church records. Some ministers recorded marriage entries in their private diaries or journals; copies are occasionally found at the church or in a local library. In some churches the recording of marriage was a personal choice of the minister. He may or may not have kept such records, and the records may or may not have been left with the church when the minister retired or moved to another parish.

Church records of deaths and burials are perhaps more prevalent than entries of births, even in churches that did not practice the rituals and ordinances of Catholicism. Deaths, burials, funerals, and memorials have always been important events, and church officials usually have been responsible for consoling the family and conducting the proceedings.

Attempts have been made to centralize and preserve some church records for the benefit of history, but many remain in the custody of local congregations or their officials.

The Genealogical Society of Utah has microfilmed many church records and has, perhaps, the greatest single collection in the world. It has excellent holdings pertaining to the colonial American states and continues to acquire church records from other parts of the United States and Canada. It was permitted to film Catholic parish registers in Mexico, and presently has more than 100,000 reels of microfilm in that collection.

Most Catholic church records in America remain in their respective parishes or in the diocesan headquarters. No attempt has been made to gather them to a central repository. The same is true of most of the larger religious groups of America. On the other hand, Quaker records have been centralized at Swarthmore College in Swarthmore, Pennsylvania, with microfilm copies on file at Salt Lake City. The Presbyterian Church South, headquartered at Montreit, North Carolina, has been gathering Presbyterian church records for several years, as has the Presbyterian Church North, at Philadelphia.

State libraries, archives, and historical societies have also been successful in collecting and preserving church records, particularly for older and defunct organizations. The Connecticut State Library at Hartford has several hundred church records in its collection; the LDS genealogical library also has copies on microfilm. Other repositories have similar collections.

Cemetery records. The custom of burying the dead in public cemeteries prevailed among ancient peoples, including the Romans, who afterward burned them and kept the ashes in urns in tombs. The Germans buried their dead in groves consecrated by their priests. With the advent of Christianity, consecrated places were set aside for the purpose of general burial in most nations where it was prevalent. Not to be buried in consecrated ground was considered ignominious in the early Christian era, and deprivation of the sacred rites of burial was part of the punishment of excommunication.

Churches often were built over the burial places of early martyrs; some early Christian leaders were buried in the church or under the altar itself. However laws were passed in Europe during the first part of the eighteenth century forbidding the erecting of sepulchres in churches and providing for the foundation of burial places outside the city.

Burial in the churchyard cemetery has been commonplace in America, usually carried out under the supervision and direction of the minister or parish priest—but some burials under the altars or in churches also took place in this country. Many cities maintain and operate cemeteries, as do most smaller towns and villages. County cemeteries exist in many states, and a surprising number of family or private burial grounds also exist. State and national cemeteries are maintained for the burial of those who have performed meritorious service.

In instances of natural or man-made disaster, mass burial has taken place at the scene, or individuals have been laid to rest in obscure places without record or recognition. Fire and holocaust have taken the lives of many and prevented physical burial, while some have requested that their bodies or those of their loved ones be cremated. An urn sitting on a mausoleum shelf or on the hearth at home may contain an ancestor's physical remains, or the ashes may have been scattered to the four winds, no trace of them remaining.

From a genealogical point of view, useful cemetery records include tombstones with inscriptions or epitaphs, sextons' records of burial or interment, and records pertaining to plot ownership and upkeep.

Family members often kept records of death and burial in Bibles, diaries, journals, and other record books; some conscientious citizens kept personal records of interments in particular cemeteries or burial grounds. I once talked to a farmer in Ohio who had maintained a book of burials in a certain cemetery because he was employed to dig the graves with his backhoe. A man in Indiana was able to show me the location of his grandparents' graves and recite for me their statistics of birth, marriage, and death even though no tombstone had been erected for them.

Church records are a primary source for death and burial information but do not always indicate the place of burial. A French Protestant church in Charleston, South Carolina, inscribed birth, marriage, and death information on plaques in the main chapel, even though the deceased members are not buried in the church cemetery. On the other hand, an Episcopal church in New York listed genealogical and historical facts about its early members on plaques in the main chapel, and the deceased members are all buried in the churchyard cemetery.

Various chapters of the Daughters of the American Revolution have projects to locate and mark the burial places of war veterans; they have also copied and published records and inscriptions from cemeteries throughout the country. Similar work has been done by other groups and individuals, and consequently a large amount of material relating to burials is in print.

Morticians', coroners', and state medical examiners' records can also be used to find dates and places of death and burial; the local headstone dealer might also have records that are pertinent. Mr. Sprague of Gouverneur, New York, was able to identify the cost, origin, and purchasers of certain peculiar tombstones in the Riverside cemetery. These facts, added to family information, helped us determine the Irish place of birth for an immigrant to New York in 1840.

Even though much cemetery information has been copied and published, much still remains at the location of burial; a personal visit may be necessary to accomplish your objectives. Burial plots adjoining an ancestor's grave may belong to close relatives, and copied records might not make this clear when the surnames are different.

Markers sometimes have been removed and placed in other locations by sextons' or even by vandals. Some headstones are buried, the information from them obtainable only with a shovel and brush. Weathering and other natural forces may have destroyed the legibility of the inscription, and only skill and special techniques can restore the information. By chalking a very badly weathered headstone at a church cemetery in central New York, I was able to calculate a 1732 birthdate—thus locating an ancestor in a church record in Connecticut.

Sometimes cemeteries are hidden away in woodlots or fields and are difficult to locate. My second great grandmother, Polly Ann Haines, was buried in the Elliot cemetery in Wayne Township, Ohio, in 1843. My wife and I visited the area in 1978, attempting to locate the cemetery and grave. This proved to be a difficult task. We finally determined that the old Elliot cemetery was located in a grove of trees in the center of a hog-feeding operation. The area had once been fenced and cared for, but when we visited it the fence was down and the hogs had rooted among the grave markers, tipping most of them over and burying many. It was only after purchasing a delving fork that we were able to locate, unearth, and identify the markers.

Sometimes a central family marker has been placed in a cemetery, with surrounding individual headstones for each family member; at other times determining whether individuals buried in surrounding plots are related is impossible. More than 95 percent of the people buried in the Traylor Union Church Cemetery at Otwell, Indiana, are descendants or relatives of Joel and Catherine Traylor, who moved there from Spartenburg, South Carolina.

Names, birthdates, birthplaces, marriage dates and places, death dates and places, names of parents, and other kinship information are the prime facts to be obtained from cemetery records, but other useful historical information can also be found. An ancestor's occupation, his social status, his church affiliation, his national or ethnic origin, or the names of friends and associates sometimes may be determined. When used in conjunction with other sources, cemetery records become extremely important to family history.

5 Census Records

Census records can provide some of the best individual and family identification obtainable—particularly where vital, church, or family records were not kept or are missing. They are good finding tools for the family historian, and they often contain kinship information that cannot be found in other sources. Names, ages, relationships, places of birth, marital status, occupation, citizenship, military status, economic conditions, residence information, evidence of death, and a variety of other facts sometimes can be found in them.

The government has used census records to establish political representation, to determine population for territorial status or statehood, for military purposes, and for the allocation of resources. Sociologists have used them for projects on family reconstitution; to determine ethnic distribution; and for studies on fertility, mobility, and longevity. The American family historian has found them invaluable in writing family history, and they have been used in writing local and regional history as well.

The census is an especially important primary source for Black American family history and other minority groups. Unfortunately American Indians were not enumerated in regular federal censuses but special lists exist for many of them. Records dating as early as 1818 are available for certain members of the Five Civilized Tribes of the southern states (Cherokee, Choctaw, Chickasaw, Creek, and Seminole), and annual enumerations beginning in 1886 exist for many western tribes on reservations.

The population of the United States has been enumerated by the federal government every ten years since 1790, but state and local censuses have also been taken at various times and in various places. Some predate the American Revolution, while others correspond to the establishment of territories or statehood. A few states have conducted decennial enumerations at regular intervals following statehood—usually alternating between federal enumerations—but others have taken censuses inconsistently or not at all.

Federal Returns

The federal government has authorized an enumeration of the population decennially since 1790; existing returns for the period 1790 through 1900 are presently available for public use. Some have been published, most have been microfilmed, and many can be found in local libraries. Those newer than 72 years are classified confidential.

The first six federal enumerations (1790–1840) give mostly statistics. That is, they list by name only heads of families with all other persons in the household accounted for numerically by sex and age groupings. In 1850 and thereafter each person was listed by name, age, sex, color, state or country of birth, and other useful information depending on the year. Until 1820 the census year ended in August of the year the census was taken, but after 1820 the census year was from June 1 of the previous year through May 31 of the census year. Beginning in 1880 enumerators were instructed to disregard children born within the census year, but returns before that date usually include them.

Federal census enumerators also completed mortality schedules as part of the 1850–1900 census enumerations. These corresponded closely in format to the population schedules just described but listed only those persons who died during the census years. These schedules include the deceased person's name, age, sex, color, occupation, birthplace, month and year of death, cause of death, number of days ill, and—in some cases—the name of the doctor or physician.

Colorado, Minnesota, Nebraska, and the Territory of North Dakota conducted special mortality censuses in 1885, but other regions did not take advantage of that government-sponsored listing. The 1890 and 1900 federal schedules were accidently destroyed, and no mortality schedules were included in the post-1900 censuses. Surviving mortality schedules are scattered in various state libraries, archives, and historical societies, or are in the custody of the Daughters of the American Revolution in Washington, D.C.

Several years ago the Daughters of the American Revolution learned that the 1850–80 schedules were no longer considered useful by the government. They therefore requested custody. After due consideration by appropriate congressional committees, the Director of the Census was authorized to offer the schedules to the respective states. The schedules that were not requested by their states were given to the Daughters of the American Revolution.

The Genealogical Society of Utah microfilmed many federal mortality schedules and also obtained copies of several that were published. Original returns are located in the following repositories:

Alabama
- State Department of Archives and History, Montgomery, Alabama, 1850–80

Arizona
- National Archives, Washington, D.C., 1870–80.
- Library, National Society, Daughters of the American Revolution, Washington, D.C., 1870–80.

Arkansas
  Department of Archives and History, Little Rock, Arkansas, 1850–80.
California
  California State Library, Sacramento, California, 1850–80.
Colorado
  National Archives, Washington, D.C., 1870–85.
  Library, National Society, Daughters of the American Revolution, Washington, D.C., 1870–80.
Connecticut
  Connecticut State Library, Hartford, Connecticut, 1850–80.
Delaware
  Public Archives Commission, Hall of Records, Dover, Delaware, 1850–80.
District of Columbia
  National Archives, Washington, D.C., 1850–80.
  Library, National Society, Daughters of the American Revolution, Washington, D.C., 1850–80.
Florida
  National Archives, Washington, D.C., 1885.
Georgia
  National Archives, Washington, D.C., 1850–80.
  Library, National Society, Daughters of the American Revolution, Washington, D.C., 1850–80.
Idaho
  Idaho Historical Society, Boise, Idaho, 1870–80.
Illinois
  Illinois State Archives, Springfield, Illinois, 1850–80.
Indiana
  Indiana State Library, Indianapolis, Indiana, 1850–80.
Iowa
  State Historical Society of Iowa, Iowa City, Iowa, 1850–80.
Kansas
  Library, National Society, Daughters of the American Revolution, Washington, D.C., 1870–80.
  Kansas State Historical Society, Topeka, Kansas, 1860–80.
Kentucky
  National Archives, Washington, D.C., 1850–80.
  Library, National Society, Daughters of the American Revolution, Washington, D.C., 1850–80.
Louisiana
  National Archives, Washington, D.C., 1850–80.
  Library, National Society, Daughters of the American Revolution, Washington, D.C., 1850–80.
Maine
  Office of Vital Statistics, Department of Health and Welfare, Augusta, Maine, 1850–80.
  Genealogical Society of The Church of Jesus Christ of Latter-day Saints, Salt Lake City, Utah, 1850–70.
Maryland
  State Library, Annapolis, Maryland, 1850–80.
Massachusetts
  National Archives, Washington, D.C., 1850–70.
  Library, National Society, Daughters of the American Revolution, Washington, D.C., 1850.

Massachusetts State Library, State House, Boston, Massachusetts, 1850–80.

Michigan

National Society, Daughters of the American Revolution, Washington, D.C., 1860–80.

Michigan Historical Commission, Lansing, Michigan, 1860–80.

Minnesota

National Archives, Washington, D.C., 1870.

Library, National Society, Daughters of the American Revolution, Washington, D.C., 1850–70.

Minnesota Historical Society, Saint Paul, Minnesota, 1850–70.

Genealogical Society of The Church of Jesus Christ of Latter-day Saints, Salt Lake City, Utah, 1850–70.

Mississippi

State Department of Archives and History, Jackson, Mississippi, 1850–80.

Missouri

Missouri Historical Society, Saint Louis, Missouri, 1850–80.

Montana

National Archives, Washington, D.C., 1870–80.

Historical Society of Montana, Helena, Montana, 1870–80.

Nebraska

National Archives, Washington, D.C., 1885.

Nebraska State Historical Society, Lincoln, Nebraska, 1860–80.

Nevada

Library, National Society, Daughters of the American Revolution, Washington, D.C., 1870.

Nevada Historical Society, Reno, Nevada, 1860–80.

New Hampshire

New Hampshire State Library, Concord, New Hampshire, 1850–80.

Genealogical Society of The Church of Jesus Christ of Latter-day Saints, Salt Lake City, Utah, 1850–70.

New Jersey

Library, National Society, Daughters of the American Revolution, Washington, D.C., 1850–80.

New Jersey State Library, Trenton, New Jersey, 1850–80.

New Mexico

National Archives, Washington, D.C., 1885.

New York

New York State Library, Albany, New York, 1850–80.

North Carolina

National Archives, Washington, D.C., 1850–80.

Department of Archives and History, Education Building, Raleigh, North Carolina, 1850–80.

North Dakota

Library, State Historical Society, Bismarck, North Dakota, 1885.

Genealogical Society of The Church of Jesus Christ of Latter-day Saints, Salt Lake City, Utah, 1880.

Ohio

Ohio Historical Society, Columbus, Ohio, 1850–60, 1880.

Oregon

Oregon State Archives, Salem, Oregon, 1850–80.

Pennsylvania

Pennsylvania State Library, Harrisburg, Pennsylvania, 1850–80.

Rhode Island
- Library, National Society, Daughters of the American Revolution, Washington, D.C., 1860–80.
- Rhode Island State Library, Providence, Rhode Island, 1850–80.

South Carolina
- Library, National Society, Daughters of the American Revolution, Washington, D.C., 1850–80.
- South Carolina Archives Department, Columbia, South Carolina, 1850–80.

South Dakota
- South Dakota Historical Society, Memorial Building, Pierre, South Dakota, 1885.
- Genealogical Society of The Church of Jesus Christ of Latter-day Saints, Salt Lake City, Utah, 1880.

Tennessee
- National Archives, Washington, D.C., 1850–60, 1880.
- Library, National Society, Daughters of the American Revolution, Washington, D.C., 1850–60, 1880.

Texas
- National Archives, Washington, D.C., 1850–80.
- Archives Division, Texas State Library, Austin, Texas, 1850–80.

Utah
- National Archives, Washington, D.C., 1870.
- Archives Division, Texas State Library, Austin, Texas, 1870.

Vermont
- National Archives, Washington, D.C., 1870.
- Library, National Society, Daughters of the American Revolution, Washington, D.C., 1850–60.
- Archives Division, Texas State Library, Austin, Texas, 1870.
- Vermont State Library, Montpelier, Vermont, 1850–80.

Virginia
- National Archives, Washington, D.C., 1860.
- Library, Duke University, Durham, North Carolina, 1860.
- Genealogical Society of The Church of Jesus Christ of Latter-day Saints, Salt Lake City, Utah, 1870.

Washington
- Library, National Society, Daughters of the American Revolution, Washington, D.C., 1860–80.
- State Library, Olympia, Washington, 1860–80.

West Virginia
- State Department of Archives and History, Charleston, West Virginia, 1860–80.

Wisconsin
- Library, National Society, Daughters of the American Revolution, Washington, D.C., 1850–70.
- State Historical Society, Madison, Wisconsin, 1850–80.
- Milwaukee Public Library, Milwaukee, Wisconsin, 1860–70.

Wyoming
- Library, National Society, Daughters of the American Revolution, Washington, D.C., 1870–80.

As previously mentioned, federal census records dating after 1900 are presently classified confidential and are available only under special conditions. Individual applications must be submitted for authorized searches, and a special fee is required. The present right-of-privacy law governing access to federal censuses covers seventy-two years. The 1910 census will presumably be released in 1982. Until that time, access is limited to individuals listed in the censuses or their immediate families. Parents or legal guardians may file applications for information that concerns minor children. If the desired record relates to someone who is deceased, the application must be signed by a blood relative in the immediate family (parent, brother, sister, or child); the surviving husband or wife; the administrator or executor of the estate; or a beneficiary by will, intestacy, or insurance. In all cases involving deceased persons, a certified copy of the death certificate must be furnished. Legal representatives must furnish a certified copy of the court order naming such legal representation, and beneficiaries must furnish legal evidence of such relationship (U.S. Department of Commerce, Bureau of the Census, Form BC-600).

Soundexes (a system of indexing surnames by sound) are available for the 1880, 1900, and 1920 federal census records, but information usually can be located only when the person's name and state of residence are known. Because no such indexes exist for other twentieth century censuses, even more information is required to locate someone in the 1910, 1930, and later schedules. If the individual being researched lived in a city, the Census Bureau must be furnished with the house number, the name of the street, the city, and the name of the parent or other head of household with whom he was living. If he lived in a small town or rural area, such information as cross streets, roads, township, district, precinct, or beat is necessary. If the district or township is not known, the distance and direction from the nearest town should be included. Application forms and schedule of fees may be obtained from the Bureau of Census, Pittsburg, Kansas 66762.

The 1790 federal census. The first federal census of the United States was authorized in March 1790—when George Washington was president—and commenced in August of the same year. It was the first attempt to enumerate the entire white population of the country and was ordered completed in nine calendar months, though some returns are dated several months after that time. It included inhabitants of the present states of Connecticut, Delaware, Georgia, Kentucky, Maine, Maryland, Massachusetts, New Hampshire, New Jersey, New York, North Carolina, Pennsylvania, Rhode Island, South Carolina, Tennessee, Vermont, and Virginia.

When the bill authorizing the 1790 census was approved, the Union consisted of only twelve states. Rhode Island, the last of the original thirteen, was admitted 29 May 1790, and Vermont was added 4 March 1791, shortly before the results of the first census were announced. Maine was then part of Massachusetts, and Kentucky was part of Virginia. The present states of Alabama and Mississippi were part of Georgia, and Tennessee was part of North Carolina. The present states of Ohio, Indiana, Illinois, Michigan, Wisconsin, and part of Minnesota were known as the Northwest Territory and were not enumerated. Neither was the vast region west of the Mississippi River and south of Georgia; it belonged to Spain.

The census returns were compiled by marshals and their assistants,

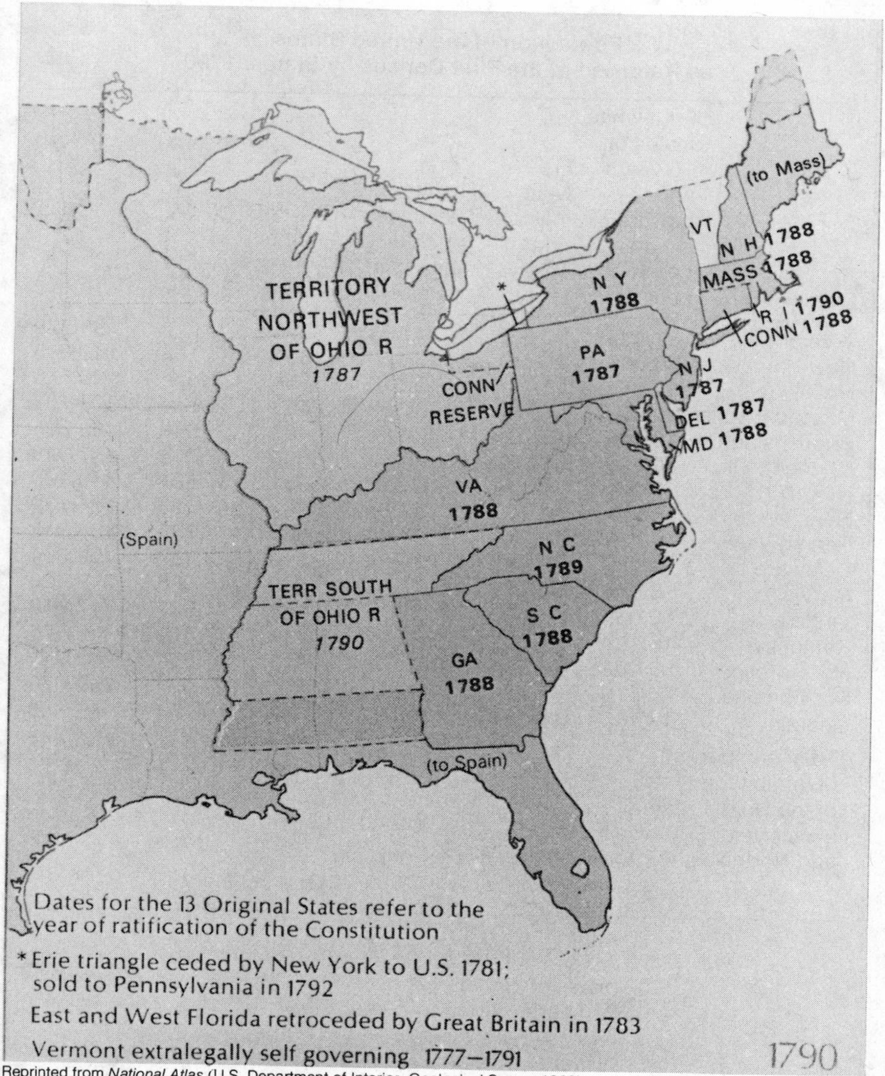

Reprinted from *National Atlas* (U.S. Department of Interior; Geological Survey 1969).

who prepared summaries for the inspection of the president. The originals were evidently filed with clerks of the district courts in the respective states. The returns were arranged by state and county, except for those of North and South Carolina, Georgia, and Tennessee (the Southwest Territory), which were grouped under districts.

Authorities have some question about the disposition of the original 1790 census schedules. Undoubtedly they were filed with the clerks of the various district courts in the first instance, but under an act of 28 May 1830, Congress directed that the originals be transmitted to the secretary of state. This was not completed until 1849, and not until 1904 were the

Population of the United States as Returned at the First Census by States: 1790

District	Free white males of 16 years and upward, including heads of families.	Free white males under 16 years.	Free white females, including heads of families.	All other free persons.	Slaves.	Total.
Vermont	22,435	22,328	40,505	255	16	85,539
New Hampshire	36,086	34,851	70,160	630	158	141,885
Maine	24,384	24,748	46,870	538	None	96,540
Massachusetts	95,453	87,289	190,582	5,463	None	378,787
Rhode Island	16,019	15,799	32,652	3,407	948	68,825
Connecticut	60,523	54,403	117,448	2,808	2,764	237,946
New York	83,700	78,122	152,320	4,654	21,324	340,120
New Jersey	45,251	41,416	83,287	2,762	11,423	184,139
Pennsylvania	110,788	106,948	206,363	6,537	3,737	434,373
Delaware	11,783	12,143	22,384	3,899	8,887	59,094
Maryland	55,915	51,339	101,395	8,043	103,036	319,728
Virginia	110,936	116,135	215,046	12,866	292,627	747,610
Kentucky	15,154	17,057	28,922	114	12,430	73,677
No. Carolina	69,988	77,506	140,710	4,975	100,572	393,751
So. Carolina	35,576	37,722	66,880	1,801	107,094	249,073
Georgia	13,103	14,044	25,739	398	29,264	82,548
Total number of inhabitants of the United States exclusive of Southwest and Northwest territories.	807,094	791,850	1,541,263	59,150	694,280	3,893,635

	Free white males of 21 years and upward.	Free males under 21 years of age.	Free white females.	All other persons.	Slaves.	Total.
Southwest Territory	6,271	10,277	15,365	361	3,417	35,691
Northwest Territory	. . .	. . .	. . .	. . .	. . .	. . .

early schedules placed in the custody of the Census Bureau.

A survey by the Census Bureau in 1897 showed that the 1790 census schedules for Delaware, Georgia, Kentucky, New Jersey, and Tennessee (Southwest Territory) were missing. The counties of Granville, Caswell, and Orange were missing from the North Carolina schedules. Only the following schedules remain:

Connecticut	3 volumes
Maine	1 volume
Maryland	2 volumes
Massachusetts	2 volumes
New Hampshire	2 volumes
New York	3 volumes
North Carolina	2 volumes
Pennsylvania	8 volumes
Rhode Island	1 volume
South Carolina	1 volume
Vermont	2 volumes

Reconstructed schedules for Delaware, Kentucky, and Virginia have been compiled from state and local tax lists. Those for Delaware and Kentucky are reasonably complete, but those for Virginia are estimated to be only two-thirds complete. Tax lists for New Jersey, referred to as "ratables," have been published and microfilmed for the period 1773–1822, but they also are incomplete. Land lottery lists, including the names of persons who drew land in seven lotteries between 1803 and 1832, have been published and microfilmed for Georgia, serving as an incomplete substitute for the missing 1790 schedules for that state.

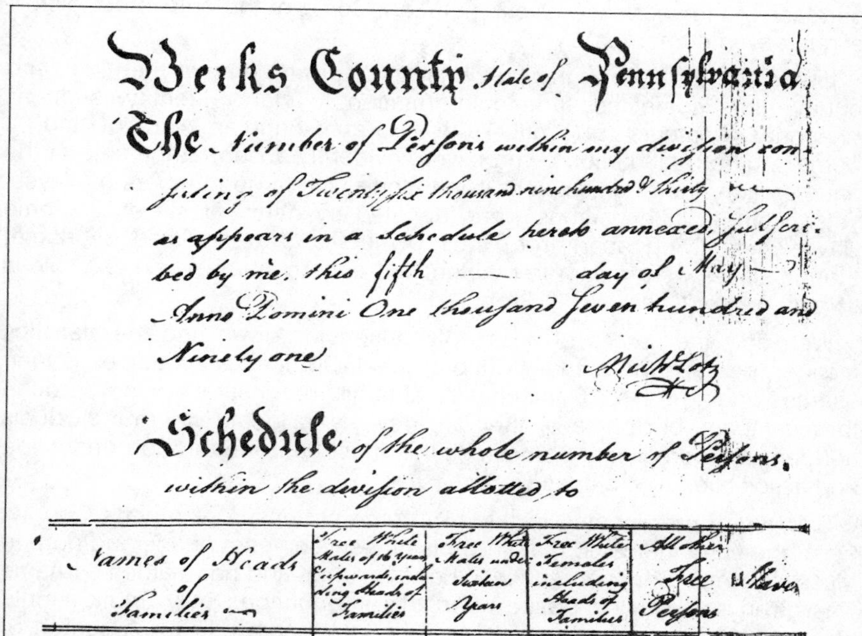
Berks County State of Pennsylvania

The Number of Persons within my division consisting of Twenty six thousand nine hundred & thirty as appears in a Schedule hereto annexed, subscribed by me this fifth day of May Anno Domini One thousand seven hundred and Ninety one

Nich Lotz

Schedule of the whole number of Persons within the division allotted to

Names of Heads of Families	Free White Males of 16 years & upwards, including Heads of Families	Free White Males under Sixteen Years	Free White Females including Heads of Families	All other Free Persons	Slaves
Borough of Reading					
Nicholas Lotz	2	1	2		
Margt. Bingeman		1	3		
Michael Lotz	1	1	6		

Content of the 1790 federal census. Each 1790 schedule identified the state, county, date, and name of the marshal or his assistant at the top of the return; the city, town, borough or other subdivision was usually identified in the left margin.

The first major column gave the names of heads of households, including women; the five additional columns provided statistical information. The first statistical column enumerated free white males of sixteen years and upwards, including heads of families; the second enumerated free white males under sixteen years; the third enumerated free white females, including heads of families; the fourth enumerated all other free persons; and the fifth column enumerated slaves.

Instructions to enumerators of the 1790 census were evidently not as detailed as those of later enumerations; some took liberties in their work that did not result in uniform procedures. In some cases, for instance, the name of the local minister or other chief townsperson was listed first, regardless of the sequence of enumeration. Some of the entries are picturesque—even humorous.

Few men had more than one Christian or given name at that time, and enumerators sometimes added information to clarify identity, such as "Leonard Clements (of Walter)" or "Sarah Chapman (wid. of Jno.)." Some southern plantation owners were evidently absent at the time of the enumeration; their names were listed along with large numbers of slaves, yet no other white persons were identifed by name or statistics. Some slaves were living apart from their owners and were listed by name, though slaves were meant to be identified only by number. An example is "Peter, negro (Chas. Well's Property)."

With only the names of heads of households given and the statistics meager, perhaps the primary value of the 1790 census schedules is their use as "finding tools." Some statistical family reconstitution can be done through them, but primarily they are devices to locate where individuals and families were living. Sometimes this must be done through deduction and association, but it does work.

Sally Long was located in the 1850 federal census of Athens County, Ohio; the entry indicated that she was fifty-seven years of age and born in Massachusetts. She married Isaac Long in Ohio, and her maiden surname was given as "Paulk." Based upon this information, Sally Paulk should have been born somewhere in Massachusetts about 1793. A search of the 1790 census returns for Massachusetts—which are published and indexed—showed only three persons by that surname in the state. Each was investigated further, and one seemed very likely to be Sally's father. "Xerxes Paulk" was listed as a resident in the town of Springfield, Hampden County; a check of published vital records for that town disclosed an entry for Sally Paulk, daughter of Xerxes, born in 1793. Could that be Sally Paulk Long of Athens County, Ohio?

The 1790 federal census returns do not always provide the information you seek for family history, but used with other records they can help you along the way to a better finished product.

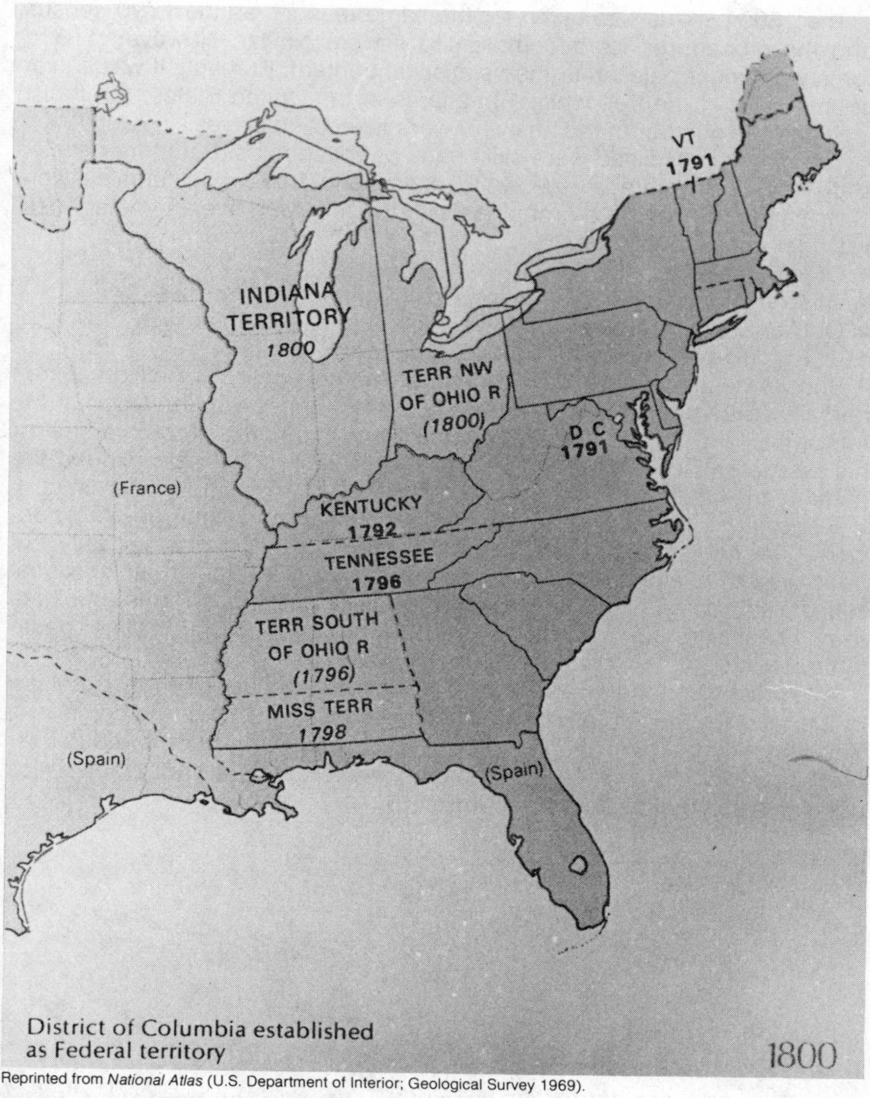

Reprinted from *National Atlas* (U.S. Department of Interior; Geological Survey 1969).

The 1800 federal census. The second federal census was begun on 4 August 1800, when Thomas Jefferson was president. The population was given as 5,308,483, nearly double that of 1790. Vermont had officially become a state, and the District of Columbia was added in 1791. Kentucky was admitted to the Union in 1792, Tennessee in 1796, and the Mississippi Territory was created in 1798. Indiana Territory was created in 1800 from the territory northwest of the Ohio River, comprising most of the present states of Indiana, Illinois, Wisconsin, part of Minnesota, and half of Michigan. France still claimed the area west of the Mississippi River, and Spain controlled Florida.

The 1800 census was taken for the same reasons as the 1790 census, and the procedures for accomplishing it were similar. However, the returns were more detailed in their statistical content. Primarily it was still an enumeration of the free white inhabitants in the United States, but it also included the number of Indians who were taxed and slaves.

The only names listed were still heads of households, but more detailed statistics were entered. Free white males and free white females were classified in two separate groupings with the following five age categories:

- Under ten years of age
- Of ten and under sixteen
- Of sixteen and under twenty-six, including heads of families
- Of twenty-six and under forty-five, including heads of families
- Of forty-five and upwards, including heads of families

Special columns were provided to show the number of all other free persons, except Indians not taxed and slaves. Space was provided at the top of the form for the name of the state and the name of the marshal or his assistant; a column at the left margin of each schedule provided the name of the city, town, borough, township, county, or other subdivision.

It is evident that some returns are summaries rather than originals, because the names are alphabetized and the population was certainly not enumerated in alphabetical sequence. It is also evident that individual states had some latitude in designing their own census forms, because they differ slightly in format—though all call for the same basic information.

A few early schedules are difficult to interpret because of the condition of the records, the microfilming, or the poor penmanship of the compilers. You may need some experience before you can easily raed the older records; developing a skill for comparing individual writing characteristics will also help you master the records.

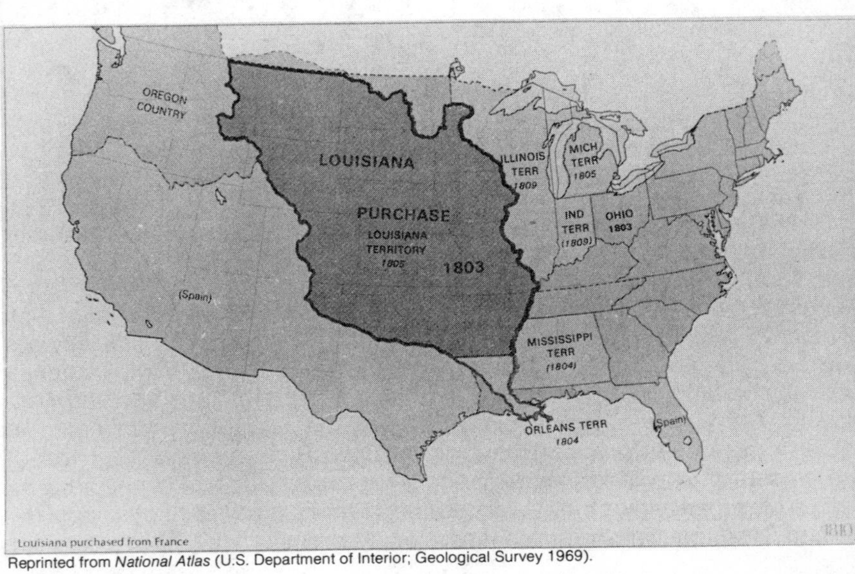

Reprinted from *National Atlas* (U.S. Department of Interior; Geological Survey 1969).

The 1810 federal census. The third U.S. Federal Census was begun 6 August 1810, under the presidency of James Madison. It showed a total population of 7,239,881. Ohio became a state in 1803, and the Louisiana Purchase was negotiated with France the same year. The Mississippi Territory was expanded in 1804, and Orleans Territory was organized. Michigan Territory was carved from Ohio and Indiana territories in 1805, and Indiana Territory was reduced to make way for Illinois Territory in 1809. Oregon country had been explored by both the United States and Great Britain, but neither had complete control until much later.

The 1810 federal census returns were identical in content to those of 1800 though not necessarily the same in format. The 1810 federal census for Hancock County, Maine, included a special column for "The Place from Whence Emigrated," but no other states provided for that information.

The example below shows a slightly different format for the 1810 census in contrast to the 1800, but the same basic information is included.

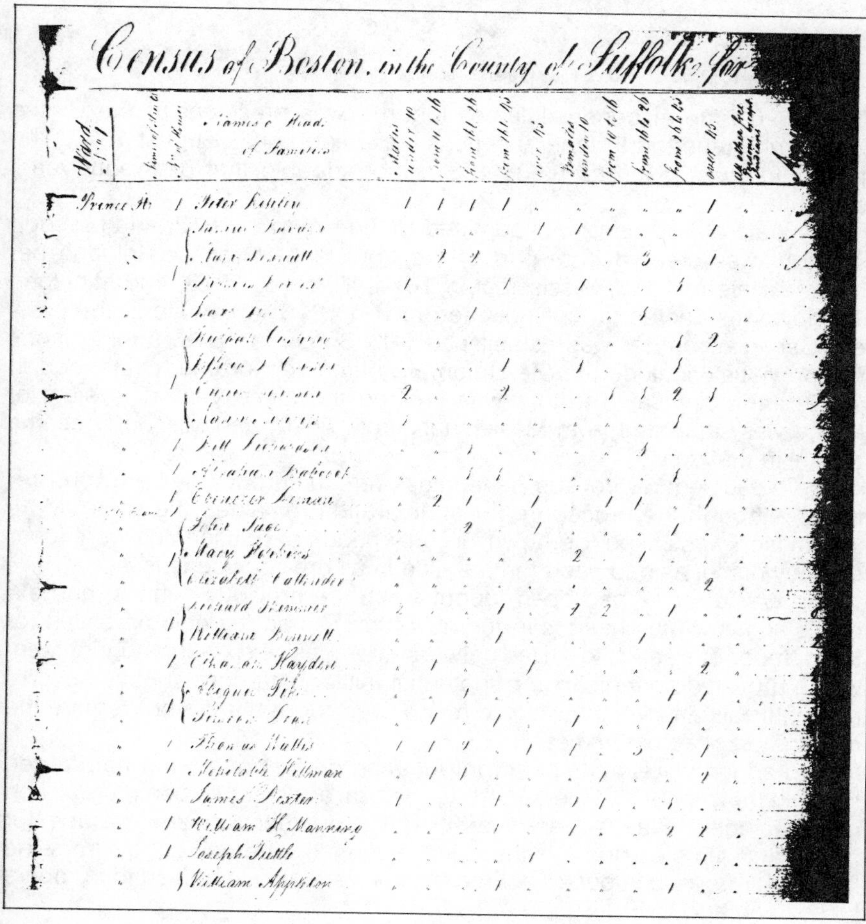

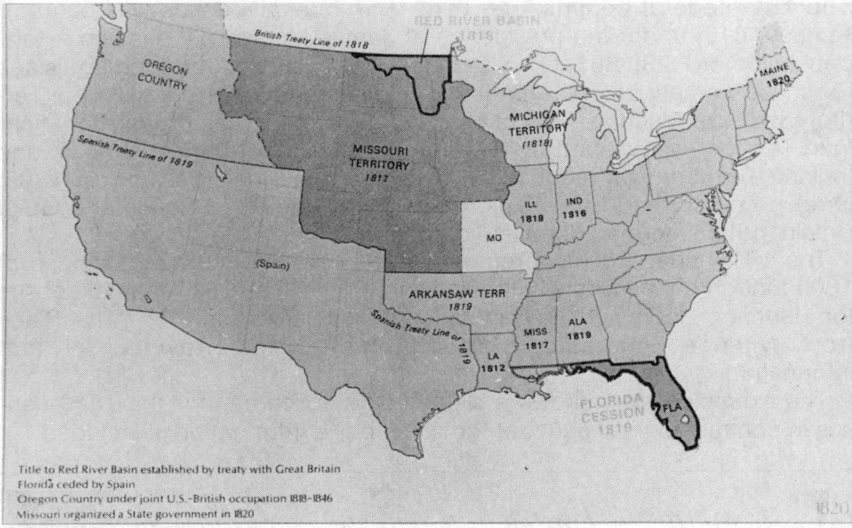

Reprinted from *National Atlas* (U.S. Department of Interior; Geological Survey 1969).

The 1820 federal census. James Monroe was president of the United States when the fourth federal census was begun on 7 August 1820. The population was given as 9,638,453, almost double that of twenty years earlier.

The state of Louisiana was admitted to the Union in 1812, and Missouri Territory was created from part of the Louisiana Purchase. Indiana became a state in 1816, Mississippi in 1817, Illinois in 1818, and Michigan Territory was carved from Illinois Territory in 1818. A line along the present Canadian border was established with Britain in 1818, adding lands not previously included in the Union. Alabama was granted statehood in 1819, and Arkansas Territory was created the same year. The state of Maine was separated from Massachusetts in 1820, and Missouri became a state in that year.

The 1820 federal census schedules were different from previous returns, although the procedure for enumeration remained the same. More information was asked for; however, only heads of households were identified by name, as had been the practice in all previous censuses.

The War of 1812 had been fought since the previous census, and explains some of the changes in the new form. An added column called for the number of free white males between the ages of sixteen and eighteen, which provided an indication of potential military strength. It gave government officials an idea of available manpower, though it did not require the registration of actual names.

Also added were columns for information on foreigners not naturalized and on the number of persons engaged in agriculture, commerce, and manufacturing. Slaves were classified by numbers in age groups for males and females, though the age categories differed slightly from the listings for free white persons. Free blacks were also identified in numbers by sex and age.

The additional information gathered on the 1820 census can prove very helpful to family historians. The added column identifying young white males between sixteen and eighteen could provide the solution to difficult kinship problems, and facts relating to naturalization and occupation also could be very important. The additional details on slaves and free blacks could be useful, especially combined with information from probate court records giving names of slaves.

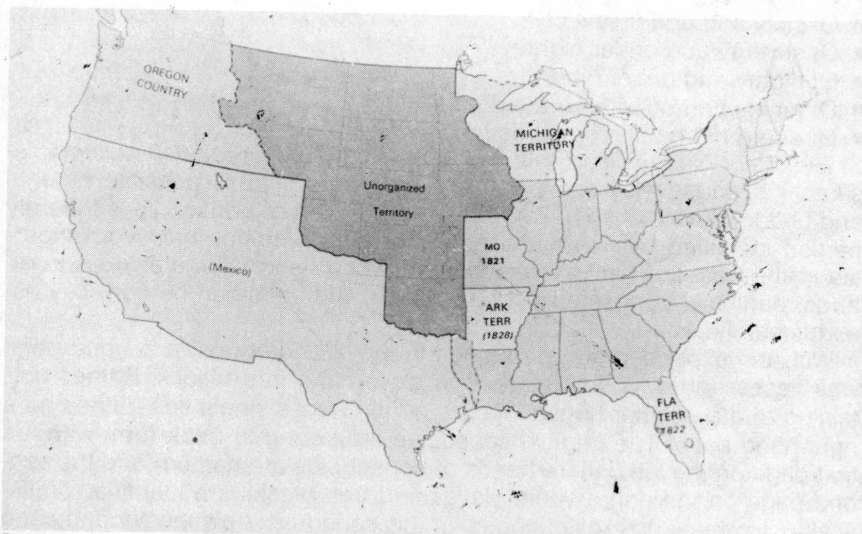

Reprinted from *National Atlas* (U.S. Department of Interior; Geological Survey 1969).

The 1830 federal census. Beginning in 1830, the population of the United States was enumerated beginning 1 June each census year. Andrew Jackson was president when the fifth federal census was taken, and the population was given as 12,866,020 inhabitants.

The country was experiencing increasing migration to the Mississippi valley, and westward movement also was increasing from the Appalachian plateau and Ohio country. Missouri became a state with the Compromise of 1821, and the previous "Missouri Territory" of 1820 was known as the "Unorganized Territory" in 1830. Florida Territory was established in 1822, and Arkansas Territory was reduced to about the size of the present state in 1828. Michigan Territory remained about the same, but the vast Spanish domain was now Mexico. Oregon country was still influenced by both British and American fur traders; controlling possession by the United States was yet to come.

As had been the practice in previous federal census returns, only identified heads of households were identified by name and age group; others were listed as statistics only. Each schedule provided space to list the state and county, as well as the district or subdivision of the county, as had been done in previous returns, but the statistical categories for persons enumerated were expanded as follows:

- Under five years of age
- Of five and under ten
- Of ten and under fifteen
- Of fifteen and under twenty
- Of twenty and under thirty
- Of thirty and under forty
- Of forty and under fifty
- Of fifty and under sixty
- Of sixty and under seventy
- Of seventy and under eighty
- Of eighty and under ninety
- Of ninety and under one hundred
- Of one hundred and upwards

The statistical details of this census are very useful to family history research, because they allow you to narrow the field of possible parents and better identify kinship. Even though the head of household is the only person identified by name, the sex and age groupings help you understand the possible family makeup. And when used with later census returns, particularly those after 1850, names and ages can be correctly ascertained and listed.

With the expanded age groupings in the 1830 returns, a second page was necessary to list information on slaves and free blacks. Entries pertaining to a particular household are continued as single line entries on a right-hand page. The original schedules are bound in book form with the first page on the left (where heads of households are named) and the second page on the right (where slaves and free blacks are identified statistically). However, microfilm copies of this schedule show the second page under the first one.

The age groupings for slaves and "free colored persons," both male and female, differed slightly from those for free whites. Black males and females were numbered by household in the following age groups:

- Under ten years of age
- Of ten and under twenty-four
- Of twenty-four and under thirty-six
- Of thirty-six and under fifty-five
- Of fifty-five and under one hundred
- Of one hundred and upwards

Totals were listed in a separate column in from the right margin of the second page; totals were also accumulated for each vertical column, thus showing totals by age group as well as by household. Special columns were provided on the second page showing the following statistical information in each household:

Free White Persons Included in the Foregoing

- Who are deaf and dumb, under fourteen years of age
- Who are deaf and dumb, of the age of fourteen and under twenty-five
- Who are deaf and dumb, of twenty-five and upwards
- Who are blind
- Aliens—foreigners not naturalized

Slaves and Colored Persons Included in the Foregoing

- Who are deaf and dumb, under fourteen years of age
- Who are deaf and dumb, of the age of fourteen and under twenty-five
- Who are deaf and dumb, of twenty-five and upwards
- Who are blind

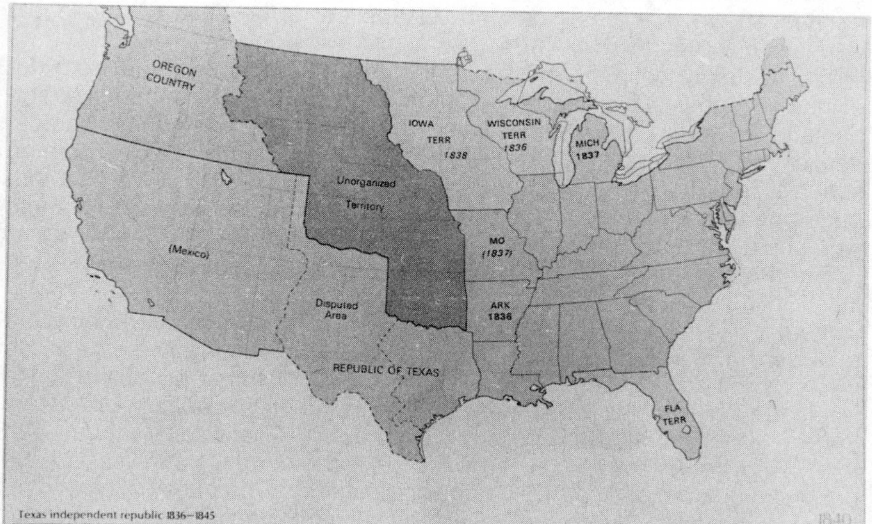

Reprinted from *National Atlas* (U.S. Department of Interior; Geological Survey 1969).

The 1840 federal census. William Henry Harrison was president when the sixth federal census was announced in 1840, and the population was 17,069,453. The strong tide of westward movement continued, and the boundaries of several states and territories changed.

Texas had become an independent republic by 1836, separating from Mexico—though much of its territory remained in dispute. Wisconsin Territory was organized in 1836, primarily from Michigan Territory, and Michigan gained statehood in 1837. Arkansas was granted statehood in 1836, and Missouri's border was enlarged the following year. Iowa Territory was organized in 1838, with great numbers of settlers beginning to enter from the southeast.

Although the format was changed somewhat, the federal census returns for 1840 were similar to those of 1830. Only the heads of households were listed by name and age, as had been the practice in all previous enumerations. Information on free blacks was brought to the first page. Information on employment, military status, and education took more than half the second page. The number of persons in each family employed in the following professions and industries were identified:

- Mining
- Agriculture
- Commerce
- Manufactures and trades
- Navigation of the ocean
- Navigation of canals, lakes, and rivers

- Learned professions and engineers

Statistics on persons who were deaf, dumb, and blind again were gathered as they had been in 1830, and statistics were added on those persons—black or white—who were insane or idiots in the public charge. This could prove interesting to some of us. Names were not listed in these categories, so whether classification ever applied to the head of household will have to be left to conjecture.

The last eight columns on the right side of the second page were designed to gather statistics on education and schools. The number of students in universities or colleges was listed, as well as the number in academies and grammar schools, the number in primary and common schools, and the number on public charge. The last column on the second page asked for the number of white persons over twenty years of age who could not read and write.

Perhaps the most important addition to the 1840 census is the column in the middle of the second page listing the names and ages of "Pensioners for Revolutionary or Military Service Included in the Foregoing." If a person in a particular household was a pensioner, his name and age was entered. The government published a list of these pensioners in a single volume titled *A Census of Pensioners for Revolutionary or Military Service, with Their Names, Ages, and Places of Residence, Under the Act for Taking the Sixth Census.* It was arranged by state, county and town but was not indexed. The LDS genealogical library compiled a typescript index to it, and in 1965 the Genealogical Publishing Company of Baltimore, Maryland, published the work in hardback cover.

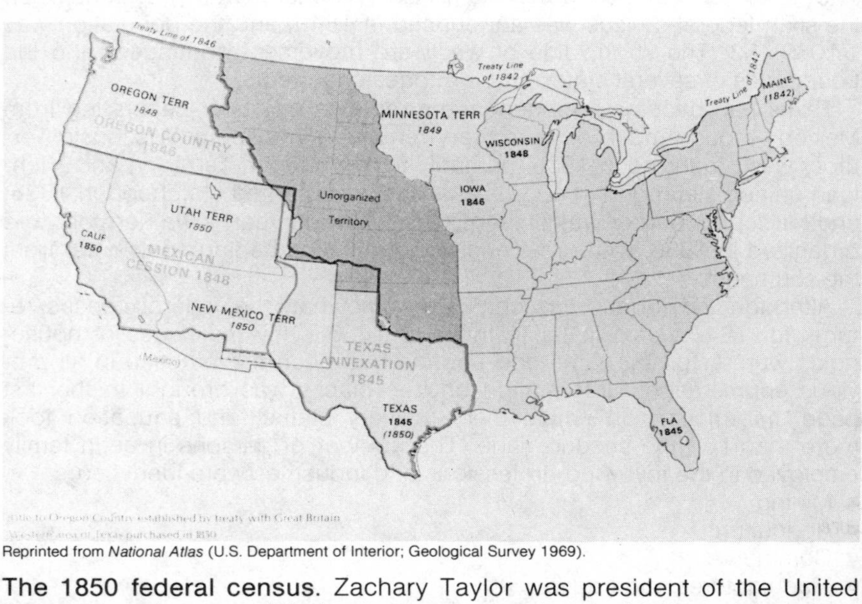

Reprinted from *National Atlas* (U.S. Department of Interior; Geological Survey 1969).

The 1850 federal census. Zachary Taylor was president of the United States when the seventh federal census was taken in 1850, and the population was 23,191,876.

By 1850 Americans had settled from the Atlantic to the Pacific and from the Canadian border to Mexico. Under the Act of 1842 donation lands were granted to settlers who would emigrate to Oregon country or to Florida; the Mormons began their 1847 movement to the Great Salt Lake basin; in 1848 war with Mexico resulted in the acquisition of New Mexico territory; California became a state in 1850; and settlers were pushing into unsettled areas throughout the nation's borders.

Texas—an independent republic since 1836—was annexed to the Union in 1845, and Florida became a state the same year. Iowa was reduced from a very large territory to its present size in 1846 and granted statehood, while its vast territory to the north was organized as Minnesota Territory in 1849. Wisconsin received statehood in 1848, and Oregon County—acquired by treaty with Great Britain in 1846—became Oregon Territory in 1848. The Mexican cession in 1848 resulted in the organization of Utah and New Mexico territories in 1850.

The 1850 federal census was a major departure from those of the previous six decades; enumerators identified each member of the household by name, age, sex, color, place of birth, and other important details. It was the first federal census to do this and is an excellent substitute for or supplement to official vital records at a time when county and state registration programs were just getting started.

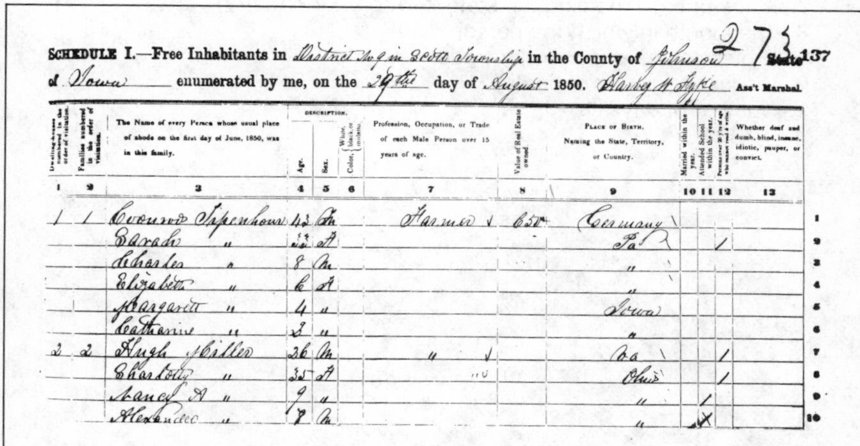
273 137

SCHEDULE I.—Free Inhabitants in District No 9 in Scott Township in the County of Johnson State of Iowa enumerated by me, on the 29th day of August 1850. Harvey W. Fyke Ass't Marshal.

Dwelling-houses numbered in the order of visitation.	Families numbered in the order of visitation.	The Name of every Person whose usual place of abode on the first day of June, 1850, was in this family.	Age.	Sex.	Color, { White, black, or mulatto.	Profession, Occupation, or Trade of each Male Person over 15 years of age.	Value of Real Estate owned.	Place of Birth. Naming the State, Territory, or Country.	Married within the year.	Attended School within the year.	Persons over 20 y'rs of age who cannot read & write.	Whether deaf and dumb, blind, insane, idiotic, pauper, or convict.	
1	2	3	4	5	6	7	8	9	10	11	12	13	
1	1	Conrad Sipenhour	43	M		Farmer	650	Germany					1
		Sarah "	33	F				Pa			1		2
		Charles "	8	M				"					3
		Elizabeth "	6	F				"					4
		Margarett "	4	"				Iowa					5
		Catharine "	2	"				"					6
2	2	Hugh Miller	26	M		"		Pa			1		7
		Charlotty "	35	F				Ohio			1		8
		Nancy A "	9	"				"		1			9
		Alexander "	7	M				"		1			10

Content of the 1850 federal census.

Heading:	Name of the district, precinct, ward, city, or town; the county and state; the day, month, and year of enumeration; and the name of the assistant marshal.
Column 1.	Dwelling numbered in the order of visitation.
Column 2.	Families numbered in the order of visitation.
Column 3.	Name of every person whose usual place of abode on the first day of June 1850 was in this family.
Column 4.	Age.
Column 5.	Sex.

Column 6. Color (white, black, or mulatto).
Column 7. Profession, occupation, or trade of each male over fifteen years of age.
Column 8. Value of real estate owned.
Column 9. Place of birth (naming the state, territory, or country).
Column 10. Married within the year.
Column 11. Attended school within the year.
Column 12. Persons over twenty years of age who cannot read and write.
Column 13. Whether deaf and dumb, blind, insane, idiotic, pauper, or convict.

Content of the 1850 federal census mortality schedules.

Heading:
Name of the town, city, district, or other subdivision.
Name of the county and state.
Name of the assistant marshal.

Column Number:

1. Name of every person who died during the year ending 1 June 1850 whose usual place of abode at the time of his death was in this family.
2. Age.
3. Sex.
4. Color (white, black, or mulatto).
5. Free or slave.
6. Married or widowed.
7. Place of birth (naming the state, territory, or country).
8. The month in which the person died.
9. Profession, occupation, or trade.
10. Disease or cause of death.
11. Number of days ill.

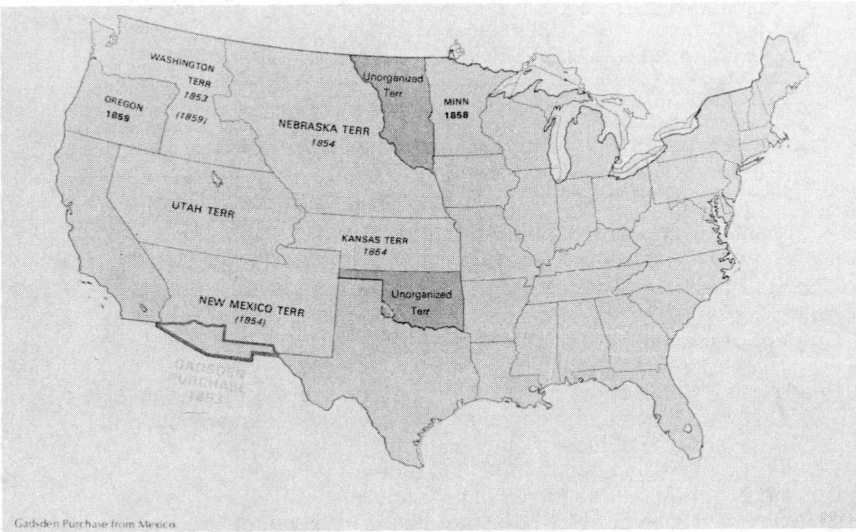

Gadsden Purchase from Mexico

Reprinted from *National Atlas* (U.S. Department of Interior; Geological Survey 1969).

The 1860 federal census. The eighth federal census was taken in 1860 during the presidency of Abraham Lincoln; the population of the United

States was 31,443,321 persons.

America continued to move west, and the Civil War was shortly to commence. Washington Territory was organized from Oregon Country in 1853; the Gadsden Purchase was made the same year, adding to New Mexico Territory. Kansas and Nebraska territories were also created in 1854, with parts of present-day North and South Dakota and Oklahoma remaining unorganized territories. Minnesota attained statehood in 1858, and Oregon in 1859.

The 1860 federal census schedules were the same in format as those of 1850, with three minor changes. The page number was given in the upper right-hand corner of the schedules, the name of the post office was listed under the left side of the heading, and a column was added to show the value of personal property in addition to the value of real estate owned.

Content of the 1860 federal census.

Heading:
- Page number.
- Name of the town, city, district, or other subdivision.
- Name of the county and state.
- Date of the enumeration and name of the assistant marshal.
- Name of the post office.

Column Number
1. Dwelling numbered in the order of visitation.
2. Families numbered in the order of visitation.
3. The name of every person whose usual place of abode on the first day of June 1860 was in this family.
4. Age.
5. Sex.
6. Color (white, black, or mulatto).
7. Profession, occupation, or trade of each person, male and female, over fifteen years of age.
8. Value of real estate owned.
9. Value of personal estate owned.
10. Place of birth (naming the state, territory, or country).
11. Married within the year.
12. Attended school within the year.
13. Persons over twenty years of age who cannot read and write.
14. Whether deaf and dumb, blind, insane, idiotic, pauper, or convict.

The information on the 1860 Federal Census Mortality Schedules is almost identical with that provided on the 1850 schedules.

The 1870 federal census. The ninth federal census was taken in 1870, when Ulysses S. Grant was president. The population of the United States was announced as 39,818,449.

In the decade preceding the 1870 census, America experienced the agony of the Civil War. Several states withdrew from the Union to form the Confederacy, then petitioned for readmission. South Carolina was readmitted in 1865; Tennessee in 1866; Alabama, Arkansas, Florida, Louisiana, and North Carolina in 1868; and Georgia, Mississippi, Texas, and Virginia reentered in 1870.

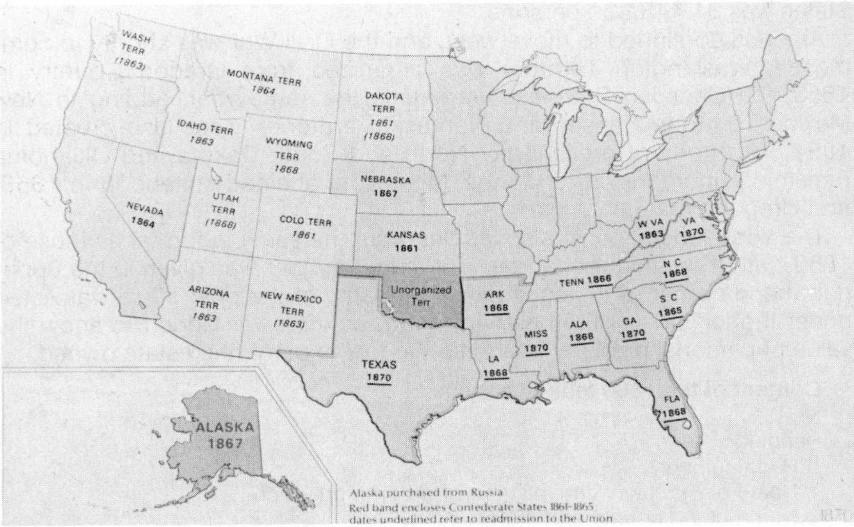

Reprinted from *National Atlas* (U.S. Department of Interior; Geological Survey 1969).

Kansas was admitted as a new state in 1861, West Virginia in 1863, and Nebraska in 1867, and several new territories were organized by the time the 1870 census was announced. These included Colorado and Dakota in 1861, Arizona and Idaho in 1863, Montana and Nevada in 1864, and Wyoming in 1868. New Mexico and Washington territories underwent boundary changes in 1863, with Utah and Dakota territories changing in 1868. Alaska was purchased in 1867, and Oklahoma remained an unorganized territory.

Some minor changes in format were made in the 1870 federal census schedules, but in content they remained very similar to the 1850 and 1860 returns. The page number was changed from the right to the left side in the headings, and the name of the assistant marshal was listed on a line opposite the post office entry. Names were entered surname first, and the occupation for all persons except infants was called for. The 1850 and 1860 returns listed names in the order spoken and called for the occupation or trade of only those persons over fifteen years of age. Two new columns were added to show if parents were of foreign birth, and a column was added to show the month of birth for children born within the census year. A column was added to identify male citizens of the United States who were twenty-one years of age and upwards, and another to identify male citizens of the United States twenty-one years of age and upwards whose right to vote had been denied or abridged.

The content of the 1870 federal mortality schedules was very similar to those of 1850 and 1860 except for columns added to indicate whether the father and mother of the deceased were of foreign birth. There was also a "Remarks" column at the bottom of the schedules where the marshal could note special situations and circumstances. The marshal who completed one Arizona schedule for 1870 wrote: "In making the enumeration, I find a very few deaths when they are of any family so I am not able to fill Column No. 1 as required by the regulations. I report a great many violent deaths, this being a frontier country where all disputes are settled by the use of weapons and occur between transients and single men who have no families." The last entry on the schedule lists the man "stabbed," giving some credence to the marshal's statement.

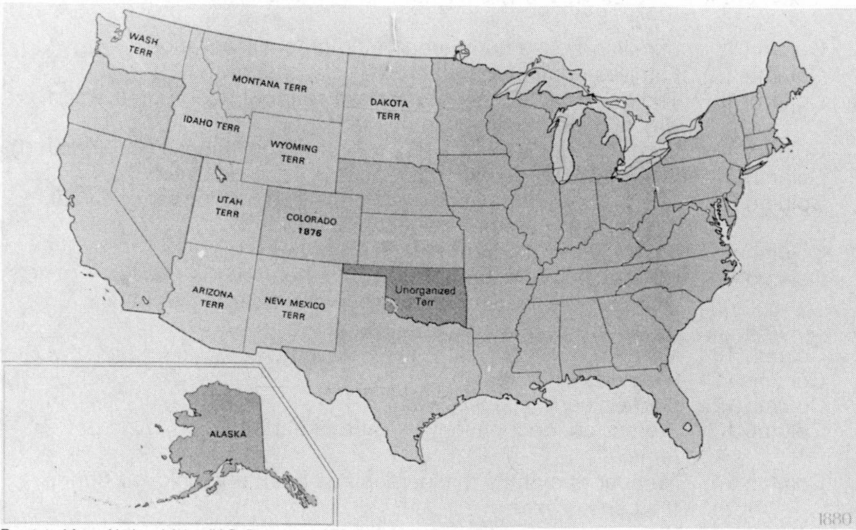

Reprinted from *National Atlas* (U.S. Department of Interior; Geological Survey 1969).

The 1880 federal census. The tenth federal census of the United States was taken in 1880 when Rutherford B. Hayes was president; the population that year was listed as 50,155,783. Colorado was the only new state admitted to the Union since 1870, but the West was on the verge of a great population expansion that would continue for decades.

The 1880 census schedules went through some interesting changes and contained new information that is helpful to family history. It was the first federal census to include relationship to the head of household, and the first to list the birthplace of each person's parents. It was also the first to be soundexed—though only partially—with the index limited to households where children of ten years of age and younger were living. It is a definite improvement over earlier federal census records, and fills a void at a time when official vital records are rather incomplete.

Content of the 1880 federal census.

Note A: The census year begins 1 June 1879 and ends 31 May 1880.

Note B: All persons will be included in the enumeration who were living on the first day of June 1880. Children born since 1 June 1880 will be omitted. Members of families who have died since 1 June 1880 will be included.

Note C: Questions 13, 14, 22, and 23 are not to be asked in respect to persons under 10 years of age.

Heading: Name of the district, precinct, ward, city, township, town; county and state; the day, month, and year of the enumeration; and the name of the enumerator.

An unnumbered column on the left side of each schedule was to contain the name of the street and the house number of the resident when living in a city, but few entries have any information recorded in that column.

Column 1. Dwelling-house numbered in the order of visitation.
Column 2. Families numbered in the order of visitation.
Column 3. The name of each person whose place of abode on the first day of June 1880 was in this family.
Column 4. Color: white (W), black (B), mulatto (M), Chinese (C), Indian (I).
Column 5. Sex: male (M), female (F).
Column 6. Age at last birthday prior to 1 June 1880. (If under one year of age, give month in fractions: 3/12).
Column 7. If born within the year give the month.
Column 8. Relationship of each person to the head of the family, whether wife, son, daughter, servant, boarder, or other.
Column 9. Single.
Column 10. Married.
Column 11. Widowed or divorced.
Column 12. Married during census year.
Column 13. Profession, occupation, or trade of each person, male or female.
Column 14. Number of months this person has been unemployed during the census year.
Column 15. Is the person (on the day of the enumerator's visit) sick or temporarily disabled so as to be unable to attend to ordinary business or duties? If so, what is the nature of the disability?
Column 16. Blind.
Column 17. Deaf and dumb.
Column 18. Idiotic.
Column 19. Insane.
Column 20. Maimed, crippled, bedridden, or otherwise disabled.
Column 21. Attended school within the census year.
Column 22. Cannot read.
Column 23. Cannot write.
Column 24. Place of birth of this person, naming state or territory of United States or the country if of foreign birth.
Column 25. Place of birth of the father of this person, naming the state or territory of United States or the country if of foreign birth.
Column 26. Place of birth of the mother of this person, naming the state or territory of United States or the country if of foreign birth.

A soundex (partial index) to the 1880 federal census was made, and film copies are available at the LDS genealogical library and at Brigham Young University. The index is by state or territory and is arranged phonetically by the name of the heads of households. It includes all persons living in households where there were children ten years of age or younger. Old couples living alone and families not having a member ten years of age or under were not indexed and must be located in the original schedules.

The soundex cards do not show all facts contained in the originals, so they must be used with the original schedules for maximum benefit. Reference to the original record is listed in the upper right-hand corner of each card, giving volume number, enumeration district, sheet number (page number), and the line number of the original entry. The name of the head of the family is listed at the top of each card and shows color, sex, age, and birthplace. The county of residence is listed along with the "M.C.D." (Municipal Civil District), usually the township. Space for the house number, street number, and the city is also provided. The lower half of each card is used to identify other members of the family by name and relationship to the head of the family, as well as by age and birthplace. The place of birth of parents is not included on the soundex cards and must be determined from the original schedules. Continuation cards are used when additional space is necessary, and cross-reference cards are filed for children when the surname is different than that of the head of the family with whom they are living.

The soundex filing system is alphabetical for the first letter of the surname and then numerical as indicated by special divider cards in the original file. This keeps names of the same and similar sound, but of variant spellings, together. A guide to the soundex system follows.

Code	Key Letters and Equivalents
1	b, p, f, v
2	c, s, k, g, j, q, x, z
3	d, t
4	l
5	m, n
6	r

The letters a, e, i, o, u, y, w, and h are *not* coded.

The first letter of a surname is *not* coded.

Every soundex number must be a three-digit number. A name yielding no code numbers, as Lee, would thus be L 000. One yielding only one code number would have two zeros added, as Kuhne, coded K 500. One yielding two code numbers would have one zero added, as Ebell, coded E 140. Not more than three digits are used, so Ebelson would be coded E 142—*not* E 1425.

When two key letters or equivalents appear together, or one key letter immediately follows or precedes an equivalent, the two are coded as one letter as follows: Ke*ll*y, coded 400; Buer*ck,* coded 620; *Ll*oyd, coded 300; and *Sc*haefer, coded 160.

If several surnames have the same code, the cards for them are arranged alphabetically by given name. There are divider cards showing most code numbers but not all. For instance, one divider may be numbered 350 and the next 400. Between the two divider cards may be names coded 353, 350, 360, 364, 365, and 355, but instead of being in numerical order they are interfiled alphabetically by given name.

Such prefixes as "van," "Von," "Di," "de," "Di," "D'," "dela," or "du" are sometimes disregarded in alphabetizing and in coding.

The following names are examples of soundex coding and are given only as illustrations.

Name	Letters Coded	Code No.
Allricht	l, r, c	A 462
Eberhard	b, r, r	E 166
Engebrethson	n, g, b	E 521
Heimbach	m, b, c	H 512
Hanselmann	n, s, l	H 524
Henzelmann	n, z, l	H 524
Hildebrand	l, d, b	H 431
Kavanagh	v, n, g	K 152
Lind, Van	n, d	L 530
Lukaschowsky	k, s, s	L 222
McDonnell	c, d, n	M 235
McGee	c	M 200
O'Brien	b, r, n	O 165
Opnian	p, n, n	O 155
Oppenheimer	p, n, m	O 155
Riedemanas	d, m, n	R 355
Zita	t	Z 300
Zitzmeinn	t, z, m	Z 325

The soundex to the 1880 census is an excellent finding tool, and each person born in the 1870s should be included. When the town or county of birth is not known but the state is, the soundex can be used to locate the family. It also might be possible to locate the family even when the state is not known, if you are willing to search the alphabetical listings for several states.

Content of the 1880 federal census mortality schedules.

Heading:
Pesons who died during the year ending 31 May 1880.
Name of the town, city, district, or other subdivision.
Name of the county and state.
Name of the assistant marshal.

Column Number:
1. Number of the family as given in column number 2 of schedule I.
2. Name of the person deceased.
3. Age at last birthday. If under one year, give months in fractions thus: 1/12; if under one month, give days in fractions thus 1/30.
4. Sex: male (M), female (F).
5. Color: white (W), black (B), mulatto (M), Chinese (C), Indian (I).
6. Single (/).
7. Married (/).
8. Widowed (/), divorced (D).
9. Place of birth of this person, naming the state or territory of the U.S. or the country if of foreign birth.
10. Where was the father of this person born?
11. Where was the mother of this person born?
12. Profession, occupation, or trade (not to be asked in respect to persons under ten years of age).
13. The month in which the person died.
14. Disease or cause of death.

15. How long a resident of this county? (If less than one year, state months in fractions thus: 1/12.)
16. If the disease was not contracted in place of death, state the place.
17. Name of attending physician.

Note E: Upon this schedule should be carefully noted (a) every death that occurred in this enumeration district during the census year, whether the deceased was or was not a member of any family that resided in the district 1 June 1880, and (b) every death that occurred outside this enumeration district during the census year, the deceased being at date of death a member of a family that resided in the enumeration distict 1 June 1880.

The enumerator should make these entries upon this schedule with great care, seeking every source of information. When a positive statement is impossible, as when an age can only be estimated or a birth place must be conjectured, the entry may be inclosed in parentheses thus: "age (25)," meaning that the best estimate of the age that can be given is 25 years. (Column lower center.)
Of the deaths reported above, the following occurred in this enumeration district, but the families to which the deceased belonged resided 1 June 1880 out of the enumeration district. Of the deaths reported above, the following occurred outside this enumeration district, though the families to which the deceased belonged resided in this enumeration district 1 June 1880. (Town, county, and state identified.)

The 1890 federal census. The eleventh federal census of the United States was taken in 1890 when Benjamin Harrison was president; the population was 62,947,714.

Unfortunately, the 1890 federal census was accidentally destroyed, except for fragments, and a veterans' enumeration for that year survives only for those states ranging alphabetically from Kentucky to Wyoming. The fragments have been microfilmed, and copies are available in the National Archives, the LDS Genealogical Society library in Salt Lake City, Brigham Young University in Provo, Utah, and other libraries. The fragments include part of Perry County, Alabama; part of the District of Columbia; part of Muscogee County, Georgia; part of McDonough County, Illinois; part of Wright County, Minnesota; part of Hudson County, New Jersey; parts of Westchester and Suffolk counties, New York; parts of Gaston and Cleveland counties, North Carolina; parts of Hamilton and Clinton counties, Ohio; part of Union County, South Dakota; and parts of Ellis, Hood, Rush, Trinity, and Kaufman counties, Texas.

The 1890 census was the first to use a family format with separate forms to enumerate each family.

Content of the 1890 federal census.
(Family schedule—One to Ten persons)

Heading:
Supervisor's district number.
Enumeration district number.
Name of city, town, township, precinct, district, beat, or other minor civil division.

Name of the county and state.
Street and number, name of ward, or name of institution.
Date and name of enumerator.

Column Content:

A. Number of dwelling-house in the order of visitation.
B. Number of families in this dwelling-house.
C. Number of persons in this dwelling-house.
D. Number of family in the order of visitation.
E. Number of persons in this family.

1. Christian name in full, and initial of middle name, then surname.
2. Whether a soldier, sailor, or marine during the Civil War (U.S. or Confederacy) or widow of such person.
3. Relationship to head of family.
4. Whether white, black, mulatto, quadroon, octoroon, Chinese, Japanese, or Indian.
5. Sex.
6. Age at nearest birthday. If under one year, give age in months.
7. Whether single, married, widowed, or divorced.
8. Whether married during the census year (1 June 1889 to 31 May 1890).
9. Mother of how many children, and number of these children living.
10. Place of birth.
11. Place of birth of father.
12. Place of birth of mother.
13. Number of years in the United States.
14. Whether naturalized.
15. Whether naturalization papers have been taken out.
16. Profession, trade, or occupation.
17. Months unemployed during the census year (1 June 1889 to 31 May 1890).
18. Attendance at school (in months) during the census year (1 June 1889 to 31 May 1890).
19. Able to read.
20. Able to write.
21. Able to speak English. If not, the language or dialect spoken.
22. Whether suffering from acute or chronic disease, with name of disease and length of time afflicted.
23. Whether defective in mind, sight, hearing, or speech, or whether crippled, maimed, or deformed, with name of defect.
24. Whether a prisoner, convict, homeless child, or pauper.
25. Supplemental schedule and page.

1890 federal census veterans' schedules. Persons who served in the U.S. Army, Navy, or Marine Corps during the Civil War or who were survivors and widows of such persons were enumerated on a special veteran's schedule in 1890. Only the schedules of states ranging alphabetically from Kentucky to Wyoming escaped the fire that burned the regular 1890 census. However, they are not as inclusive as the regular census schedules, and they list no vital statistics.

This schedule includes the names of surviving veterans or their widows; rank, company, regiment or vessel; date of enlistment; date of discharge;

and length of service. The post office address of the person is listed at the bottom of the schedule, and space is provided for special remarks about disabilities and other important circumstances that affected the veteran.

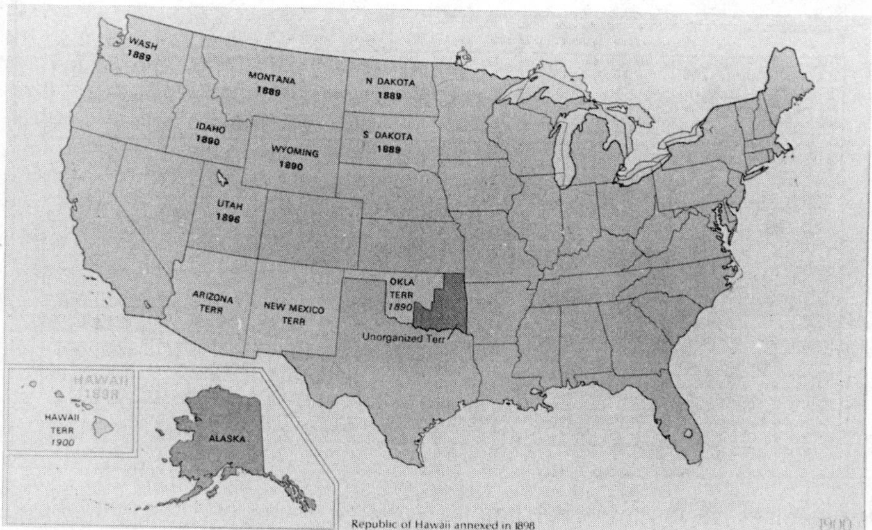

Reprinted from *National Atlas* (U.S. Department of Interior; Geological Survey 1969).

The 1900 federal census. The twelfth federal census of the United States was taken in 1900 when William McKinley was president; the population was announced to be 75,994,575. Several more territories had become states, and the Republic of Hawaii had been annexed.

Montana, North Dakota, South Dakota, and Washington were admitted to statehood in 1889; Idaho and Wyoming were admitted in 1890; and part of present-day Oklahoma was organized as a territory in 1890. Utah was granted statehood in 1896, but Arizona and New Mexico remained territories.

In December 1973, the 1900 federal census returns were opened for public use, though certain restrictions at first limited their inspection to historians, genealogists, and sociologists. Also, for a short time the records could be searched only at the National Archives or one of its branches. More recent legislation modified those requirements, making the records available for purchase by any individual or organization. Microfilm copies of the complete 1900 federal census—plus the soundex to it—are presently available for use at the LDS Genealogical Society library in Salt Lake City, Utah, or through any of its branch libraries. Brigham Young University is in the process of acquiring it.

The 1900 federal census is without doubt the most informative census presently available for family history. Among the more important genealogical details contained in it are the month and year of birth, relationship of each person to the head of the family, state or country of birth, state or country of birth for parents, the year of immigration to the United States, the number of years in the United States, whether a naturalized citizen,

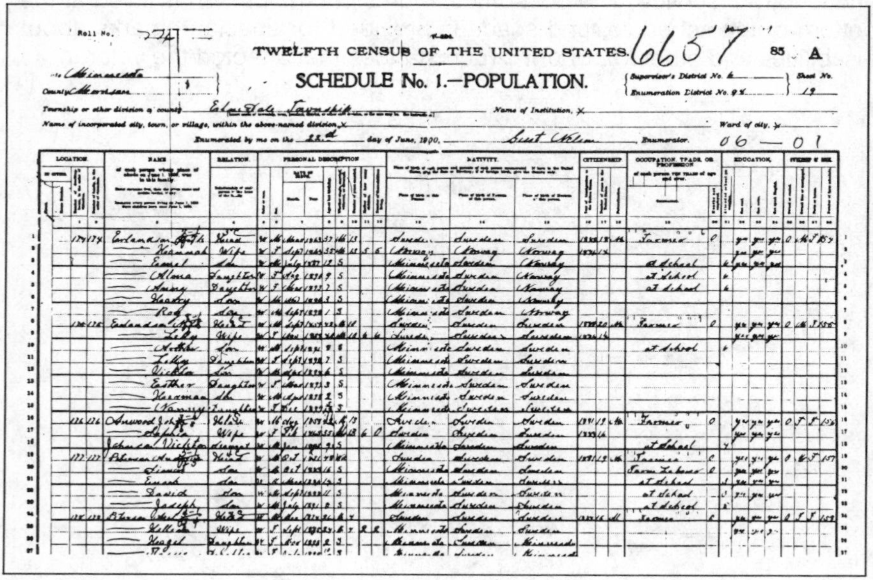
TWELFTH CENSUS OF THE UNITED STATES. 6657 85 A

SCHEDULE No. 1.—POPULATION.

the number of years married, mother of how many children, and how many of those children were living at the time the census was taken.

Content of the 1900 federal census.

General Information

a. State, county, township, or other division of county.
b. Name of incorporated city, town, or village.
c. Name of institution.
d. Enumeration date and enumerator.
e. Supervisor's district number and enumeration district.

Location

a. Street.
b. House number.
c. Number of dwelling-house in the order of visitation.
d. Number of family in the order of visitation.

Name

a. Each person's name whose place of abode on 1 June 1900 was in that family.
b. Every person living on 1 June 1900.
c. Children were omitted when born after 1 June 1900.

Relationship

Relationship of each person to the head of the family.

Personal Description

a. Color or race.
b. Sex.
c. Date of birth (month and year).
d. Age at last birthday.
e. Whether single, married, widowed, or divorced.

f. Number of years married.
g. Mother of how many children.
h. Number of these children living.

Nativity
a. Place of birth of this person (state or country).
b. Place of birth of father of this person (state or country).
c. Place of birth of mother of this person (state or country).

Citizenship
a. Year of immigration to the United States.
b. Number of years in the United States.
c. Naturalization.

Occupation, Trade, or Profession (each person ten years old and over)
a. Occupation.
b. Months not employed.

Education
a. Attended school (in months).
b. Can read.
c. Can write.
d. Can speak English.

Ownership of Home
a. Owned or rented.
b. Owned free or mortgaged.
c. Farm or house.
d. Number of farm schedule.

You should locate your people in the 1900 census returns and study the information listed very carefully. In many instances important names, dates, and places can be added to your records, and gaps in your pedigree can be filled. Locating information on other relatives, friends, neighbors, and family associates is also advisable, because their listings may provide additional helpful information. Spouses of ancestors and other relatives often lived in close proximity, and family associates were often natives of the same states and countries.

State and Local Returns

State and local census records—including territorial listings—are good supplements to federal census records, and many have been published or microfilmed. A few predate the American Revolution, but most were taken later and correspond closely to the federal returns, both in time period and content. Some alternate decennially with the federal censuses, thereby providing five-year listings.

Most state records taken before 1850 are statistical in format—much like the federal returns of corresponding periods—but some are as inclusive as the federal records of 1850 or later. Some were taken to determine territorial status or statehood, while others were taken to determine representation in state legislatures or for other political purposes. One early Maryland census was taken to determine the names of those who did not take an oath of loyalty during the Revolution. Some states took them at regular intervals following statehood, while others took them only periodically or not at all.

Fortunately, two useful bibliographies of state and local census records have been compiled to guide researchers in their use: one as recently as 1973 and the other in 1948. The most comprehensive is John D. Stemmons' *The United States Census Compendium: A Directory of Census Records, Tax Lists, Poll Lists, Petitions, Directories, Etc., Which Can Be Used as a Census.* The earlier work is Henry J. Dubester's *State Censuses: An Annotated Bibliography of Censuses of Population Taken After the Year 1790 by States and Territories of the United States.*

Colonial census enumerations. Census enumerations of the population during the colonial period were not regular, though some names and numbers of inhabitants were recorded at various times and places for different reasons. Writers have gathered and recorded a fair amount of this information, and historians have provided us with some names and numbers of early settlers in America during the earliest history.

Charles M. Andrews frequently makes reference to inhabitants of the colonies in *The Colonial Period of American History,* (1964, vol. 1), sometimes giving detailed classifications. Other historians have done the same, but perhaps not in as much detail. For example, while writing about the early Virginia land-tenancy system, Andrews refers to a letter from John Rolfe to Richard Warwick in 1616: "The main body of planters was divided into officers, laborers, and farmers. The total number of colonists at this time was three hundred and fifty-one—two hundred and five officers and laborers and eighty-one farmers, and the rest women and children" (page 125).

At another point, while explaining the merits of the joint stock company organized to settle the colony, he quotes from the Virginia Company Records: "A year after the annulment of the charter, the population had risen to nearly eleven hundred. The colony already possessed all the essentials of a permanent settlement—family and agricultural life, men, women, and children, artisans, hired laborers, and indentured servants, and a few negroes . . . forty-two sail of ships were reported in 1623 as plying back and forth between England and Virginia; and in the main the people were peaceful and contented. It looked as if the Virginia colony had actually taken root" (page 140).

Most of Andrews' references to names and numbers of colonial inhabitants come from volumes one and two of the *Virginia Company Records,* and volume one of Alexander Brown's *Genesis of the United States*—both of which should be found in any good historical library. He also refers to other early publications and documents of the colonial era, but many of them can be found only in special libraries and historical societies.

Most early colonial sources making specific reference to names and ages of inhabitants come from land and court records, ship passenger lists, militia lists, or the private diaries, journals, and papers of early settlers. They are not census enumerations in the strictest sense, but they do provide the primary lists of names and ages of inhabitants in the earliest periods of colonial history.

Charles Edward Banks provides alphabetical lists and background information on many early New England inhabitants in *The Winthrop Fleet of 1630; The English Ancestry and Homes of the Pilgrim Fathers; Planters of the Commonwealth;* and *Topographical Dictionary of 2885 English Emigrants to New England 1620–1650;* while Azel Ames' *The Mayflower and her Log* provides excellent detail on the earliest settlers of the Plymouth Colony.

The names of more than fifty thousand early immigrants to Pennsylvania in the colonial period are contained in Ralph Beaver Strassburger and William John Hinke's *Pennsylvania German Pioneers: A Publication of the Original Lists of Arrivals in the Port of Philadelphia from 1727 to 1808,* and in Israel Daniel Rupp's *A Collection of Upwards of Thirty Thousand Names of Germans, Swiss, Dutch, French and Other Immigrants into Pennsylvania from 1727 to 1776.*

George Cabell Greer's *Early Virginia Immigrants 1632–1666;* Nell Marion Nugent's *Cavaliers and Pioneers;* William Glover Stanard's *Some Emigrants to Virginia;* and William Armstrong Crozier's *Virginia Colonial Militia 1651–1776* are good examples of published lists showing early inhabitants of the South. A few publications also are in print dealing with ethnic or regional groups, such as R. A. Brock's *Huguenot Emigration to Virginia,* or Worth S. Ray's *The Mecklenburg Signers and Their Neighbors.*

Local tax lists, tax digests, rate lists, land lottery lists, petitions, and state militia lists can also be used as substitute census records. *New Jersey in 1793* by Norton and Richards and *Virginia Tax Payers 1782–87* by Fothergill and Naugle are good examples. Stemmon's *Census Compendium* cited previously is an exhaustive guide to this type of record.

A few local census enumerations taken prior to the Revolution have been published or microfilmed. A 1701 census for Long Island, New York, is on file at the LDS Genealogical Society library in Salt Lake City, as are printed copies of the 1774 and the 1776 censuses for Rhode Island. The state of Maryland took a census in 1776 and another in 1778 to ascertain which persons failed to take an oath of fidelity. North Carolina enumerated her population between 1784 and 1786, as have other states named in Dubester and Stemmons' works.

State and territorial census enumerations. After the colonies obtained their independence from Great Britain, a number of states and territories enumerated their populations to determine territorial status or in preparation for statehood.

In 1787 Congress established the Territory Northwest of the Ohio River from which the states of Ohio, Indiana, Illinois, Michigan, and Wisconsin were taken. In 1790 the Territory South of the Ohio River was created from which the states of Tennessee, Alabama, and Mississippi evolved. By 1800 Indiana Territory had been carved from the Territory Northwest of the Ohio River, and Mississippi Territory had been carved from part of the Territory South of the Ohio River.

The United States acquired the vast Louisiana Purchase from France in

1803, enlarged the Mississippi Territory in 1804, created the Orleans Territory the same year, and established the Louisiana Territory in 1805. Michigan Territory was also created in 1805 from part of Indiana Territory, and a new Indiana Territory was formed in 1809, with Illinois Territory coming into existence the same year. America was on the move west, and censuses of the population were important factors in establishing territories and states. Family history has benefited from them.

Several of the territorial census enumerations have been published, microfilmed, and indexed. Current holdings at Brigham Young University include territorial listings for Arizona, Illinois, Iowa, Kansas, Michigan, Minnesota, Montana, Nebraska, North Dakota, Oklahoma, and Wisconsin. The Oklahoma territorial census at BYU is an enumeration of the inhabitants in Indian land west of Arkansas in 1860, but covers the present state of Oklahoma.

Territorial Census of Arizona: 1864

Fort Buchanan—Continued

Name	Age (years)	Sex	Occupation	Value of property	Place of birth
Cross, Edward E.	30	Male	Editor	7,500	New Hampshire
Doyle, John	27	"	Wagon master	500	Tennessee
Everett, Alice	25	Female	Housewife	350	Ireland
Laura E	2	"			New Mexico
Faringhy, L. O	30	Male	Bookbinder	5,000	France
Gonzales, Damiana	40	Female	Seamstress	100	Mexico
Anselma	40	"	Washwoman		"
Gonzales, Porfirio	25	Male	Laborer	200	"
Klein, Harrison	27	"	Blacksmith		Pennsylvania
Lindsay, John H	28	"	Carpenter	200	"
Longmire, Guadalupe	27	Female	Laundress		New Mexico
Mary	7	"			"
Andrew	3	Male			"
Eliza A	1/12	Female			"
Márquez, Josefa	23	Female	Washwoman		"
Felipe N	4	Male			"
Miller, August	31	"	Laborer	250	Hesse-Darmstadt, Germany
Moore, Margaret A	20	Female	Milliner		England
Randal, Julia	24	"	Housewife		Massachusetts
Ray, John	35	Male	Teamster		New York
Reed, James M	27	"	Blacksmith	180	Tennessee
Robles, Francisco	17	"	Servant	100	Mexico
Ryan, William	26	"	Shoemaker		Ireland
Kate	25	Female	Laundress		"
William	1/12	Male			New Mexico
Spinning, Mary F	21	Female	Housewife		Kentucky
W. M	2	Male			New Mexico
Thompson, W. R	32	"	Merchant	20,000	Virginia
Trojel, Teodora	18	Female			Mexico
Vásquez, Guadalupe	10	"			New Mexico
White, F. F	45	"	Sutler	20,000	Massachusetts

Kansas, Minnesota, and New York are examples of states that took local census enumerations decennially between federal census enumerations. Those for Kansas and Minnesota are available on microfilm for the period 1865–95, and those for New York date from 1825–1925. An 1851 census for Utah has been published (Utah was still a territory at the time), and a state census for California is on microfilm for 1852. The 1875 state census for Nevada and 1885 censuses of Colorado and Nebraska have also been microfilmed. These state enumerations dating after 1850 are very similar in content to the federal returns of corresponding periods. Exceptions generally favor the state schedules containing more genealogical information than the federal returns.

Special Census Indexes

Perhaps the best thing that has happened to family history and census records in recent years is the profuse number of census indexes that have been published. Over one hundred volumes are currently on the reference shelves of the library at Brigham Young University; ten years ago there were very few. Individuals and organizations with varied interests have been responsible, some using modern computer technology to accomplish their purposes.

These indexes take much of the drudgery out of census searching, allowing researchers to locate names that otherwise would be lost in numerous record listings. Mistakes of omission and commission have been made in some of the indexes, but their value far outweighs their failings. We all owe a special note of gratitude to those who labored so long and so hard to accomplish this arduous task.

At this writing, most of the federal census records prior to 1850 have been indexed, as have several territorial enumerations. Only a few state enumerations dating after 1840 have been completed, but most of the early state lists have been done. All the 1850 federal census enumerations have been indexed, and recently the 1860 federal census index for Ohio was acquired by Brigham Young University. Other libraries undoubtedly have similar collections.

Searching Census Records Effectively

Methods vary from problem to problem in census searching, but an accepted practice among professionals is to search modern returns first, then search the earlier listings. Modern census records (1850–1900) contain more genealogical information than those prior to 1850, and they often provide important facts that can guide you as research continues. It is much easier to identify families and individuals in the earlier records after you have noted the structure of the family you are researching in modern census listings. Of course sometimes the only pertinent census listings are in the early records, and searches should be made accordingly.

Individuals and families should also be located in more than one census whenever possible, because important facts may be missed if other entries are ignored. Names, dates, places, and other facts may vary from record to record, depending on the knowledge and intent of the informants and the ability of the enumerators. If the informant did not have the correct facts, or did not wish to give them, the records will reflect it; if the enumerator had poor penmanship or could not spell, the records will show it.

At times the enumerators were not able to question family members personally, but relied on a neighbor's statements or omitted information on that family entirely. Perhaps some families living in remote areas also were overlooked. Omissions and incorrect information can sometimes be rectified when individuals are located in more than one census listing. Also names may be illegible in some entries because of ink blots or damaged records, whereas in other entries they may be clear.

In modern census records where names and ages are listed, the age usually refers to the person's last birthday, but it is not uncommon to find ages varying several years from the correct age. Women typically are less than ten years older each decade, while men might age as much as twelve or fifteen years in the same period! Locating individuals in two or more census records can help establish the correct age.

At times you will be unable to locate your people in a particular record, even though you are sure they resided in that county and state. Sometimes you must search the entire county, or even surrounding counties, to locate them. Enumerators were not always consistent in their entries, and schedules are sometimes filmed out of their original sequence. Some records are copies rather than originals, which also can account for errors and omissions. One of my ancestral families was enumerated in two different counties the same census year. Evidently they lived in the first locality when the census was taken there, then moved to the second city and were enumerated again.

You should carefully note the dates counties were formed, too, because families may have resided in a particular county when one census was taken, but may have fallen under the jurisdiction of another county after a division was made. Some families resided in the same home over a long period but were listed under the jurisdiction of several different counties because of reorganization and division. Guidebooks—such as George B. Everton's *Handy Book for Genealogists*—can provide the information necessary to determine dates of county organization.

More often than not enumerators did not omit families; rather the searcher overlooked the entry or searched the wrong records. Places of birth of other family members, friends, and associates can sometimes provide the clues necessary to locate people in the census. The enumerators often spelled names the way they sounded (phonetically) rather than according to recognized spelling standards. Verbalize each name you are seeking several times before and during your census searches. If you will follow that practice, your reflexes are more apt to respond to entries similar in sound to the one you are seeking.

Sometimes the entries are so faded or illegible that you cannot be certain of them. You may find it necessary to compare writing characteristics of the enumerator from one entry to another to decipher the entry. A careful analysis of letter formations in other entries can help you identify hard-to-read entries. Sometimes by placing a bright yellow or red paper on the reading surface you can read the entry more clearly when working with microfilms. Many researchers try to make something out of the name that is not really there. Look at a particularly difficult entry from several different angles—also from a more relaxed viewpoint. Too rigid an attitude cannot be objective. You may even ask someone sitting near you to view the entry and give his opinion. He could approach it from an entirely fresh perspective, interpreting a difficult entry with relative ease.

Some enumerators used abbreviations or ditto marks, or they omitted details that should have been recorded. It is common to find the surname listed only once with each family entry, then ditto marks or blank spaces used under the first entry. Entries for color or sex also were often omitted or entered incorrectly. Some enumerators left the color column blank when the individual was white, entering the appropriate letter only when the person was black, mulatto, or Indian.

Unfortunately American Indians were not enumerated in regular federal census returns because they were not considered citizens. However when they were married to whites or when they had severed their connections with the parent tribe, they were sometimes listed. Combination entries in regular federal census returns and in special Indian enumerations occasionally exist. A white man married to an Indian might be enumerated alone in the regular federal census while his wife and children were enumerated in special Indian returns—or they all may be listed in one or both enumerations. It is worthwhile to search both the regular federal returns and the special Indian census records if your people lived on or near Indian reservations.

Federal, state, territorial, and local census records stand out as prime sources for family history. Used in conjunction with other available sources, they will help you meet your goal of compiling a well-documented family history.

6 Court Records

Perhaps no other official public records contain as much useful information for family and local history as American court records, yet often they are neglected by researchers. Until recently, most of the records were available for research only through personal inspection at the courthouse or town hall—making research difficult for some—but with the current interest shown in records preservation by public officials, many records now have been microfilmed and are accessible through local libraries, archives, and historical societies. This is particularly true of earlier records.

All kinds of genealogical and historical information can be found in court records—including basic facts for personal or family identification and social, economic, and political information. Name, age, and place of residence are usually listed when the record concerns an individual, and kinship information is provided when disputes between family members and relatives are arbitrated in court. Often the occupation, social status, military status, political or religious affiliation, and other conditions also are given. Previous places of residence and family migration patterns can sometimes be determined, as can death or burial information.

Court actions of special interest to family and local history research include adoption, change of name, divorce, naturalization and citizenship, guardianship, estate settlement, bankruptcy and foreclosure, as well as various disputes regarding real and personal property. They result in the creation of permanent court records that with very few exceptions are open to the public.

Though our court system has undergone considerable change, its fundamental objectives and concepts have remained the same: to adjudicate disputes, to decide the guilt or innocence of persons accused of crime, to protect personal property rights, and to determine the constitutionality of laws (Abraham 1959, p. 2).

The courts operate under either a federal or state system, and their records usually remain in custody of the respective court. The records created under the state system are the most popular with family historians, but useful information also can be found in the federal records. In the federal system, cases originate in the district courts, with circuit courts and the United States Supreme Court handling appeals. Special courts also exist under the federal system to handle foreign cases, but their work usually is less important to family and local history. In the state system, minor courts operate at the town or city level, with major trial courts at the county or district level. The major trial courts have appellate jurisdiction and are required by law to keep permanent records.

Cases pertaining to common law, equity, criminal prosecutions, and probate may be brought before the courts. Of the four, probate is probably the most important to family history—but the other records may contain genealogical information, and they certainly contain excellent historical background. In some jurisdictions special courts handle only probate, while in others a single court may hear civil, criminal, and probate cases. Courts typically handling probate cases include the probate court, orphans court, surrogate court, ordinary court, county court, and circuit court. Those handling civil and criminal cases as well as probate include the county court, circuit court, court of common pleas and quarter sessions, court of oyer and terminer, and superior and inferior courts. Their records include docket books, journals, indexes, order books, will books, volumes of miscellaneous content, and case files containing loose documents relating to the respective cases brought before them.

Probate Law and Custom

Probate concerns itself with the proving of wills and with administering the estates of persons who have died. It also hears cases concerning orphans and guardianship, insanity, lunacy proceedings, and heirship matters. It falls under control of the state court system and is handled at the county, town, or district level, depending on the state. Its records are closely allied to land records and those of the other courts and with few exceptions are open to public inspection.

Any responsible adult can make and leave a will (testate estate), and of course many people die without leaving wills (intestate estates). Not every estate is probated, for various reasons, but officials are interested in probating all estates because when no legal heirs can be found the remaining wealth accrues to the state. Some individuals dispose of all their property before death, while others provide for disposition through written (holographic) or oral (nuncupative) wills. State law provides for the legal and equitable distribution of property where no will exists or where existing wills are proven invalid.

The probate court records in a case usually began with someone presenting a will for probate or petitioning the court to administer the estate of someone who died without leaving a will. Any interested person could initiate the action: family members, relatives or friends, family associates, creditors, or local officials. It could be done immediately after the principal's death or years later and might involve any number of persons.

The process continued with the court issuing letters testamentary or letters of administration—depending on the type of estate—directing the executor or administrator to carry out the terms of the will or administer the estate according to prescribed laws. If the executor or administrator was unable or unwilling to carry out the assignment, a document of renunciation might be filed with the court; then another administrator would be appointed with new letters issued and the will annexed, if appropriate.

The executor or administrator may have been required to take out bond or otherwise guarantee his qualifications, but some testators stipulated in the will that the executor was to act without bond. After preliminaries were taken care of, the property was located, inventoried, appraised, and accounted for. Sometimes real or personal property had to be sold to complete the probating process, and special documents and accounts were effected. The widow may have been given allowances in money or kind for her support during the process, in which case additional documents would be created.

In some instances the court may have held probate in abeyance while some other matter of law regarding the case was settled. Perhaps a son or daughter was left out of the will or contested the proceedings for some other reason; the court would be obliged to settle that matter first. In the recent probate case involving multimillionaire Howard Hughes, the court spent more than three years deciding whether a valid will existed; thirty separate documents were submitted as authentic wills, but all were determined to be invalid by the court. At the time of this writing, members of Hughes's family are contesting other actions relating to the case, and the probate process will undoubtedly continue for several more years before it is settled.

Heirs and other interested persons might also submit letters, affidavits, depositions, or other documents to the court for consideration and hearing; any of these might contain valuable genealogical and historical information. In some cases, one hundred or more documents are on file. Finally, however, the estate is settled, proceeds are distributed, and the probate process is completed.

Donald Lines Jacobus, often called the father of American genealogy, wrote an informative article on peculiarities of the American probate system that is as meaningful today as when it was written in 1932.

> Aside from the vital records kept in early days by the towns and churches, no source of information is so important genealogically as the probate records; and even the vital statistics cannot as a rule be distributed correctly into family groups without the aid of the probate entries. When a man's will named each child specifically, as well as his wife, we know that we have a family group proved by sound legal evidence, and the same is true in intestate estates when the court ordered the estate distributed to the widow and children.
>
> An estate, in legal parlance, is testate when there is a will, and intestate when there is not. A will has to receive the approval of the court, and if not approved, the estate becomes intestate. It is customary for the will to name one or more executors to carry out its provisions; when not named, or if the executor named died before the testator (maker of the will), the court

appoints an administrator "cum testamento annexo" (with the will annexed). In intestate estates, the court appoints an administrator, whose duties are similar to those of the executor in testate estates, except that there being no will, the estate will have to be distributed in accordance with the laws of inheritance of the time and place.

A nuncupative will is one which is expressed by word of mouth in the presence of witnesses, instead of being committed to writing. In former days, wills of this type were more common than today, and courts often admitted the wills, not only of soldiers and sailors before going into action, but those of any person who thus expressed his will orally in expectation of dying soon.

Differing according to the time and place, either two or three witnesses were required for the making of a valid will whether written or oral. These witnesses, when the executor presented the will in court, were required to acknowledge their signatures and to express their belief that the testator was of sound mind when he signed the will or expressed it orally in their presence. Sometimes a young woman witness had married in the interval between the making and proving of the will, and proof of her marriage is thus afforded by the records of an estate in which she had no personal interest.

In early days in some parts of the country, wills were proved by witnesses before a magistrate in the town where they and the testator lived, and the magistrate then certified their acknowledgement to the probate court. This was a matter of convenience, since the probate district often covered an entire county or at least several towns. In such cases, the acknowledgement of the witnesses may be dated several days before the will was presented for probate. The important dates to note are that on which the will was made (specified in the will itself), that on which the witnesses made acknowledgement, and that on which the will was presented in court. Of these three dates, the testator certainly died between the first and the last, and thus the date of his death is often fixed within a period of a week or a month if he died soon after the will was made. The acknowledgement of the witnesses when made after the testator's death, often enables us to fix the date of death within an even more narrow limit.

But it later became the practice (and in some sections may have been the practice quite early) to have the witnesses make their acknowledgement before a notary or other qualified officer at the time the will was signed. Amateurs when making rapid notes of an estate sometimes discover that they have taken down the same date for the making of the will and its probation (proving). This is because for the second date they have noted the date on which the witnesses acknowledged their signatures, in one of the instances where this was done the day the will was made. The genealogist should be careful to watch for this, and where the dates are identical, to make sure that they have found the date on which the will was approved by the court. When using a record volume in which will and probate proceedings were entered, it may be found that the probate clerk entered first the will and acknowledgment of witnesses and last of all the probation of the will with the date of the court; on the other hand, he may have entered at the head or in the middle of a page the words "At a Court of Probate held in XYZ the second Tuesday in March 1723/4" and then entered records for several pages pertaining to several estates which came before that court hearing. In the latter case, it is necessary to look back carefully through several pages until the date is found.

In New York State, the surrogate's court corresponds roughly to the probate court of other sections.

It was customary in intestate estates for a relative of the deceased to petition the court for administration. In some sections, a written petition, naming all who had an interest in the estate, was required, but in most sections of the country, this was not required at a very early date. When such a petition is found, it is extremely valuable, for it usually states the names and places of residence of the heirs, and specifies how they were related to the deceased.

If an estate proved to be insolvent, then, unless there was a will or a petition naming the heirs, the records of the estate are very disappointing to the genealogist. The widow was allowed her dower (or third) and the rest of the estate went to the creditors.

In quite early days, it was customary, when a girl married, for the father to give her part of the "portion," usually in movables, so as to help her set up housekeeping. The bridegroom's father might aid by conveying land to his son on which to build a house. Because of these customs, the inventories of estates in early days do not give us a fair idea of the actual wealth of many decedents, since the property inventoried was merely what was left after providing at least partially for several children. When a child had received its full portion during the father's lifetime, his will may fail to make any mention of that child. This is particularly true when the will was nuncupative or written hastily when the man was dying. As it was the custom to keep an account book in which the value of property "advanced" to each child was carefully entered, the executor of the estate, if a child omitted from the will made a claim, could produce the dead man's own account book in court to prove that the child was entitled to nothing further.

In intestate estates, the court gave an order for distribution, after hearing the testimony of heirs and examining deeds and account books. Sometimes the court order specifies that John, the eldest son, has received his full portion, that Joseph has received $10 towards his portion, and so on, and directs what amount each child is to receive. The distribution made by the administrator carries out the order, but shows just what property was "set out" to each child. Where some of the children had received their full portions during the lifetime of the deceased, the court order may make reference to this fact, while the distribution may omit any mention of them. Hence, the genealogist who uses only the files may be misled by the distribution into believing that there were no other surviving children than those named therein while an examination of the court order in the record volumes would prove the contrary.

In New England, the general rule of distribution was for the widow to receive as her "dower" the use of one-third of the realty for life, and one-third of the movables absolutely. The children received two-thirds of the movables and realty as well as an interest in the one-third of the realty which was subject to the widow's dower. Where there were no children, a man's brothers and sisters usually came in for the two-thirds interest. If a will gave a wife less than the dower allowed her by law, she had a good legal claim to refuse the legacy given her by will and to demand her legal dower.

It was a somewhat general practice in the very early colonial period for sons to receive their portions in realty and for daughters to receive theirs in movables. The eldest son by English law received the landed estate; but in this country land was so plentiful at first that it was not considered good public policy in the development of an unsettled region to entail estates for the benefit of the eldest son. In New England he received a double portion in consideration of his "birth-right." Therefore, when the genealogist finds in a deed that Samuel Smith conveyed a one-seventh interest in the estate of his father John Smith deceased, he may conclude that John Smith left six surviving children, each of whom received one-seventh except the eldest son who received two-sevenths.

It is usually easier to trace male lines than female, as the surname did not change. Daughters may have been unmarried when the father's will was made, or even if married, the will and distribution may fail to specify anything but their Christian names. When a will states that "my daughters Mary and Martha shall have five shillings apiece, which with what they have received heretofore shall be their entire portion out of my estate," and that "my daughter Grace shall have $30 to make her equal with her sister," the genealogist may assume that Mary and Martha were married before the will was made and had received their portions at marriage, and that Grace was an unmarried daughter.

While a wife who was the mother of the children could claim her legal "thirds," an exception should be noted when a widower married a widow above child-bearing age. It was customary in such cases, since the widower wanted his estate to go to his children, and the widow wanted her movables to go to her own, to draw up "article," an antenuptial agreement specifying what each party reserved. It might be that the elderly bridegroom allowed the widow $10 and a cow out of his estate at his death, in return for the use of such movables as she brought into his house, and that she reserved the movables to herself and her heirs if she survived the second husband, or to her children if she died before him. Such second marriages were almost an economic necessity to our ancestors who lived under primitive conditions and it was quite usual for agreements to be made prior to the second marriage, to protect the interest of the children of the contracting parties. These agreements were binding in law, and precluded the claim to legal dower. Sometimes they were recorded at the time, or in the probate records after the second husband had died. Again, they were merely referred to in the will without ever being recorded. The writer has seen one will which does not even make mention of the testator's wife, yet there is other evidence to show that he had married a widow who survived him. She was doubtless provided for by one of these antenuptial agreements, which in this case was not recorded or referred to in the public records.

Early wills often named more than one executor, and quite frequently a man named a relative of his own and a relative of his wife to serve together. This was done to safeguard the interests of everybody concerned. In addition to executors, two or three overseers were also named in many early wills or were appointed by the courts. Their duty was advisory, and often they were prominent men of the community, though occasionally they were related to the testator or to his wife.

It is well to examine the bond of the executor or administrator, because the law required that one or more persons should endorse the bond as sureties. These bondsmen, since there were no professional bonding houses until a late period, were most often relatives of the decedent; if a man's wife was executrix, very often her relatives signed her bond. Thus, when the identity of a man's wife is unknown, the bond sometimes affords a clue. This should be sought in the files, because in most probate districts the record volumes only specify that the bond was accepted without a copy being entered; and the names of the bondsmen are not always stated in the record of acceptance. The originals are also useful because of the autographs of the executors and bondsmen.

Guardians were appointed by the court for children under fourteen years of age; at fourteen or over, the child was allowed to choose his own guardian, subject to the approval of the court. Hence, if a guardian was appointed, it is usually safe to assume that the child was under fourteen. If the record reads that James Johnson was allowed guardian to Jane Robinson, the inference is that she chose him and hence was over fourteen. Although as a rule children chose their guardians when they reached fourteen or a little over, it is never safe to assume this unless the record states the age, for circumstances not known to us may have deferred the choice of guardian until the child was fifteen, sixteen, or even twenty.

Considerable study and knowledge of English law of the earlier centuries is needed to arrive at correct deductions when ususual probate cases are found. At the death of a young unmarried man named Farnes, the court granted the estate to his paternal uncle, to the exclusion of his sister of the half-blood. Why? Well, we may suspect that the matter of ''public policy'' entered into the decision, for the uncle was an incompetent who might become a town charge, while the half-sister lived outside the jurisdiction of the court. But the legal point made was that the property came from the paternal side, while the half-sister was related only through the mother.

The amateur should not feel too secure in the deductions he makes from probate records until his personal research is sufficiently extensive to provide many examples of the various types of legal procedure, as well as an occasional exception to the more familiar types. Differences in law and methods of procedure are to be found in different colonies, and although most of the information given in this paper applies pretty generally, and I did not wish to confuse the reader by noting too many exceptions, the practicing genealogist will know offhand of a few exceptions, and the amateur will have to watch for differences or exceptions in the specific locality where he is working. [Jacobus 1932, vol. 9]

Probate Court Records

Any number of records and documents may be created in the probate process, though they vary in content and value with each case. Some probate court records have been lost through negligence or such destructive forces as fire or flood, and some have been microfilmed and put in storage, but most remain at the courthouse or town hall and are accessible for research. Probate entries might be found in any court records, but those of primary importance are the general indexes to estates, will books or records of wills, court order books, and case files or probate packets containing the original documents relating to individual cases. Guardianship accounts, heirship matters, insane cases, and lunacy proceedings vary in application and may be located in separate volumes or among other records.

It is not uncommon to find mixed entries in the records. Wills may have been recorded in deed books, for instance. Orphan and guardianship matters might be found in the will books or scattered throughout the order books; marriage or divorce entries may be listed in the will books, deed books, court order books, or in separate books of entry. Also, finding probate entries in books classified as "miscellaneous records," is not unusual. Evidently some clerks made entries in any record book that was convenient, under the assumption that they were all official records.

Perhaps the best place to begin searching for probate information is in the will books or record of wills, generally indexed. These are special volumes where handwritten or typed copies of the original wills have been recorded.

The same procedure should be followed whether you are searching microfilm copies of probate records or the records themselves; search the will books or record of wills first, then proceed to the other records. The will books or record of wills are usually lettered or numbered in chronological sequence. Each volume is usually indexed—either at the front or back of the book—and a general probate index often exists also, referring to other probate documents and court actions as well as to the will.

GENERAL INDEX TO PROBATE, GUARDIANSHIP AND INSANE CASES
UTAH COUNTY, UTAH

PLAINTIFF

SURNAME	GIVEN NAMES ABCDEFGH	GIVEN NAMES IJKLMNO	GIVEN NAMES PQRSTUVWXYZ	DOCKET NUMBER	REGISTER OF ACTIONS
Andrus	Amos	Oscar		1	2 p 73
Andrew	Daniel S.			2	2 p 81
Anderson		John		7	3 p 11
Anderson			Thomas	14	3 p 122
Anderson		Larcine Maria (Inc)		16	3 p 145
Anderson	Edith M.			17	1
Anderson		John		919	4
Anderson	Andrew			1047	4
Anderson	C.J.			1284	5
Anderson	Hans C.			1304	5
Anderson		John		1337	5
Ambrosen	Herman C.J.			1400	5
Anderson	Hans C. (s)			1737	6
Anderson	Emil			2214	6
Angelini			Rosa Marioni(s)	2255	6
Anderson	A. Wilford (s)			2484	7

Sometimes entries have been made in various books, and documents have been placed in files or probate packets; the general indexes often refer to them. In some jurisdictions, separate indexes exist for testate and intestate estates; in others a single index identifies all entries.

Some probate actions may have been recorded in civil court records among nonrelated items and cannot be identified in the general probate indexes. You may find it necessary to search court order books or docket books and journals to locate pertinent entries. In Beaver County, Pennsylvania, matters pertaining to intestate estates were recorded in regular civil court order books and were indexed in the register's dockets.

Several years ago I found a published probate index to Virginia records that listed an inventory for John Dubberly of Accomack County—possibly ancestral to one of my clients. In the index John's inventory was dated in 1734, but no further information was provided. A search of microfilm copies of early Accomack county records failed to locate the entry in the usual probate books. However, a page-by-page search of county court order books revealed a full-page entry for John that identified his wife Grace and his children John, William, Thomas, and Mary. Further research in records of Virginia and North Carolina proved the family connection.

Individual documents created during the probate process are usually consolidated and placed in special files for safekeeping and future reference. All loose documents and papers relating to a particular case generally are clipped together and arranged in numerical or alphabetical sequence in folders or file boxes. They might include the original will, letters of administration, renunciations, bonds, applications, inventories, appraisals, support bills, sales and accounts, letters and notices from creditors or relatives, affidavits, depositions, powers of attorney, and various other documents. In New York, New Jersey, Pennsylvania, and several other states, probate documents are placed in small packet boxes, or they are folded and tied with ribbon or string then placed in specially designed metal file boxes. New York files are numbered in chronological sequence and identified in the general probate indexes.

Probate files in some counties, districts, or towns are nonexistant or very incomplete—particularly for the colonial period; wills and inventories are often the only probate documents remaining. In other jurisdictions the files have been retired to inaccessible places or have been removed from the courthouse or town hall. The early probate files for Grant County, Indiana, for example, were literally dumped in a dusty attic room of the courthouse at Marion. When I visited in 1968, I was able to investigate the records only after obtaining special permission from reluctant county officials. The files were in no logical order or sequence and were in a terrible state of preservation. On the other hand, probate files for Connecticut districts have been placed in the Connecticut state library in Hartford, and courteous officials will search their files and copy selected documents at a very reasonable fee.

To give yet another example, officials of the Oneida county courthouse at Utica, New York, were unable to direct me to the probate files for the earliest period of the county's history—but a custodian took me to the basement vault where the records were housed.

The Genealogical Society of Utah has microfilmed probate court records from many states and several foreign countries. Early records for most of the eastern states have been filmed, and several of the midwestern and southwestern states as well. Unfortunately, the entire probate files were seldom filmed, but indexes, will books, and some court order books were regularly included.

The will. As stated previously, any person who is of sound mind and legally of age can leave a will, whether written (holographic) or oral (nuncupative). A written will can be made anytime during the life of the testator, but often is made shortly before death. An oral will is usually given shortly before death and is recorded by the witnesses at or near the time of death.

As far as family history is concerned, the contents of a will can vary from the ridiculous to the sublime, but every will provides certain basic genealogical and historical information. The name of the testator, his place of residence, the date the will was made, the names of any witnesses, and facts pertaining to the proving of the will are basic to the document when it has been probated. Other important names, dates, places, events, and circumstances also may be listed. The name of the spouse is commonly entered, as are the names and places of residence of children and grandchildren. Brothers and sisters, parents, aunts and uncles, even cousins and other relatives might be identified, as well as friends, family associates, and other persons who have influenced the testator's life. Step-relationships and illegitimacies can be determined from some wills.

Elizabeth Downs married, lived to a ripe old age, then died—all in the state of New York. During her life she stated that she was the daughter of Ebenezer Downs and was born in Southbury, Connecticut, during the middle of the eighteenth century. A search of vital records for Southbury—which are rather good—failed to list her, though they did include other members of the family. A reading of Ebenezer's will disclosed a step relationship. He left goods and chattel to "Elizabeth Jarrot"—whom he did not otherwise identify though he left her items equivalent in value to the bequests given his children. Further research disclosed that Ebenezer had married "the Widow Jarrot," who evidently had a child from her former marriage. Elizabeth was actually Ebenezer's stepdaughter but had considered herself his daughter.

Used in conjunction with other sources, wills can be very helpful in proving difficult genealogical connections. For several years my family sought information about the parents of Abraham Haines who married Nancy Ann Doty 1 July 1793 in Greene County, Tennessee, and died there sometime after 1840. In 1974 with the assistance of John W. Haines, author and genealogist from New Jersey, we were able to extend Abraham's line to the immigrant Haines who was in New Jersey in the late 1680s.

John Haines directed us to the will of Ezekiel Haines of Culpepper County, Virginia, who died in 1781 leaving land and money to his grandson Abraham—who was the right age to be our Abraham of Greene County, Tennessee. We already knew the Doty family—including Abraham's wife—moved from New Jersey to Virginia and later to Greene County, Tennessee; so if we could find some connection between the Haines family of Culpepper County, Virginia, and that of Greene County, Tennessee, we might have a good lead. To shorten a long story, we learned that Ezekiel's son Abraham married Hannah Painter in New Jersey, dying a few years later. Hannah then married Godfrey Antrim and moved with her new husband and young son Abraham to Culpepper

County, Virginia. We learned that Godfrey and Hannah also had issue: Thomas B. Antrim, Robert Antrim, and Nancy Antrim. Research in Greene County marriage records disclosed that each of these children married in Greene County, Tennessee, in the first decade of 1800. The clincher was the third marriage of Hanna Antrim. On 13 March 1802 in Greene County,

Will of James W. Taylor deceased

Know all whom this may concern:

That I James W. Taylor of Lehi City Utah Co. Utah Ter being of sound & disposing mind & memory do make publish & declare this to be my Last Will & Testament, My Will is that all my just debts & funeral expenses shall be paid by my Executors hereinafter mentioned & named to be paid out of my Estate as soon after my decease as shall by them be found convenient I give devise & bequeath to my beloved wife Ann Taylor all my household Furniture, all my money, Shares in the Peoples Coop Institution all my Real Estate & all Property Real & Personal That I am possessed of at death to be used by her during her life. after her death the whole to be Equally divided between my children for the benefit & their heirs & asigns forever, their names as follows Sarah Jane Taylor Harwood, Samuel Taylor Margret Taylor Wines, Ester Ann Taylor Roberts, Alice Ann Taylor Roberts, James Taylor, Deseret Taylor Austin, Florence Taylor Jones, Rose Taylor Wadsworth, & furthermore after the decease of my wife I bequeath all my household Goods & Chattles of Every Kind Furniture Beds & Bedding, Cloths & Every Household utensse, to be equally divided between my Daughters only. Real Estate consist of Lot 4 B. 17. Lots 7 & 8 on B 25 Plat "A" Lehi Survey of building lots also 10 acres of farming land situated in Section 18 Township 5 S. R. 1 East U.S. also 8½ acres Pasture 4½ acres of Grass land in Sec 19 the pasture in Section 16. And Lastly I do nominate & appoint my Soninlaw James Harwood & Samuel Taylor my Son to be the Executors of my last Will & Testament In Witness Whereof I the said James W. Taylor have to this my last Will & Testament consisting of one sheet of Legal Cap, Subscribed my name & affixed my seal this Eighteenth day of March 1891.

Signed James W. Taylor Seal

Signed, Sealed published & declared by the said James W. Taylor of Lehi City Utah County as for his last Will & Testament in the presence of us who at his request & in his presence, & in the presence of each other [illegible] subscribed our names as witnesses thereto

Signature of Witnesses

[illegible] Lehi City Utah

Richard [illegible] " " "

Tennessee, was recorded the marriage of Hannah Painter Haines Antrim to Philip Babb.

Some wills are long and extensive; others are brief and general. One testator left his entire estate to his "beloved wife and loving children," but failed to name any of them. Another—more esteemed by genealogists—listed his seven children by name and residence then identified each of his several grandchildren through individual bequests. It is not unusual for a testator to identify deceased children then name their living heirs. On the other hand, it is not unusual for a testator to name only part of his family in his will. A child might be omitted for any number of reasons; perhaps he already received his share of the estate, or perhaps in the mind of the testator he forfeited his right to inherit.

A bachelor who died in LaSalle County, Illinois, in 1911 left considerable property to his nieces and nephews. He was very discriminating in the disposition of his property and made the following stipulation in his will:

> Should any of my heirs at law, devisees or legatees, or any person in this will mentioned, or any person having an interest in my estate, by proceedings in court, attempt to contest or set aside this will, or object to the probate of same; or shall by legal proceedings attempt or endeavor to have this will declared of no force or null and void, or shall endeavor to have set aside any conveyance of property made by me, it is my desire and I hereby direct that he or she, or they shall receive nothing from my estate, and any portion herein devised or bequeathed to him or her, or them, shall pass to and vest in my residuary legattee and divisee, Leonard Johnson. [Will of Austin Sanderson, LaSalle County, Illinois]

The testator could make any stipulation he desired in the will, and he could recount any number of events and circumstances. Each will should be read and analyzed.

In style and format, the testator usually followed the pattern of the day. He probably expressed the desire that his body be buried in "a decent and Christian manner," and that his spirit be committed to "that God which gave us life." He typically stated that he was "of sound mind and memory, though weak in body," and usually stipulated this was his "last will and testament, revoking all former wills." A codicil (an addition to a will) also could be part of the record, or listed in close proximity to the will. It was used to change or add something without the necessity of rewriting the entire will.

The petition to probate. When a person died leaving property and effects, someone usually petitioned the court for letters to probate the estate. Petitions have been located for both testate and intestate cases, but are more common for those that are intestate.

Usually the spouse or some other member of the family petitioned, but a collateral relative, a friend or family associate, a creditor, or some local official could also do so. The petition itself is usually found in the probate files or recorded in the court order books, though some New York petitions are recorded in the record of wills preceding the will. Petitions do not exist for every estate probated—especially during the colonial period or in the South—but they are extremely valuable when they can be found.

They are good substitutes for the will in intestate cases, generally listing the heirs and giving their relationship to the deceased. Some list the addresses or places of residence of the heirs, and the date and place of death of the deceased. Sometimes a summary or general statement of the property or wealth is also listed.

Petitions exist as early as 1790 in New York files and perhaps earlier than that in some other states. In some cases in New York, a copy of the newspaper account of the probate proceeding is attached to the petition. Evidently it was a common practice to publish facts regarding probate in the local newspaper. This is certainly true today, and often those accounts are useful.

PETITION OF Jane Cadwallader in the matter of the Estate of John Cadwallader deceased for Letters of Administration. To the Hon. Thompson Chandler Judge of the County Court of McDonough County

The Petition of the undersigned Jane Cadwallader respectfully represents that John Cadwallader late of McDonough County deceased, died at Praire City in said County on or about the first day of October A.D. 1859 leaving property and effects in this County but leaving no last Will and Testament as far as known to and believed by this petitioner. That said deceased left him surviving your petitioner Jane Cadwallader, as his widow, and the following named children, towit: Morris, George, Eva May, and Luella Carrie Cadwallader

Your Petitioner being the widow of said deceased, therefore prays that Letters of Administration upon the Estate of the said John Cadwallader deceased may be granted to her

Macomb, October 31st 1859 — Jane Cadwallader

STATE OF ILLINOIS)
) SS.
MCDONOUGH COUNTY)

Jane Cadwallader being duly sworn, deposes and says that the facts averred in the above petition are true according to the best of her knowledge, information and belief.

Sworn to and subscribed before me J.H. Baker)
Clerk of the County Court of McDonough County,)
this 31st day of Oct A.D. 1859) — Jane Cadwallader

J.H. Baker
CLERK

S.H. Bradbury)
Edward Reed) Appraisers
Ezra D Smith)

Proof of heirship. Miscellaneous letters and documents proving heirship may also be found among the probate records. They consist of official papers, documents, and informal letters purporting kinship to the deceased.

In the following document, the heirs of Austin Sanderson are identified. Of special significance is the statement: "Austin Sanderson departed this life, testate, at his late home at Leland in this County, on or about March 10th, 1911, leaving him surviving no widow, and no child or children, and no descendant or descendants of any deceased child or children, and no father, and no mother, and no brother, and no sister." There were three typewritten pages in the file naming heirs to his estate, primarily his nieces and nephews.

In the Matter of the Last Will and)
) Proof of Heirship.
Testament of Austin Sanderson, Deceased)

Now on this day comes Edward H. Farley, executor of the last will and testament of Austin Sanderson, deceased, in his own proper person and by Al. A. Clapsaddle his attorney, and makes proof of heirship in the estate of said Austin Sanderson, deceased; and the Court having heard the testimony of said Edward H. Farley, a competent witness of lawful age, produced, sworn and examined on oath in open court, finds therefrom that the said Austin Sanderson departed this life, testate, at his late home at Leland in this County, on or about March 10th, 1911, leaving him surviving no widow, and no child or children, and no descendant or descendants of any deceased child or children, and no father, and no mother, and no brother, and no sister, and Austin Sanderson, Seward Sanderson, Josephine Richolson, Isabelle Richolson, Martha Halverson and Mary Oakland children and only surviving children of Sander Sanderson a deceased brother of said Austin Sanderson, and Harvey Sanderson, Sander Sanderson, Eva Hill, Kinne Sanderson, Lester Sanderson and Vira Sanderson children and only children of Samuel Sanderson a deceased son of Sander Sanderson, and Mabel Knutson, Silas Sanderson, Otto Sanderson, Alma Sanderson, Edith Sanderson, Curtis Sanderson, Myrtle Sanderson, Herbert Sanderson, and Kenneth Sanderson children and only children of Charles Sanderson a deceased son of Sander Sanderson, and no descendant or descendants of any other deceased son or daughter of said Sander Sanderson;

Letters testamentary and of administration. After the will has been submitted for probate or after a petition to probate the estate has been received, the court generally issues letters testamentary (in a testate estate) or letters of administration (in an intestate estate). Letters of administration with the will annexed might also be issued in a testate estate when the executor or executrix fails to act. These documents give authorization for the executor or administrator to carry out the probating process and contain useful information for family or local history. A number of different documents might be found in the probate files relating to the issuance of the letters: the order for notice of application for letters of administration, the notice of application for letters, an order appointing the administrator, the actual letters, and the bond for the executor or administrator. The genealogical and historical value varies with each document, and the records must be studied individually.

Conducting research in the office of the register of wills in Beaver County, Pennsylvania, I was unable to locate probate files pertaining to several intestate estates—though there was indication they had been probated in 1872. Questioning the clerk, I learned the information had been copied into civil court order books and indexed in the register's dockets.

I found an entry showing that T. S. Javins came into the register's office on 10 January 1873 and claimed administration upon the estate of Henrietta Javins, his wife, who died intestate in 1872. The court granted the husband letters of administration after he posted a $2600 bond. Thomas Javins and Jesse Hannah acted as sureties. I found no other documents relating to the case in the probate files or record books.

Inventories, appraisals, sales, and accounts. After the executor or administrator has been appointed and the necessary letters have been granted, one of the first probating actions they oversee is the appointment of persons to locate, inventory, and appraise the real and personal property of the deceased. Several different documents and records might be affected in the process, and any of them might contain useful information. They do not always contain genealogical information, but they are usually excellent historical sources.

In some of the southern states, probate files are incomplete or nonexistent; the only probate records on file are the inventories, appraisals, sales, and accounts. In some instances, the inventory is the only existing record showing an individual's estate was probated. It also may be the closest thing to a death record obtainable, though it seldom contains the exact date and place of death. More often it gives the place of death, but even that may not be certain.

In the Haines case cited previously, an inventory proved valuable in helping reconstruct the family. As mentioned, Hannah Painter Haines Antrim married her third husband, Philip Babb, of Greene County, Tennessee, in 1802. Philip died sometime before 1813, the date an inventory of his personal property and an account of sales were recorded. The widow, Hannah Babb, is mentioned as are several other relatives of interest: Robert Antrim, a son of Hannah and stepson of Philip; Nancy Haines, a daughter-in-law of Hannah and stepdaughter-in-law of Philip; and Christian Leaky, father of a son-in-law of Hannah Painter Haines Antrim Babb.

Orphans and guardianship, minors, and insane persons. The probate court has jurisdiction in orphan and guardianship cases, minor children involved in court cases, and insane persons. Documents relating to any of them might be found in the probate files, the will books, or court order books. Sometimes special volumes and indexes deal exclusively with each classification, but more often they are combined with other probate records and documents.

In the probate court of Utah County I discovered two pertinent examples of this type of record. In the first example, George Baum petitioned the court to be made guardian for his father who was old and infirm and not capable of managing his own business affairs. Later George's father died and George again petitioned the court, this time to be made administrator of his father's estate. However, the court did not confirm the petition after hearing objections from another brother, Isaac Baum.

In a second example, John S. Friel petitioned the court to be made guardian of his own children, Emily and Sarah. They had been given a legacy by their late grandfather, John Hafer, but were not of age. After a hearing, the court granted the father's petition for guardianship.

During the eighteenth century in York County, Maine, Henry Pendexter petitioned the court to be made guardian of his younger brother Sibley. The request was recorded immediately following the entry of their father's will in the record of wills, but additional hearings and accountings were entered in later volumes as they happened.

Division and distribution. Sooner or later, the probate process is completed and the estate is settled. The proceeds are distributed to the legal heirs and assigns, and the records are filed for future reference. The court may have directed that all property be sold to the highest bidders and the money distributed according to law, or the will may have stipulated the way the estate was to be divided and distributed. The records must be consulted to determine the story. Sometimes they are voluminous with detail; other times they contain meagre information.

Civil and Criminal Court Records

Court records are created for reasons other than probate, and any of them may be useful for family and local history. Records pertaining to disputes, adoption, change of name, divorce, naturalization and citizenship, and criminal prosecution are all important. Loose documents may be found in case files, and record entries in registers, docket books, journals, day books, court order books, or other records.

As a rule, no general index is made of all civil and criminal court actions, but usually indexes or registers exist for certain types of cases. For example, a special index to divorce hearings might exist, but entries for adoption might be located only through a chronological search of the docket books or court order books. Indexes to some civil actions might exist, but matters relating to naturalization and citizenship might be located only in special district court volumes.

Adoption. Modern adoption records usually are sealed by court order and inaccessible to the public, though some earlier adoption records are open. Special indexes usually exist for the modern records, but others must be located through a chronological search of docket books, journals, order books, or case files.

A few years ago I remarried and had the opportunity to adopt Marie-Agnes Magali Marguerite Marie-France Bearnson, daughter of my wife Daniele. Four documents were created in the process: a petition for adoption, an agreement to adopt, a consent for adoption, and a decree of adoption. By order of the court, the records were sealed, but each of the participants were provided copies prior to the court order.

The petition for adoption was my official request to adopt Marie-Agnes. It listed Marie-Agnes's date and place of birth, the fact that her mother and I were now married, and our marriage date. It also indicated that I was more than ten years older than the adoptee and that I agreed to assume all legal obligations and responsibilities outlined. It included the mother's consent and changed the adoptee's name to Marie-Agnes Magali Marguerite Marie-France Wright.

The agreement to adopt indicated that I had petitioned the court for adoption and would treat the adoptee as my own child, that she would become a child of the Wright family, and her name would henceforth be known as Marie-Agnes Magali Marguerite Marie-France Wright.

The consent for adoption was essentially the adoptee's signed statement that she sought to be adopted by me and that she had read all the appropriate documents relating to the case.

The decree of adoption indicated that the case had been heard by the court; gave the day, month, and year of hearing; and summarized the status of the adoptor and the adoptee. It also indicated that the required evidence had been presented to the court and gave the names and residences of each party involved. The decree was dated and signed, as were the other documents, and recorded and sealed by the court.

Divorce and marriage annulment. Divorce is a civil court action, and though the records might prove embarrassing to some, they are public records. They often contain valuable genealogical and historical information. Modern divorce records are indexed, but some for earlier periods are not. Documents and record entries include a petition for divorce, the findings of fact and conclusions of law, and the decree of divorce.

The petition for divorce contains the plaintiff's charges and grievances against the defendant, and usually includes names, dates, places, events, and circumstances. Often the marriage date and place are given, and the maiden surname of the wife may be listed.

The findings of fact and conclusions of law are equally valuable in content; they list the conclusions and rulings of the court. Here the essential names, dates, places, and particulars are recorded.

The decree of divorce outlines what should take place with regard to property, child support, and alimony. It may include details relating to the status of children or other conditions. Usually there is a relisting of facts from the other documents, too.

Legal change of name. Some people petition the court for a legal change of name; in so doing, they create helpful records for future researchers. Many people assume different given names and surnames during their lifetime, but for the name to be legal, there must be a court action. The resulting records are public, except in most cases of adoption, but they are seldom indexed. Finding the records is usually a matter of searching the docket books, journals, court order books, or case files.

One of my first courthouse research experiences made me acquainted with such records. A colleague and I were trying to locate the early probate files in Oneida County, New York, and were directed to a basement vault by the janitor. We finally found what we were looking for in records at the bottom of the elevator shaft, but only after checking through box after box of change of name records of Italian immigrants to the area.

Sometimes a name change is not known by descendants until they get involved in family history research. A close friend of mine recently discovered that his christening name was entirely different from his present name. He was adopted shortly after birth, and even his birth record was changed to show his present name. This is a common practice in modern adoptions.

Naturalization and citizenship. Perhaps there is more interest shown in this record group by family historians than any other, yet most Americans did not go through a court action to become citizens. They attained citizenship by birth or by special proclamation.

During the colonial period no laws requiring residents of this country to become citizens existed, though certain groups had to take oaths or make declarations of loyalty. The English merely were coming to English colonies, and other immigrants were establishing homes in a new territory open to most ethnic groups. It was not until 1790 that Congress enacted legislation for the naturalization of aliens. After the Revolution all residents (except Indians) were declared citizens of the United States by national proclamation.

On 26 March 1790 Congress passed the first naturalization act, which provided that aliens who desired to become citizens could apply at any court of common law after residing in the country for at least one year. Under this law aliens were naturalized in federal or state courts, and the records may still be in custody of those courts. Some records have been forwarded to the National Archives or federal records centers operated by the General Sevices Administration.

Many laws have been passed regarding immigration, naturalization, and citizenship, but most records dating before 1906 are in custody of the local state courts, even though they were created in federal courts. Records since 1906 are in the custody of the Commissioner of Immigration and Naturalization, Washington, D.C., and are confidential.

Some early naturalization and citizenship records have been copied and filed in the National Archives—including those from 1787 through 1906 filed by courts in Maine, Massachusetts, New Hampshire, and Rhode Island. Records for some people who took civil service examinations in 1905 or 1906 were also sent to the National Archives, and some naturalization records relating to the District of Columbia also are there (Colket and Bridgers 1964, p. 142).

Naturalization or citizenship records in the courthouses and town halls are seldom indexed and must be located in the same way as other unindexed civil court records: through a chronological search of the dockets, registers, journals, or court order books. In some cases special entry books have been kept, but more often than not the records are filed or recorded among other civil court actions. Also keep in mind that your ancestor may have initiated action in one town or county, then moved to another where the naturalization process was completed. A number of records and documents may have been created during the citizenship process: declarations, petitions, applications, lists, and orders.

The example shown below was located among court records in Jay County, Indiana, while I was searching for a probate record. Two dusty volumes of naturalization and citizenship records were shelved with the will books in the county clerk's office, and the entry for John Remakles was obtained from them.

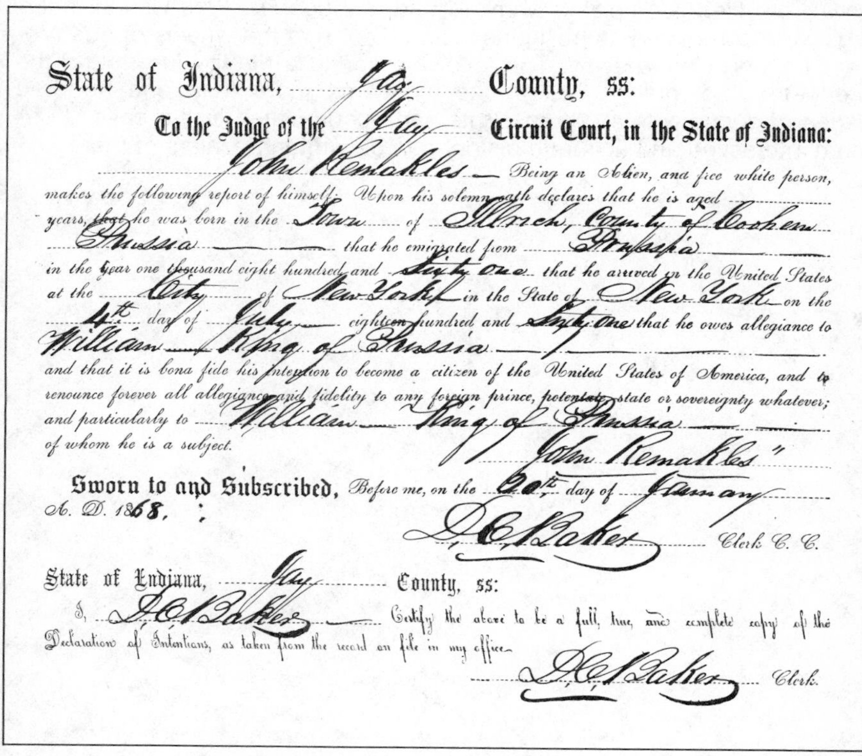

State of Indiana, Jay County, ss:

To the Judge of the Jay Circuit Court, in the State of Indiana:

John Remakles Being an Alien, and free white person, makes the following report of himself. Upon his solemn oath declares that he is aged — years, that he was born in the Town of Illrich, County of Cochem Prussia that he emigrated from Prussia in the year one thousand eight hundred and Sixty one that he arrived in the United States at the City of New York in the State of New York on the 4th day of July eighteen hundred and Sixty one that he owes allegiance to William King of Prussia and that it is bona fide his intention to become a citizen of the United States of America, and to renounce forever all allegiance and fidelity to any foreign prince, potentate, state or sovereignty whatever; and particularly to William King of Prussia of whom he is a subject.

John Remakles

Sworn to and Subscribed, Before me, on the 20th day of January A. D. 1868.

D. C. Baker Clerk C. C.

State of Indiana, Jay County, ss:

I, D. C. Baker Certify the above to be a full, true, and complete copy of the Declaration of Intentions, as taken from the record on file in my office.

D. C. Baker Clerk.

Other court actions. Any number of other interesting civil or criminal court actions might be filed in the courthouse or town hall; some may be indexed, some even may be published, but most will be located only through personal inspection and digging through the records. Disputes between neighbors and relatives, matters of equity, contests with the law, criminal prosecutions—even murder—may be involved.

A close friend of mine discovered after twenty years of personal history research that his grandfather was murdered in 1901 in Park City, Utah. According to court records, the man had been drinking at a local bar, then entered a livery stable to rent a horse. He wanted to ride it to work at the Silver King Mine higher in the canyon.

Evidently the proprietor had had problems with my friend's grandfather before. He refused to rent him a horse, saying he didn't have one available. But while the rejected customer was still standing there, another man came into the stable and obtained a horse with no trouble. My friend's grandfather struck the proprietor and accused him: "You can give anyone a horse but me, can't you!" The proprietor drew a revolver and shot him through the neck, wheeling him around, then pulled the trigger again and shot him through the back near the spine. That wound was fatal; the victim died a few hours later in the Park City Hotel and was buried in the old Park City cemetery.

The local police were called in, and charges of murder in the first degree were filed. Complaints were signed, subpoenas were issued, hearings were conducted, depositions were taken, and the wheels of due process began to grind away. The following spring a trial by jury found the proprietor "not guilty," but in the meantime more than one hundred pages of documents and transcripts had accumulated in the case file. A more interesting and accurate history can be written because of them.

7 Land Records

The story of America is really the story of land, and considering the entire spectrum of American family and local history, land records probably have been more useful in research than any other major record group. Traditionally land has been rather easily obtained by the ordinary person, and its ownership and use has been a matter of public record. This has not always been the case in other countries.

Land records contain a variety of genealogical and historical information and have met the needs of researchers in different ways. They have been the major source of information for many family history studies and have provided primary source material for local history as well. They are considered by many to be the foundation upon which an acceptable family or local history should be built. They are closely related to probate and other official court records, and should be investigated in connection with them. Land and property are paramount issues in the settlement of estates, and a majority of the civil cases before our courts deal with real and personal property or their use.

In periods where vital records are missing or are incomplete, land records provide some of the best kinship information obtainable. Names of family members and former spouses, clues to the maiden surname of a wife, the names of friends and associates, and the names of collateral relatives are some of the more important genealogical facts contained in them.

When it comes to time and place, land records identify previous places of residence, dates of settlement or removal from a particular area, places of residence of friends and relatives, and other useful facts. Evidence of marriage, occupation, church affiliation, social or political status, and military condition may be found in them, in addition to clues to death and burial. They might also contain facts that can be used for other social studies, including civil rights, the distribution of wealth, family mobility, and the like. The more that land records are studied, the more possibilities are seen for their use.

Land Title Origin

Title to American lands originally rested with God and the Indians, but certain European powers laid claim to them during the sixteenth and seventeenth centuries by right of exploration and settlement. Then they began programs of expansion through conquest, settlement, and treaty until they claimed the entire country and certain adjacent lands. Through charters and grants from rulers and monarchs, title passed to the colonies or their proprietors, then in turn to the individual.

After the Revolution, the United States acquired title to certain western lands and continued a program of territorial expansion and land control. Titles to some lands were gained through cessions from the colonial states; others were acquired through purchase, annexation, conquest, and treaty. Territories and states were carved from the vast public domain, and title to land was granted to them or to individuals through special acts of Congress. The territories and states in turn granted or sold land to individuals, giving them title. The federal government also continued programs to place public domain lands in the hands of citizens.

The purpose and contents of land records in the colonial states are similar to those in the public domain states, but policies and procedures for distribution have been different. Jurisdictional control and recording practices also have varied. In theory, the title to any parcel of land in the United States or its possessions is traceable—through town, county, district, state, territorial, or national records—to the original owner. However, in practice that isn't always possible because of inaccurate, incomplete, or missing records.

The Colonial States

The thirteen original colonies obtained title to their lands through charters and grants from the English Crown, then in turn passed title to the individual. The New England colonies were comprised of Connecticut, Massachusetts, New Hampshire, and Rhode Island. Maine was a province of Massachusetts until 1802, and Vermont did not receive independent status until 1770. The middle colonies consisted of Delaware, New Jersey, New York, and Pennsylvania—though Delaware was known as the "South Counties of Pennsylvania" until 1701. The southern colonies were made up of Georgia, Maryland, North Carolina, South Carolina, and Virginia. Kentucky and West Virginia were originally part of Virginia, Tennessee was part of North Carolina, and the area south and west of Georgia belonged to Spain.

Three types of colonies administered land and property prior to the Revolution: royal, proprietary, and corporate. Georgia, New Hampshire, New Jersey, New York, North Carolina, South Carolina, and Virginia were royal colonies at one time or another, with title to lands and responsibility for administration resting with the Crown and its governors. Delaware, Maryland, Pennsylvania, New Jersey (for a time), and the Carolinas (for a time), were proprietary colonies. Land and property in those colonies were the responsibility of selected proprietors and their agents. Connecticut, Massachusetts, Rhode Island, and Virginia (for a time) were corporate colonies with land ownership and its administration resting with various merchants and individuals in England, as well as with certain colonial leaders in America.

Individuals within the three types of colonies gained title to their lands in different ways—through special purpose grants, through the head-right system, or through private purchase. Special purpose grants were usually given for military or meritorious service, or for being a recognized member

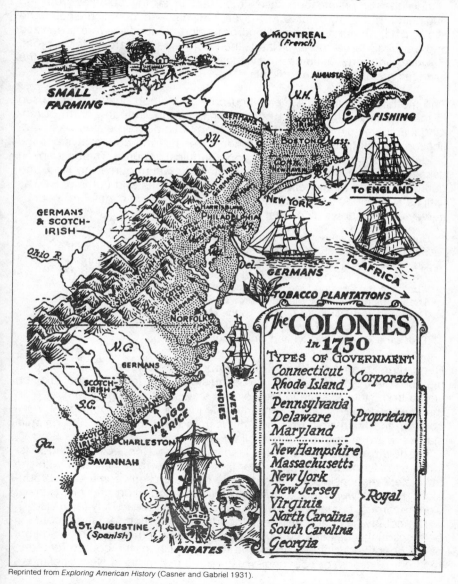

Reprinted from *Exploring American History* (Casner and Gabriel 1931).

of the community. They were also given—to extend the frontier—for protecting the colonies from Indians or other outside forces.

The head-right system was practiced in early Virginia, the middle colonies, and New England. Under this system, all persons were treated alike; land was granted in stated quantities to individuals settling or bringing others to settle in the colonies. No orderly pattern was followed under the system, and it was abused by some. However, it served to attract many settlers to America and to one colony from another.

Individual or private purchase—important in all the colonies from the beginning and in the states to the present day—accounts for most land title transfer. In certain periods land or trading companies were organized and acquired large tracts of land, then sold smaller parcels for a profit. However, in many instances individuals purchased land directly from the town fathers or from other officials.

The method of survey. A metes-and-bounds method of survey was used in the colonies during most of the colonial period, though a form of rectangular survey similar to that used in the public domain states was practiced in New England for a time. Under the metes-and-bounds system, the land was described by physical or topographical features. The description usually included the name of the tributary or watercourse the land bordered and listed measurement details of boundaries and rights-of-way as well as restrictions or limitations for use. The following metes-and-bounds survey extract shows a colonial New York survey record:

> Surveyed and Laid out as of Land according to the Map or Chart. Beginning at the Mouth of The Wapinger's Creek Then Running as the Creek Runs Sexteen Miles To a Large White Oak Marked on four Sides Thence South Twenty Degrees East Three Hundred and Thirty Eight Chains to the Division Line Between Van Pla__ith (?) and Courtland Thence along a Line of Marked Trees South Fifty Two Degrees West one Thousand and Thirty five Chains To the Mouth of the Honey Creek Thence along or up Hudson's River to Where it first Begins Containing Fourteen Thousand Three Hundred and ninety Eight acres.

Recording methods and jurisdictional differences. The recording methods and procedures for land acquisition, title transfer, and taxation varied from state to state in the colonial states but remained consistent in the public domain states. Similarly, the jurisdictions responsible for recording and maintaining records differ from state to state in the colonial states but are the same in the public domain states.

The town was responsible for land records in Connecticut, Rhode Island, and Vermont—with the records kept at the town hall and with the town clerk responsible for recording. In Massachusetts some early proprietors' records were kept at the town where acquisition and title transfer were recorded, but land records were recorded at the county level also.

The county has been the most important jurisdiciton for land records in both colonial states and public domain states, with the records being kept at the county courthouse under the responsibility of the county recorder, recorder of deeds, or county clerk. (In some instances in New England, a shiretown is the equivalent of the county courthouse.) In Delaware, Kentucky, Maine, Maryland, Massachusetts, New Hampshire, New Jersey, New York, North Carolina, Pennsylvania, South Carolina, Tennessee, Virginia, and West Virginia recording responsibility for land records is given to the county. Prior to 1772, New Hampshire records were kept on a provincial basis, but between 1769 and 1772 counties were established and given recording responsibility. Prior to 1702 in New Jersey and 1783 in South Carolina, the proprietors were responsible for land transactions; after those dates such responsibility fell to the counties.

Searching the Records. A number of different records and documents dealing with land acquisition, title transfer, and taxation were created in the colonial states, and many are conveniently available for research. They include charters, grants, memorials, patents, warrants, survey records, plat books, deed books, mortgage records, leases, contracts, agreements, and miscellaneous tax records. Some of the same records can be found in the public domain states, but some are peculiar to the colonial states.

Most land records in the courthouses or town halls have been bound in large volumes, indexed, and placed on special shelves for public use, but some are found among other loose court records and are not indexed. Some have been copied and published, and some have been microfilmed, but a majority of those available for use are the originals or certified copies. County and town officials will usually check their indexes and cooperate in providing copies of existing records through correspondence for a fee, but they are seldom able to make exhaustive searches for inquiring researchers. Because of the nature of family history and the complexity of land records, personal inspection of the records or research through a qualified agent is advisable.

The LDS genealogical library in Salt Lake City has an excellent collection of land records from the colonial states dating—with few exceptions—from the earliest colonial period to the Civil War. A few collections extend to the 1960s and 1970s, but the filming cutoff date for most land records was about 1860.

In New England, early settlement took place on a town basis with individuals or groups petitioning the general assembly (governor and council) for settlement rights. The names, and sometimes the previous places of residence, of these people were recorded in the town meeting books or proprietors' records. It was the practice to grant town lots to those in good standing—such as "freemen" or those who had "owned the covenant" of the church—and also to give them rights to the town common. They could build homes and plant gardens on their individual lots and graze their animals on the town common.

It was a general practice in Massachusetts towns to record individual land allocations in the proprietors' records, then make additional entries each time title to the land changed hands, which often occurred between family members or relatives. Excellent kinship information can be determined in these instances, sometimes helping to extend an ancestral line several generations. Land entries were also recorded on a county basis in that state, and when disputes were taken before the courts involving land already recorded in the proprietors' records, the facts in those records were usually given legal precedence.

The town meeting books also contain many other entries that may or may not pertain to land ownership and use but can be useful. Fence viewers, road watchers, hog reavers, jurors, moderators, and other persons are named and identified. Cattle brands were assigned, vital statistics were recorded, and many other interesting genealogical and historical facts were recorded.

In the middle and southern colonies, special purpose grants were often the earliest records of land title transfer from the government to the individual. They included head-right grants, royal grants, memorial grants, military grants, land-bounty warrants, and special grants or patents of land for political or meritorious service. They are often the documents of original title found in the courthouses of the middle and southern states.

Head-right grants were given as early as 1623 in Virginia, where an individual could gain title to fifty or more acres merely by showing his presence. They were also made in other colonies, and many ship's captains brought people from England to collect their head right in exchange for passage to the new world. Others obtained grants in their own behalf and established residence on the land, expanding their holdings through cash purchase or other means as economic success permitted and reducing them as economic depression or other difficulties necessitated.

Many of the earliest head-right grants for Virginia have been published in Nell Marion Nugent's Cavaliers and Pioneers covering the period 1623–1732. They are really abstracts of Virginia land patents and grants in paragraph form, giving the full names of the patentee, the number of acres in the patent, the metes and bounds, the date of settlement, and the names of family members and owners of adjoining properties. The records have been supplemented from marriage contracts, wills, deeds, and other legal instruments. The names of five thousand persons transported to the colony at the expense of planters are listed; total names equal sixteen thousand five hundred.

North and South Carolina granted thousands of acres of land to settlers after 1670, not only to British subjects but immigrants from other parts of Europe and America as well. Huguenots (French Protestants) settled on the Ashley and Cooper Rivers—also at Bath on Pamlico Sound beginning in 1680. At the same time, English settlers from the Chesapeake region were moving from the James River south along the Chowan to Albemarle Sound. The town of Edenton was settled before 1690. By 1700 German and Swiss-German Palatines settled at New Bern on the Neuse River in North Carolina, and many of their countrymen migrated from Pennsylvania down the Great Valley Road through Virginia to take advantage of Carolina grants. The Scotch-Irish followed the same pattern, and later great numbers of Scottish Highlanders took up lands along the Cape Fear River. Within a few more years, settlers from Maryland and Virginia were pulling up roots and migrating to the coastal counties of North Carolina to take advantage of generous land grants. By 1750 settlers were also taking up lands along the Savannah River on both the South Carolina and

Georgia sides.

Most were attracted to the area because of the generous land grants available; it was not uncommon to get two hundred or more acres for less than ten shillings per one hundred acres granted. Later grants were as high as fifty shillings per one hundred acres. In the 1750s and 1760s, many South Carolina memorial grants were made for one shilling per one hundred acres.

After the Revolution, the federal government and some colonial states initiated programs to place lands in the hands of veterans who fought in the war. The federal bounty-land warrant program began in 1789 and did not terminate until 1856; lands were granted in Virginia and North Carolina as early as 1784. Under the federal grants, a private could receive from fifty to one hundred acres and a field officer up to five thousand acres. In the Virginia grants, privates and noncommissioned officers could receive one hundred acres or more, depending on their service, and field officers up to seventeen thousand acres, depending on their service. These programs resulted in the migration of many families to western lands, both in the colonial states and the public land states. The entries are often the documents of original title in the courthouse.

Virginia granted lands in Kentucky, and North Carolina granted lands in Tennessee, creating thousands of records and giving clues to migration in the process. Most of these early grants have been published or microfilmed and are readily available for research. An example is Samuel M. Wilson's *Catalogue of Revolutionary Soldiers and Sailors of the Commonwealth of Virginia to Whom Land Bounty Warrants Were Granted by Virginia for Military Service in the War for Independence.* It lists hundreds of veterans, giving their names, the number of acres received, the date, and the location of the grant.

The LDS genealogical library in Salt Lake City has an excellent microfilm collection of these early southern states land grants and patents, as well as county land records. At this writing there are more than two hundred reels of microfilm for Kentucky land grants alone, and a similar number for North and South Carolina combined. Originals are found with the Kentucky State Land Office at Frankfort; the Virginia State Library at Richmond; the Department of Archives and History at Raleigh, North Carolina; the Department of Archives and History at Columbia, South Carolina; or at the Georgia Department of Archives and History at Atlanta.

Special purpose grants and patents were also given settlers in New York and Pennsylvania, which encouraged migration to their western lands. However, many large land-holding companies were organized and also sold lands in those states on a cash or credit purchase plan. The original records of lands obtained in that manner are not centralized. The LDS genealogical library has microfilm copies of most county land records for New York and Pennsylvania before the latter half of the nineteenth century, but it does not have many records of private companies.

The Bureau of Land Records, Department of Community Affairs, Harrisburg, Pennsylvania, has records of all grants and conveyances from the proprietors or commonwealth to the purchasers—including original surveys, warrants, patents, maps, and indexes. Few of these records are presently on microfilm in Salt Lake City. Papers of the Holland Land Company that sold lands in western New York shortly after the Revolution are at the Buffalo Historical Society in Buffalo, New York. Records of the Phelps and Gorham purchases are at the state library in Albany, New York. Neither of these collections presently is available at Salt Lake City.

Land survey records and plat books also contain important genealogical and historical information; they are located among the records at each jurisdictional level. They typically describe a certain parcel of land, either by a metes-and-bounds method or by rectangular survey. They also give the name of the purchaser or receiver and a physical description of the land in word and pictorial form. They seldom contain vital statistics, but the name of the individual, his place of residence, the date, and the description of property all are valuable information.

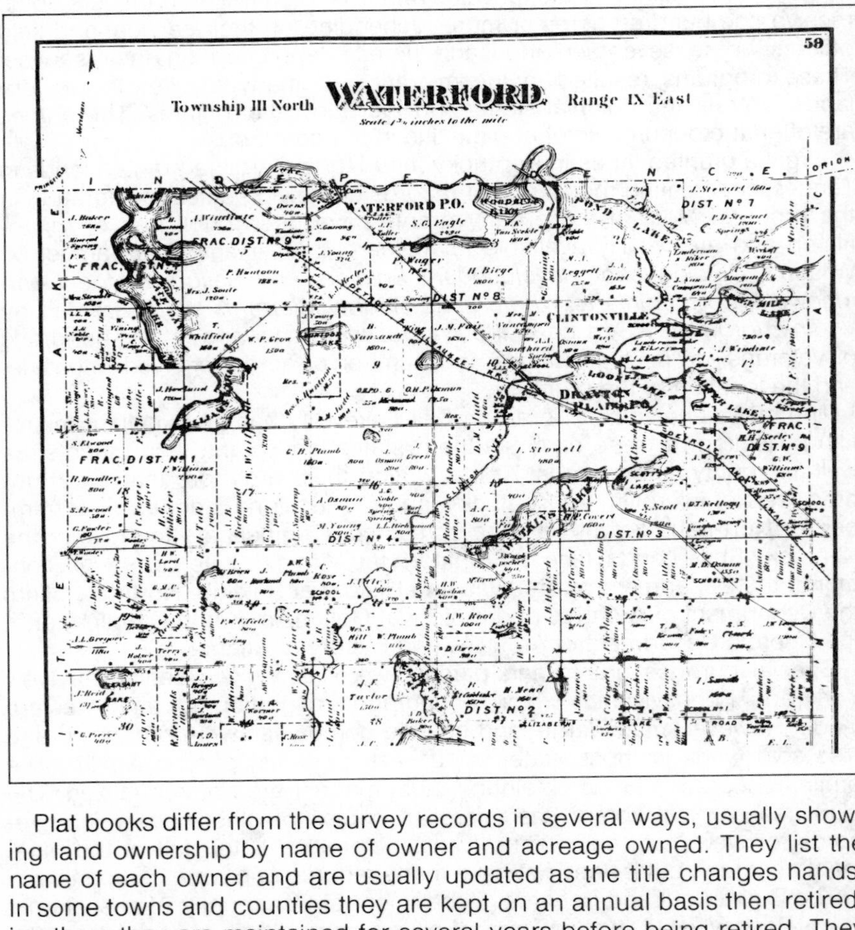

Plat books differ from the survey records in several ways, usually showing land ownership by name of owner and acreage owned. They list the name of each owner and are usually updated as the title changes hands. In some towns and counties they are kept on an annual basis then retired; in others they are maintained for several years before being retired. They are not generally indexed, so investigators must often search several volumes of records to find a particular individual listed. It is sometimes possible to determine the names of relatives, the maiden name of a spouse, and the names of friends and associates through the plat book listings.

Land records created in the colonial states subsequent to the documents of original title include deeds of conveyance, mortgages, leases, contracts and agreements, and taxation records. The deeds are perhaps the most important, but any of the others might help solve a difficult family history problem or provide valuable information for local history.

In most counties (or towns in New England), the deeds, mortgages, leases, contracts, and agreements are all recorded in the deed books and are indexed. The tax records are generally kept in separate volumes and are seldom indexed—though some Kentucky tax lists are arranged alphabetically. In New York counties and a few others, the mortgage records are kept in separate volumes with separate indexes and begin almost as early as the deed records.

The deeds are written instruments designed to transfer ownership of real and personal property, while mortgages are pledges of property to creditors as security for the payment of debts. Leases are contracts by which landlords rent lands and buildings to tenants for a specified time; contracts and agreements are legal documents specifying other conditions and considerations between individuals. An antenuptual agreement is often found among land records and specifies conditions and considerations between two individuals before marriage. Perhaps a widow desires that land owned by her before marriage should be vested in her children by her first marriage, but land owned jointly after the new marriage might be shared by the issue of the second marriage. Powers of attorney are also found recorded among land records, whereby individuals delegated others to act in their behalf in matters of land ownership and use.

Deeds of conveyance are written instruments designed to transfer the ownership of real and personal property. They usually consist either of warrantee deeds or quit-claim deeds, but finding deeds of gift or deeds of trust among the town and county land records is not uncommon. A warrantee deed indicates the owner has clear and legal title to the land; he owns it in fee simple and guarantees the title to the point that he will uphold it in court. A quit-claim deed merely releases whatever right or title the person or persons held in the property. When an individual died owning real estate but did not leave a will, it is common to find quit-claim deeds from his heirs relinquishing their right and title to the land.

A deed of conveyance is often similar in format to a business letter or report; it contains an opening or salutation, the body, and a closing. The opening usually gives the date it was made, the names and places of residence of the persons involved, and the consideration or payment that changed hands to make it a legal transaction. Sometimes the date of recording is listed in the opening of the deed, but more often it is given at the end.

The body of the deed gives a legal description of the land and property and outlines all limitations or restrictions that might be placed in effect. Some deeds detail the past history of that particular parcel of land, naming previous owners and listing important circumstances under which the title was obtained. Where the land had been owned by several family members in succession, excellent pedigree information can be documented. Almost anything can be found in a deed, and though there is often repetition of legal terms, the entire document should be carefully read for pertinent facts.

The closing of the deed usually contains information about the time and place and includes the names of any witnesses and signers of the instrument. The date of the deed may be mentioned again in the closing, and the date of recording also can appear there. The dower release might be listed when appropriate, but usually it is a separate entry following the signatures.

A former client from Oregon desired to learn the parentage of her ancestor, Ezra S. E. Davis, who died in 1857 in Amador County, California, after coming west during the gold rush. My client descended through Isaac Ely Davis, a son of Ezra and his wife Catherine Stattler Davis. According to family records, Isaac was born in 1845 in Iowa Territory. Family records also indicated Ezra and Catherine resided in Dubuque County, Iowa, before Ezra journeyed west, and Ezra's mother was stated to be "Mary Davis of Philadelphia."

A search of the 1850 federal census for Dubuque County, Iowa, listed the following two households of likely interest:

Name	Age	Birthplace
#1582 Benjamin F. Davis	45 M Painter	Pa.
Rachel	45 F	N.J.
William M. G.	17 M	Pa.
Lafeyette	13 M	Pa.
John W. F.	11 M	Iowa
Martha M.	9 F	Iowa
Julia B.	7 F	Iowa
#1583 Ezra S. E. Davis	35 M Carpenter	Pa.
Catherine	33 F	Pa.
Marion	11 M	Iowa
Harrison	7 M	Iowa
Isaac	5 M	Iowa
Mary	1 F	Iowa

A search of Philadelphia deed indexes (on file at the LDS genealogical library in Salt Lake City for the period 1682–1932) disclosed two entries in 1844 of special interest. The first was between "Benjamin F. Davis et. al. and Mary Davis," and the second was between "Samuel M. Davis et. al. and Mary Davis." Both were recorded in deed book RLL #35 on succeeding pages—but at that time the library did not have copies of the deed books for the period of interest, only for 1682–1832. It was therefore necessary to write to the recorder of deeds at Philadelphia for photocopies—but the results were well worth the effort and expense ($5.00 each). The following extract is from the first page of the deed from "Benjamin F. Davis et. al. to Mary Davis."

STATE OF PENNSYLVANIA, CITY OF PHILADELPHIA, COUNTY OF PHILADELPHIA
Deed Book R.L.L. #35, page 55

BENJAMIN F. DAVIS et. al.
to
MARY DAVIS

This indenture made the thirteenth day of December in the year of our Lord one thousand eight hundred and forty four, Between BENJAMIN FRANKLIN DAVIS of the City of Dubuque in the County of Dubuque and the Territory of Iowa, teamster, and RACHEL his wife, and EZRA STILES ELY DAVIS of the same place, house carpenter, and CATHARINE A. his wife, of the one part, and MARY DAVIS, of the township of Mayaminsing in the County of Philadelphia and State of Pennsylvania, widow, (the Mother of the said BENJAMIN FRANKLIN and EZRA STILES ELY DAVIS), of the other part. Whereas Joseph Couperthwart Esquire, High Sheriff of the City and County of Philadelphia, by deed poll dated the fifth day of March Anno Domini one thousand seven hundred and eighty eight, duly acknowledged in and entered among the records of the Court of Common Pleas for the City and County of Philadelphia, granted and conveyed unto SAMUEL DAVIS in fee simple, a certain lot or piece of ground situate, lying, and being in Wiccacoe in the County of Philadelphia, then and now called the District of Southwick, containing in breadth. . . . Subject to the yearly rent of eight pounds fifteen shillings payable to the Rector Church Wardens and Vestrymen of the United Swedish Churches of Wiccacoe, seized and sold as the property of Emanuel Bryan and Mary his wife by a writ . . . out of the Court of Common Pleas . . . at the suit of Paul Esling, Jacob Cline, and Bartholomew Becker, executors of Francis Sennie (?), deceased. And whereas the said SAMUEL DAVIS, being legally seized in his demise . . . died having first made and published his last will and testament in writing, dated the eighth day of December Anno Domini one thousand eight hundred and ninety nine, duly proved and remaining in the Registers's Office at Philadelphia wherein and whereby he intercited and willed thus: "Item: I do give to my son ISAAC DAVIS all those my two northern houses and lots of ground thereto belonging situate on the east side of Second Street in Southwick . . . to have and hold to him my son ISAAC and to the heirs of his body lawfully begotten, but if he should die without issue then to the use of his brother JOHN and sister HANNAH and to the heirs of their bodies lawfully begotten and for want of said issue then to the use of my own rightful heirs forever . . ." And whereas the said ISAAC DAVIS died seized of the two frame tenements and lots of ground . . . died leaving a widow, the said MARY DAVIS and issue four children, namely the said BENJAMIN FRANKLIN DAVIS, SAMUEL MEEKER DAVIS the said EZRA STILES ELY DAVIS and CAROLINE H. M. SHUBERT, to which issue the same two frame tenements and lot of ground . . . descends in fee . . . subject to the dower in thirds for life of their said mother . . ."

Among other things, the two deed records confirm that Benjamin Franklin Davis of Dubuque County, Iowa, was a brother of Ezra S. E. Davis; that Ezra's middle initials stood for "Stiles and Ely" (possible maiden surnames of progenitors); that Mary Davis of Philadelphia in 1844 was the mother of Benjamin and Ezra; that Benjamin's wife was Rachel and Ezra's was Catharine A; that Benjamin and Ezra also had a brother Samuel Meekers Davis and a sister Caroline H. M. Davis Shubert; that the father of Benjamin, Ezra, Samuel, and Caroline was the deceased Isaac Davis, formerly of Philadelphia; and that Samuel Davis whose will was proved in Philadelphia County, Pennsylvania, in 1799 was the father of Isaac Davis and grandfather of Benjamin and Ezra. What more could be wanted from two deed records?

Special attention should be given transactions where the consideration (payment) is unusually small or large, because this may indicate a special family relationship. The father may sell his son or son-in-law a sizable parcel of land for "one dollar and other good and valuable consideration," or he might indicate that the consideration was for "the love and affection" he held for the individual. On the other hand the amount might have been very large in relation to the land's apparent value, but the body of the deed might indicate some other consideration was involved (such as care and support in old age). Today it is common for the consideration to be "for ten dollars and other good and valuable consideration" because the persons involved do not care to reveal to the public the entire amount of the transaction. Often no kinship exists in these instances, so other sources must be used to determine whether any relationship exists between the parties.

Some deeds were not recorded until several years after they were made, so a wide range of time should be considered when searching the records. Progenitors on my mother's side were Mennonites from Lancaster County, Pennsylvania, and though they failed to leave wills or get involved in civil or criminal court records, they do appear in land records. My immigrant ancestor, Christian Musser, purchased two hundred acres shortly after Lancaster County was organized in 1729 but left no will when he died in 1755; no record of the land's disposition appeared in the deed records during the time I would normally expect it to—between 1729 and 1811. But nearly one hundred years after Christian purchased the land, a series of documents were recorded showing that the land had been used by the families of descent—the son of Christian, then the grandson, and so on—each without effecting an official record of title transfer. It was simply by family agreement. However, in 1811 it became necessary to clear the title to sell part of the land, and in so doing each son and father relationship was detailed, enabling us to document four generations from land records.

Most deed books are indexed either individually or in a general manner by the names of the buyers and sellers (grantee-grantor indexes). In a few instances the indexes have been destroyed or have not been kept in an efficient manner, but most are excellent and enable the researcher to locate any record of title transfer. In some parts of the public domain, land records are filed by description of the land rather than by the names of the persons buying or selling; this makes it more difficult to locate a particular record without knowing the physical location of the land. However in the colonial states records are generally indexed by the names of the buyers and sellers.

Some town and county land records have been indexed under a phonetic system with similar sounding surnames listed together. This makes it easier to locate entries when variations occur in the spelling of surnames. Often a key on the inside cover of the first index book explains the system. By noting the first letter of the surname and by considering consonant sounds, you can follow the grid lines to a meeting point where page numbers are listed; then by turning to the page indicated, you can locate each name of interest and find the book and page number where the actual information is recorded. Both New York and Pennsylvania use this system to index deed and mortgage records.

Virginia and several other southern states also consider given names in their land record indexes; transactions are indexed by given name as well as by surname. This is efficient when locating records where the given name is known but makes it difficult to locate all entries for a particular surname. To do that, you must check every given name in alphabetical sequence, which can be frustrating and very time consuming. In some cases it is wise to start in the earliest indexes and copy all references that seem significant to a particular problem, then read each record and copy those that are pertinent. In other cases it might be better to locate references only in the time period of interest and investigate them on a selective basis.

By paying special attention to names and places in the records and by noting the description of the property, it is sometimes possible to gain kinship information that could not otherwise be obtained. Also, by noting the names listed in the body of the record and the names of witnesses, other genealogical conclusions can be reached. The fact that a person signed his name by using his mark might help distinguish him from other persons of the same name in the same records.

Usually it is a good practice to copy references from the indexes over a wide time period before checking the actual records, unless you are looking for a specific record. Careful evaluation of the index entries will allow you to be selective in your reading and may save valuable time. You should evaluate both grantor and grantee indexes to make sure important entries are not missed; some indexes are incomplete in cross referencing. After the index references have been copied, search the actual records, copying or extracting entries of interest. When the surname and given names are common, it may be necessary to do selective reading and copying; at other times it is advisable to read and copy each record. When a record is known to be relevant, it should be photocopied or copied verbatim but when you are not sure the record pertains, you might want to copy extracts only. Sometimes after extracting all entries pertaining to the same surname, you can determine valuable relationships and other important facts.

Any extract should include the volume and page number, the date the instrument was made and recorded, the names and places of residence of all persons involved, the consideration, a brief description of the property, any unusual conditions listed in the body of the deed, the names of the witnesses, and the signatures or marks of the participants. It should be remembered that the deed book entries are actually copies of the original instruments written in the hand of the clerk; they do not represent the actual penmanship of the record makers, and the signatures are not those of the actual participants. More recently, county or town records are photocopies of the originals and do represent the actual signatures of the makers.

The methods, procedures, and techniques of search are the same in public domain states as listed here; in fact, many of the recording practices are the same in all counties. However, descriptions of land and real property might vary because of the method of survey.

Records relating to taxation of real and personal property exist in all states, but they vary in their content and accessibility. As a general rule, they exist in all the colonial states, and most early records have been microfilmed or published and are available for research. Most of them are of value only in locating individuals in particular places and time periods, but a few provide sufficient detail to establish ages and calculate kinship—for instance those for Virginia and Kentucky. Virginia Pope Livingston had the following to say about Virginia tax records:

> When one considers the peculiarities of genealogical research in Virginia in the post-Revolution period, one set of records springs immediately to mind. In the year 1782, the Commonwealth of Virginia instituted an annual series of tax lists, land taxes, and personal property taxes. These are state records, are not to be found for the early years in the counties, and are not, so far as I know, available on microfilm. [Many are now available in Salt Lake City on microfilm.] The tax lists can be examined in the State Archives in Richmond.
>
> These records are an invaluable source of genealogical information, particularly when used, as of course all records should be, in conjunction with other types of records. The regulations for listing taxable property, both land and personal property, varied from year to year. It is, therefore, essential that every time you pick up a tax list, you examine carefully the headings of each column. Even in the same county, the enumerators of different districts may arrange their columns in a different order. One very important feature of the tax lists is that the date of enumeration is entered in the margin for each entry.
>
> The land tax lists generally show the acreage, the assessed valuation and the amount of tax. In some years, they show the distance from the court house, in some the name of the nearest watercourse; both of these are extremely helpful in locating your families. Perhaps the most useful feature is the section, supposed to be annual, but unfortunately seldom so, called "Alterations." This section shows changes in title or tax responsibility, and frequently shows the means by which the change occurred, as by deed, will, division, and so on. Sometimes the grantor's name is given—a great boon, especially in the counties whose records have been destroyed. The Alterations may show that a man received land by the division of an estate, and this can often lead to identification of his wife or maternal grandparent.
>
> Finally, the land tax lists also include business licenses issued during the year; these, followed through other records, may show that the business partner by the name you are looking for actually resided elsewhere, though licensed to do business in this particular county.
>
> The personal tax lists are perhaps even more useful genealogically. In Virginia, all white males became taxable, or "Tithable," at age 16. Women, who are still considerably ignored in Virginia, were not taxable themselves, though they may appear on the land tax list if they owned land, or on the

personal tax lists if they owned taxable personal property or had taxable males under 21 in their households. Slaves were taxable at 12. In practically all years, I believe, stud horses and cattle were taxed.

When searching early tax records, it is a good practice to extract entries for all persons by the same surname and also to cover a wide time period. Individuals may not be located every year, even though they were known to be resident in that county, and some cannot be located because certain records are missing. People were no different in the early days than they are now, and anyone who could avoid the tax lists undoubtedly tried to do so. Sometimes by noting when a person first appears in the tax records and by noting that he was merely a "poll" or "tithable," and then by following him through each list for a number of years and identifying his taxable real estate, one can determine parentage and other important kinship information. In Kentucky tax records it is often possible to determine a young man's age and his father's name from the lists. Kentucky lists included free white male persons twenty-one years of age and upward, and when the person first turned twenty-one he was usually listed immediately under his father's entry. By following the records in succeeding years it is also possible to show a father's ownership of land decreasing by an amount equal to a son's newly acquired land. The land may also be shown to be entered in the same name and be situated on the same watercourse. In some cases, the records can be used to identify a female spouse or a widow, while in other instances the records might lead to the maiden name of the wife. [Livingston 1969.]

The Genealogical Society of Utah has completed the filming of early tax records for New England and many records for the middle and southern states. It has an excellent collection for early Pennsylvania counties and "ratable lists" for New Jersey counties covering the period 1772–1822. Very few tax lists of any type are currently on film for New York counties. However, good collections exist for Virginia, West Virginia, Kentucky, North and South Carolina, Georgia, and Tennessee. Few pertaining to Maryland are on file at Salt Lake, but a good collection exists for Delaware.

The Public Domain States

Following the Revolution title to the public domain was vested in the United States government through cession from the colonial states, then later through purchase, annexation, conquest, and treaty. The Treaty of Paris, signed by the United States and Great Britain in September 1783 and ratified by Congress at Philadelphia in January 1784 recognized American independence and granted title to all territory west to the Mississippi River. The northern boundary of the United States was a hazily defined line of lakes and rivers, and the southern boundary was set at the thirty-first parallel—a line agreed upon if England ceded Florida to Spain, which was done (Hofstadter, Miller, and Aaron 1959, p. 190).

The question of the United States gaining title to certain colonial lands was considered even before the Treaty of 1783. Maryland refused to ratify the Articles of Confederation until the "landed" states of New York, Virginia, North and South Carolina, Georgia, Massachusetts, and Connecticut ceded their claims of western lands to the federal government.

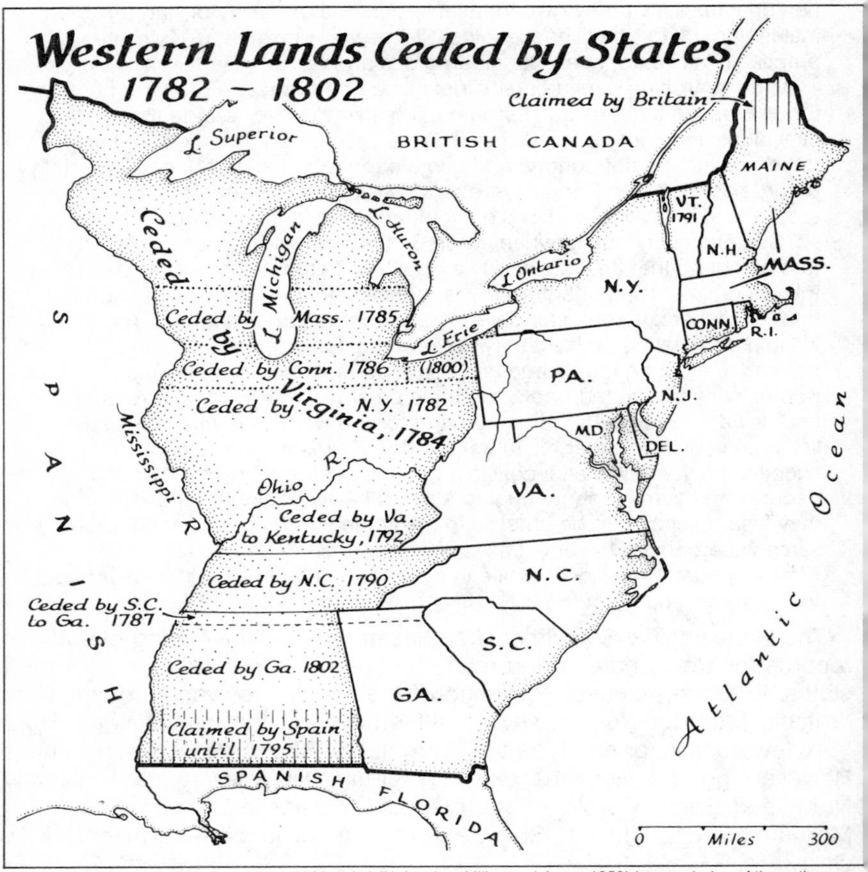

Reprinted from *The American Republic to 1865*, vol. 1 (Hofstadter, Miller, and Aaron 1959) by permission of the authors.

Their western boundaries were fixed by original charters at the Mississippi River or the Pacific Ocean. Maryland argued that since the war was a common effort, new territories should be considered common property. In 1780 Virginia broke ranks with the others and by 1784 renounced her vast western territories; New York and Connecticut followed. By 1802 Georgia ratified the cession agreement, being the last of the states to do so (Hofstadter, Miller, and Aaron 1959, p. 206).

When Georgia ceded her lands in 1802, the western boundary of the United States was the Mississippi River—but westward expansion had just begun. In 1803 the Louisiana Purchase brought vast territories in middle America under U.S. control; then in 1819 Florida and the southern parts of Alabama and Mississippi were obtained from Spain. Mexico gained independence from Spain in 1821, and Texas gained independence from Mexico in 1836 and was annexed to the United States in 1845. In 1846 Oregon country came under American control; and in 1848 the war with Mexico brought the great southwest into the United States. The Gadsden Purchase in 1853 extended the border south of the Gila River in southern

Arizona, and some adjustments were also made on the northern border with Great Britain around that time. In 1867 Alaska was purchased from Russia; Hawaii was annexed as a territory in 1898. The Spanish American War brought territory in the Caribbean and the Pacific under U.S. control. Certain of these territories obtained their independence, but others remained under United States trusteeship.

Historical and Statistical Table of the U.S. and Territories in 1880

Colonial States	Date of Ratification or Organization
Connecticut	9 Jan 1787
Delaware	7 Dec 1787
District of Columbia	16 July 1790
Georgia	2 Jan 1788
Kentucky	4 Feb 1791
Maine (Province of Mass. to 1820)	3 Mar 1820
Maryland	28 Apr 1788
Massachusetts	6 Feb 1788
New Hampshire	21 June 1788
New Jersey	18 Dec 1787
New York	26 July 1788
North Carolina	21 Nov 1789
Pennsylvania	12 Dec 1787
Rhode Island	29 May 1789
South Carolina	23 May 1788
Tennessee	1 June 1796
Vermont	18 Feb 1791
Virginia	26 June 1788
West Virginia	31 Dec 1862

Public domain states	Date of Ratification or Organization
Alabama	3 Mar 1817
Alaska*	27 July 1868
Arizona*	24 Feb 1863
Arkansas	2 Mar 1819
California	9 Sept 1850
Colorado	28 Feb 1861
Dakota*	2 Mar 1861
Florida	30 Mar 1822
Illinois	3 Feb 1809
Indiana	7 May 1800
Iowa	12 June 1838
Kansas	30 May 1854
Louisiana	3 Mar 1805
Michigan	11 Jan 1805
Minnesota	3 Mar 1849
Mississippi	7 Apr 1798
Missouri	4 June 1812
Nebraska	30 May 1854
Nevada	2 Mar 1861
New Mexico*	9 Sept 1850
Ohio	30 Apr 1802
Oregon	14 Aug 1848
Texas	29 Dec 1845
Utah	9 Sept 1850
Washington*	2 Mar 1853
Wisconsin	20 Apr 1836
Wyoming*	25 July 1868

*Territory

Source: Adapted from *The public domain: its history with statistics in 1880* by The Public Land Commission (GPO 1880).

On 20 May 1785 Congress passed the first national land act, after long debate about whether public lands primarily should be sold for revenue or to actual settlers. The act favored the latter, and authorized lands were to be surveyed in Ohio and sold at open auction in Philadelphia, Pittsburgh, and Cincinnati. One-twentieth of the purchase price was to be paid at the time of application, with half the remainder to be paid in thirty days and the final half within a year. This was a compromise between the speculators, who would provide revenue by making large purchases, and the actual settlers, who desired smaller tracts for homes. However the compromise proved unsatisfactory to both groups; it was superseded in 1800 by an act that reduced the minimum tract that could be purchased to a half section and extended credit to a four-year period. In 1804 the mini-

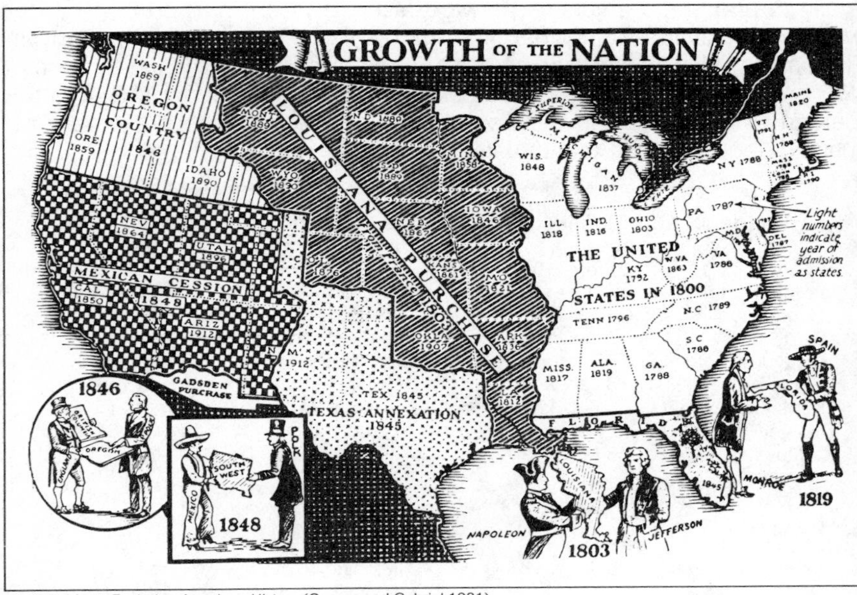

Reprinted from *Exploring American History* (Casner and Gabriel 1931).

mum tract was reduced still further to a quarter section of 160 acres. Both the reduction in size and the extension of credit were concessions to the settlers and were supposed to check speculators. However the results were not satisfactory, and in 1819 hard times brought demands for new legislation. In 1820 the minimum price was cut to $1.25 per acre, to be paid in one cash payment, and the smallest unit of purchase was reduced to 80 acres (Craven and Johnson 1952, p. 263).

On 13 July 1787 Congress created the Northwest Territory, the first commonwealth in the world recognizing every man to be free and equal. The ordinance established temporary government and outlined laws controlling the districts established, even affecting the descent and conveyance of property, both real and personal. It also extended the fundamental principles of civil and religious liberty to inhabitants of the territory and provided for the establishment of states with permanent governments to share in the federal councils on an equal footing with the original states. It provided that states from the territory could be admitted to the Union when they reached a population of sixty thousand free inhabitants, and this served as a guide for subsequent territorial acquisitions (Rhodes 1960, pp. 8–12).

The method of survey. A rectangular method of survey was used in the public domain rather than the metes-and-bounds system used in the colonies. It provided more accurate measurements and a more uniform system for surveying land. Principal meridian and base lines were established as needed, with range lines every six miles east and west and township lines every six miles north and south. The rectangles between the range and township lines were numbered in rows north and south with reference to range lines east and west, and the sections were numbered in sequence. The sections could be further subdivided into half sections, quarter sections, and so on.

This method of survey had been used earlier in Vermont and some of the other northeastern states, but it did not become a widely accepted mode of land measurement there. Five-mile townships were the norm in the northeastern states, but six-mile townships became popular in the

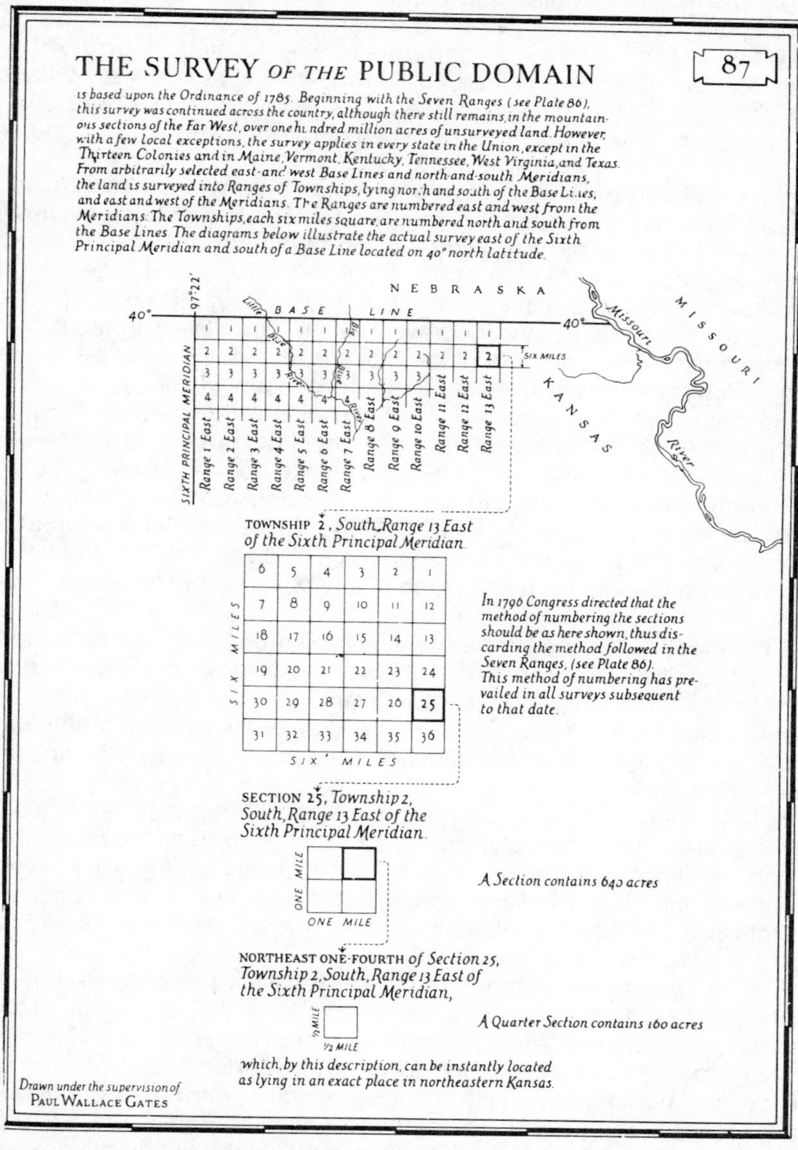

THE SURVEY OF THE PUBLIC DOMAIN
87
is based upon the Ordinance of 1785. Beginning with the Seven Ranges (see Plate 86), this survey was continued across the country, although there still remains, in the mountainous sections of the Far West, over one hundred million acres of unsurveyed land. However, with a few local exceptions, the survey applies in every state in the Union, except in the Thirteen Colonies and in Maine, Vermont, Kentucky, Tennessee, West Virginia, and Texas. From arbitrarily selected east-and west Base Lines and north-and-south Meridians, the land is surveyed into Ranges of Townships, lying north and south of the Base Lines, and east and west of the Meridians. The Ranges are numbered east and west from the Meridians. The Townships, each six miles square, are numbered north and south from the Base Lines. The diagrams below illustrate the actual survey east of the Sixth Principal Meridian and south of a Base Line located on 40° north latitude.
NEBRASKA
MISSOURI
KANSAS
BASE LINE
40°
97°22'
Little Blue River
Big Blue River
Missouri River
SIX MILES
SIXTH PRINCIPAL MERIDIAN
Range 1 East
Range 2 East
Range 3 East
Range 4 East
Range 5 East
Range 6 East
Range 7 East
Range 8 East
Range 9 East
Range 10 East
Range 11 East
Range 12 East
Range 13 East
TOWNSHIP 2, South, Range 13 East of the Sixth Principal Meridian.
SIX MILES
SIX MILES
In 1796 Congress directed that the method of numbering the sections should be as here shown, thus discarding the method followed in the Seven Ranges, (see Plate 86). This method of numbering has prevailed in all surveys subsequent to that date.
SECTION 25, Township 2, South, Range 13 East of the Sixth Principal Meridian.
ONE MILE
ONE MILE
A Section contains 640 acres
NORTHEAST ONE-FOURTH of Section 25, Township 2, South, Range 13 East of the Sixth Principal Meridian,
½ MILE
½ MILE
A Quarter Section contains 160 acres
which, by this description, can be instantly located as lying in an exact place in northeastern Kansas.
Drawn under the supervision of
PAUL WALLACE GATES

Reprinted from *Atlas of American History* (Adams 1943) by permission of C. Scribner's Sons.

public domain. The numbering of sections was changed to a serpentine sequence after the system was first used, and that has been a uniform practice since. The system must be understood by researchers because many land records in the public domain are filed by description rather than by the names of buyers and sellers, as is the case in the colonial states.

Ohio was the first to qualify for statehood under the Northwest Ordinance and became the first public domain state to enter the Union. Congress approved the constitution and admitted Ohio as a state on 19 February 1803. The first seat of government was located at Chillicothe in Ross County, where it remained until 1810; then it was moved to Zanesville until 1812, when it was returned to Chillicothe. In 1816 the seat of government was permanently established at Columbus.

Virginia military lands. This area represented a body of lands containing just over four million acres lying between the Scioto and Little Miami Rivers. It was bounded by the Ohio River on the south and the counties of Auglaize, Hardin, and Marion on the north. Virginia claimed the area under charter from King James I of England in 1609. However, the state agreed to relinquish all land northwest of the Ohio River in favor of the federal government upon condition that these military lands be guaranteed to Virginia troops who served in the revolutionary war.

The district was not surveyed into townships of any regular form, and any individual who held a Virginia military land warrant could locate wherever he chose within the district. He could take up land in any dimension he desired wherever land had not been previously entered into the records by someone else. In consequence, some sections encroached upon others. There has probably been more litigation between the holders of conflicting titles in this district than in any other part of the state.

The Connecticut western reserve and fire lands. This area consisted of over three million acres in the northeastern corner of the state and was often called "New Connecticut." It was surveyed into townships five miles square rather than six miles square, and Connecticut was guaranteed the exlusive right of soil in 1786, although the United States government reserved the right of jurisdiction.

In 1662 King Charles II of England granted Connecticut all lands between the forty-first and forty-second parallels of north latitude from Providence plantations on the east to the Pacific Ocean on the west, with exception of the New York and Pennsylvania colonies. These rights were relinquished only after considerable altercation and after the United States became an independent nation.

The "fire lands" adjoined the reserve to the west and consisted of most of the present counties of Erie and Huron. In 1792 the State of Connecticut granted these lands to certain citizens. Benedict Arnold is credited with leading a British force of raiders into Connecticut during the Revolution and burning several towns; as a result Connecticut granted 781 square miles from the west side of the Connecticut Reserve to 1,870 persons residing in nine Connecticut towns that suffered fire losses.

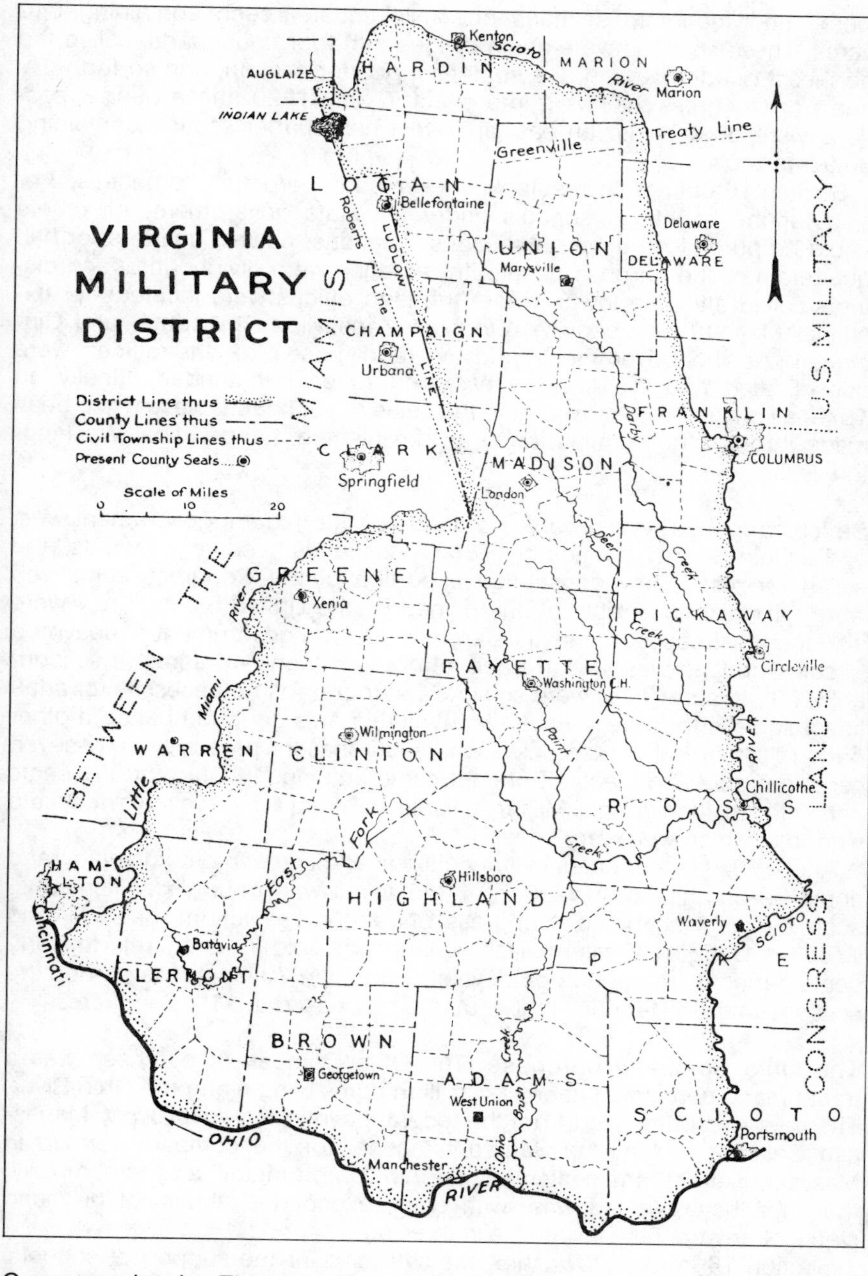

Congress lands. These lands were called "Congress lands" because they were sold directly to purchasers by the United States government. They were surveyed into townships of six square miles each, under the authority and at the expense of the national government. The townships were subdivided into sections one mile square, each containing 640 acres. These sections were again divided into four equal parts, called the northeast quarter section, the southeast quarter section, and so forth. By a law of Congress that went into effect in July 1820, these quarter sections were divided into an east and west half-quarter section containing 80 acres each.

Section 16 of each township was reserved in perpetuity to be leased or sold for the benefit of schools under the state government. All others could be purchased either in sections, fractions, halves, quarters, or half quarters. For the purpose of sale, these lands were divided into land districts called after the towns where the land offices were located—for example, Marietta, Steubenville, Wooster, Zanesville, Chillicothe, and Cincinnati. As the government lands were disposed of, the offices were consolidated and the territory assigned to each extended. Finally, in 1876, all offices were closed, and the sales of such lands have since been made through the commissioners of the General Land Office, Washington, D.C.

Seven ranges. The first survey of lands by the federal government west of the Ohio River was made in 1786. These lands became known as "the seven ranges." They constituted a portion of the Congress lands and were the most accessible of any owned by the United States. They were also the most desired by settlers and the first the government endeavored to sell. The land was sold in tracts of not less than 640 acres (a section) at $2.00 per acre; sales were so slow that there was no necessity for additional surveys for several years. Many immigrants could do better in other parts of Ohio and in Kentucky, where purchasers paid only sixty-seven cents per acre. Connecticut offered some holdings in Ohio for fifty cents per acre. In the Virginia Military District all land was available for state warrants, which were very cheap.

After 1796 United States military district land came into competition and could be purchased in tracts of 4,000 acres with bounty certificates issued by the Continental Congress under the resolutions of 1776 and 1780. In 1795 the Western Reserve land was sold in its entirety for forty cents per acre. To encourage development, in 1820 Congress divided the sections into smaller units that could be purchased at $1.25 per acre.

The Ohio Company purchase. The Ohio Company's purchase was a tract of land containing about 1.5 million acres lying along the Ohio River. The tract was purchased from the federal government in 1787 by Manassah Cutler and Winthrop Sargeant, agents for the company formed in Massachusetts for the settlement of Ohio. Unfortunately for the company, the tract they selected was—with some exceptions—the most hilly and sterile of any tract of similar size in the state.

Section 16 in each township was set apart for the support of schools, as in the Congress lands, and Section 29 was set apart for the support of religious institutions. Also, two townships six miles square were granted for the use of colleges; this is where the present Ohio University at Athens is located. The price was to be not less than one dollar per acre (except-

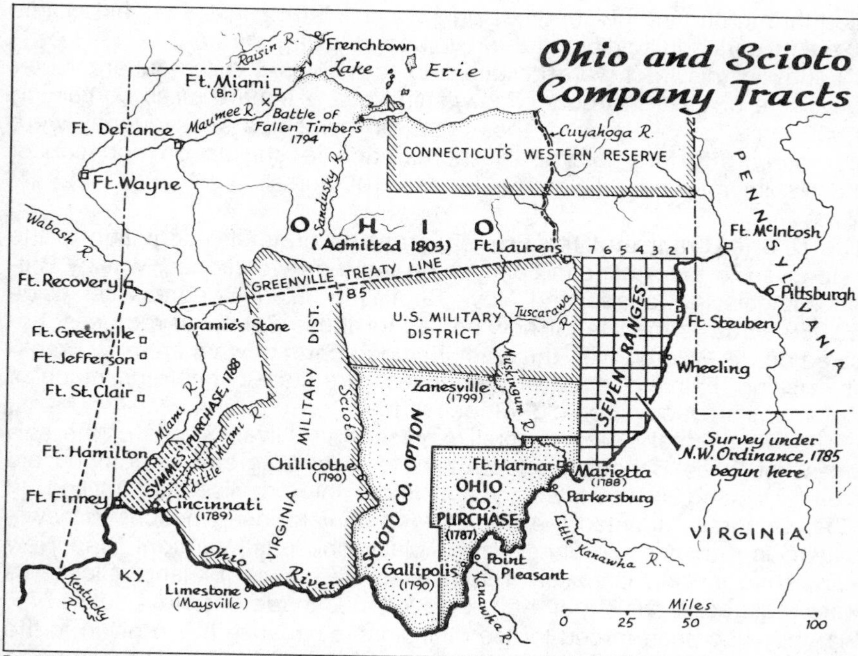

Reprinted from *The American Republic to 1865*, vol. 1 (Hofstadter, Miller, and Aaron 1959) by permission of the authors.

ing the reservations and gifts mentioned) payable in specie loan office certificates reduced to specie value or certificates of liquidated debts of the United States with a reduction of one-third dollar per acre for bad land.

The first settlement took place in 1788 at Marietta. In 1792—when the patents were issue—the number of shares in the company was 822 with each share entitled to 1,173 acres. The land was divided upon that basis, and settlers from New England moved in at a rapid pace.

Symmes purchase. In 1794 Judge John Cleve Symmes of New Jersey purchased 311,682 acres of land for sixty-seven cents an acre. This tract, historically known as the "Symmes purchase," is located in the southwestern corner of the state between the Great and Little Miami rivers and borders on the Ohio River for twenty-seven miles. Judge Symmes contributed liberally to the support of the Continental army under George Washington and received certificates of indebtedness for his help. Noting the Ohio Company's use of Continental army bounty warrants and similar documents for purchasing large tracts of Congress lands, he petitioned Congress for similar rights on 29 August 1787. The contract was made in October 1788, and the patent for his purchase was given on 13 September 1794.

The United States military lands. These lands consisted of 2.5 million acres located east of the Scioto River in the central part of the state. They were called "United States military lands" because they were appropriated through an act of Congress on 1 June 1796 to satisfy certain claims of the officers and soldiers of the revolutionary war.

Lands in this tract were divided into townships 5 miles square. Later they were divided into quarter townships of 2½ square miles containing 4,000 acres each. Some of these quarter townships subsequently were subdivided into forty lots of 100 acres each for the accommodation of those soldiers who held warrants for only 100 acres.

The refugee tract and the French grant. In grateful recognition of the help given to the American colonies during the revolutionary war by British subjects in Canada and Nova Scotia, in 1798 Congress set aside 50,080 acres as the site for new homes for these Canadian refugees. Located on the Scioto River, this tract included parts of what are now Franklin, Licking, Fairfield, and Perry counties. The state capitol and much of Columbus are located on old refugee lands.

The Continental Congress first expressed its "lively sense of the services" of these Canadian refugees in 1783 and agreed to compensate them with land; it was fifteen years before this promise was fulfilled. In 1798 Congress directed the Secretary of War to insert notices in newspapers in New York, Pennsylvania, Massachusetts, Vermont, and New Hampshire inviting Canadian refugees to file claims for land. Claimants were required to show that they had lived in Canada prior to 4 July 1776, that they had been forced to flee their homes because of aid given to the colonies during the revolutionary war, and that they had not returned to Canada to live prior to 25 November 1783.

Sixty-seven such claimants were awarded 50,080 acres of land, most of which was in tracts of 320, 640, 1280, and 2240 acres. About half this land was claimed. That which was not claimed later was sold at the Chillicothe land office to the highest bidder, but for not less than two dollars an acre.

In 1795 Congress donated a tract of 24,000 acres in Scioto County to a number of French people who had been swindled out of their money by a land company that in reality held no lands. An additional 1,200 acres adjoining the first lands was granted by Congress in 1798.

Searching the Records

Land records in the public domain states differ from those of the colonial states primarily in title origin. The documents of original title differ, but those after the initial acquisition are about the same: deeds, mortgages, leases, contracts, agreements, and tax records. Of course the method of survey is different—therefore the description of real estate will be different in deeds—but other information is similar.

The county has jurisdiction for recording land transactions in the public domain states after initial title has been acquired; prior records are found in state and federal land offices. The county recorder is usually responsible for recording after the document of original title (usually the patent) has been obtained, and the books of entry are similar to those already explained under records of the colonial states.

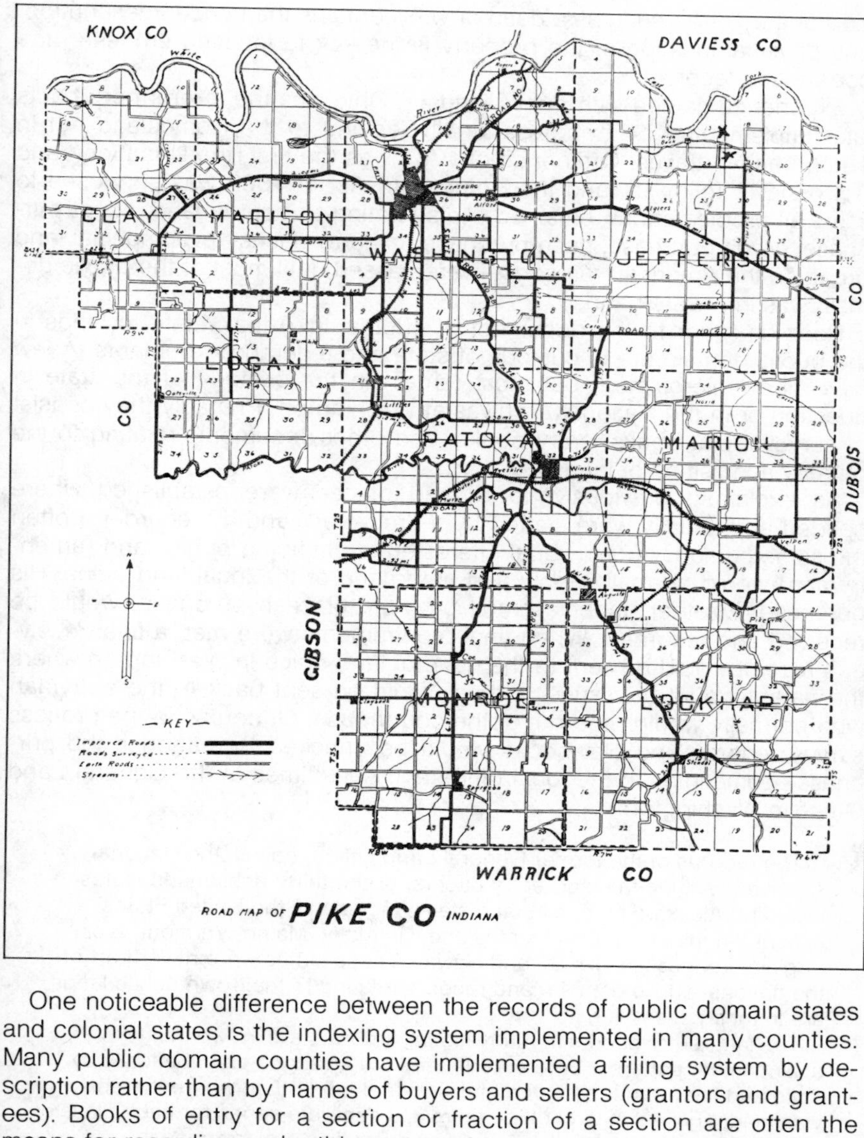

One noticeable difference between the records of public domain states and colonial states is the indexing system implemented in many counties. Many public domain counties have implemented a filing system by description rather than by names of buyers and sellers (grantors and grantees). Books of entry for a section or fraction of a section are often the means for recording under this system. A particular parcel of land is identified, then all transactions are listed in sequence. This makes it convenient when the description is known, but without knowing at least the quarter section locating records is quite impossible. Usually you can obtain a township map from the auditor's office for a reasonable fee; this identifies township lines and sections, enabling you to determine the proper section when the physical location of the property is known. When it is not, you must question old-timers in the area or search county histories to find a reference to the home or farmstead. Sometimes a document in possession of the family, such as a deed or will, contains the needed description. The physical location of the property is the key to locating entries in the courthouse records.

Experience gained with public lands in Ohio was the forerunner of acts later implemented by Congress, finally leading to the Homestead Act in 1862. The Northwest Ordinance of 1787 was the first, the Donation Land Act of 1841 followed, and the Homestead Act of 1862 was supposed to solve all problems that remained. Acts relating to bounty land, script purchase, credit purchase, cash purchase, mineral claims—even special land grants to the American railroads—were passed until most of the public domain was in private hands.

Records (prior to the document of original title) that relate to lands in the public domain are in custody of state and federal governments. A few have been microfilmed, but most remain in the custody of the state in question or in the National Archives at Washington. Primarily they consist of surveys, plat books, entry books, and other documents relating to the primary acquisition of land.

As explained previously, local land offices were established where needed and usually were staffed by a "receiver" and a "recorder," often the same person. An individual interested in obtaining public land (an entryman) would normally apply and enter land at the local land office. His purchase, whether under a credit program or cash purchase, would be received and recorded. When final requirements were met, a final receiver's receipt would be sent to the general land office in Washington where the patent would be issued. It then would be sent back to the entryman who normally would record it at the courthouse. Of course in the process survey records and plat books would be checked to authorize the purchase—sometimes at the local office and sometimes at the General Land Office in Washington.

> The records of the former General Land Office, now in the National Archives, include the land-entry papers for the thirty public-land states including Alaska. The public-land states include all the United States except the thirteen original states and Kentucky, Maine, Vermont, West Virginia, Tennessee, Texas, and Hawaii. These states were never part of the national public domain, and records relating to their own public lands are in their possession.
>
> The land-entry papers in the National Archives are in two main arrangement patterns. Before 1908 they are arranged alphabetically by state and thereunder by name of the district land office where the entry was made. For each land office there is a separate series for each class of entry. Within each series the individual entry files are arranged in numerical order according to the number assigned to each entry at the time the final certificate was issued by the register of the local land office. With minor exceptions, warrants, scrip, mineral, lieu selection entries, and all patented cases after 1908 are arranged in an unbroken numerical series, regardless of state or land office, according to the number assigned at the time of patenting.
>
> There is no general overall index to entrymen or patentees for land-entry papers prior to 1908. There is such an index in the Bureau of Land Management, Department of the Interior, for the patented cases after

1908. There are partial indexes, however, either in the Bureau of Land Management or in the National Archives for the following series prior to 1908: (1) warrants under the Military Bounty Land Act of 1788 (incomplete), (2) Virginia military-bounty-land warrants, (3) private land claims, (4) coal cash entries, and (5) mineral entries. There is also a consolidated name index (by name of entryman or patentee) for those land entries that are arranged by district land office in Alabama, Arizona, Florida, Louisiana, Nevada, Utah, and Alaska. This index does not include names of persons who "located" land under military bounty-land warrants. As the index is consolidated and the names are in one alphabetical sequence, it is not possible to select all entries for any particular state. Each index card shows the name of the entryman, description of the land, name of land office, date, type and number of entry. No personal information of any kind regarding the entryman appears on these cards. Among the records of the Veterans Administration in the National Archives, there is an alphabetical index to applications for military bounty-land warrants issued under the acts of 1847, 1850, 1852, and 1855.

For all land-entry files other than those covered by name indexes, it is necessary, in order to find a file relating to a particular entry, to know (1) the legal description of the land in terms of township, range, section, and fraction of section of (2) the date (or approximate date) of the entry and the name of the land office through which the entry was made. A legal description of the land can usually be obtained from the recorder of deeds of the county in which the land is located.

The federal land records document only the initial transaction whereby the land was transferred from the Government to the first owner; whether that first owner was a state government, a railroad company or a private individual. Information concerning all later transactions in the chain of title to that land must be looked for among local records.

The land-entry papers in the National Archives include (1) records relating to entries based on purchase or special conditions of settlement, 1800–1951; (2) bounty-land-warrant records, 1789–1908; (3) homestead entries; and (4) private land-claims records, 1789–1908. The first class, records relating to entries based on purchases or special conditions, may be divided into several groups. The credit entry files and the cash entry files contain relatively little information of genealogical value; the donation entry files contain genealogical data in varying amounts.

The Bureau of Land Management has retained all record copies of patents issued for all types of land entries, 1800 to date. No personal information about the entryman, however, appears on these record copies. To obtain information from these record copies it is necessary to have the date of the patent and the volume and page number of the record copy as shown on each individual land-entry paper now filed in the National Archives. [Wright and Pratt 1967]

Credit prior entries. Most land sold by the federal government between 1800 and 1820 was sold on credit at no less than two dollars an acre in accordance with provisions of the Act of 10 May 1800. The act allowed land to be bought in installments, with the purchaser paying one-third of the price with each installment. Upon making the final payment, the purchaser received a credit prior final certificate. These final certificates show the name of the purchaser, county of residence he stated at the final payment, date of certificate, description of the tract in terms of subdivision, section, township and range, name of the land office, the amount paid, and a reference to the record copy of the patent. No other personal information about the purchaser is given in these certificates.

Credit under entries. Entries made under the Act of 3 March 1821, which granted longer terms for the credit purchase of land, are known as "credit under entries." Upon making the final payment the purchaser received a credit under final certificate similar in all respects to credit prior certificates. Most entries consist solely of the final certificate.

Cash entries. Nearly all public land sold by the federal government to individual settlers after the Act of 21 April 1820, was sold for cash at no less than $1.25 per acre. The cash entry files, which cover roughly 1820–1908, consist generally of a receiver's receipt for the money and a register's receipt registering the land purchases and authorizing the claimant to obtain a patent. Each receipt shows the name of the purchaser; the county of residence stated at the time of purchase; the date of purchase; name of land office; description of the land in terms of fraction of section, section, township, and range; the number of acres in the tract; the amount of money paid, and the volume and page of the record copy of the patent. No personal information concerning the entryman was required in cash entries, and little genealogical data appears in them. If the tract paid for was claimed on the basis of a preemption claim, the cash entry may include a preemption proof or similar document that may show the name of the claimant, his age, citizenship, date of entry on tract, number and relationship of members of his household, and the nature of his improvements. If the tract paid for was entered originally as a homestead

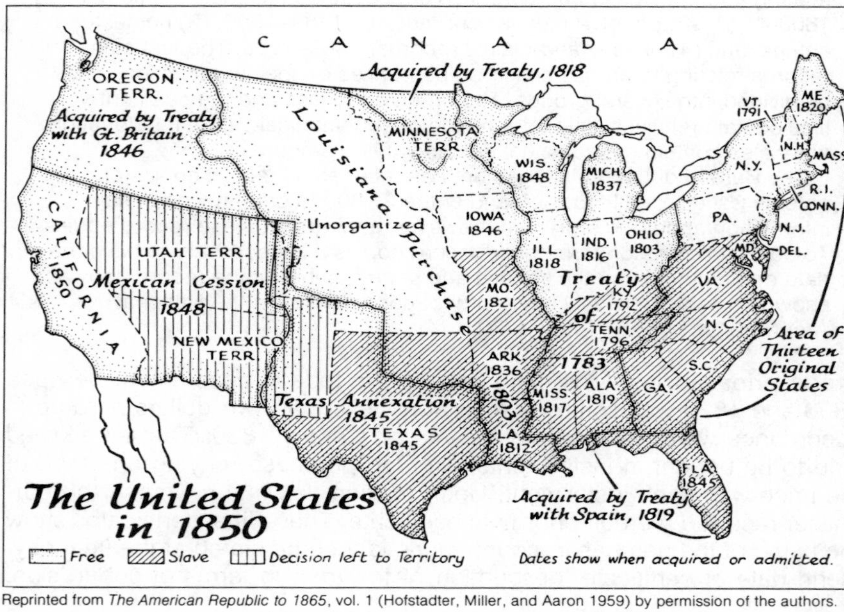

Reprinted from *The American Republic to 1865*, vol. 1 (Hofstadter, Miller, and Aaron 1959) by permission of the authors.

and later commuted to a cash entry, the cash entry file may include the homestead entry documents. If, however, the homestead entry was commuted to cash, the final proof testimony, which is the important source of genealogical information, was not taken.

Donation land claims files: Florida, Oregon, and Washington. The donation entry files pertain to land donated to settlers in return for certain conditions of settlement. They consist of Florida, Oregon, and Washington donation entry files. The Florida files usually include a permit to settle, an application for a patent, a report by the land agent, and a final certificate authorizing the issuance of patent. A permit to settle shows the name of the applicant, his marital status, the month and year he began residing in Florida, and a legal description of the land.

The Oregon and Washington donation files for each land office are filed in two numerical series, one relating to complete entries and the other to incomplete entries. A file for a complete entry usually contains a notification of the settlement of public land and the donation certificate. The notification shows the legal description of the land, the name of the entryman, how long a resident of the land, date of application, place of residence, citizenship, age, place and date of birth, and—if married—the date and place of marriage. Sometimes the given name of the wife also appears. The National Archives has a microfilm copy of the Index to Oregon Donation Land Claims prepared by the Oregon State Library. This index is in two parts, one arranged alphabetically and the other geographically. There are also several indexes to registers of these donation claims, but they contain gaps.

The Genealogical Forum of Portland has abstracted Oregon donation land claims and published them in three volumes with alphabetical and geographical indexes available. An extract from the foreword of volume 1 follows:

> Much genealogical data is to be found in the papers filed for the Oregon donation land claims granted to settlers of the Oregon Territory before 1853. Original papers, made in duplicate, are located at the Land Office in Portland, Oregon (those used by the Surveyor General's Office) and the National Archives, Washington, D.C. (those used by the Register and Receiver's Office). The genealogical material abstracted from the papers in the Land Office at Portland by members of the Genealogical Forum of Portland is the subject matter of this book.
>
> This volume contains abstracts of the first 2500 claims filed at the Oregon City Land Office. A total of 5289 claims were filed at this office; 2141 claims were filed at the Roseburg Land Office, 5 at The Dalles Land Office, and 2 at the La Grande Land Office. The Forum plans to continue with the abstracting and printing of these claims.
>
> The books should be of interest to genealogists because of the family data contained and to historians everywhere because proof of Oregon settlers and their paths of migration are shown. A survey of the records indicate that at least 45 percent of the settlers were not born in the same state as the one in which they were married. All states existing in 1853 are represented in the list from which Oregon settlers emigrated, with the greatest number coming from Missouri, Kentucky, Virginia, Ohio, Indiana,

Tennessee, Illinois, New York, Pennsylvania, North Carolina, South Carolina, Connecticut, Iowa, Maryland, Massachusetts, and Vermont.

Bounty land warrants and scrip. The entry papers for the Virginia revolutionary warrants are dated chiefly 1795–1830 and include such documents as a surrendered warrant, a certificate of location, a survey, power of attorney, assignment, and possibly an affidavit concerning the veteran's heirs. Most Virginia warrants were used in the Virginia Military District of Ohio prior to 1830 and were exchanged for scrip after that date. By the five acts beginning in 1830, Congress provided tha holders of unused Virginia and United States revolutionary war warrants could surrender them for scrip certificates. These certificates could be used for land location anywhere on the public domain that land was offered for selection. A scrip application file includes such documents as the surrendered bounty land warrant, power of attorney, assignments, an affidavit of relationship, and related correspondence.

The records relating to revolutionary war warrants surrendered for land in the Military District of Ohio are dated chiefly 1789–1833. In most instances the surrendered warrant and the certificate of location are the only documents filed but occasionally an affidavit, power of attorney, or similar document is filed with the warrant. Warrants based upon the Act of 1803 as extended in 1806 show the location of the tract in terms of lot, subdivision, township, and range.

The records relating to War of 1812 warrants include the notification of the filing of the warrant with the general land office, a power of attorney, and a letter of transmittal. A typical file contains such information as the name of the veteran, the location of the land, date of patent, and volume

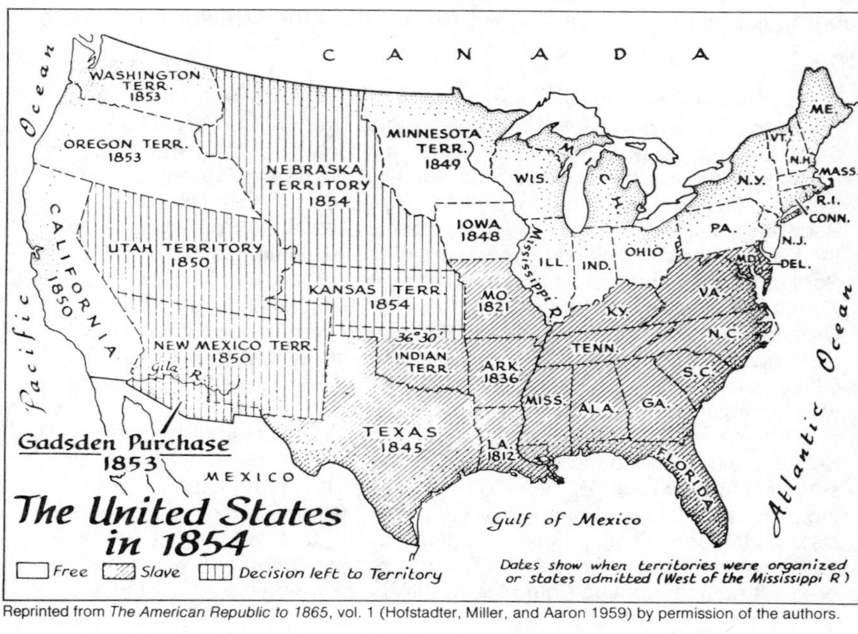

Reprinted from *The American Republic to 1865*, vol. 1 (Hofstadter, Miller, and Aaron 1959) by permission of the authors.

and page number of the record copy of the patent.

The last important group of warrant files consists of records relating to United States warrants issued for unspecified land based on a series of acts passed between 1847 and 1855. Many of these warrants involve veterans of the Mexican War. The Mexican War is the last war for which veterans were granted bounty lands; no warrants have been issued for any service after 3 March 1855, the date of the last set. The Homestead Act enacted in 1862 served to take the place of bounty land acts.

Homestead entries. Under the Homestead Act of 20 May 1862, citizens and persons who had filed their intentions to become citizens were given 160 acres of land on the public domain provided they fulfilled certain conditions, such as building a house on the land, cultivating the land, and residing on the homestead for five years.

The homestead entry papers, filed by names of land office, are dated 1863–1908. They are usually two separately numbered series for each land office, one relating to complete homestead entries, the other to unperfected entries. A complete file includes the homestead application, the certificate of publication of intention to make a claim, the homestead final proof, and a final certificate authorizing the claimant to obtain a patent. The homestead final proof testimony, the only document in the file that includes personal information about the claimant, shows the name, age and post office of the claimant, a description of the tract, a description of the house and the date when residence was established, the number and relationship of members of the family (but seldom their names), evidence of citizenship, the nature of the crops and number of acres under cultivation, and testimony of witnesses as to the truth of the claimant's statements.

Private land claims. These are claims to land made on the basis of grants or settlements that occurred before the United States acquired sovereignty. These claims relate chiefly to persons who claimed to have received grants from foreign sovereigns to their descendants and to pioneer citizens of the United States who settled in these lands with the permission of the foreign governments.

The private land claims in the National Archives relate to land in portions of fourteen states: Alabama, Arizona, Arkansas, California, Colorado, Florida, Illinois, Indiana, Iowa, Louisiana, Michigan, Mississippi, Missouri, New Mexico, and Wisconsin.

The claims papers of the general land office are filed in separate dockets containing such documents as correspondence, affidavits, and copies of court decisions. Since all these dockets are poorly indexed with regard to the personal names of the applicants or grantees, it is essential to have a legal description of the land in order to locate an individual docket. Records relating to individual claims presented between 1790 and 1837 were reported to Congress and transcribed and indexed in the *American State Papers Class VIII Public Land,* Gales and Seaton, 8 vols.

Sequence for search. The sequence of search may vary with each gene-

HOMESTEAD PROOF—TESTIMONY OF CLAIMANT

James L. Wells, being called as a witness in his own behalf in support of homestead entry, No. 4235, for SW¼ Sec. 12, T. 28N., R. 9 W. testifies as follows:

Ques. 1.—What is your name, age, and post-office address?

Ans. James L. Wells, age 41 years, Manchester, Okla

Ques. 2.—Are you a *native-born* citizen of the United States, and if so, in what State or Territory were you born?*

Ans. I am. Kansas.

Ques. 3.—Are you the identical person who made homestead entry, No. 4235, at the Alva Okla Ty land office on the 17 day of Jany, 1894, 18 , and what is the true description of the land now claimed by you?

Ans. I am. I claim the SW¼ Sec. 24, T. 28N., R. 9 W.

Ques. 4.—When was your house built on the land and when did you establish actual residence therein? (Describe said house and other improvements which you have placed on the land, giving total value thereof.)

Ans. Dug out, 12 x 16, built Sept. 27, 1893, and actual residence established therein same date. Stone house, 16 x 33, addition, 14 x 16, stone hen house, stables, well, 65 acres cultivated, 15 acres fenced, 2300 fruit and forest trees. Value $800.

Ques. 5.—Of whom does your family consist; and have you and your family resided continuously on the land since first establishing residence thereon? (If unmarried, state the fact.)

Ans. Wife and six children. We have.

Ques. 6.—For what period or periods have you been absent from the homestead since making settlement, and for what purpose; and if temporarily absent, did your family reside upon and cultivate the land during such absence?

Ans. None

Ques. 7.—How much of the land have you cultivated each season, and for how many seasons have you raised crops thereon?

Ans. 65 acres cultivated to crops each season.

Ques. 8.—Is your present claim within the limits of an incorporated town or selected site of a city or town, or used in any way for trade and business?

Ans. No sir

Ques. 9.—What is the character of the land? Is it timber, mountainous, prairie, grazing, or ordinary agricultural land? State its kind and quality, and for what purpose it is most valuable.

Ans. Prairie land, most valuable for farming.

Ques. 10.—Are there any indications of coal, salines, or minerals of any kind on the land? (If so, describe what they are, and state whether the land is more valuable for agricultural than for mineral purposes.)

Ans. None

Ques. 11.—Have you ever made any other homestead entry? (If so, describe the same.)

Ans. No sir

Ques. 12.—Have you sold, conveyed, or mortgaged any portion of the land; and if so, to whom and for what purpose?

Ans. No sir

Ques. 13.—Have you any personal property of any kind elsewhere than on this claim? (If so, describe the same, and state where the same is kept.)

Ans. No sir

Ques. 14.—Describe by legal subdivisions, or by number, kind of entry, and office where made, any other entry or filing (not mineral), made by you since August 30, 1890.

Ans. No sir

(Sign plainly with full christian name.) James L. Wells

*(In case the party is of foreign birth a certified transcript from the court records of his declaration of intention to become a citizen, or of his naturalization, or a copy thereof, certified by the officer taking this proof, must be filed with the case. Evidence of *naturalization* is only required in final (*five-year*) homestead cases.)

6—577

alogical problem, but usually it is best to locate the individual of interest through the use of tax lists or deed indexes. In New England, search town meeting books and proprietors' records when they are indexed. But since the majority are not, tax lists or deed indexes will serve the purpose. Plat books and surveyors' records might also be useful as locating tools, but they are not always indexed or convenient to use.

Once the county or town of residence has been established, investigate the deeds and mortgages. If there are only one or two entries for the surname, they should be evaluated and copied verbatim; if many entries are located, copy the index references and make extracts of the actual records. Tape recorders and cameras make excellent copy tools for land records, but be careful of spelling and arrangement when using the tape recorder.

After the deeds, mortgages, and leases have been examined, plat books, surveyors' records, special agreements and contracts, and related records should be searched. Documents relating to antenuptial agreements and powers of attorneys should be noted when they are filed among the other land records; otherwise they should be located in their respective record volumes.

After searching local land records, you should search existing state records, then federal or national land records. However, keep in mind that land records pertaining to the public land states are in the National Archives while those for the colonial states remain in their respective town, county, and state land offices.

Documents and records other than those explained in this chapter may also be found among local, state, and federal land records; methods regarding their use may be determined that will supersede or supplement those listed here. However, the information presented serves as a guide and provides new motivation for research.

8 Military Records

Military records may not provide the solution to every family history problem in America, but they can certainly be used as a research supplement. The amount of genealogical and historical information contained in military records is surprising, and the number of persons who have been involved with the military since colonial times is astonishing.

A recent newspaper article indicated that more than 14 million veterans of World War II, 5 million veterans of the Korean conflict, and two hundred thousand veterans of the Vietnam War are still living in America. About 1.8 million veterans of World War I are still on government pension rolls, and ten thousand veterans of the Spanish-American War are still with us. Fewer then ten veterans of the Indian wars are still living, but even though the last veteran of the Civil War died in 1959, several widows of Civil War veterans are still collecting pensions.

Thousands of Americans were involved with the military prior to the Civil War, too, and Congress passed numerous acts providing benefits for them. No official records exist relating to veterans of the early colonial wars before the Revolution, but government records do exist after that date. A few local and state militia lists have been preserved that contain the names of some early colonial war participants—and some public records at the town, county, and state level give reference to them. But most personal information relating to the early periods is found in compiled regional and local histories or in specialized publications dealing with the conflict. *Soldiers in King Philip's War* by George Madison Bodge is an example.

Official military records have been preserved for the revolutionary war and later periods, though compiled service records for the Revolution are fragmentary. Some of the original records were lost in a fire that occurred in the offices of the Secretary of War on 8 November 1800. Other records were destroyed in 1814 when government buildings in Washington were ransacked and burned by the British, and another fire in 1973 destroyed many records at the National Personnel Records Center in St. Louis, Missouri.

Compiled service and pension files provide the most important information for family and local history. Some of the records contain considerable information; others contain very little. The service files are perhaps the greatest in number but are not necessarily the best in genealogical content. They relate to military personnel during their time in the service and include such records as enlistment and induction notices, registers and rosters, muster rolls, payrolls and vouchers, orders and citations, applications and recommendations for promotion, requests for leave, oaths of loyalty for some officers, disciplinary proceedings, medical histories, separation notices, and discharge papers.

The pension files usually pertain to individuals after separation from active service, but they are as important to family and local history as the service files—perhaps more so. They relate primarily to the obtaining and receiving of benefits by veterans, their widows, children, and other dependents. The files contain a variety of affidavits, depositions, claims, letters, personal documents, agency reports, and miscellaneous records.

Location and Accessibility

The National Archives and Records Service (NARS) is the official depository for records of military personnel separated from the U.S. Air Force, Army, Coast Guard, Marine Corps, and Navy. The records are housed mainly in two locations: the National Archives in Washington, D.C., and the National Personnel Records Center in St. Louis, Missouri. Some records are at the Washington National Records Center in Suitland, Maryland, and some World War I draftee records currently are housed at a federal records center in East Point, Georgia. The records of military personnel who are presently on active duty or in the Reserves or the National Guard remain with their respective organizations and units.

Records relating to military service that ended more than seventy-five years ago are available for public examination and copies can be provided, but records of military personnel who served within the last seventy-five years are subject to restrictions imposed under the Public Information Act of 1966. Although such records cannot be copied or made available for public examination, information from them may be furnished to searchers on request.

Military records in the National Archives may be inspected in person, and copies may be obtained without restriction. Copies also may be obtained through correspondence upon proper application. However limitations are in effect for records at the National Personnel Records Center in St. Louis, Missouri. Generally only requests from official sources and from members of veterans' immediate families—such as the father, grandfather(s), brother(s), and uncle(s)—will be honored. If the person whose records are requested is living, his written consent is required before any information will be supplied. The information furnished is usually limited to complete name and dates of service, but if needed to assure identification of the person or if specifically requested, such information as date and place of birth and name of father, mother, and wife is furnished.

Photocopies of unrestricted original documents are available for a fee. NARS will conduct a search for the documents if—in addition to the full name of the serviceman, the war in which he served, and the state from which he entered service—an inquirer can supply other identifying information. If the request concerns a navy enlisted man, the name of at least one vessel on which he served must be given, with approximate dates and, if possible, his place of enlistment.

If a file is found for the veteran in question, NARS will supply photocopies of documents that provide pertinent information about the veteran and his family. The inquirer will be billed for copies provided. The NARS staff is not permitted to read all documents in a file or to answer specific questions about them; however, if the inquirer wishes to have photocopies of all the papers in a file, they will be furnished for a moderate additional cost. If the name supplied by an inquirer is not the same as the name carried on the rolls, or if the unit is not known or is given incorrectly, the NARS staff may find it difficult to identify the serviceman's record. There are usually many servicemen with the same or similar names, and the name a serviceman listed on the rolls may differ from the name by which he was known to his family.

NARS can establish only relatively easy identifications. It cannot undertake extensive research or lengthy evaluation of conflicting or uncertain evidence in the records. If such research or evaluation is necessary, it will offer to furnish reproductions of all the records. In attempting to identify a serviceman when the information supplied is not sufficient, the NARS staff will try to match initials and spelling of the surname given in a standard list of variant spellings. If the staff is able to reduce the possibilities to a few individual records, it will attempt identification by comparing the records with any information the inquirer supplies that is likely to be useful for the purpose. If the serviceman's identity seems obvious or probable, NARS will furnish a photocopy of the record it thinks is correct.

Records in the National Archives

Military records in the National Archives at Washington, D.C., relate to (1) *volunteers* who performed service during an emergency and whose service was considered to be in the national interest during the period 1775–1902; (2) *regular army* enlisted personnel who served between 1789 and 31 October 1912 and officers who served between 1789 and 30 June 1917; (3) *navy* enlisted personnel who served between 1789 and 31 December 1885 and navy officers who served between 1789 and 31 December 1902; (4) *Marine Corps* enlisted personnel and officers who served between 1789 and 31 December 1895; (5) *Coast Guard* personnel who served in the Revenue Cutter Service, the Life Saving Service, and the Lighthouse Service between 1791 and 1919; (6) *Confederacy* personnel who rendered military service for the Confederate States between 1861 and 1865; and (5) *veterans pension files* based on federal military service 1775–1916 and *bounty land warrant application files* relating to claims based on wartime service 1775–1885.

Service files relating to volunteers. Service records of volunteer soldiers who fought in various wars from the revolutionary war through the Philippine insurrection cover the period 1775–1902. The compiled military service record consists of a card or cards on which is recorded information collected from muster rolls, returns, hospital registers, prison records, and other records. Cards for each war are arranged by state, military unit, and alphabetically by surname. The War Department program for compiled service records began some years after the Civil War to permit more rapid and efficient checking of military and medical records in connection with claims for pensions and other veteran's benefits.

The compiled military service record of each volunteer soldier is filed with similar records for other soldiers who fought in the same war and regiment or other unit. In addition to information about the soldier abstracted from original rolls, returns, registers, or other records, it sometimes contains—particularly for later wars—one or more original documents relating to the soldier. The record usually shows a soldier's presence or absence on certain dates. Typically, it also shows his rank, military organization, and term of service; sometimes it shows age, place of enlistment, and place of birth. Although it is of value for proving military service, it usually contains little genealogical information.

It should be noted that despite the War Department's efforts to assemble available information, many compiled service records are not complete. Full records of the participation of a given unit may not have been available. Also, a soldier may have served in a state militia unit that was not called into the service of the Continental, federal, or Confederate States governments. Records of such service, if available, are most likely to be in state archives or in the custody of the state adjutant general.

Service files relating to regular army personnel. Records at the National Archives relating to service in the regular army cover 1789–1917 for officers and 1789–1912 for enlisted men. They include service rendered during peacetime as well as wartime.

Records relating to officers are scattered among many files and vary in content, but usually they contain orders, muster rolls, returns of posts and military units, station books, War Department correspondence, and medical records.

Records relating to enlisted men include registers of enlistments, muster rolls of regular units, and medical records. The registers of enlistment are best for family history purposes, usually showing the soldier's name, age, place of birth, date and place of enlistment, occupation at enlistment, regiment and company, physical description, and date and reason for discharge or—where applicable—date of death or date of desertion (and sometimes of apprehension or return after desertion). The information in these diverse and scattered sources was never collected and organized into compiled service records as was done for volunteer soldiers.

Personnel records of officers separated from service after 30 June 1917, and of enlisted personnel separated after 31 October 1912, are in the National Personnel Records Center in St. Louis, Missouri, explained later in the chapter.

REGISTER OF ENLISTMENTS, UNITED STATES ARMY.

NO.	NAMES		When (1865)	Where	By Whom	Period	Town or County	State	AGE	OCCUPATION	Eyes	Hair	Complex'n	Height	REGIMENT	CO.	REMARKS
1041	Lathrop	Albert C.	December 8	Buffalo N.Y.	Capt. Kellogg	3 yrs	[illegible]	N.Y.	31	[illegible]	Blue	Dark	Dark	6	16 Inf.	F	Discharged Dec. 8 '68 by expiration of service at Memphis Tenn. a Pvt.
	Lengert	[illegible]	18				[illegible]	Germany	18	Laborer		Brown	Fair	5	16 Inf.	E	[illegible]
	Lake	George	5	Chicago Ill.	Lieut. [illegible]		Chicago	Ill.	20		Grey	Black			13 Inf.	H	Died Dec. 13 1865
	Leize	Robert	25					Germany	23	Shoemaker	Blue	Brown			36 Inf.	G	Discharged Dec. 25 '68 by expiration of service at Camp Douglas U.T. a Pvt.
	Lynch	Thomas	28					Ireland	2[illegible]	Soldier		[illegible]			13 Inf.	E	Discharged Dec. 28 '68 by expiration of service at Fort Bridger Wyo. T. a Sgt.
	Lord	Thomas	22	[illegible]	Lieut. [illegible]		[illegible]		[illegible]	Laborer	Grey				2d [illegible] Inf.	F	[illegible]
	Lacrs	William	[illegible]	[illegible] Mass.	[illegible]		[illegible]	Ireland	[illegible]	Soldier	[illegible]		Ruddy	2	G.S.		[illegible]
	Louis	Albert	[illegible]				Boston	Mass.	20	[illegible]		Dark	Light	2	11 Inf.	F	Died [illegible]
	Lockhart	David	22				[illegible]	[illegible]	[illegible]	Soldier	Dark	Brown	Ruddy		11 Inf.	F	Died July [illegible]
1050	Leonard	James	26				Boston	Mass.	[illegible]	Laborer	Blue		Light		G.S.		[illegible] Boston [illegible]
	Lacomte	Simon [illegible]	[illegible]	New Bedford Mass.	Lieut. [illegible]		Montreal	Canada	26	Clerk	Dark	Dark	Dark		2d Arty.		Died June [illegible]
	Long	James F.	27				New Bedford	Mass.	2[illegible]	Seaman	Grey	Black		3	5 Arty.		[illegible]
	Lyons	William	2	[illegible] Tenn.	Lieut. [illegible]		[illegible]	N.J.	[illegible]	Laborer	Blue	Dark			13 Inf.		Discharged [illegible] for Disability at Jefferson Bks. [illegible] a Pvt.
	Lenwood	[illegible]	[illegible]				Stockholm	Sweden	[illegible]	Sailor		Light	Light	5	1[illegible] Inf.	C	Discharged [illegible] by expiration of service at Fort [illegible] a Pvt.
	Lang	George	1	[illegible]	Capt. [illegible]		Stuttgart	Wurtemburg	2[illegible]	[illegible]	Grey	[illegible]	[illegible]	6	1 Cav.		Died [illegible]
	Lammerzahl	Albert	4	Chicago Ill.	[illegible]		[illegible]	Germany	[illegible]	Blacksmith	Blue	Dark	Light		2 Cav.		[illegible]
	Lilly	John	15				Fort Stanley	Canada	[illegible]	[illegible]	Hazel	Light			4 Inf.	A	[illegible]
	Lindgren	Johan	26				[illegible]	Sweden	[illegible]	[illegible]	Blue			7	1[illegible] Inf.	F	Died May [illegible]
	Lynch	Patrick	4	[illegible] Ky.	Lieut. [illegible]		New York	City	2[illegible]	Farmer		Brown			2d Inf.	[illegible]	Discharged [illegible] by expiration of service at Lebanon Ky. a Pvt.
1060	Lagren	[illegible]	2[illegible]	Springfield Ill.	Capt. Marshall			Norway	22	Laborer		Light			1[illegible] Inf.	F	Discharged [illegible] by expiration of service at Fort [illegible] a Pvt.
	Leonard	Robert	[illegible]	New York City	[illegible]		Dublin	Ireland	2[illegible]	[illegible]	Grey			6	10 Inf.	G	Discharged [illegible] by expiration of service at Fort Wadsworth [illegible] a Pvt.
	Denel	William	[illegible]				[illegible]	Germany	[illegible]	[illegible]		Brown			10 Inf.	F	Discharged [illegible] by expiration of service at Fort Wadsworth [illegible]
	Lane	John	4		Lieut. Merrill			N.Y.	2[illegible]	Laborer		Sandy		5	5 Arty.	K	Died June [illegible]
	Lockwood	Nathaniel	[illegible]	[illegible]			[illegible]		[illegible]	Soldier	Dark	Dark	Fair		1 Arty.	F	Died March [illegible]
	Larkin	[illegible]	30				[illegible]	[illegible]	[illegible]	Laborer	Blue	Brown			5 Cav.	F	Discharged [illegible] by expiration of service [illegible]
	Lasner	Thomas	2[illegible]	[illegible]	Lieut. [illegible]			Canada	21	Farmer	Dark	Dark			4 Inf.	F	Died March [illegible]
	Langerman	[illegible]	2[illegible]	[illegible]	[illegible]			Ireland	[illegible]	Farmer	Grey	Brown			1[illegible] Inf.	F	Discharged [illegible] by expiration of service at Fort [illegible]
	Lauder	James M.	2[illegible]	Cincinnati O.	[illegible]		[illegible]	[illegible]	2[illegible]	Soldier	[illegible]	Light			[illegible]		Discharged [illegible] by expiration of service at [illegible] a Sgt.
	Lauck	[illegible]	[illegible]	[illegible]	[illegible]		New York	N.Y.	21	Seaman		Brown			5 Arty.	H	Died June 20 '66
1070	Long	George W.	2[illegible]				[illegible]		22	Laborer	Hazel				10 Inf.	F	Discharged [illegible] by expiration of service at Fort Abercrombie D.T. a Pvt.
	Lanited	John	[illegible]				Lancaster	Penn.	21	[illegible]	Brown				10 Inf.	G	Discharged [illegible] by expiration of service at Fort Ripley Minn. a Pvt.
	Leane	[illegible]	2[illegible]				[illegible]		[illegible]	Laborer	Blue				[illegible] Inf.	K	Discharged June 26 [illegible] Charleston S.C. a Pvt.
	Larsens	[illegible]	2	[illegible]	Lieut. [illegible]		Dublin	Ireland	23		Grey	Light		6	[illegible] Arty.	F	Discharged [illegible]
	Lyndholm	John A.	2	[illegible]			[illegible]	Switzerland	33			Brown	Sandy	5	[illegible]		Died [illegible]
	Latchford	William	30	[illegible]			[illegible]	[illegible]	2[illegible]	Soldier	Blue	Brown	Fair	5	2[illegible]		Discharged [illegible] by expiration of service [illegible]
	Lee	George W.	1[illegible]	Sacramento Cal.	Lieut. McElroy		New Orleans	La.	20	Clerk	Hazel	Dark	Ruddy		2 Cav.		Discharged [illegible] by expiration of service at [illegible]
	Loebel	John	15				[illegible]	Saxony	35		Blue	Brown			2 Cav.		Discharged [illegible] by expiration of service at [illegible]
	Lorotte	[illegible]	2	[illegible]	Capt. [illegible]		[illegible]	[illegible]	2[illegible]	Soldier	[illegible]	[illegible]	Dark		8 Cav.	F	Died [illegible]
	Lowry	Albert	[illegible]				[illegible]	[illegible]	2[illegible]	Farmer	Blue	Light	Fair		8 Cav.		[illegible]
1080	Lee	Washington	[illegible]				[illegible]	[illegible]	[illegible]	[illegible]	[illegible]	Dark	[illegible]		8 Cav.		[illegible] Fort [illegible] a Saddler

The registers for the period 1789–1821 are arranged in two groups. The first group relates to service from 1789 to the end of the War of 1812 (15 May 1815). The second group relates to service from 17 May 1815 to 30 June 1821. One or more registers relate to soldiers whose surnames begin with a particular letter of the alphabet.

Registers of enlistment for the period 1 July 1821 through 31 October 1912 are arranged by the initial letter of the soldier's surname and chronologically by the month of enlistment. A single register may relate to a part of a year, a whole year, or more than one year. As the soldier's enlistment was received, an entry was made in the register and the number corresponding to the entry was added to it. The basic entries of name, enlistment date, place and period, nativity, age, and physical description were made from the enlistment papers. Other details were added later. The registers for the period 1821–1912 reflect, as do subsequent entries, the various organizations in which the soldier served and the date, place, reasons for, and character of his discharge. Most enlistment papers have two or more numbers, and it is presumed they were separately arranged at one time and then renumbered to correspond with their enlistment register entry number.

Enlistment papers were prepared for all enlisted men serving in the regular army except for principal musicians and drum majors. The enlistment papers reflect the agreement to serve a specified number of years and contain the soldier's name, date and place of enlistment, age and birthplace, brief physical description, and—in the case of a minor—the consent of his parent. In 1885 the name of an emergency addressee was added. The enlistment officer's signature and the signature or mark of the enlistee also appear on each enlistment paper. A new paper was prepared for each subsequent enlistment, and the reverse side included the name of the serviceman and his organization.

In 1894 a physical description and assignment card was prepared and filed with the enlistment papers. Such cards do not add materially to the personal data found on the enlistment paper, but they do show the name of the organization to which a soldier was initially assigned. Beginning in 1894 a station card is also found in the enlistment papers of hospital corps personnel. When a soldier served more than one enlistment, his enlistment papers are filed together in a single jacket. Enlistment papers are arranged in two series—1818 through 14 July 1894 and 15 July 1894 through 31 October 1912.

Records of army officers are found in the registers of enlistment, consolidated files, and official military communications. The adjutant general was charged with matters pertaining to the command, discipline, and administration of the military establishment; he has had the duties of recording, authenticating, and communicating to troops and individuals in the military service. His records relating to officers included enlistment papers, muster rolls, returns, reports of battles, official reports of all officers, reports of the status of the militia, reports of absences, records of court-martials, inventories of the effects of deceased soldiers and officers, communications relating to appointments, requests for warrants for soldiers, and requests for promotion.

Each communication received and retained was filed by the serial assigned chronologically each year. In 1863 efforts were made to create consolidated files relating to individual officers, but this was usually done only when such papers were needed in the course of regular business. Otherwise, the records of officers can be located only by a detailed search of the annual registers of letters sent and received by the adjutant general. In some instances military histories of officers were prepared, usually by the bureau or special office to which they were assigned.

In 1890 a new record-keeping system was employed by the War Department—the record card system, allowing for the continuous indexing and referencing of communications received. The records were not always filed together, but the system facilitated continuous referencing of communications about an individual and resulted in most officers' files being consolidated.

By a special act in 1815, annual registers of officers serving in the U.S. Army were published under the title *The Official Army Register.* Other published sources containing biographies and histories of officers are as follows:

Historical Register and Dictionary of the U.S. Army 1789–1903 by Francis B. Heitman (1903).

Biographical Register of the Officers and Graduates of the U.S. Military Academy by George W. Cullum (1891).

Army List and Directory by the War Department (1891–1942).

Official Army Register of the Volunteer Force of the United States Army for the Years 1861–65 (8 vols.) by the War Department (1865).

Official Register of Officers of Volunteers 1899–1900 in the Service of the U.S. by the War Department (1900).

Records of all officers whose service terminated during the period 1789 through 31 October 1916 are on file in the National Archives, but if service terminated after 1916, papers have been transferred to the National Personnel Records Center at St. Louis, Missouri.

Service files relating to navy and Marine Corps personnel. Records in the National Archives relating to navy and Marine Corps personnel include those pertaining to service in the revolutionary war during the period 1775–83; navy officers during 1798–1902 and enlisted men 1798–1885; and Marine Corps personnel during 1798–1895.

Records for the revolutionary war period are very fragmentary, including only such information as the serviceman's name and rank, the name of the vessel on which he served, and the dates of his service or the dates he was paid. The fires in 1800 and 1814 that were mentioned previously also took their toll among navy and Marine Corps personnel records.

Records relating to the service of commissioned officers in the navy after the Revolution but before 1846 give each officer's name, rank, state of birth, sometimes his age or date of birth, state of residence, and dates of service. Records for 1846 and later contain the above information and occasionally give the date and place of an officer's death in service or the date of his retirement.

Records relating to a navy enlisted man's service before 1846 usually give only his name and rating, the names of the vessels on which he served, and the dates of his service. Later records also give the enlisted man's age and place of birth and occasionally his place of enlistment.

Records of commissioned officers in the Marine Corps usually show each officer's name and rank and the date of his appointment or acceptance of a commission. They may also give his age and residence. Service records for enlisted marines usually show the man's name and age, and the date, place, and term of enlistment.

Service files relating to Coast Guard personnel. The United States Coast Guard was not created until 28 January 1915, but prior to that time it consisted of the Revenue Cutter and Life-Saving Services of the Department of the Treasury. The Bureau of Lighthouses of the Department of Commerce also became a part of the Coast Guard on 1 July 1939. Inspectors and engineers of the Lighthouse Service districts were officers of the army and navy; their records will be found under the branch they served in, but all other employees of the Lighthouse Service and inspectors, superintendents, keepers, and other employees of the Life-Saving Service were civilians. Their records are housed in the Washington National Records Center at Suitland, Maryland.

Records in the National Archives relating to Revenue Cutter Service officers date from 1791 to 1919. They usually show the date and place of birth and death for each officer, and they always show his date of appointment, promotions, special duty assignments, and names of vessels he served on. There are also applications for appointments and commissions as officers or cadets for the period 1833–90, copies of officers' commissions 1791–1909, and muster rolls and payrolls for the period 1832–1914. The muster rolls show each crew member's name, rating, number of days served during the reported month, transfers, and often termination of service. The muster rolls for enlisted men usually also show date and place of enlistment, place of birth, age, and physical description.

Service files relating to the Confederacy. Compiled service records for some individuals who served in the Confederate States army are in the National Archives at Washington, D.C. They contain little or no genealogical information, but they are of value for proving military service. Confederate pensions were issued by most of the southern states, but those records are in custody of the respective states. Details are included later in this chapter.

Before the Confederate government evacuated Richmond, Virginia, in April 1865, President Jefferson Davis directed all department heads to complete arrangements for leaving the capitol. Some records were boxed for rail transportation, clerks piled other records in the streets and set them afire, and other records were simply abandoned in the government offices. The central military records of the Confederate army were taken to Charlotte, North Carolina, by the adjutant and inspector general, who then transferred them to the Union commander. The records were taken to Washington, D.C., where they were preserved by the War Department along with other Confederate records captured by the Union army. In

1903 the Secretary of War persuaded the governors of most southern states to lend the War Department the Confederate military personnel records in possession of the states so they could be copied.

Over the years the records were arranged in various groupings with several thousand index cards created to identify facts pertaining to a particular individual. In 1903 legislation authorized the creation of Compiled Military Service Records for Confederate Veterans. They are in three parts, and each has been microfilmed. Part 1 consists of jacket envelopes for men who served in organizations connected with one of the Confederate states during 1861–1865; they are arranged alphabetically by state, branch of service, designation of organization, and alphabetically by the name of the individual. Part 2 consists of jacket envelopes for men who served in organizations raised directly by the Confederate government and not identified with any particular state. Part 3 consists of jackets known as the "General and Staff Officers' Papers," containing carded records of general officers, officers and enlisted men of the staff departments, and officers attached to other units.

A Consolidated Index to Confederate Veterans' Compiled Military Service Records has been created, and the microcopy numbers for it and for the three record groups follow:

Group 1:	
Alabama	M 311 (508 rolls); Index M 374 (49 rolls)
Arizona Territory	M 318 (1 roll); Index M 374 (1 roll)
Arkansas	M 317 (256 rolls); Index M 376 (26 rolls)
Florida	M 251 (104 rolls); Index M 225 (9 rolls)
Georgia	M 266 (607 rolls); Index M 226 (67 rolls)
Kentucky	M 319 (136 rolls); Index M 377 (14 rolls)
Louisiana	M 320 (414 rolls); Index M 378 (31 rolls)
Mississippi	M 269 (427 rolls); Index M 232 (45 rolls)
Missouri	M 322 (193 rolls); Index M 380 (16 rolls)
North Carolina	M 270 (580 rolls); Index M 230 (43 rolls)
South Carolina	M 267 (392 rolls); Index M 381 (35 rolls)
Tennessee	M 268 (359 rolls); Index M 231 (48 rolls)
Texas	M 323 (445 rolls); Index M 227 (41 rolls)
Virginia	M 324 (1,075 rolls); Index M 382 (62 rolls)
Group 2:	M 258
Group 3:	M 331 (275 rolls)
Consolidated Index:	M 253 (535 rolls)

The Consolidated Index contains the names of all military personnel in the compiled military service records. The cards give the name of the soldier, his rating or rank, the designation of the unit with which he served, and often information concerning the origin of the unit.

Other compiled records relating to the Confederacy also are available in the National Archives; under certain conditions they might help solve a particular pedigree problem. They include special files about individuals and businesses compiled by the War Department, Union provost marshals' records concerning certain individuals from the South, and special records relating to military and civilian personnel in prisons and in other situations.

A file compiled by the War Department on individual Confederate citizens or business firms 1861–65 is available on 1,240 rolls of microfilm (M 346). It contains original documents with cross-references to other compiled files and book records. Vouchers, receipts, affidavits, and correspondence relate to payments for materials purchased by or services performed for the army and navy. Other documents include abstracts of expenditures, contracts for armament, contractors' bonds, certificates of deposit, passes, powers of attorney and other documents.

The Union provost marshals' papers relating to civilians 1861–67 are available in two microfilm collections (M 345 and M 416) and might also be useful for genealogy. They contain papers relating to the arrest and trial of persons suspected of aiding or spying for the enemy, of disloyalty, and of other war crimes.

A file has also been compiled relating to military and civilian personnel 1861–65 (M 347). It contains correspondence, card abstracts, and cross-reference slips relating to officers, soldiers, civilian employers, citizens, Confederates in Union prisons, federals in Confederate prisons, and British subjects in Confederate service. The files are arranged alphabetically by surname (Colket and Bridges 1964).

Records relating to veterans who applied for pensions or bounty land. From the earliest days of English settlement in America, the colonies gave financial aid to persons disabled in military service and to dependents of persons killed in service. After the colonies declared their independence, the Continental Congress passed resolutions promising compensation to all who were disabled in the revolutionary war, to those who continued in service to the end of the war, and to widows or orphans of officers killed in the war. Compensation could be in money or land or both. Because the Continental Congress lacked funds, it first relied on the states to provide compensation but later took over the responsibility itself.

The first Congress under the Constitution approved an act making the United States responsible for payment of disability pensions that had been granted by states for service in the revolutionary war. Acts passed during the next three decades limited benefits to those disabled in service and to dependents of those who were killed in service or who died as a result of service. In 1818, however, Congress provided that every person who had served in the revolutionary war for nine months or until the end of the war and who was "in need of assistance from his country for support" should be pensioned. Later legislation removed the requirement of need.

Following the precedent set for revolutionary war veterans, Congress authorized pensions for those who served in succeeding wars, including the Indian wars, and for those who served in peacetime. Pensions for peacetime service have been limited to veterans who suffered service-connected disabilities or to dependents of men who died as a result of service. The records of pensions granted or applied for under many of these laws are in the National Archives. The pension files relate to claims based on service in the U.S. Army, Navy, or Marine Corps between 1775 and 1916.

Applications and supporting papers that the Secretary of War received through 8 November 1800 apparently were destroyed in the War Department fire of that date and in the fire of 1814. A few records relating to early claims still exist, and information from them has been summarized on cards filed with the revolutionary war pension and bounty-land warrant application files.

A typical pension file contains the application of the claimant, documents submitted as evidence of identity and service, and records of action taken on the claim. The claimant may have been a veteran or his widow, minor children, or other dependent. Since a claimant could have applied for a pension under several different acts, a pension file may contain more than one application from a claimant. It may also contain applications from several claimants because applications for pensions based on the service of one serviceman for a certain period were usually filed together. Documents submitted in support of some pension claims include affidavits attesting to service, pages from family Bibles, and copies of records or birth, marriage, and death. For service in the Civil War and later, a pension file may also include Bureau of Pensions' questionnaires sent out in 1898 and 1915, which contain genealogical information.

Pensions based on military service to the Confederate States of America were authorized by some southern states but not by the federal government until 1949. Inquiries about state pensions should be addressed to the state archives at the capitol of the veteran's state of residence after the war.

In 1776 and later the Continental Congress granted public land to those who remained in the armed forces until the end of the war or until discharged by the Congress and to dependents of those killed in the war. Laws passed between 1796 and 1855 also granted warrants for land to those who had served in the revolutionary war, the War of 1812, the Indian wars, and the war with Mexico. Bounty-land warrant application files relate to claims based on wartime service between 1776 and 3 March 1855.

The documents in a bounty-land warrant application file are similar to those in a pension file. They include the application of the claimant, who may have been a veteran or a veteran's widow or heirs, affidavits attesting to service, and the jacket on which action taken on the claim is noted. Since Congress enacted many laws relating to bounty lands, more than one application may be found in a file. Many of the application files relating to service in the revolutionary war and the War of 1812 have been combined with pension files.

Both pension and bounty-land warrant application files usually show the name, rank, and military unit of the veteran and the period of his service. If a veteran applied, the file usually shows his age or date of birth and place of residence at the time he applied, and sometimes his place of death. If his widow applied, the file shows her age and place of residence, her maiden name, the date and place of their marriage, and the date and place of her husband's death. When application was made on behalf of minor children or by heirs of the veteran, their names and sometimes their ages or dates of birth are shown.

A summary of the more important pension acts passed prior to the Civil War follows:

On 18 March 1818 Continental soldiers and marines were allowed pensions provided they were "in need of assistance from their country for support." This did not entitle any of the men serving in the militia or state troops to a pension, nor could the pension be given to anyone who was not in actual need.

On 1 May 1820 an additional act was passed stating that no person should receive a pension after 4 March 1820 "unless he exhibits a schedule of his whole estate and income, clothing and bedding excepted," and that the Secretary of War could strike from the pension list the names of persons who, in his opinion, were not in indigent circumstances.

On 15 May 1826 each surviving officer of the Revolution in the Continental Line who was enlisted to receive half pay by the Resolve of 21 October 1780 was allowed half pay for life beginning 3 March 1826—provided that no officer should receive more than full pay of a captain.

On 7 June 1832 surviving Indian spies and soldiers in the Continental Line, state troops, volunteers, or militia, were placed on the pension list, provided they had served six months; the amount of pay was to increase for length of service up to two years. In case of the death of the soldier between the times of payment of pension, his widow or his children were entitled to the amount due.

On 4 July 1836 a law was passed granting half pay for life to widows of revolutionary soldiers, provided they were married before the last term of service was performed. This privilege was extended on 3 March 1837 to those widows who had remarried after their husband's death, provided they were widows on 4 July 1836 and continued to remain widows thereafter.

On 7 July 1838 a pension for five years was granted to those widows who were married before 1 January 1794, and on the same day another act was passed granting the pension to widows whose husbands had died after 4 July 1836.

On 23 August 1842 the remarriage of widows claiming pensions under the Act of 7 July 1838 was not considered a bar to the pensions, provided the applicant was a widow at the time she made application; in any event, marriage caused a pension to stop automatically.

On 3 March 1843 the time of widows' pensions granted under the Act of 7 July 1838 was continued for one more year and on 17 June 1844 for four more years. On 2 February 1848 the pensions were continued for life, and on 29 July 1848 the date of marriage was extended to 1 January 1800. Not until 1853 were all restrictions as to date of marriage removed.

On 3 March 1855 Congress voted bounty land to all soldiers and sailors (or their legal representatives) who had served six weeks or more in any of the wars of the United States. Thus, some who could not obtain pensions because they had not served six months could and did obtain bounty lands.

The basic congressional act designed to benefit Civil War veterans, their widows, and certain other dependents was the Act of 14 July 1862. This act granted pensions to all veterans disabled in service after 4 March 1861 and to widows and children under sixteen years of age and other dependents of veterans who died in or as a result of such service. In an act of 27 June 1890, Congress extended pension benefits to veterans of the Civil War who had served ninety days and were honorably discharged and could not earn a living because of disabilities not service connected. Widows and minor children were also eligible for pension under certain conditions.

Disabled veterans of the Spanish-American War, the Philippine insurrection, and the Boxer uprising—and widows, minor children, and other dependents of veterans who were killed in or died as a result of service rendered in these wars—were eligible for pensions under the Act of 14 July 1862, which applied not only to the Civil War but also to all future wars in which the United States might engage. It was not until 16 July 1918 that the widows and minor children of these veterans could apply for pensions on the basis of the veterans' service alone. Surviving veterans of these wars did not receive pensions on the basis of service alone until the passage of a congressional act dated 5 June 1920.

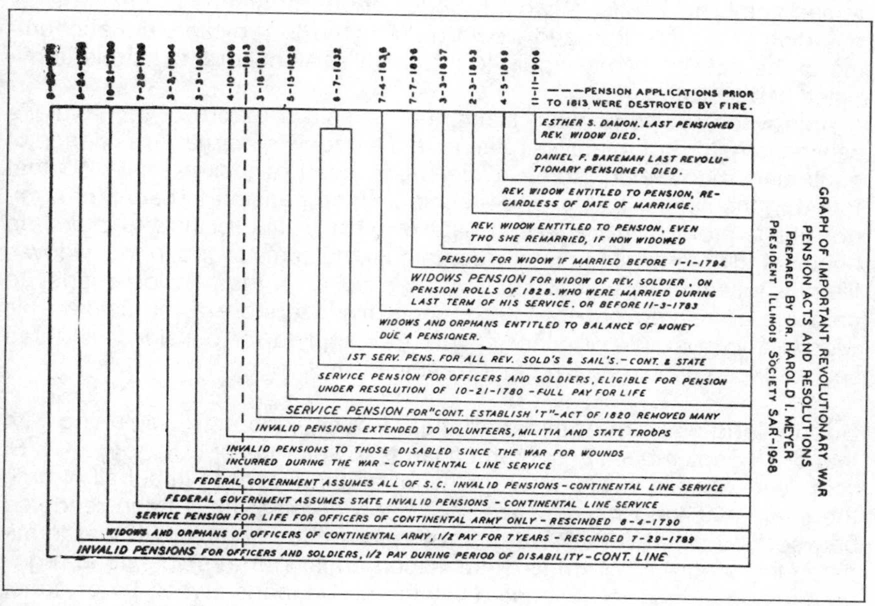

GRAPH OF IMPORTANT REVOLUTIONARY WAR PENSION ACTS AND RESOLUTIONS
PREPARED BY DR. HAROLD I. MEYER
PRESIDENT ILLINOIS SOCIETY SAR–1958

Revolutionary war pension records. Pension records relating to the revolutionary war were created under various congressional acts beginning 26 August 1776 and continuing into the twentieth century (the last revolutionary war widow did not die until 11 November 1906). The burden to provide the actual benefits first rested with the states and applied mainly to officers, but by 1818 pensions were provided others who served and were based upon need and length of service. The rate of pay was twenty dollars per month for officers and eight dollars for others. No provisions were made in the first laws to establish need, and as funds became limited some pensioners were dropped from the rolls. An act in 1821 restored many persons who had been previously dropped from the rolls, and pension requirements were gradually liberalized, especially by acts in 1828 and 1832. They allowed for widows' and orphans' benefits, though various later acts altered the requirements for proving a claim.

The Act of 1832 set guidelines by which applications for pensions were to be made. They required (1) a declaration of service rendered and proof of discharge or commission, (2) certification of an evaluation of evidence given by the court, (3) relinquishment of prior claims, (4) evidence of a minister or other witnesses acknowledging acquaintanceship with the claimant, (5) certification by the court of the veracity of the witnesses, and (6) statements as to birthplace, age, residence at the time of application, form of enlistment, names of officers under whom each period of service was rendered, and certification of the court clerk by signature and seal.

An application by a widow or by another in behalf of orphaned children required additional evidence. An application for a minor required all information to be furnished about a widow, and also evidence of her death or remarriage. The applicant would, under court appointment, be the legal guardian of the children and would be required to provide strict accounting of the pension monies paid to the minors. All minors' pensions terminated at age sixteen.

Approved widows pension claim files contain a record of the soldier's service, a record of affidavits relating to the widow's marriage, evidence of continued widowhood, some evidence of need, a jacket similar to that found in the soldier's files, and—if she claimed pension in behalf of a minor child—proof of his age and date of birth. A file relating to claims in behalf of minors would normally contain all the items found in the widow's file plus letters of guardianship. It was the policy of the pension agency to combine all related papers into a single file; therefore if the soldier, his widow, and guardian of minor children all applied for pensions, all three sets of papers would be filed in the same claim folder.

Bounty-land warrant application files. Bounty-land acts, beginning with that of 16 September 1776, granted lands to veterans of U.S. service, U.S. volunteers of state militia, or others who rendered service in behalf of or in the interest of the United States. Such service must have been rendered between the revolutionary war and passage of the act in 1856 that terminated the program. Warrants were issued entitling the recipients to a given acreage of land to be located within and on lands owned by or under the jurisdiction of the federal government. By the Act of 1776 warrants for the following acreages of land were granted to each qualified veteran upon the presentation of satisfactory evidence of service terminated by honorable discharge or death:

major general	1100 acres
brigadier general	850 acres
colonel	500 acres
lieutenant colonel	450 acres

major	400 acres
captain	300 acres
lieutenant	200 acres
ensign	150 acres
noncommissioned officer	100 acres
private	100 acres

Unfortunately, all papers relating to land warrants received in Washington, D.C., prior to the fire of 8 November 1800 were destroyed.

Bounty-land laws served to foster enlistments and to deter desertions or resignations. They were also given at subsequent dates as a reward for service rendered. Relatively few veterans applied for regular pensions, but many applied for and received bounty lands. As in the case of the pension certificate, the warrant was a negotiable instrument, and many warrants were sold for their ready cash value to land speculators.

After the revolutionary war, grants of land based upon military service were limited to 160 acres. During the Mexican War (1856–48) noncommissioned officers and other enlisted men serving in either U.S. or volunteer regiments were entitled to receive 160 acres of land or one hundred dollars in script for twelve months' service. Those serving less than twelve months were entitled to twenty-five dollars in script or forty acres of land.

An act of 3 March 1855 provided 160 acres to all who had served fourteen days or more in any battle in any war in which the United States had been engaged from 1790 to the passage of the act. Revolutionary war veterans who had received less than 160 acres could also apply under the act.

A claim file for bounty land may include several approved claims and some disapproved claim papers. As in the case of a pension claim, satisfactory evidence of service was required. The files contain little more genealogical information than is normally found in the service files except in the case of a claim by a widow or legal guardian—then additional genealogical data might be included. A soldier's claim will, if based upon volunteer service, contain an application stating his age, residence, alleged service, reference to previous warrants issued, and certification by a court clerk. A regular army soldier generally proved his service by presentation of his original discharge certificate. A widow or legal guardian had to follow almost the same process of assembling and submitting evidence to prove relationship as that followed in a pension claim.

There are 450,000 separately filed bounty-land claim folders in the National Archives, and all papers relating to a particular claim have been filed together. Each file includes the warrant number, the act, the acreage granted, the name of the veteran, his rank, and his organization.

The revolutionary war pension files and bounty-land warrant application files are serviced by both a published and microfilmed index. The National Genealogical Society in Washington, D.C., published an index to the files serially in their *Quarterly* beginning in March 1943. In 1966 they published the same information in a single volume; the Genealogical Publishing Company of Baltimore published the serial index in one volume the following year. The National Archives also created a microfilm copy of the index.

As part of their contribution to the American bicentennial celebration, the National Archives microfilmed the jacket covers and all documents in the revolutionary war pension and bounty-land warrant application files and made them available to the public. The LDS genealogical library in Salt Lake City acquired the collection on two thousand reels of microfilm; it is arranged alphabetically by the name of each applicant.

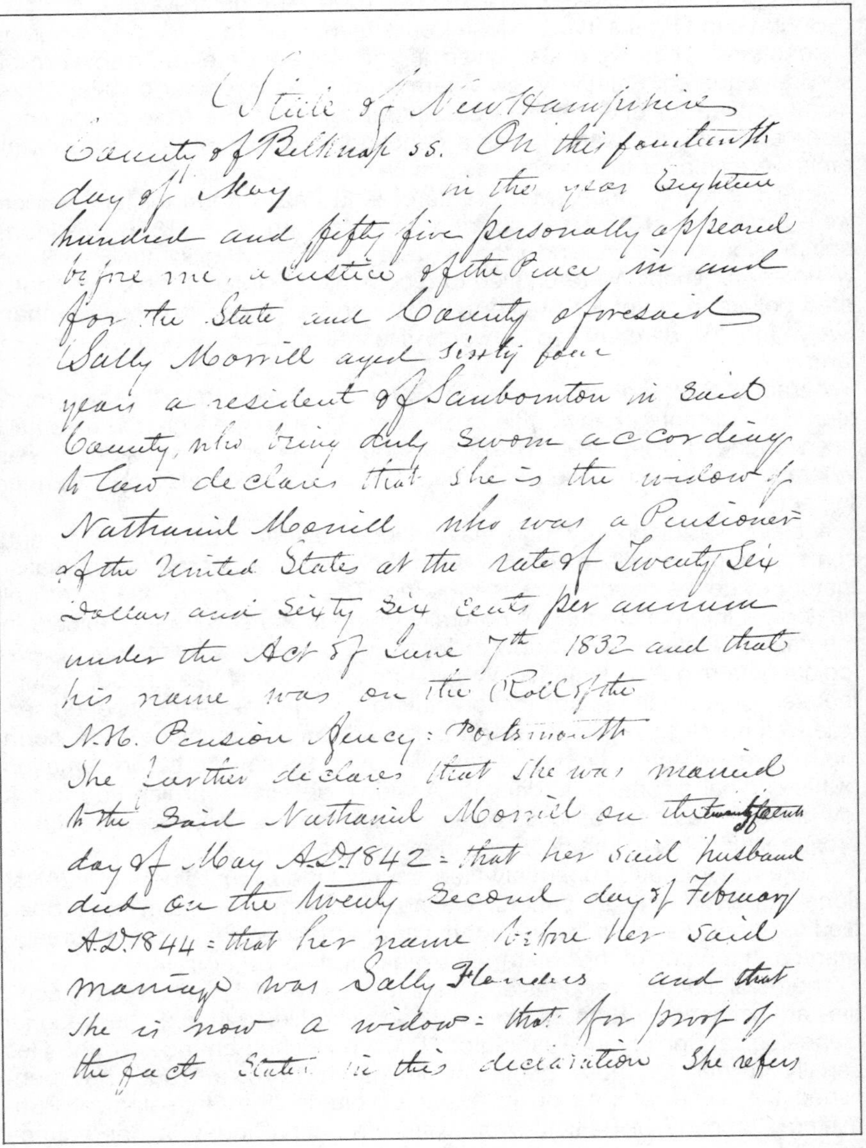

State of New Hampshire
County of Belknap ss. On this fourteenth
day of May in the year Eighteen
hundred and fifty five personally appeared
before me, a Justice of the Peace in and
for the State and County aforesaid
Sally Morrill aged sixty four
years a resident of Sanbornton in said
County, who being duly sworn according
to law declares that she is the widow of
Nathaniel Morrill who was a Pensioner
of the United States at the rate of Twenty Six
Dollars and Sixty Six cents per annum
under the Act of June 7th 1832 and that
his name was on the Roll of the
N.H. Pension Agency: Portsmouth
She further declares that she was married
to the said Nathaniel Morrill on the fourteenth
day of May A.D. 1842 = that her said husband
died on the twenty second day of February
A.D. 1844 = that her name before her said
marriage was Sally Flanders and that
she is now a widow = that for proof of
the facts stated in this declaration she refers

For more details consult *Guide to Genealogical Records in the National Archives* by Colket and Bridgers and *U.S. Military Service and Pension Records Housed at the National Archives* by James D. Walker.

United Empire Loyalists. After the Treaty of Paris in 1783, both the United States and Great Britain provided means for those who suffered losses because of their loyalty to the British Crown to claim compensation from the British government. Records created as a result of the claims have been filed in the Public Record Office, London, as part of the records in the custody of the Exchequer and Audit Department. They are titled Claims, American Loyalists, Series I (A.O. 12) and Series II (A.O. 13); they consist of 146 volumes and more than 140 bundles of records. The collection was microfilmed in London on behalf of the Public Archives of Canada, and the LDS genealogical library in Salt Lake City acquired a copy.

A typescript name index to both series has been microfilmed and is available at Salt Lake City (GS Film 162,010). The collection at Salt Lake City is on 173 reels of microfilm (GS Film 366,693—366,869) and was microfilmed according to bundle numbers as follows:

1–10	Supplied donations
11–16	New York claims
17–20	New Jersey claims
18–22	New Brunswick claims
23	New Hampshire claims
24–26	Nova Scotia claims
27–33	Virginia claims
34–38	Georgia claims
39–40	Maryland claims
41–42	Connecticut claims
43–51	Massachusetts claims
51–52	New Hampshire claims
54–57	New York—temporary assistance
58	Virginia claims
59	Virginia, Rhode Island, Vermont, New Hampshire, and Bahamas claims
59–62	Maryland support claims
63–67	New York support claims
68–69	Rhode Island support claims
70–72	Pennsylvania claims
73–75	Massachusetts assistance
76	Connecticut claims
79	Miscellaneous letters
80	Late Claims, South Carolina and Pennsylvania
81–85	Canada claims
86–107	Miscellaneous letters
108–116	New York assistance
117–24	North Carolina assistance
125–35	South Carolina assistance
136	South Carolina and Georgia assistance
137–40	Miscellaneous papers

The genealogical library in Salt Lake City also has an excellent collection of compiled and published material relating to Loyalists.

Old wars series pension records. The "old wars" pension application files relate to claims based on death or disability incurred in service, both peacetime and wartime, between the end of the revolutionary war (11 April 1783) and 4 March 1861. The series does not include files relating to claims based on death or disability incurred in service in the War of 1812. It does, however, include a few files for those whose death or disability claims are based on service in the Civil War before 14 July 1862. The series consists of several subseries: Mexican War death or disability files, Civil War death or disability files, and miscellaneous service death or disability files. The miscellaneous subseries contains claims relating to service in the various Indian wars and in the regular establishment. All War of 1812 death or disability claims are interfiled with the War of 1812 pension application files whose claims are based on service alone. Some death or disability claims based on service in the War of 1812, the Mexican War, the Civil War, and the Indian wars have been consolidated with other pension application files relating to claims based solely on service rendered.

The files within each of the subseries of the old wars pension application files are arranged alphabetically by name of veteran. Within the miscellaneous subseries, the files are arranged not only alphabetically but also chronologically by the period of service. An alphabetical name index on seven rolls of microfilm covers the period 1815–1926 (microcopy T-316).

War of 1812 pension records. The War of 1812 pension application files relate to claims based on service between 1812 and 1815. The claims include those based on death or disability incurred in service as well as those based on service alone. Some War of 1812 bounty-land warrant application files are interfiled with the pension files. The application files are arranged alphabetically by the name of the veteran. The face side of each jacket or envelope has been reproduced on 102 rolls of microfilm and arranged alphabetically by the name of the veteran (microcopy M-313).

The records are similar to those of the revolutionary war period, though the pension acts relating to the War of 1812 were passed several years after termination of the war. The first service pension act exclusively for veterans of the War of 1812 was passed on 14 February 1871, fifty-six years after the war ended. It granted pensions to those who served sixty days or to their widows if married prior to the treaty of peace that took place on 17 February 1815. An act on 9 March 1878 reduced the service provision to fourteen days and removed the marriage date restriction.

Indian wars pension records. The pension application files in the Indian wars series relate to claims based on service performed in various Indian wars and disturbances between 1817 and 1898. The claims are primarily those based on service alone and were filed from 1892 to 1926.

The files are arranged in four subseries numerically by either the application number or the certificate number, depending on the class of the claim. The four subseries are designated as (1) Indian survivors' originals, (2) Indian survivors' certificates, (3) Indian widows' originals, and (4) Indian widows' certificates. An alphabetical name index on twelve rolls of microfilm covers the period 1892–1926 (microcopy T-318).

Mexican War pension records. The Mexican War pension application files relate to claims based on service between 1846 and 1848. The claims are chiefly those based on service alone and filed between 1887 and 1926. Pension legislation for Mexican War veterans and their widows was passed on 29 January 1887, thirty-nine years after the war. It provided pensions to soldiers and sailors who had served at least sixty days—if they had reached age sixty-two or were disabled or dependent—and to their widows or orphans.

The Mexican War pension application files consist of four subseries: (1) Mexican survivors' originals, (2) Mexican survivors' certificates, (3) Mexican widows' originals, and (4) Mexican widows' certificates. The files in the series of originals are arranged numerically by the original numbers assigned the claims when they were submitted, and the files in the certificate series are arranged numerically by the certificate numbers assigned the claims when they were approved.

An alphabetical name index on fourteen rolls of microfilm covers the period 1887–1926 (microcopy T-317).

Civil War pension records. The basic act of Congress designed to benefit Civil War veterans was dated 14 July 1862. It applied not only to the Civil War but also to all future wars in which the United States might become engaged. It authorized pensions to veterans disabled in service after 4 March 1861, to their widows, to their children under sixteen years of age, and to other dependents. Under the Act of 27 June 1890, Congress extended pension benefits to any veteran who had served ninety days, who was honorably discharged, and who could not earn a living because of nonservice disabilities. Widows and minor children were also eligible under certain conditions.

Under the Act of 14 July 1862, disabled veterans of the Spanish-American War, the Philippine insurrection, and the Boxer uprising, their widows and minor children, and dependents of veterans who were killed in or died as a result of service rendered in these wars, were also eligible for pensions. It was not until the Act of 16 July 1918 that widows and minor children of these veterans could apply for pensions on the basis of the veteran's service alone. And surviving veterans of these wars did not receive pensions on the basis of service alone until the Act of 5 June 1920.

Service and pension files of volunteers serving in the Civil War with the Union army contain more personal information than those pertaining to earlier wars. Some early enlistments (1861–62) were for very short periods and reflect little more than enlistment and discharge information, but records for longer periods are more comprehensive. The files in the Civil War and Later series chiefly relate to claims based on service between 1861 and 1934, excluding Confederacy and World War I veterans. The files in this series may, however, include some papers based on service rendered as early as 1817.

The pension files are divided into nine subseries, each arranged numerically. The subseries are (1) navy survivors' originals, (2) navy survivors' certificates, (3) navy widows' originals, (4) navy widows' certificates, (5) survivors' originals, (6) survivors' certificates, (7) widows' originals, (8) widows' certificates, and (9) C and XC files. The first four subseries relate to claims submitted between 1861 and 1910 and are based on service in the navy between 1861–1910. The next four subseries relate to claims submitted between 1861 and 1934 for service in the United States Army and to claims submitted between 1910 and 1934 for service in the United States Navy. These claims were based on death or disability incurred in service and on service alone from 1861–1917. The C and XC subseries include all types of claims filed between 1861 and 1934 and are based on service between 1817–1934, excluding World War I service.

There is an alphabetical index on 544 rolls of microfilm covering the period 1861–1934 (microcopy T-288) for pensions based on Civil War service in the Union forces. There is also an Organization Index on 764 rolls of microfilm (microcopy T-289) arranged alphabetically by name of state, numerically by regiment, alphabetically by company, and alphabetically by the veteran's name.

There is also a card index known as the Remarried Widow's Index and one known as the C and XC Index. The Remarried Widow's Index is an incomplete listing of widows' pension claims based on their first husband's service. The index lists a widow's remarried name and the name of her former husband. The C and XC Index shows the new numbers assigned to some previously approved claims originally numbered under an elaborate system employed by the Pension Bureau prior to the introduction of the flat file or C and XC system. A Pension Payment Card Index also exists for files after 1907, listing the pensioner's name, pension agency, amount of payment and increases, payments made, and the individual's date of death. Occasionally the name of the heir who received the death benefits is listed.

Documents contained in the pension claim files can be as few as six pages and as many as several hundred, but significant genealogical data usually can be found on fewer than ten pages. The documents are similar in format and content to those contained in pension files of earlier wars, but sometimes are a little more inclusive.

Civil War draft records also were created under the Act of 3 March 1863. They relate to the part of the United States under Union control and include single men between the ages of twenty and thirty-five years and married men between thirty-five and forty-five years. The records include consolidated lists and descriptive rolls.

The consolidated lists are the principal records of the Washington, D.C. office of the Provost Marshal General's Bureau relating to individual men. They are arranged by name of state and enrollment or congressional district. Most are bound volumes. They are divided as follows: (1) persons subject to military duty between the ages of twenty and thirty-five and unmarried persons subject to military duty above age thirty-five and under

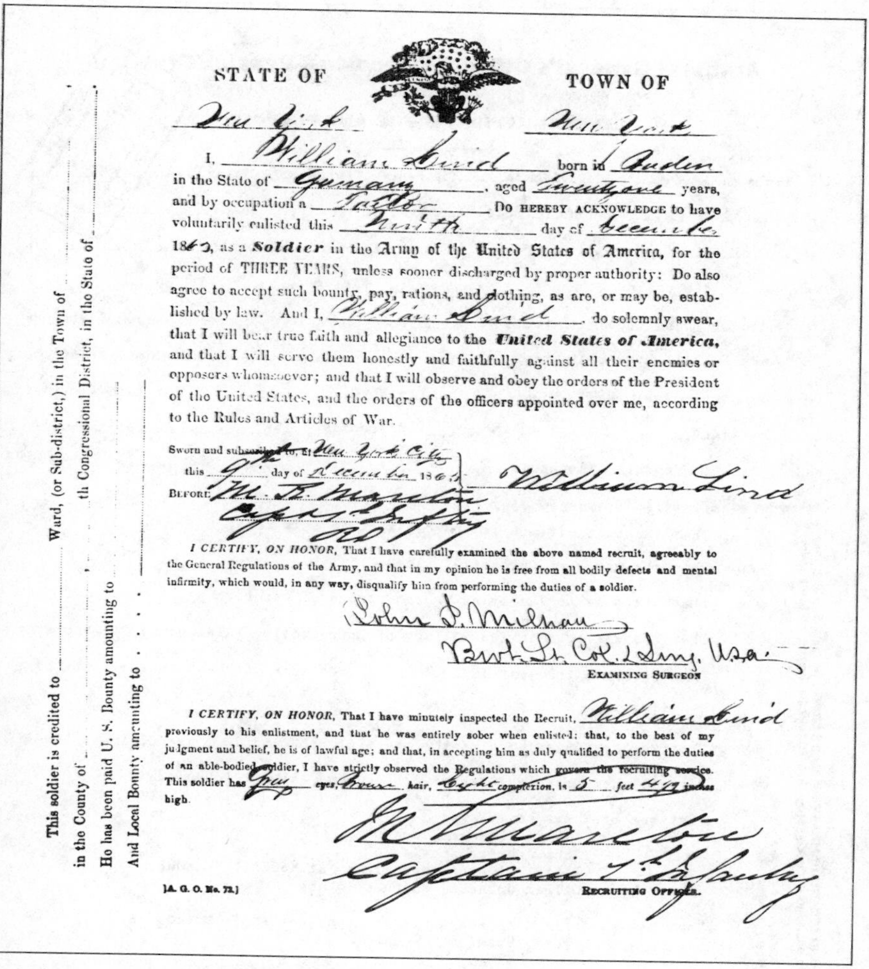

STATE OF New York TOWN OF New York

I, William Lind born in Baden in the State of Germany, aged Twenty one years, and by occupation a Tailor Do hereby acknowledge to have voluntarily enlisted this Ninth day of December 186_, as a **Soldier** in the Army of the United States of America, for the period of THREE YEARS, unless sooner discharged by proper authority: Do also agree to accept such bounty, pay, rations, and clothing, as are, or may be, established by law. And I, William Lind, do solemnly swear, that I will bear true faith and allegiance to the **United States of America**, and that I will serve them honestly and faithfully against all their enemies or opposers whomsoever; and that I will observe and obey the orders of the President of the United States, and the orders of the officers appointed over me, according to the Rules and Articles of War.

Sworn and subscribed to, at New York City this 9th day of December 186_ BEFORE M. R. Marston Capt 1st Infty [illegible]

William Lind

I CERTIFY, ON HONOR, That I have carefully examined the above named recruit, agreeably to the General Regulations of the Army, and that in my opinion he is free from all bodily defects and mental infirmity, which would, in any way, disqualify him from performing the duties of a soldier.

John S. Milhau
Bvt. Lt. Col. & Surg. USA
EXAMINING SURGEON

I CERTIFY, ON HONOR, That I have minutely inspected the Recruit, William Lind previously to his enlistment, and that he was entirely sober when enlisted; that, to the best of my judgment and belief, he is of lawful age; and that, in accepting him as duly qualified to perform the duties of an able-bodied soldier, I have strictly observed the Regulations which govern the recruiting service. This soldier has Grey eyes, Brown hair, Light complexion, is 5 feet 4½ inches high.

M. R. Marston
Captain 1st Infantry
RECRUITING OFFICER.

[A. G. O. No. 72.]

This soldier is credited to ____ Ward, (or Sub-district,) in the Town of ____
in the County of ____ th Congressional District, in the State of ____
He has been paid U. S. Bounty amounting to ____
And Local Bounty amounting to ____

age forty-five, (2) married men over thirty-five and under forty-five, and (3) volunteers. Entries in each class are arranged alphabetically by the initial letter of the surname. A typical entry shows each man's name; place of residence; age as of 1 July 1863; occupation; marital status; state, territory, or country of birth; and—if a volunteer—the designation of his military organization.

The descriptive rolls or lists are the principal records of the enrollment districts relating to individual men. They are arranged by name of state and the number of enrollment or congressional district. The rolls are chiefly in the form of bound volumes, but the entries vary considerably from district to district. Some are not indexed, some are indexed by the initial letter of the surname, and some are indexed according to the place of residence. In addition to information corresponding to the consolidated lists, the records include a personal description, the exact place of birth,

Adjutant General's Office, Wisconsin—Pension Division

CIVIL WAR DIVISION 1917

GENERAL AFFIDAVIT FOR ANY PURPOSE

In the matter of the Widow's Pension Claim Mary P. Dill

No. 1,095,057 account of Daniel J. Dill (Here give soldier's name.)

late a Colonel (Grade), of Co "____," 30th. Regiment Wisconsin Vol. Inf.

State of Wisconsin, County of Pierce } ss.

On this 15th. day of June, A. D. 1917, personally appeared before me Mary P. Dill, the claimant, a respectable citizen, entitled to credit, who being duly sworn, says that she is a resident of Prescott, in the County of Pierce, State of Wisconsin, her postoffice address is Prescott, Wisconsin, and is 72 years old; [illegible] dec[illegible].

That the said affiant is the claimant in this case;

That she was born October 22, 1844;

That there is no family or church record of her birth;

That she was born in the Village of Griggsville, Pike County, Illinois;

That prior to the year 1878 birth records were not kept in the State of Illinois;

That during the summers of the years of 1850 and 1860 the claimant lived with her parents, Stephen Johnson and Abigail Johnson;

That her brothers names are;
William Johnson, now dead,
John Johnson, now dead,
Elliot Johnson, now living at Kendall, Kansas,
Oliver Johnson, address unknown,

That her sister's name was Annie Johnson, now Annie Morris, of Ogden, Utah.

Mary P. Dill

WITNESSES MUST STATE THEIR MEANS OF KNOWLEDGE of facts to which they testify, and write their names immediately after their statements, leaving no blank space over their signatures.
When affiant signs by mark two witnesses attest.
Jurat and Seal of Magistrate on other side.

PENSION L JUN 22 1917 U. S. OFFICE.

and whether he was accepted or rejected for military service. Some of the entries are incomplete. To use the records, you must know the congressional district in which the man was living. This can be determined from the Congressional Directory for the Second Session of the Thirty-Eighth Congress of the United States of America (Washington, D.C., 1865).

The National Archives also has other miscellaneous record collections relating to Civil War servicemen, including records of Burials at U.S. Military Installations and Applications for Headstones. The records of burials at U.S. military installations are dated chiefly from 1861 through 1914 and include burial registers, compiled lists of Union soldiers buried at the U.S. Soldiers' Home, and compiled lists of Union soldiers buried at national cemeteries.

The burial registers contain records of burials from 1861 through 1914 (with a few as late as 1939) at the U.S. Soldiers' Home in Washington D.C., and at national cemeteries, forts, and post cemeteries in Cuba, the Philippines, Puerto Rico, and China. Filed also are a few registers for burials at private cemeteries. Most registers are arranged alphabetically by the name of the installation; as a minimum they show each soldier's name, military organization, and date and place of burial. The registers for the U.S. Soldiers' Home also show the soldier's rank; the town, county, and state of residence before enlistment; the name and residence of his widow, relative, or friend; his age; his nativity; the cause, date, and place of his death; the date of his burial; and sometimes the place of his burial.

The compiled lists of Union soldiers buried at the U.S. Soldiers' Home relate to burials between 1861 and 1918. The entries are arranged alphabetically by initial letter of the surname, and there are separate lists arranged by the name of the state. A typical entry usually shows the name of the soldier, his military organization, the date of his death, and the place of his burial.

The compiled lists of Union soldiers buried in national cemeteries relate chiefly to burials during the years 1861 through 1865, but some are as late as 1886. They are arranged alphabetically by state of burial. The lists for each state are divided into three parts; on one the names are arranged by cemetery, on another by military organization, and on another alphabetically by the initial letter of the surname of the soldier. Lists arranged by surname, however, exist only for Connecticut, Delaware, District of Columbia, Iowa, Maine, Maryland, Massachusetts, Michigan, New Hampshire, New Jersey, Pennsylvania, Rhode Island, Vermont, and Wisconsin. A typical entry usually shows the name of the soldier, his military organization, the date of his death, and the place of his burial.

Lists of Union soldiers buried in public and private cemeteries during the Civil War are published in Quartermaster General's Office *Roll of Honor* (Washington, D.C., 1865–1871). Entries are arranged by the name of the cemetery and alphabetically by the name of the soldier, showing his date of death. Accompanying the volumes is a place index to volumes one through thirteen entitled *Alphabetical Index to Places of Interment of Deceased Union Soldiers* (1868). The National Archives has an unpublished place index to all volumes. The Memorial Division, Quartermaster General's Office, Washington, D.C., has an alphabetical card file identifying nearly all soldiers who were buried in national cemeteries and other cemeteries under its jurisdiction from 1861 to the present time.

The Applications for Headstones are dated 1879 through 1925 and relate to servicemen who were buried in private village or city cemeteries. Under terms of an act approved 3 February 1879, headstones were erected by the government at the graves of Union servicemen. Headstones later were erected at the graves of servicemen of the revolutionary war and other wars in which the United States engaged. Most applications are arranged by the state of burial and the name of the county, giving the date of application. A few applications relating to servicemen buried at branches of the National Home for Disabled Volunteer Soldiers are arranged by the name of the branch and the date of application. Each application shows the name of the serviceman, his rank and military organization, the date of his death, the name and location of the cemetery in which he was buried, and the name and address of the applicant for the headstone.

Records in the National Personnel Records Center

Modern military records relating to the United States Army, Air Force, Navy, Marine Corps, and Coast Guard are housed at the National Personnel Records Center in St. Louis, Missouri, except records for those who are currently on active duty, in the reserves, or in the National Guard. Their records remain in the custody of their assigned organizations and units.

Records at the National Personnel Records Center include those relating to army officers separated from the service after 30 June 1917 and enlisted personnel separated after 31 October 1912; Air Force officers and enlisted personnel separated after September 1947 (date the Department of the Air Force was established); naval officers separated after 1902 and enlisted personnel separated after 1885; Marine Corps officers and enlisted personnel separated after 1895; and Coast Guard officers separated after 1928 and enlisted personnel separated after 1914. Records of civilian employees of preceding agencies of the Coast Guard (Revenue Cutter Service, Life-Saving Service, and Lighthouse Service) for the period 1865–1919 are also at St. Louis.

For the most part, records at the National Personnel Records Center consist of individual files in which significant papers pertaining to service are filed. They are usually in a single jacket or folder known as the Service Record or 201 File. Officers' personnel records cover separated regular army officers and active duty National Guard officers; reserve officers if deceased; nurses, contract surgeons, field clerks, and Public Health Service officers commissioned in the U.S. Army; and officers of the Philippine Scouts. Enlisted men's records cover members of the Specialist Corps, Russian Railway Corps, Student Army Training Corps, Philippine Scouts, former members of the National Guard, and reservists if deceased. A clear-cut distinction between regular and nonregular service does not persist after 1917.

As mentioned previously, a fire at the National Personnel Records Center destroyed many records in 1973.

9 Miscellaneous Sources and Applied Research

Several other record groups that do not fall conveniently under any of the categories covered in previous chapters contain useful information for family and local history—such miscellaneous sources as those relating to private social and commercial establishments, the North American Indians, and immigration.

Records relating to private social and commercial establishments can be further subdivided as follows:

- business and employment records
- school records
- medical records
- records of morticians, coroners, and medical examiners
- records of fraternal, patriotic, and hereditary societies

Sources pertaining to North American Indians are classified under the following:

- oral history and tradition
- tribal and agency records
- Indian census records
- overlapping records of the white man

Sources dealing with American immigration include the following:

- ship passenger lists
- oaths and declarations
- records referring to the immigrant ancestral home

Outlining the Problem

Each family or local history problem must be considered individually and evaluated according to time and place, and all pertinent information should be listed before the actual investigation of source material begins. After basic genealogical and historical facts are identified and listed, then possible sources can be outlined to guide you in a logical research procedural pattern.

The following example shows how one student outlined a research problem and listed possible sources for investigation:

Social-Commercial Records That Might Exist for One of my Ancestors, William Stennett Poppleton, Who Lived from 1844 to 1923

William Stennett Poppleton was born 14 August 1844 in Moulton, Lincs., England. He was the oldest of six children born to William Poppleton and Sarah Stennett. His father became a member of the Church of Jesus Christ of Latter-day Saints in 1852 and emigrated to America that same year, leaving his family in England. He at first located near St. Louis, Missouri, where he worked to earn money to bring his family to America.

His wife and family arrived in America in the fall of 1853 and joined young William's father near St. Louis. The family next lived near Genoa, Nebraska, from 1856 to 1860. In the spring of 1860 a member of the Church hired young William to drive a four-mule team across the plains to Utah. Young William separated from his family and arrived in Bountiful, Utah, the fall of 1860 and soon after moved to Cache Valley.

On 9 December 1865 he married Celia Knox Riggs of Wellsville, and they had eleven children. On 6 June 1884 he married Emma Mitton as a plural wife, and they had nine children.

About 1886 the anti-polygamy crusade started. William went underground using the assumed name of Wm. Grey. With some other men of the Church he went to Mexico, but he did not stay long. He returned to Utah and worked as a carpenter for the Union Pacific Railroad. In 1888 he went to Rock Springs, Wyoming, with some other Church men and worked in the mines.

During 1888 he returned and was arrested three times for polygamy and paid a fine of eighty dollars each time. In 1890 he was arrested again for polygamy and served forty-five days in the state penitentiary. After the manifesto he was permitted to live with his wives in Wellsville.

He worked in various stores and small businesses in Wellsville. For sixteen years he was Cache County road superintendent and for eight years a town councilman. He was a prominent member of the Home Dramatic Company, and for thirty years he was a member of the Brass and String Band. He held numerous church positions in the Wellsville Ward.

He enjoyed remarkable health until he was seventy years old when his health became poor and he underwent several critical bladder operations.

He died 27 August 1923 in Wellsville, Cache County, Utah.

From this sketch of the life of William Stennett Poppleton I would hope that information of a genealogical nature would be found concerning him in social and commercial records at the following general locations:

a. School administration offices (1) near St. Louis where the family lived from 1853 to 1856, (2) near Genoa, Nebraska, where the family lived from 1856 to 1860, and (3) from 1860 on in the Bountiful and Wellsville, Utah, areas.
b. The Union Pacific Railroad offices in Ogden, Utah; the Cache County Road Commission in Logan; offices of a mine in Rock Springs, Wyoming; Wellsville town offices where he served as a councilman; and possibly some of the small business firms where he worked in Wellsville. A note in his wife's file indicates that he worked at Baugh Bros. store in Wellsville at one time.

c. With his active participation in dramatic and musical organizations in Cache Valley there should be considerable information about him in newspapers and possibly local histories of the area to be found in libraries in Logan, Salt Lake City, and possibly elsewhere.
d. The state penitentiary where he served time for practicing polygamy and other offices where he paid fines.
e. Doctors offices in Wellsville, Logan, and possibly other towns where he worked during his life.
f. The hospital in Logan where his bladder operations likely were performed as this is the only place closer than Ogden where there was a hospital at the time.
g. The mortuary offices in Logan, the nearest to Wellsville.
h. Coroner's office only if further search should indicate something unusual or extreme about his death.
i. Possibly insurance records in Logan or Salt Lake City.
j. Possibly suppliers of road building supplies in the Cache Valley, Ogden, and Salt Lake areas.

Private Social and Commercial Sources

Ours has been a free enterprise system, with small private organizations as well as large corporate entities influencing the social and economic lives of the people. Whether large or small, public or private, social or commercial, all have used individuals and families to accomplish their goals—if not through labor and management, then as purchasers and users of available goods and services. If an individual did not build cars and wagons, he bought them; if he was not the doctor, he may well have been the patient. If he did not preach the sermons, perhaps he became a member of the congregation. If he was not the mortician, he may have been the embalmed. From the point of view of the researcher, these actions and circumstances have resulted in records that can benefit family and local history.

Business and employment records. Most private organizations have maintained records of their members and employees by name, date, and place. Records relating to labor and management are commonplace in our economic system, and those pertaining to cash or credit purchases also are important. Some of the more important deal with employment and termination of employment; the training and advancement of personnel; payroll, insurance, and retirement records; social security records; affiliation with union and labor organizations; and association with fraternal orders.

If the individual being researched was a professional—such as a doctor, lawyer, or engineer—special records may exist. Membership and biographical forms may have been completed, and educating or training organizations may have maintained records. Insurance may have been purchased or money borrowed from some institution that recorded personal information. Some businesses have maintained ledgers and account books containing names, dates, and addresses. However, this is not a modern practice for some large commercial organizations unless credit

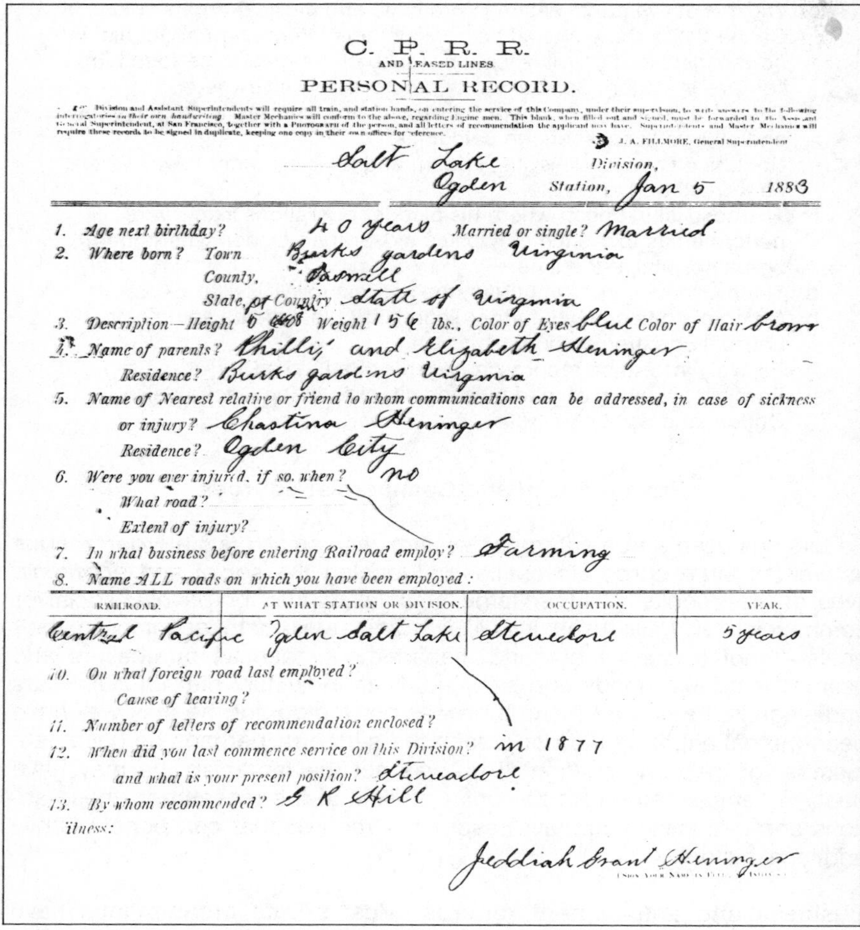

C. P. R. R.
AND LEASED LINES
PERSONAL RECORD.

Division and Assistant Superintendents will require all train, and station hands, on entering the service of this Company, under their supervision, to write answers to the following interrogatories *in their own handwriting*. Master Mechanics will conform to the above, regarding Engine men. This blank, when filled out and signed, must be forwarded to the Assistant General Superintendent, at San Francisco, together with a Photograph of the person, and all letters of recommendation the applicant may have. Superintendents and Master Mechanics will require these records to be signed in duplicate, keeping one copy in their own offices for reference.

J. A. FILLMORE, General Superintendent

Salt Lake Division,
Ogden Station, Jan 5 1883

1. *Age next birthday?* 40 years *Married or single?* Married
2. *Where born? Town* Burks gardens Virginia
County, Taswell
State, or Country State of Virginia
3. *Description—Height* 5 [illegible] *Weight* 156 *lbs., Color of Eyes* blue *Color of Hair* brown
4. *Name of parents?* Phillip and Elizabeth Heninger
Residence? Burks gardens Virginia
5. *Name of Nearest relative or friend to whom communications can be addressed, in case of sickness or injury?* Chastina Heninger
Residence? Ogden City
6. *Were you ever injured, if so, when?* no
What road?
Extent of injury?
7. *In what business before entering Railroad employ?* Farming
8. *Name ALL roads on which you have been employed:*

RAILROAD.	AT WHAT STATION OR DIVISION.	OCCUPATION.	YEAR.
Central Pacific	Ogden Salt Lake	Stevedore	5 years

10. *On what foreign road last employed?*
Cause of leaving?
11. *Number of letters of recommendation enclosed?*
12. *When did you last commence service on this Division?* in 1877
and what is your present position? Stevedore
13. *By whom recommended?* G K Hill

Witness:

Jedidiah Grant Heninger
(SIGN YOUR NAME IN FULL, WITH INITIALS)

purchasing is an important facet of their business. Such records are private and usually remain in the custody of the owners or managers, but many will open their records for family history purposes when courteously approached. A personal contact in a forthright but respectful manner is often the key in gaining access to the records.

School records. Records relating to students, faculty, and administrators of American schools, colleges, academies, universities, and other educational or training institutions also are possible sources for family and local history. Some have records dating to the earliest colonial periods while others exist only after World War II. Records may pertain to student admission, registration, attendance, graduation, and dismissal; records also exist relating to faculty, administrators, and staff personnel. Even though such records are usually private, they are often available for legitimate research. Some are public and have been published.

Harvard University at Cambridge, Massachusetts, has published biographies of some students dating from 1642 and retains admission books dating from 1725; records since 1820 include the names of parents. The University of Alabama at Tuscaloosa has published *Register of the University of Alabama 1831–1901* in four volumes, containing vital statistics and historical information on former students. Brigham Young University at Provo, Utah, has detailed records of students, faculty, administrators, and staff personnel dating from 1879, and its modern records have been computerized.

Brigham Young University also has collected information relating to former students and filed it in the university archives. An example pertains to Alma Richards, one of Brigham Young University's greatest athletes. A file donated by his widow, Lenora Richards, contains his personal correspondence, records of athletic accomplishments, news clippings, and photographs. Similar files probably have been received by other institutions.

Records pertaining to some early primary schools in America have been preserved and deposited in public libraries, but many others have been lost or destroyed. The records of those schools still operating usually remain in custody of the school or its officials. One 1830 Illinois school record included a list of poor children whose tuition had been paid by the local school commissioners; the record included each student's name, age and date of entrance into school, and names of parents or guardians.

Detailed applications were required for admittance to some schools, and supporting documents often were preserved. The records usually are in custody of the registrar or archivist at the school, and family history research holds a high priority with many administrators.

Medical records. Records of physicians and surgeons, dentists and orthodontists, chiropractors, and other medical practitioners are also possible sources for family history, as are the records of hospitals, medical clinics, nursing homes, and other health-care facilities. These records are strictly confidential in most instances, but sometimes information can be released from their files for family history purposes if the individual concerned is deceased and no personal harm would result from the disclosure.

Both doctors' and hospitals' records are very comprehensive, usually containing vital statistics, kinship information, and medical history relating to the person and his family. Sometimes the files include records and reports of several different family members, especially where the family had the same doctor over a long period or where sickness and accident affected more than one family member. In some instances the oral testimony of the doctors and nurses is a primary source in its own right.

Some hospitals issue birth records and also will provide essential facts on deaths occurring in their facilities. Records in doctors' files might include the same information. Although the diagnostic and medical records are confidential, registers or admittance records usually are accessible. They often contain the name, age, and address of the person admitted plus kinship information. The records of nursing homes and other health-care facilities also are possible sources and contain similar personal information. In each instance a personal visit to the facility is advisable, but courteous requests by correspondence can also bring good results.

Records of morticians, coroners, and medical examiners. The records of local morticians, county coroners, and state medical examiners are good supplements to official vital records, and provide primary source information where official records were not kept or are missing. The mortician has long been an integral part of the official vital statistics recording process, and many were keeping comprehensive records prior to state or local registration. County coroners and state medical examiners also have contributed to the vital statistics recording process in certain instances; their records are of equal importance.

The mortician often is responsible for initiating the death record and for placing the obituary or death notice in the local newspaper. He also handles the funeral and burial arrangements in most cases and sees to the inscription and placement of the tombstone. His records can include complete vital statistics on the deceased, names and addresses of next of kin, names of friends and associates, names and addresses of those who contributed or assisted in any way with the funeral, and other information. Some morticians' records date to the middle of the 1800s, and they are usually accessible to family members and researchers.

The names and addresses of morticians and funeral directors can be determined from the National Directory of Morticians to which most local funeral directors subscribe. The records usually remain in the custody of the present proprietor, though cases are known where records of former owners have been deposited at the town hall or county courthouse.

Where the cause of death was in doubt or where unusual circumstances surrounded a death, an inquest may have been held by the county coroner or the state medical examiner, resulting in other records. In some states an inquest is mandatory if a physician is not present at death, but that has not been a common practice in all states. It is a fact, however, that crimes of violence—including murder, rape, felonious assault, and robbery—have been on the increase in recent years. Therefore such records are becoming more and more prevalent.

A typical file concerning a coroner's inquest includes a *necropsy report* giving the technical causes of death, *pathology* and *toxology reports* supporting the findings, *testimony* about the circumstances surrounding the death, and a *jury report.* With few exceptions, the records are public and can be used by researchers for family history purposes.

During World War II a Utah family received information that their son had died in San Francisco, California, while in military training. The official death record indicated he took his own life by jumping from the San Francisco Bay Bridge, but family members questioned this. However, records obtained from the coroner's office confirmed the situation. Documents included testimony from a Coast Guard officer stating he was on a routine patrol in the Bay area when he sighted "the body of the deceased, fully dressed, except for coat, lying face downward in the rocks about fifty feet southeast of the shoreline" and that he found identifying papers on the

Place of Death	Usual Residence
City State	City State
Name	
Birth Place City State	
Sex Color	Single, Married, Widowed, Divorced
Husband or wife Age	
Date of Birth	
Age — Years Months Days	Social Security Number
Occupation	
Father's Name	
Birth Place	
Mother's Maiden Name	
Birth Place	
Informant	Address Phone No.
Date of Death — Year Month Day	Place Burial
Date of Burial — Year Month Day	Cemetery
Duration of Illness	
Principal Cause of Death	
Doctor's Signature	Address
Funeral Director's Signature	Address
Funeral Director No.	Embalmer No.

body. Testimony of a fellow soldier indicated the deceased "was a very quiet man and no one got to know him very well," and that "during the last week of his life he seemed depressed over an impending divorce." Testimony also indicated the young man had been seen "walking on the Bay Bridge before his death" and likely jumped from it. An extensive necropsy report indicated that death was caused by fractures, contusions, and injuries to internal organs, all due to "trauma."

The following newspaper account reports a coroner action:

> Body of missing man found on Spruce Mountain. Wells inquest set to learn cause of death. An inquest was planned at Wells this afternoon to determine the cause of death of a man identified as Vincent Gustafson, fifty-year-old itinerant miner from Ely.
>
> Gustafson's badly decomposed body was found Saturday in a desolate region of the Spruce Mountain area by government trapper Ed Taylor of Wells.
>
> According to information reported by Elko County Sheriff J. Harris, Gustafson had been reported missing from the Monarch Mine in the Spruce Mountain Mining District on July 10. Identification of the body was made by Monarch Mine employee Robert Griggs.
>
> Sheriff Harris revealed that Taylor came upon Gustafson's body on a little-used road about ten miles northeast of the Monarch Mine. Harris said Gustafson's body was clad only in a tee shirt. His pants and one shoe were found nearby.
>
> The sheriff said his office is investigating the death to determine if there is any evidence of foul play. He said however that the condition of the body made it difficult.
>
> After being notified of the body's discovery, Sheriff Harris said that the investigation was held off until yesterday morning so that a thorough search of the area could be made in full daylight. [*Elko Daily Free Press,* December 9, 1957]

Of course not all deaths result in a coroner's inquest, and such unusual circumstances seldom surround our ancestors' deaths, but these records should certainly be considered by researchers as possible sources for family history.

Records of fraternal, patriotic, and hereditary societies. Such fraternal and social orders as the Masons, Odd Fellows, Elks, Mystic Shrine, or Grange keep membership records that can be used for family history, and membership records of hereditary and patriotic organizations have long been regarded as good sources for genealogy. Although their records are confidential, many organizations are happy to cooperate with researchers seeking family history.

Most of these organizations require formal application for membership and also maintain continuing records. Some societies include connections with a particular colonial group or citizen, such as a revolutionary war veteran or a colonial patriot; others are founded on common beliefs and purposes.

The Daughters of the American Revolution is perhaps the most widely known patriotic organization and has actively recruited members for many years. Not only has it kept membership records, it also has located, compiled, indexed, and preserved hundreds of volumes of genealogical and historical records. Charts have been published showing members and their ancestry, and in 1966 a Patriot Index was published containing the names of more than one hundred thousand patriots—men and women who served the nation in some capacity.

The Sons of the American Revolution maintain similar records of membership but have not engaged in as many gathering and publishing programs; however, they do maintain a card index for ancestors from the Revolution showing the membership number of each person who has claimed that ancestor. They also have published some lists showing members' ancestral connections.

The following list gives the names and addresses of several hereditary societies in America and shows their dates of organization.

The Society of the Cincinnati, organized 1783; 2118 Massachusetts Ave. N.W., Washington, D.C. 20008

Daughters of the Cincinnati, organized 1894; 122 E. 58th Street, New York City, New York

National Society Daughters of the American Revolution, organized 1890; 1776 D Street, N.W., Washington, D.C. 20006

National Society Daughters of the Revolution, organized 1891; 66 Heights Road, Ridgewood, New Jersey 07450

National Society Sons of the American Revolution, organized 1889; 2412 Massachusetts Avenue N.W., Washington, D.C. 20008

General Society Sons of the Revolution, organized 1876; Fraunces Tavern, 54 Pearl Street, New York, New York 10004

Descendants of the Signers of the Declaration of Independence, organized 1907; 1300 Locust Street, Philadelphia, Pennsylvania 19107

General Society of the War of 1812, organized 1814; Secretary General, 3311 Columbia Pike, Lancaster, Pennsylvania 17603

National Society U.S. Daughters of 1812, organized 1892; 1461 Rhode Island Avenue N.W., Washington, D.C. 20005

Aztec Club of 1847, organized 1847; 5225 Westpath Way, Washington, D.C. 20036

Military Order of the Loyal Legion of the United States, organized 1865; 1805 Pine Street, Philadelphia, Pennsylvania 19103

Dames of the Loyal Legion of the United States, organized 1899; P.O. Box 24, Gettysburg, Pennsylvania 17225

Auxiliary to Sons of the Union Veterans of the Civil War, organized 1883; 2025 Cleveland Avenue, West Lawn, Pennsylvania 19609

Ladies of the Grand Army of the Republic, organized 1886; 90 Conestoga Boulevard, Lancaster, Pennsylvania 17602

Sons of Confederate Veterans, organized 1896; Southern Station, Box 1, Hattiesburg, Mississippi 39401

Order of Stars and Bars, organized after 1889; Southern Station, Box 1, Hattiesburg, Mississippi 39401

United Daughters of the Confederacy, organized 1894; 328 North Boulevard, Richmond, Virginia 23220

Spanish War Veterans United, organized 1898; 810 Vermont Avenue N.W., Box 1915, Washington, D.C. 20013

Military Order of the World Wars, organized 1920; 910 Seventeenth Street N.W., Washington, D.C. 10006

The records of other fraternal and social orders generally remain in the custody of their respective organizations, and they may or may not open their records for history purposes. However, my experience has shown several to be cooperative when the desired information pertains to a progenitor of the inquirer and when the request is conciliatory and courteous.

Sources Pertaining to the North American Indian

Conducting applied genealogical research and teaching family history at the university level for twenty years have brought me into contact with many different people seeking to learn more about their ancestry and family heritage. None have brought more interesting, challenging, and rewarding associations than the young American Indian students at Brigham Young University. Through this contact I have gained a great admiration and respect for the Indian people—their artistry and other talents, their character and personal strengths, their love and respect for the family, and their keen desire to learn more about their ancestry and heritage.

Between 1961 and 1971 my contact was incidental, with only a half dozen Indian students enrolled in genealogical courses each semester. However, between 1971 and 1977 I had the opportunity to instruct a course each semester with enrollment restricted to students with American Indian ancestry. Here I really began to learn about this aspect of American genealogy: working closely with Indian students to evaluate and analyze their problems, then conducting actual research for and with them to extend their pedigrees. These students accomplished as much as students in other classes who had, on the average, ten times the source materials. Many Indian students were able to document three and four generations fairly quickly, and where favorable circumstances existed some were able to trace certain lines to the fifth, sixth, and seventh generations.

The classes averaged between twenty and thirty students each semester and represented several different tribes throughout the United States and Canada. Of course most were from the West—Brigham Young University being a western institution—but a fair number were from the midwestern and eastern states. The Navajo had by far the largest representation, with Hopi, Zuni, Apache, and others following. Students from Montana and the Dakotas represented the Sioux, Crow, Yanktonnai, Gros Ventre, Assiniboin, and Mandans. A few Cheyenne and Arapaho students enrolled. Several whites tried to document Cherokee ancestry ascribed to their lineage by family tradition, but very seldom were we able to verify that claim.

Indian students began their research much as others did: by recording basic facts from personal knowledge and memory, then gathering and recording oral history and tradition from family and tribal members. They were encouraged to read good books and talk with tribal members to learn more about their tribe's history and background, then to learn specific customs relating to naming, marriage, burial, and other important practices. These customs differ from tribe to tribe, and a knowledge of them is essential for successful research.

Students were also encouraged to write home for additional information, but in most instances they had to visit their families and tribes in person to gain important oral history and tradition. This type of information can seldom be obtained through correspondence by a family member, and certainly it cannot be obtained by an agent. Such information is considered sacred, and the individual must visit his own family and tribe to obtain it; moreover, family and tribal members must be in the proper frame of mind to disclose the information. In some cases it may take several sessions with a particular individual or group to obtain the desired information; in others it might be done in one sitting. An interview with an individual might be in order in one instance, and a group session with several family or tribal members might be more proper in another. We learned this work was a never-ending process and could be continued as long as anyone was interested in the subject.

The next step usually was for the individuals to contact the tribal headquarters and ask for information about themselves then about specific ancestors and relatives in the tribe. Both personal visits and requests by correspondence proved successful in doing this. The tribal offices have a wealth of information about individuals and families and often are very cooperative in dispensing it. Some have kept vital records concerning birth, marriage, and death from a fairly modern period, and many have enrollment records showing official membership in the tribe. Individual information cards have been kept in a few offices, and tribal council minutes often contain personal information. Where royalty payments and government monies have been received, annuity and payment records give excellent personal information. Other tribal records include land allotment records, heirship and probate records, and some tribal census records. Of course where tribal status has not been maintained or where Indians were not placed on reservations, such records are nonexistant. Many eastern tribes never maintained such connections.

Indian census records taken by the federal government became a primary source for many students whose ancestors were on western reservations; some of the southeastern tribes were enumerated as early as 1818. Most of the government census records relating to Indians date from 1885 to 1940, but some are rather incomplete until the 1930s. Microfilm copies are in the National Archives at Washington, D.C., and the LDS Genealogical Society library also has acquired the collection (which consists of six hundred reels). This source proved to be the single best source for most western Indian students at Brigham Young University, particularly the Sioux, Assiniboin, Gros Ventre, and Mandans.

The Bureau of Indian Affairs (BIA) also has valuable records for Indian family history, as does the Smithsonian Institution; both are in Washington, D.C. The official government records relating to treaties, Indian removal, the establishment of superintendencies and agencies, the operation of schools, and other matters are found in BIA records. Thousands have been classified and inventoried by the National Archives. For an exhaustive list of these records, see Preliminary Inventories: Records of the Bureau of Indian Affairs, compiled by Edward E. Hill (1965).

When Indians integrated with whites, the major record groups covered in previous chapters apply. Vital records of towns, counties, and states include Indian entries also, particularly in modern periods. Records of churches, hospitals, schools, private businesses, and military organizations also might include them. Some Indians appeared before various courts; others appear in land records. Newspapers have printed articles on individual Indians and on tribes and their circumstances. Almost every source already covered is a possible source for Indian family history.

The following examples showing how various sources might be used to document American Indian pedigrees have been taken from research projects of American Indians who were attending Brigham Young University.

Research project: Eleanor Boyd. Eleanor was born 29 July 1955 at Tuba City, Arizona, the daughter of John Boyd and Jennie (Lane) Boyd—both Navajo Indians. She knew her grandparents on her father's side were Dan Tacheen (born 1880) and Lutie (born 1878). She also knew her grandparents on her mother's side were Keith Lane (born 1879) and Faye (born 1891).

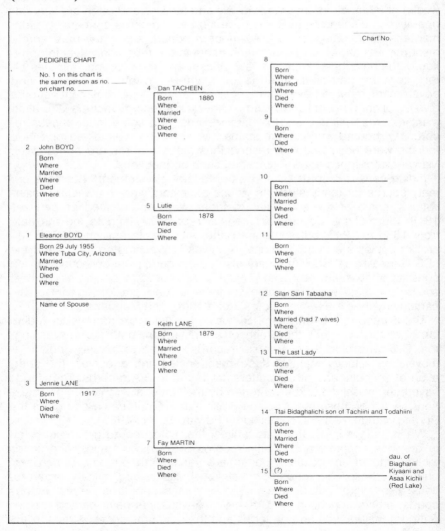

Chart No. ____

PEDIGREE CHART

No. 1 on this chart is
the same person as no. ____
on chart no. ____

1 Eleanor BOYD
Born 29 July 1955
Where Tuba City, Arizona
Married
Where
Died
Where

Name of Spouse

2 John BOYD
Born
Where
Married
Where
Died
Where

3 Jennie LANE
Born 1917
Where
Died
Where

4 Dan TACHEEN
Born 1880
Where
Married
Where
Died
Where

5 Lutie
Born 1878
Where
Died
Where

6 Keith LANE
Born 1879
Where
Married
Where
Died
Where

7 Fay MARTIN
Born
Where
Died
Where

8
Born
Where
Married
Where
Died
Where

9
Born
Where
Died
Where

10
Born
Where
Married
Where
Died
Where

11
Born
Where
Died
Where

12 Silan Sani Tabaaha
Born
Where
Married (had 7 wives)
Where
Died
Where

13 The Last Lady
Born
Where
Died
Where

14 Ttai Bidaghalichi son of Tachiini and Todahiini
Born
Where
Married
Where
Died
Where

15 (?) dau. of Biaghanii Kiyaani and Asaa Kichii (Red Lake)
Born
Where
Died
Where

Eleanor had known several aunts and uncles, and she had heard family members speak of earlier progenitors—but she had no facts concerning them. After writing home for information, she received the following photographs: one of herself; one of her family showing her parents and brothers and sisters; and one showing her grandmother, Faye Martin, her mother, Jennie Lane Boyd, her mother's half-sister, Sarah Lane, and her aunts, Ruth Kent, Margaret Manymule, and Fanny Lane.

The unusual Indian pedigree also received by Eleanor showed six generations beyond herself. It included her brothers and sisters and some nieces and nephews; her parents, Jennie Lane and John Boyd and their brothers and sisters; her grandparents, Keith Lane and Faye Martin, and information about their brothers and sisters; the parents of her grandfather, Keith Lane (The Last Lady and Silan Sani Tabaaha); the father of her grandmother Faye Martin (Ttai Bidaghalichi), and his parents (Tachiini and Todahiini); the parents of her great-grandmother whose name is unknown (Biaghanii and Asaa Kichii or Red Lake); and Asaa's mother (Asa

Balachilatani or Many Children), fourth-great-grandmother of Eleanor Boyd.

A search of Indian census records at the LDS genealogical library in Salt Lake City located the households of Keith Lane and Dan Tacheen, Eleanor's maternal grandparents. Faye Lane Boyd, Eleanor's grandmother, is shown as the second wife of Keith Lane, and Eleanor's mother—Jennie—is shown as a seventeen-year-old daughter in 1934. Dan Tacheen and Lutie, Eleanor's paternal grandparents, are shown in the same census with their family, and Dan is also shown with two wives. It is very possible that the Rex Lane shown in the household of Keith and Fay Lane is the heavyweight boxer who made headlines during the 1940s and 1950s, but that is an undocumented assumption on my part.

Indian census records. According to officials in the National Archives, the federal government did not take regular census rolls of Indians until 1884. Prior to that year, enumeration rolls were made for specific purposes, such as annuity payment rolls, rosters or muster rolls of emigrants, and allotment rolls. Before 1870 the various Indian tribes had the legal status of separate nations; it was not within the province of the federal government to take census enumerations without the consent of the tribes involved. For that reason there are few census rolls antedating 1870.

Of the earlier and specialized censuses in the BIA records of the National Archives, only those of the eastern or North Carolina Cherokees possess some degree of completeness. The earliest begin in 1818 then continue periodically until the first true census was taken of the Eastern Band of Cherokees in 1848. Three additional censuses were taken between 1848 and 1851, then on 27 July 1868 Congress authorized a census of all Cherokees east of the Mississippi. Enumerations were made of some other tribes prior to 1884, but there was no regularity in these censuses; in some cases only one census was taken.

By 1884 it was realized that more definite enumeration was needed. Section 9 of an act passed by Congress on 4 July 1884 required Indian agents to submit a census of Indians at their agencies or upon reservations under their charge. These censuses were to include the number of males above eighteen years of age, the number of females above fourteen years of age, the number of school children between the ages of six and sixteen years, the number of school houses at the agency, the number of schools in operation and the attendance at each, and the names of teachers employed and salaries paid such teachers. Censuses immediately following 1884 were individualistic and based almost entirely on the interpretations of the agents. Most were made on ordinary letter-type paper, frequently giving only Indian names (which were not arranged alphabetically). However, later directives required that the agent distinguish between different tribes and bands under his jurisdiction and that he follow an outlined format.

In 1909 agents were required to show a separate grouping of Indians residing on reservations, and in 1910 names, ages, sex, and family relationships were required. In 1919 it was stipulated that names of families be arranged alphabetically. Other stipulations were added at various other

Western Navajo Agency Census Rolls dated 1 April 1934

#	Name	Sex	Born	Age	Relationship
2063	LANE, Keith	M	1879	55	Head
2064	LANE, Emma	F	1884	50	wife #1
2065	LANE, Maude	F	1904	30	daughter
2066	LANE, Milo	M	1908	26	son
2067	LANE, Nancy	F	1909	25	daughter
2068	LANE, Henry	M	1913	21	son
2069	LANE, Sarah	F	1914	20	daughter
2070	LANE, Manly	M	1915	19	son
2071	LANE, Fred	M	1918	16	son
2072	LANE, Julius	M	1920	14	son
2073	LANE, Mary	F	1921	13	daughter
2074	LANE, Winifred	F	1925	9	daughter
2075	LANE, Lola	F	1928	6	daughter
2076	LANE, Glen	M	1924	10	grandson
2077	LANE, Thelma	F	1926	8	granddaughter
*2078	LANE, Fay	F	1891	43	wife #2
2079	LANE, Lila	F	1915	19	daughter
*2080	LANE, Jennie	F	1917	17	daughter
2081	LANE, Rose	F	1912	13	daughter
2082	LANE, King	M	1923	11	son
2083	LANE, Joseph	M	1925	9	son
2084	LANE, Ruth	F	1927	7	daughter
2085	LANE, Joe	M	1926	8	grandson
**2086	LANE, Rex	M	1927	7	grandson

*Mother and Grandmother of Eleanor Boyd
**Heavyweight boxing contender of the 1940s and 1950s?

#	Name	Sex	Born	Age	Relationship
*3417	TACHEEN, Dan	M	1880	54	Head
*3418	TACHEEN, Lutie	F	1878	56	wife #1
3419	TACHEEN, Kenneth	M	1904	30	son
3420	TACHEEN, Edwin	M	1913	21	son
3421	TACHEEN, Abel	M	1914	20	son
3422	TACHEEN, Frank	M	1920	14	son
3423	TACHEEN, Thelma	F	1895	39	wife #2
3424	TACHEEN, Susan	F	1913	21	daughter
3425	TACHEEN, Forest	M	1920	14	son
3426	TACHEEN, Ada	F	1925	9	daughter
3427	TACHEEN, May	F	1928	6	daughter
3428	TACHEEN, Emaline	F	1932	2	daughter

*Grandparents of Eleanor Boyd

times. The spelling of Indian names by the census takers was largely phonetic, and they did not always interpret sounds uniformly. This often is a source of confusion in the records, and entries of the same persons might vary from year to year.

Following 1940 censuses were no longer required by the commissioner of Indian Affairs, though some local censuses were still taken by field offices.

The first census taken by the Western Navajo Indian Agency—where the Boyd and Lane families lived—was taken in 1915. Mr. Peter Paquette was superintendent of the agency, with offices at Ft. Defiance, Arizona. He gave some interesting historical information about the Navajo Indians in that area in his first report on 30 June 1915:

> A census of this portion of the tribe is just being taken and it is impossible at this time to furnish the office a census. The work of compiling this data will require the services of the clerks for several months. At the same time accurate data relative to land under cultivation, irrigation, stock, etc. will be furnished. There is nothing to go by in the preparation of such a census. The number of Navajos so far enumerated on this reservation is 10,707 and indications are that the enumerators will find about 1,000 more Indians.

Evidently the enumeration was completed before the following winter, because on 26 December 1915 Paquette wrote the following:

> Referring to above cited office authority dated December 10, 1914, there is transmitted, herewith, a census of the Navajo Indians of this reservation together with full and complete data relative to stock owned, land farmed, fenced, plural marriages, defectives and much other data that the office has been anxious to obtain for a number of years. I respectfully call attention to the following general summary of this census:
>
> There are 11,915 Navajos—5789 males
> 6146 females
>
> There are 4,411 children eligible for school
> 63 children of school age are defective.

The Navajos own (this reservation)

406,316 head sheep	valued at $1,321,719.50
116,202 head goats	87,151.50
14,406 head cattle	432,180.00
26,255 head horses	656,375.00
2,116 head burros	4,232.00
435 head mules	8,700.00
Total live stock valuation	$2,510,358.00

The total tribal property (valuation) is $14,958,748.00 besides coal of which there are enormous quantities.

There are government school facilities now and buildings for only	870 pupils
There are mission school facilities for	260 pupils
Pupils in nonreservation schools (could be)	150 pupils
Total pupils provided for now	1280
Number pupils totally unprovided for now	3131
Valuation farm products sold this year	$990,000.00

Acreage of reservation—Navajo (in Arizona)	3,503,026 acres
(in New Mexico)	506,880 acres
Total acreage	3,009,960 acres
Number of houses	766
Number of hogans	2,075
This census cost (actual)	$1,769.50

There is now on file in the Navajo agency office a full and complete family card system covering each family in detail.

The census tabulation work which amounts to 298 typewritten pages was done entirely by the agency office in addition to their other duties.

The census submitted is the first of its kind ever taken. [Paquette 1915b]

The statement that this was the first census of its kind ever taken is interesting, and the statement that a family card system was established at the agency office is important to Navajos interested in gaining genealogical facts.

Paquette provided some excellent historical background on the Navajo people with respect to their naming customs and also gave the following short history of their earliest population:

When the Navajos came back to Fort Defiance, Arizona, from Fort Sumner, New Mexico, in 1868, where they had been held as prisoners of war for three years, the military authorities took a census—that is, they established a stockade at Fort Defiance and counted the number of persons. The military reports show that there were 7,019 Navajos at that time. Old Navajos are agreed that the military authorities were not able to capture all the Navajos when they were removed from here in 1865, and their estimates as to the number who escaped the soldiers varies from a hundred to ten or twelve hundred. Certain it is that the total number of Navajos at that time could not have exceeded 8,500 persons and forty-seven years later the population of this reservation is 11,915 persons. Besides there are the San Juan, Pueblo Bonito, Leupp, and Western Navajo reservations besides the Navajos on the Moqui reservations. [Paquette 1915b, p. 18]

The above history was especially interesting to the Boyd-Lane pedigree, because family tradition indicated Eleanor Boyd's third great-grandmother, Asaatiaai, was living "before the tribe went to Fort Sumner." It also provided excellent background on tribal clans and naming customs that helped Eleanor understand her family heritage more fully.

The following information—which should be of interest to every Navajo Indian interested in family history—was included on page 20 of the report:

Attention is called to a portion of this census wherein the spelling of names, clans, etc., is given. This data on the Navajo language is original classification work done by John G. Walker, a Navajo of half blood, formerly a clerk at the Navajo agency but now (12-20-1915) a trader on the Leupp reservation. All census work is based on this outline as to general spelling and as to clans.

Work of compiling the data, form in which submitted, and subjects covered were supervised by B. H. Dooley, clerk, Navajo agency. All work of compilation was done by the regular Navajo Agency Office force.

Every Navajo belongs to some clan, of which there are sixty. The husband belongs to one clan and the wife and children to another (never the same clan for husband and wife). The wife in nearly every instance is really the head of the family, the woman very largely controlling property. A family feature of Navajo life in the past was for a man say twenty-five to marry a woman thirty-five or forty who had a daughter or daughters growing up. When these girls reached a marriageable age the stepfather then married the girl or girls (his stepdaughters). The older men also often marry younger girls. Plural marriages do not exist to any extent, that is, to what has commonly been believed in the past. One hundred eighty-three men have two wives, seven have three wives, and one has four. No additional such marriages are allowed. A Navajo family for the purpose of this census has been defined as follows:

A man, wife, and children.
A widow with children, if any.
A widower with children, if any.
A single person, either male or female, eighteen years old and over.

All persons eighteen years old and over whether the husband and wife were living together or not. [Paquette 1915b, p. 20]

The above information on plurality of wives was especially interesting to Eleanor Boyd because both her grandfathers were shown in the 1934 census as having two wives. As she located her family in other census enumerations, she found some listed by their Indian name as well as their English name, and Mr. Paquette's explanation of naming customs was most helpful. He explained that individual names were derived principally from the clan to which the individual belonged. He listed each of the sixty clans by name, then listed the following examples of name derivation:

Names derived from a person's hair:		
Bits-Lepahe	(Bi tsi le pa he)	Gray hair
Bitsi-Lechee	(Bi tsi le chee)	Red hair
Bitsi-Letsoi	(Bi tsi le tsoi)	Yellow hair
Bitsi-Lekai	(Bi tsi le kai)	White hair
Bitsi-Nodozie	(Bi tsi no doz i)	Streaked hair
Chis Chillie	(Chis chil li)	Curly hair
Names derived from the color or number of stock:		
Bile-Lezhiny	(Bi le le zhiny)	Black
Bile-Letsoi	(Bi le le tsoi)	Sorrel horse
Bile-Lepahe	(Bi le le pa he)	Roan horse
Bile-Lekizy	(Bi le le kizy)	Pinto horse
Bile-Eskliny	(Bi le es kliny)	Speckled horse
Bile-Doklizy	(Bi le do klizy)	Gray horse
Bile-Klonny	(Bi le klony)	Many horses
Depay-Klonny	(De pay klonny)	Many sheep
Klizy-Lekai	(Klizy le ki)	White goat
Names derived from miscellaneous sources:		
Klaw	(Klaw)	Left-handed
Etsitty	(E tsi ti)	Smith
Peshlakai	(Pesh la kai)	Silversmith
Biwoshkizy	(Bi wosh kizy)	Man with one tooth gone

Nanl-hody	(Nanl ho di)	Limpy
Na-adiny	(Na a di ni)	Blind
Askee	(As ke)	Boy
Ason	(A son)	Old woman
Ated	(A ted)	Small girl
Deneh	(De neh)	Middle-aged man
Hatale	(Ha ta le)	Chanter; singer
Hoskay	(Hos ka)	A brace; a warrior
Hosteen	(Hos ten)	An old man
Natah	(Na tah)	Chief; leader
Names referring to complexion:		
Chee	(Che)	Red
Tsoi	(Tsoi)	Yellow
Zhen	(Zhen)	Black; dark; swarthy
Pahe	(Pa he)	Gray
Kai	(Ki)	White
Names denoting height, weight, and so forth:		
Dass	(Das)	Heavy
Neskahe	(Nes ka he)	Fat
Nez	(Nez)	Tall
Tso	(Tso)	Large
Tsehe	(Tse he)	Very small
Tsusie	(Tsu sie)	Slender
Yazzie	(Yaz zi)	Small
Names based on relationship:		
Begay	(Be ga)	Son of a father
Beyaz	(Be yaz)	Son of a mother
Bitse	(Bi tse)	Daughter of a father
Bitchi	(Bi tchi)	Daughter of a mother
Bikiss	(Bi kis)	A brother
Bilah	(Bi lah)	A sister
Bizhay	(Bi zhay)	Father of
Bimah	(Bi mah)	Mother of
Bitsoi	(Bi tsoi)	Grandson of
Benalli	(Be nal li)	Granddaughter of
Badaney	(Ba da ney)	Son-in-law of
Binigh	(Bi ni)	Elder brother of
Bitsilly	(Bi tsi ly)	Younger brother of
Bichi	(Bi chi)	Grandfather of

A number of other interesting things are also included in the Indian census returns after about 1900: births and deaths that occurred during the year; the number of intermarriages with whites; the number and types of houses or hogans; important geographical points and districts for enumeration purposes; the number and kinds of churches on the reservation; commercial enterprises; and information relating to farming, agriculture, irrigation, and production.

Research Project: Kenneth Dale Sekaquaptewa. Kenneth was an English major with a minor in journalism; he became very interested in tracing his ancestry while attending Brigham Young University in 1973. He is Hopi, born 26 October 1949 at Phoenix, Arizona. His father, Wayne Phillip Sekaquaptewa, was of the Oraibi village of Hopis, born 5 May 1923 at Hoteville, Arizona. His mother, Judy Chen, was born 22 June 1924 of Chinese parents in Shanghai, China.

The Hopi Indians have been centered in the northern part of Arizona since the thirteenth century and probably before then. Recently they have been involved in land disputes with their Navajo neighbors. Ken was involved in reporting congressional hearings on the subject in his journalism classes. Partially through these interests he began tracing his Hopi ancestry, and found the Indian census records very helpful.

The Hopi Indian census of Hoteville, Arizona, for 1924 showed his father, Wayne Sekaquaptewa, as a one-year-old son in the household of his parents, Emory and Duwawisnema. It gave Wayne's complete date of birth and his parent's date of marriage. In the same census Ken's great-grandfather Sam Talashonsnewa was listed, and Ken's grandmother Helen Duwawisnema was identified as Sam's child by a former marriage.

Hopi Indian census, Hoteville, Arizona (Chotevilla Indians) July 1924

325 Sekaquaptewa, Emory	Head born 1895 age 29 male
326 Sekaquaptewa, Duwawisnima Helen	Wife born 1901 age 23 female
327 Sekaquaptewa, Wayne	Son born 3 May 1923 age 1 male
Married by law Feb 14, 1919—Transferred from Bacobi census.	
369 Talashonewa	Head born 1863 age 61 male
370 Koyahonsie	Wife born 1860 age 64 female
371 Tuwahnewa, Henry	Son born 1906 age 18 male

Census Roll Number		Name		Sex	Age at Last Birthday	Tribe	Degree of Blood	Marital Status	Relationship to Head of Family	At Jurisdiction Where Enrolled
Present	Last	Surname	Given							Yes or no
1	1(a)	2	3	4	5	6	7	8	9	10
2508	2012	Seimatewa	Howard	M	1898 38	Hopi	F	M	Head	Yes
2509	2013	"	Viola	F	1899 37	"	F	M	Wife	Yes
2510	2014	"	Calvin	M	1930 6	"	F	S	Son	Yes
2511	2015	"	Violet Ethel	F	1/5/32 4	"	F	S	Dau	Yes
2512	2017	Sekatayou	Roy	M	1900 36	"	F	Wd	Head	Yes
2513	2018	"	Willard	M	7/28/22 14	"	F	S	Son	Yes
2514	2019	"	Ida Lee	F	9/8/23 13	"	F	S	Dau	Yes
2515	2020	"	Elvan	M	6/4/28 8	"	F	S	Son	Yes
2516	2021	Sekauaptewa	Emory	M	1895 31	"	F	M	Head	Yes
2517	2022	" Duwasisnim	Helen	F	1901 35	"	F	M	Wife	Yes
2518	2023	"	Wayne	M	5/3/23 13	"	F	S	Son	Yes
2519	2024	"	Eugene	M	7/7/25 11	"	F	S	Son	Yes
2520	2025	"	Emory, Jr.	M	12/29/27 9	"	F	S	Son	Yes
2521	2026	"	Abbott	M	12/4/29 7	"	F	S	Son	Yes
2522	2027	" Talashonewa	Sam	M	1863 73	"	F	Wd	Father In Law	Yes
Total										M-11 F-4 13

Henry and Helen Sekaquaptewa are children of Talashonewa by a former marriage.

The 1925 census for the same place listed both families again, and the 1926 census included Eugene, a granduncle; Talashonewa, Eugene's wife Koyahonsie, and Ken's great-granduncle, Henry Tuwahnewa. The families were located in each annual census from 1925 through 1937, adding and confirming genealogical information; the 1937 enumeration listed Ken's great-grandfather, Sam Talashonewa, in the household of Emory Sekaquaptewa, Ken's grandfather.

Research project: Charlene In The Woods. Charlene is a Sioux of the Cheyenne River agency in North Dakota; she was born 13 May 1955 in

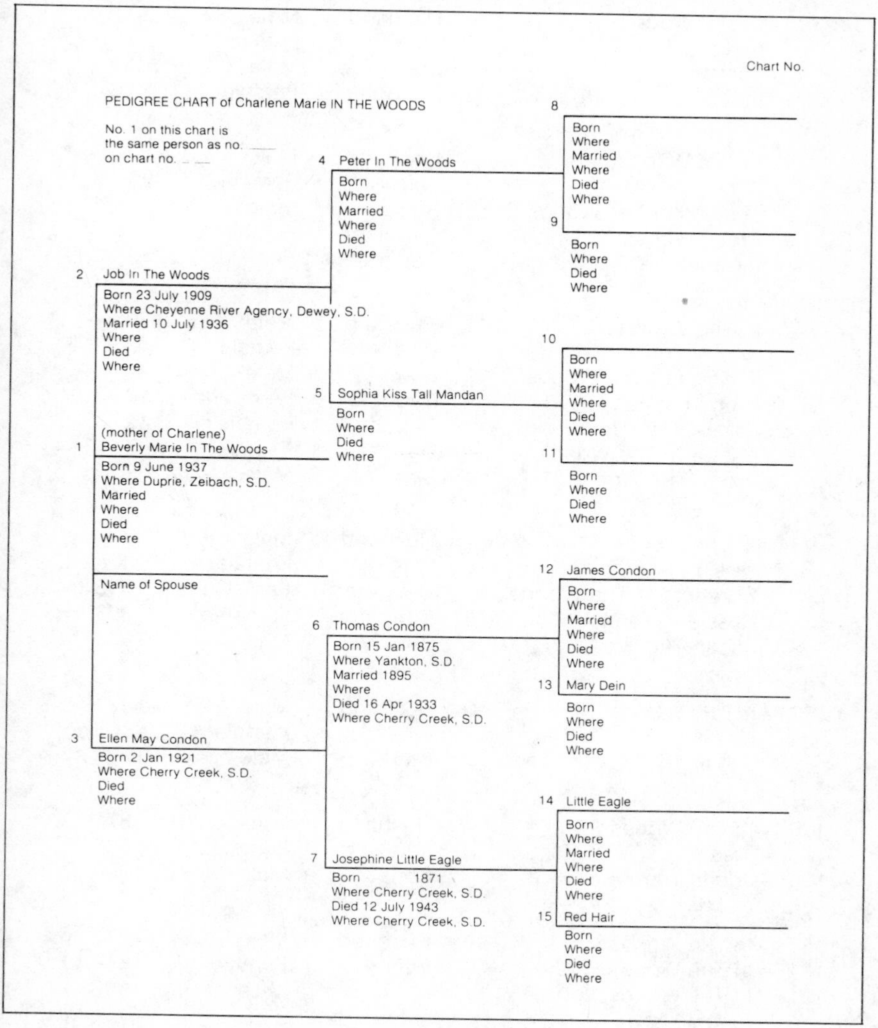

Dewey, South Dakota. Her father was Robert Ross, born 7 January 1929 at Red Elm, Zeibach, South Dakota, and her mother was Beverly Marie In The Woods, born 9 June 1937 at Duprie, Zeibach, South Dakota. While attending Brigham Young University Charlene became interested in tracing her mother's ancestry. She was able to make some interesting conclusions through the census records; combining that with information in the family's possession, she was able to document each ancestral line to the fourth generation.

A search of the Cheyenne River agency Indian census records in the Genealogical Society microfilms, Salt Lake City, Utah, disclosed the following entries for persons by the name of *In The Woods.*

1892			
2306—In The Woods	Husband	Male	30
Kiss	Wife	Female	33
Thomas	Son	Male	3
Infant	Daughter	Female	2/12
1901			
2324—In The Woods	Husband	Male	30
Kiss	Wife	Female	33
Thomas In The Woods	Son	Male	12
Pretty Woman	Daughter	Female	7
Elizabeth In The Woods	Daughter	Female	3
1910			
747—In The Woods	Husband	Male	39
Kiss	Wife	Female	42
Thomas In The Woods	Son	Male	21
Pretty Woman	Daughter	Female	16
Elizabeth In The Woods	Daughter	Female	12
Bessie In The Woods	Daughter	Female	7
Job In The Woods	Son	Male	2
1915			
1934—In The Woods	Husband	Male	1871
Kiss	Wife	Female	1868
Elizabeth In The Woods	Daughter	Female	1898
Bessie In The Woods	Daughter	Female	1903
Job In The Woods	Son	Male	1908
1921			
1521—In The Woods	Husband	Male	1871
Kiss	Wife	Female	1868
Job In The Woods	Son	Male	1908
1925			
1363—In The Woods	Husband	Male	1871
1364—Kiss	Wife	Female	1868
1365—Job In The Woods	Son	Male	1908
1928			
1314—In The Woods	Husband	Male	1871
1315—In The Woods, Mrs. Kiss	Wife	Female	1868
1316—In The Woods, Job (Crow Man)		Male	1908

1929

1347—In The Woods, Mrs. Kiss	Widow	Female	1868
1348—In The Woods, Job (Crow Man)	Single	Male	1908

1930

1519—In The Woods, Mrs. Kiss	Widow	Female	62
1520—In The Woods, Job	Single	Male	22

1934

1440—In The Woods, Mrs. Kiss	Widow	Female	66
1441—In The Woods, Job 7/21/08	Single	Male	25

1937

1535—In The Woods, Mrs. Kiss	Widow	Female	69
1536—In The Woods, Job 7/21/08	Head	Male	28
1537—In The Woods, Mrs. Ellen Condon (½ Blood), residence—Zeibach, S.D.	Wife 1/2/21	Female	15

Supplement for 1938

1536—In The Woods, Beverly Marie, Female, born 6/9/37, Sioux ¾ Blood, Single, Daughter, enrolled, residence—Zeibach, S.D.

A search of the 1880 federal census soundex for Dakota Territory listed the following household appearing to be that of James Condon and Mary, grandparents of Ellen May Condon In The Woods (third-great-grandparents of Charlene In The Woods):

Volume 3, Enumeration District 106, Sheet 7, Line 18

James Condon		White, Male, age 40 born Ireland
Mary	Wife	White, Female, age 35 born Ireland
Philip	Son	White, Male, age 22 born New York
Kate	Dau.	White, Female, age 17 born N.Y.
James	Son	White, Male, age 15 born New York
Mary Ann	Dau.	White, Female, age 12 born Wisc.
Thomas	Son	White, Male, age 3 born Nebraska

A search of the 1880 federal census records for Yankton, South Dakota, revealed the following household believed to be ancestral to Charlene In The Woods:

Condon, James	WM 40 Laborer	Ire.	Ire.	Ire.
Condon, Mary	WF 35 Wife	Ire.	Ire.	Ire.
Condon, Philip	WM 22 Son	N.Y.	Ire.	Ire.
Condon, Kate	WF 17 Daughter	N.Y.	Ire.	Ire.
Condon, James	WM 15 Son	N.Y.	Ire.	Ire.
Condon, Mary Ann	WF 12 Daughter	Wisc.	Ire.	Ire.
Condon, Thomas	WM 3 Son	Nebr.	Ire.	Ire.

According to family information, Thomas Condon, born in 1875, married Josephine Little Eagle, and they were the parents of Ellen May Condon, born 2 January 1921 (grandmother of Charlene). The Cheyenne River Indian agency census records were investigated and proved even more revealing on the *Little Eagle* line than they did on the *In The Woods* and *Condon* lines. A tie in the census records between the *Little Eagle* and *Condon* lines further substantiated the pedigree connections. See if you will agree with our deductions that the following census entries are ancestral to Charlene In The Woods:

Cheyenne River Indian Agency Census Records

1886		
553—Little Eagle	M 35	(1851)
No Name	F 32	(1854)
The Indian Came	F 11	(1875)
No Name	F 7	(1879)
No Name	F 3	(1883)
1887		
553—Little Eagle	M 35	(1852)
No Name	F 32	(1855)
The Indian Came	F 11	(1876)
No Name	F 8	(1879)
No Name	F 5	(1882)
1890		
553—Little Eagle	M 47	(1853)
Red Hair	F 37	(1853)
Her Cane	F 22	(1868)
Deer That Comes Out	F 20	(1870)
Deer That Shakes Himself	F 12	(1878)
1891		
553—Little Eagle, Head	M 48	(1843)
Red Hair, Wife	F 38	(1853)
Her Cane, Daughter	F 23	(1868)
Deer Come Out, Daughter	F 21	(1870)
Deer That Shakes Himself (Maggie), Daughter	F 13	(1878)
Cedar Eagle, Daughter	F 1	(1890)
1892		
1655—Little Eagle, Husband	M 57	(1835)
Red Hair, Wife	F 39	(1853)
Her Cane, Daughter	F 22	(1870)
Deer That Comes Out, Daughter	F 21	(1871)
Deer That Shakes Himself, Daughter	F 16	(1876)
Cedar Woman, Daughter	F 2	(1890)
1900		
1784—Little Eagle, Husband	M 65	(1835)
Red Hair, Wife	F 47	(1853)
Deer That Shows Herself (Jennie), Daughter	F 19	(1881)
Cedar Woman, Daughter	F 10	(1890)
Deer That Comes Out, Daughter	F 29	(1871)
Moses Coming Deer, Grandson	M 5	(1895)
Felix Coming Deer, Grandson	M 5½	(1899)

1901			
1727—	Little Eagle, Husband	M 64	(1837)
	Red Hair, Wife	F 48	(1853)
	Jennie Deer That Shows Herself, Daughter	F 20	(1881)
	Cedar Woman, Daughter	F 11	(1890)
	Moses Coming Deer, Grandson	M 6	(1895)
	Felix Coming Deer, Grandson	M 1	(1900)
	Deer That Comes Out, Daughter	F 30	(1871)
1910			
553—	Deer That Comes Out, Mother	F 39	(1871)
	Cedar Woman, Sister	F 30	(1890)
	Andrew Coming Deer, Son	M 15	(1895)
	Silas Coming Deer, Son	M 9	(1901)
	Felix Coming Deer, Son	M 5	(1905)
	Roscoe C. *Little Eagle,* Son	M 3	(1907)
	Kate *Condon,* Daughter	F 1	(1909)
1915			
1438—	Deer That Comes Out, Mother	F	1871
	Andrew Coming Deer, Son	M	1895
	Silas Condon, Son	M	1901
	Felix Condon, Son	M	1905
	Joseph Condon, Son	M	1907
	Eddie Condon, Son	M	1910
	Moses Condon, Son	M	1915
1921			
1181—	Deer That Comes Out, Mother	F	1871
	Samuel Condon, Son	M	1906
	Roscoe C. Condon (Joseph), Son	M	1907
	Ellen Condon, Daughter	F	1/2/1921
1930			
661—	Condon, Josephine, Married	F 59	(1871)
	Condon, Ellen, Single, Dau. (¼ P)	F 9	(1921)
	Condon, Bud, Single, Son (¼ P)	M 8	(1922)
1933			
N.E.—	Condon, Thomas, Head	M (no age listed)	
604—	Condon, Mrs. Josephine, Deer That Comes Out or Little Eagle, Wife, full blood	F 62	
605—	Ellen Condon 1/2/21, Dau. (½)	F 12	
606—	Bud Condon 12/2/22, Son (½)	M 10	
607—	Condon, Roscoe C. (Joseph) 4/30/07, Head (½)	M 25	
	Condon, Thomas Joseph 12/13/32 (3/12), Son (¼)		

So it turns out that *Deer That Comes Out* is Josephine Little Eagle who was born in 1871 and who married Thomas Condon. She is the daughter of Little Eagle and Red Hair as the pedigree indicated, and thus she is the great-grandmother of Charlene In The Woods. There might be some question whether Little Eagle in the 1886 enumeration is the same person as is shown in the 1890 entry, but the numbers are the same. It is also possible that Deer That Comes Out is one of the individuals without a name in 1886 and 1887, though the ages do not agree. Even though the names and ages vary somewhat each year, the census entries can be used to document pedigrees and establish connections.

Research Project: James David Stiffarm. James has one of the most unusual pedigrees I have seen; he claims the proud blood of four Indian tribes, a Scottish trader, a Swiss brewer, and a Frenchman. He was born 20 March 1950 at Lewistown, Fergus, Montana, the son of Moses James

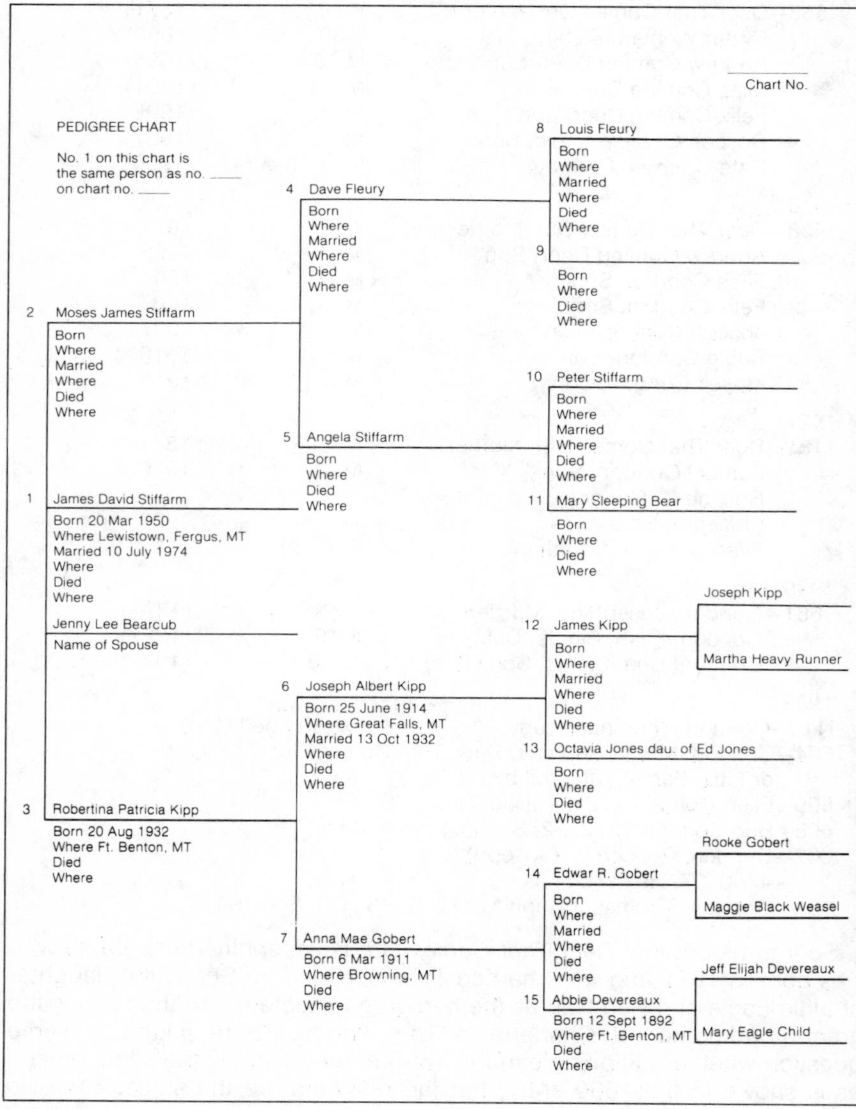

and Robertina Patricia (Kipp) Stiffarm. He married Jenny Lee Bearcub on 10 July 1974, and he has been able to document five generations of ancestry for his daughter JoDene Michelle Stiffarm, born in 1975.

James and Jenny were both enrolled in my genealogical research course at Brigham Young University. From the following newspaper account, James determined that he was descended from the Blackfoot, Sioux, Mandan, and Gros Ventre Indian tribes and a Scottish trader named Jim Kipp. From research at Brigham Young University in Indian and federal census records, he learned he is of the "Blackfeet Blood Piegan" Indians; that his second-great-grandfather, "Rooke" Gobert, was a brewer born in Switzerland; that his second-great-grandfather, Jeff Elijah Devereaux, was of French extraction; and that he probably has a little English-Welsh blood as well.

Indian Lad Born in Lewistown's Hospital This Week Is Great, Great, Great Grandson of Montana Pioneer

It was no ordinary boy who was born to Mr. and Mrs. Moses Stiffarm at Lewistown's St. Joseph's hospital a few minutes before midnight on Monday of this week.

In his veins flows the proud blood of four Indian tribes and of a pioneer trader from Scotland.

He is the great great great grandchild of Jim Kipp, a builder of the West, who is sometimes known as "Mr. Man of the Montana Plains."

Also, the little Indian lad born this week is the great great great grandson of Earth Woman, a Mandan whom the Scotsman met and married in what is now North Dakota, when he was enroute to this area.

He is the great great grandson of a Blackfoot squaw, Heavy Runner, who married Joe Kipp, son of the original Jim Kipp.

To this marriage was born another Jim Kipp who married a Sioux, adding the blood of a third tribe to the little lad now at the hospital here.

The daughter of this marriage was wooed and won by a Gros Ventre, the fourth tribe to contribute to the blood of Mr. and Mrs. Moses Stiffarm's little boy.

But this is just a bit of the Montana history that makes the little lad far from an ordinary baby.

Jim Kipp is the baby's great grandfather, though he is only 58 years old. He and his wife came here from across the Missouri river for the birth.

Jim, an intelligent, clear-eyed rancher who is as much a part of Montana as the Missouri river brakes and badlands, was willing to reminisce a bit when cornered by the Daily News.

"My grandfather, Jim Kipp, came West via Montreal, back in 1832," he said. "Representing the American Fur Company, he had three keel boats and 60 men, and made his way up the Missouri river to what is now Montana. The fur company was controlled by the Chouteaus, for which the town of Chouteau and county of Chouteau are now named. The Chouteaus named Fort Benton for Missouri's then Senator Benton, and they also named St. Louis for the king of France."

Joe Kipp, who was a son of the Scotsman, Jim Kipp, and the Mandan squaw, was once a guide for the famed Father DeSmet, and travelled much of the West, including the Bitterroot Valley, where the priest established a mission at what is now Stevensville, Mont.

When Chief Joseph made his famous flight from Oregon to Canada, via today's Yellowstone Park, Half Moon Pass and Lewistown, Joe Kipp was a scout for General Miles.

Joseph and his warriors ran into an advance party of Miles' army at Cow Island on the Missouri, a few miles above today's Power Plant ferry.

"When the skirmish started," Jim Kipp recalled, "my father was hunting deer in a bottom about a mile above the island and on the south side of the river. He swam the river and joined the soldiers in rifle pits they had dug, but the fight was soon over, and Joseph and his Nez Perce fled toward the Bear Paw mountains. Thinking they were in Canada, and safe, they paused to lick their wounds, only to have General Miles catch them and force their surrender."

The scout later ran a trading post at the mouth of Warm Spring Creek in today's Fergus county, when there were probably no more than half a dozen whites in all of Central Montana. This was in the winter of 1878–79. He traded with Indians from Fort Buford, where the Yellowstone flows into the Missouri from Fort Kipp east of Poplar, which was named for his father, and with Indians from as far west as the continental divide. James Willard Schultz, writer of many books on Indians, wintered with him that year.

Jim Kipp, the great grandfather of the little boy born this week, oddly enough owns the very land on which his father fought on the side of the soldiers against Joseph.

He "squatted" on Cow Creek in 1913, on the north bank of the Missouri and opposite Cow Island. The area, which is part of today's Blaine county, was surveyed in 1919, and Jim then filed on it.

Two whites were killed in the Cow Island fight, a nameless soldier and a paperhanger named Neubert or Schubert. They lie buried today in a double grave on the Cow Creek bottom, a quarter of a mile above the river and only about 100 yards from Jim Kipp's ranch house.

Jim Kipp also leases land on the Belknap reservation, and raises cattle, Shetland ponies and thoroughbred horses.

His grandson and granddaughter are Mr. and Mrs. Moses Stiffarm, parents of the boy that was born this week, and natives of Montana's Gros Ventre reservation. Moses Stiffarm rolled up quite a record during World War II with the 11th Airborne in the Pacific, ending up in Japan.

He moved his family south of the Missouri river recently, and has been punching cattle for Owen Anderson, a rancher in the Wood Hawk valley north of Winifred. This is how he happened to bring Mrs. Stiffarm to the Lewistown hospital for the birth of their boy.

And so it is that this lad of the "Indian league of Nations" and a Scotch great great great grandfather was born in Lewistown.

A proud day it was for the Key City, too, as the lad's ancestors played a great part in the building of Montana . . . he's no ordinary baby.
[*Lewistown Daily News,* March 1950]

The 1880 federal census for Chouteau County, Montana, listed Joseph Kipp's birthplace as Dakota, that of his father as Canada, and that of his mother as Dakota. Joseph's wife Martha (Heavy Runner) Kipp was listed as born in Montana and so were both her parents. Joseph Kipp's mother-in-law (Lee-pee-oah-see) was also living in his household; her place of birth was listed as Montana with that of her parents. She would be James David Stiffarm's third-great-grandmother.

The 1870 federal census of Big Horn County, Montana, listed "Joseph

Kip, age 23, half Indian, interpreter, born in Montana." He was living in Benton City. On page 17a of the same census, Rock Govert was listed as 34 years of age, a brewer, born in Switzerland. This is undoubtedly the Rooke Gobert who married Maggie Black Weasel and is James David Stiffarm's second-great-grandfather. One other interesting entry in the 1870 census was that for Edward Jones, age 30, a miner born in Wales; he could be the Ed Jones shown on James Stiffarm's pedigree.

Peter Stiffarm and Mary (Sleeping Bear) Stiffarm (James's great-grandparents) were located in several Indian census returns for the Gros Ventre Indians of the Fort Belknap Agency.

William F. Wheeler, the federal census enumerator for Big Horn County in 1870, reported the following interesting observation:

> In my trip down the Missouri River in April last, and at Ft. Buford, I saw several men who had spent the winter among the Crow Indians hunting buffalo for robes, and they informed me that there were no white men, except occasional hunters, who lived with the Indians, and a few near the Crow agency, anywhere on the Yellowstone or its tributaries. At the agency it was supposed there were quite a large number of white men—about 400—in the southern part of the county, who started to explore the Big Horn and other streams for gold from Cheyenne on the UPRR in May or June last; and it was feared they had been destroyed by Sioux Indians. Except with the Crows, it is not safe for whitemen any where in the County. All with whom I conversed agree in representing the valley of the Yellowstone and its tributaries as the most fertile imaginable. The grass grows to the height of four to six feet and like all the grass in Montana, cures in the stalk before frost comes and retains its nutriment all winter. . . . Coal abounds the whole length of the Yellowstone.

Miscellaneous sources. The tribal offices usually maintain enrollment, annuity, and allotment records that contain helpful genealogical information. Applications of individuals accepted by the tribe for enrollment as legitimate members contain a variety of information, including the name and residence of the person and the names of ancestors that show his connection to the tribe. In some cases the entry also indicates the number of children in the family. Entries also are filed for individuals whose application was rejected for one reason or another. The following is an extract from a Cherokee enrollment record at Salt Lake City:

> Homer Abercrombie—Mineral Bluff, Georgia
> Rejected: Applicant and ancestors never enrolled.
> No affiliation or association with Eastern Band shown.
> Applicant never recognized by Tribe as member.
> Ancestors: Sallie Reid, Robert Wright, and Riley Wright.
> Decisions: Vol. V page 304.
> [Cherokee Enrollment Records, vol. I, 1924]

Annuity payrolls and receipt rolls are also among tribal records and are similar to the modern census rolls. The annuity payrolls resulted from treaties or acts of Congress providing that the federal government make annual payments to tribal members for a stated period of time. They are usually in bound volumes arranged by the name of the tribe and chronologically. Those in the National Archives are dated 1848–1940 and are especially valuable for the period before annual census rolls were taken in 1885. The modern enrollment and annuity payment rolls sometimes include marriage information as well as the usual vital statistics.

C. George Younkin wrote an excellent paper concerning tribal and agency records for the five civilized tribes; it should be consulted by all persons interested in Indian genealogy. His paper is entitled *Historical and Genealogical Records of the Five Civilized Tribes and Other Indian Records* and was read at the 1969 World Conference on Records at Salt Lake City. He gives a brief history of each tribe and the government's association with it, then includes details on record holdings at Federal Records Center 7 in Fort Worth, Texas. He also gives suggestions for searching the records and lists reference and finding aids.

Copies of a few tribal records have been filed with the LDS genealogical library in Salt Lake City; the following entry, for example, was taken from Genealogies of the Blackfoot Indian Tribe in Browning, Glacier, Montana. The record was copied in 1956 from books in the tribal office of the Blackfoot Council at Browning by Anthony C. (Mose) Gilham; it was microfilmed by the Genealogical Society in 1968.

Rides At The Door Full Peigan 44 yrs
Father: *Lone Pity,* dead
Grandfather: *Chief Bull,* dead
Grandmother: *Spring Water,* dead
Mother: *Yellow Owl Woman,* dead
Grandfather: *Screaming Owl,* dead
Grandmother: *Dry Good Woman With The Coat,* living

The Coat, living, is a brother of *Yellow Owl Woman. Good Medicine Pipe Woman,* living, is a sister of *Yellow Owl Woman. Red Calf,* wife of *Shoots First,* living, is sister of *Yellow Owl Woman. Big Robe* was brother, no issue, dead. *Screaming Owl,* dead, brother, no issue. *Many Tail Feathers* is half brother of *Yellow Owl Woman. James Many Tail Feathers* is half brother of *Yellow Owl Woman. Fine Victory,* wife of *Big Wolf Medicine,* is half sister of *Yellow Owl Woman. Handing Back,* wife of *Spotted Eagle,* is half sister.

Wife: *Mary Grant Rides At The Door* ¾ Peigan 37 yrs
married 1887—Indian's Custom
Father: *James Grant,* dead, Blackfoot
Mother: *Mary Cadotte Grant,* living by herself.
Grandfather: *Cadotte*
Grandmother: unknown

Paternal aunts and uncles unknown. *Charles Rose,* living, is half brother of *Mary Grant. Peter Cadotte* is half brother of *Mary.* Brothers and sisters of *Mary* are *Julia Magee,* living, wife of *Tom Magee. Maggie Little Skunk* and *Cecile Little Skunk. James Grant, Richard Grant, Peter Grant,* are half brothers.

Children:

Richard Rides At The Door	*18 md to Amy Slannon*
Frank	13
James	10
Johnny	7
Joseph	5
William	2
Annie	born 1908

Lives between Willow Creek and John Vielle. Wants boys to have land on Willow Creek and will take up land above *Fox's* on upper Willow Creek.

There were several hundred entries in the above record, and the information had evidently been compiled from family knowledge and recorded in council books.

Part of another entry from the same record follows:

Little Dog Part Peigan 54 yrs

Paternal uncles and aunts all dead. *Little Dog* stated that the mother of *Walking In The Water* was *Long Time Good Success. Short Rib* says that *Walking In The Water* was daughter of *Under Petrified Rock,* a sister of his. When *Under Petrified Rock* died, the child was taken and raised by *Long Time Good Success,* a cousin of *Under Petrified Rock. Short Rib* says that *Little Dog* thinks his mother-in-law is *Long Time Good Success* but is in error. A cousin of *Long Time Good Success* was *Calf Boss Ribs,* died two years ago, leaving *Barney Boss Ribs* and *Medicine Rabbit,* a girl, and *Capturing A Gun In The Morning,* a boy. Sister of *Long Time Good Success* is *Double Blanket Woman,* living. The father of *Petrified Rock* is dead. The mother, *Victory At Home* is dead.

Family connections in the above record were cross-referenced when they appeared in more than one entry. It can readily be seen that such information is valuable to the searcher if he once finds a family connection, but very little date or place information is given.

It can also be seen that complex and unusual family relationships existed among the American Indians because of death, divorce, abandonment, and the like. Doctor James R. Clark in *The Cultural and Historical Background of the Indian People: A Vital Part of the Genealogical Research Problem* (paper read at the World Conference on Records in Salt Lake City 1969) explains the complex nature of some Crow family units:

> In a small, light blue house on the east side of the highway leading out of Crow Agency, Montana, our interviewer met *May Takes Gun Child In Mouth*. Mrs. *Child In Mouth* was seventy-three years of age at the time of the interview. She was a widow. She was a three quarters blood Crow or Absaraka. Living with her was *Ira L. Bad Bear,* a grandson, age nineteen, who was single. Also living with her was *Dennis Big Hair,* a grandnephew, age twenty-seven, who was divorced.
>
> *Andrew Bird In Ground* lived in Real Bird Land southeast of the Crow Agency. Living with him in his home was a rather typical extended family. There was his wife, *Inez,* his son-in-law, *Burton Darrow Pretty On Top,* who had married *Eleanor,* daughter of the *Bird In Grounds.* Also living at home with her daughter, *Carlen Faith Bird In Ground,* was their twenty-year-old, single daughter, *Andrea.* The *Bird In Grounds* had seven other children living at home ranging in age from nineteen to four years of age [p. 9]

When I visited the Indian archives at the Oklahoma Historical Society in Oklahoma City recently, I was overwhelmed by the amount of source material available for midwestern and eastern Indian research. According to Martha Blaine, director, the archives has well over three million pages of manuscript material and six thousand volumes—the largest collection of Indian documents in the United States outside of Washington, D.C. The records pertain primarily to the Five Civilized Tribes (Cherokee, Chick-

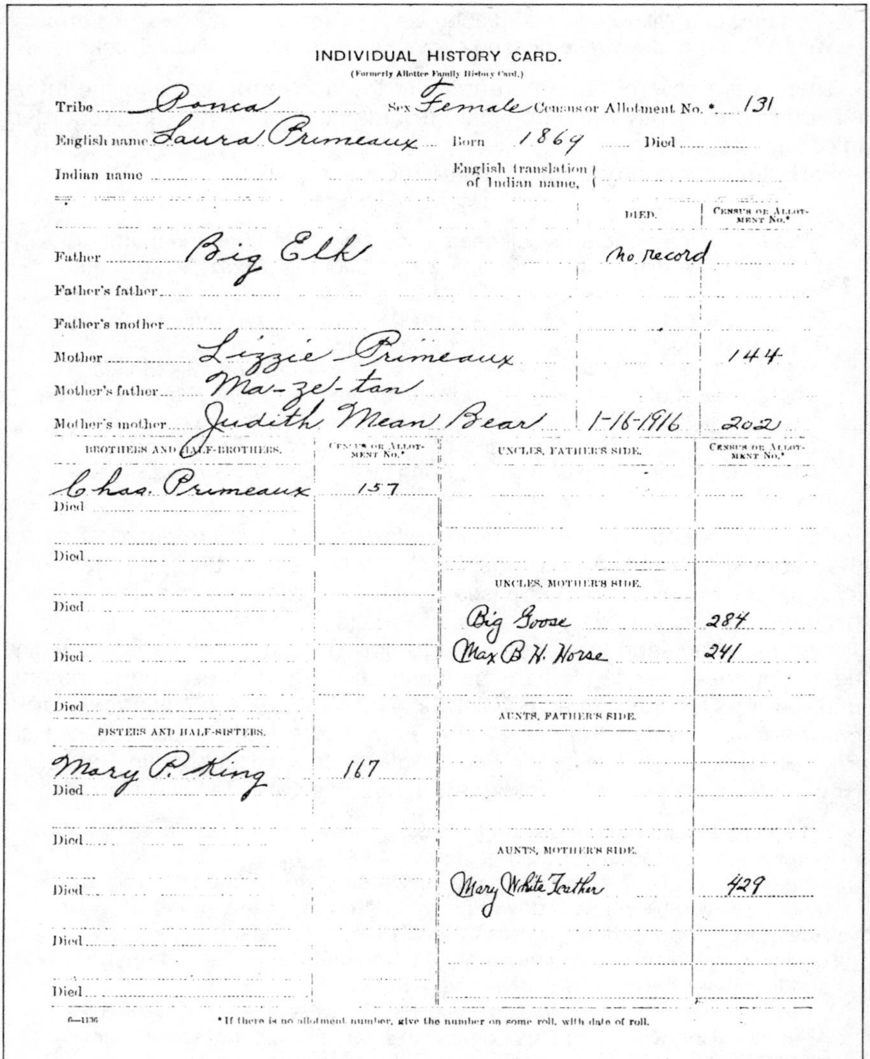

INDIVIDUAL HISTORY CARD.
(Formerly Allottee Family History Card.)

Tribe Ponca Sex Female Census or Allotment No.* 131

English name Laura Primeaux Born 1869 Died

Indian name English translation of Indian name,

		Died.	Census or Allotment No.*
Father	Big Elk	no record	
Father's father			
Father's mother			
Mother	Lizzie Primeaux		144
Mother's father	Ma-ze-tan		
Mother's mother	Judith Mean Bear	1-16-1916	202

Brothers and half-brothers.	Census or Allotment No.*
Chas. Primeaux	157
Died	
Died	
Died	
Died	
Died	

Sisters and half-sisters.	
Mary P. King	167
Died	
Died	
Died	
Died	
Died	

Uncles, father's side.	Census or Allotment No.*

Uncles, mother's side.	
Big Goose	284
Max B. H. Horse	241

Aunts, father's side.	

Aunts, mother's side.	
Mary White Feather	429

6—1136 *If there is no allotment number, give the number on some roll, with date of roll.

asaw, Choctaw, Creek, and Seminole), but also represented were the Cheyenne and Arapaho Agency, Cantonment Agency, Chilocco Indian School, Kiowa Indian Agency, Mekusukey Academy, Pawnee Indian Agency, Quapaw Indian Agency, Shawnee Indian Agency, and the Executive Library Cherokee Nation. These groups were variously represented, but all had several thousand pages of available material.

The archives also had several private collections relating to American Indians, including those of Grant Foreman and Frederick B. Severs. Foreman's publication *The Five Civilized Tribes* (1966) is a masterpiece on the subject, and Angie Debo's *The Road To Disappearance* (1967) should

(12) (5—128.)

CENSUS of the Blackfeet, Blood & Piegan Indians of Blackfeet Agency, Montana taken by George Steell, United States Indian Agent, June 30" , 1893

NO.	INDIAN NAME.	ENGLISH NAME.	SEX.	RELATION.	AGE.
	(67)				
280		Belle Ripley	F	Mother	40
281		David Ripley	M	Son	16
282		Minnie Ripley	F	Daughter	12
	(68)				
283	Na to kots i nama	Two Guns	M	Husband	25
284	Ah ke sin aki	Taking Good Camps	F	Wife	16
	(69)				
285	Aki ma kan	Many Guns	M	Father	32
286	Kunis ke naki	Moose Woman	F	Wife	29
287		Joe Many Guns	M	Son	6 mo
	(70)				
288	Se kum o makon	Hairy Running Crane	M	Father	41
289	In is kim ake	Buffalo Stone	F	Wife	37
290	Apats e kemau	Feathers Behind	M	Son	6
	(71)				
~~291~~		~~John Kipp~~	M	Father	32
292		Mary Kipp	F	Wife	27
293	*	Jack Kipp	M	Son	8
294		Joseph Kipp	"	"	5
295		Isabel Kipp	F	Adopted	13
296		Infant	M	Son	8 mo
	(72)				
297	Akop sis o	Many Cuts	F	Widow	62
	(73)				
298		Henry Lamb	M	Brother	9
299		Bessie Lamb	F	Sister	8

also be read by those interested in American Indian history. To get a background of the early history and removal of the eastern Indian tribes, read *The Trail of Tears* by Gloria Jahoda (1975). You will also cry.

Two years ago the Oklahoma Historical Society were microfilming their collection of Indian materials under a special grant, but they estimated at that time it would take from seven to ten years to complete the job. Then microfilm copies will be available for purchase.

Items included in various collections at the archives included cash property accounts, adoptions, agency purchases, allotments, agency reports, newspapers, vital statistics, divorces, enrollments, and information about estates, farmers, customs, employment fairs, exhibits, chiefs, captives, pensions, military service, medicine men, and outlaws.

One unusual collection was a volume entitled *Final Rolls of the Citizens and Freedmen of the Five Civilized Tribes of Indian Territory*. It was completed and printed by an act of Congress 21 June 1906 and lists the following: Choctaws by blood, new born Choctaws by blood, minor Choctaws by blood, Choctaws by marriage, Choctaw freedmen, minor Choctaws freedmen, Mississippi Choctaws, new born Mississippi Choctaws, minor Mississippi Choctaws, Chickasaws by blood, new born Chickasaws by blood, minor Chickasaws by blood, Cherokees by blood, Delaware Cherokees, Cherokees by intermarriage, Creeks by blood, minor Creeks by blood, Creek freedmen, new born Creek freedmen, minor Creek freedmen, Seminoles by blood and freedmen, new born Seminoles by blood, and new born Seminole freedmen. Using the Choctaw rolls as an example, the ages of the Choctaws by blood are calculated to 25 September 1902. The enrollment number is listed first, then name, age, sex, degree of blood, and census card number. The census card—on file in the Muskogee area office, Muskogee, Oklahoma—gives more information, including the names of parents, where they lived, and whether they are living or dead. The ages of the new borns are calculated to 4 March 1905, as are the ages of children born between 25 September 1902 and that date. The ages of the minors are calculated to 4 March 1906, when the rolls of the five civilized tribes were closed forever. The freedmen are the descendants of slaves of the enrollees (Colket and Bridgers 1964, p. 131).

The following maps show areas of Indian location, removal, and relocation in the United States:

Reprinted from *The American Republic to 1865*, vol. 1 (Hofstadter, Miller, and Aaron 1959) by permission of the authors.

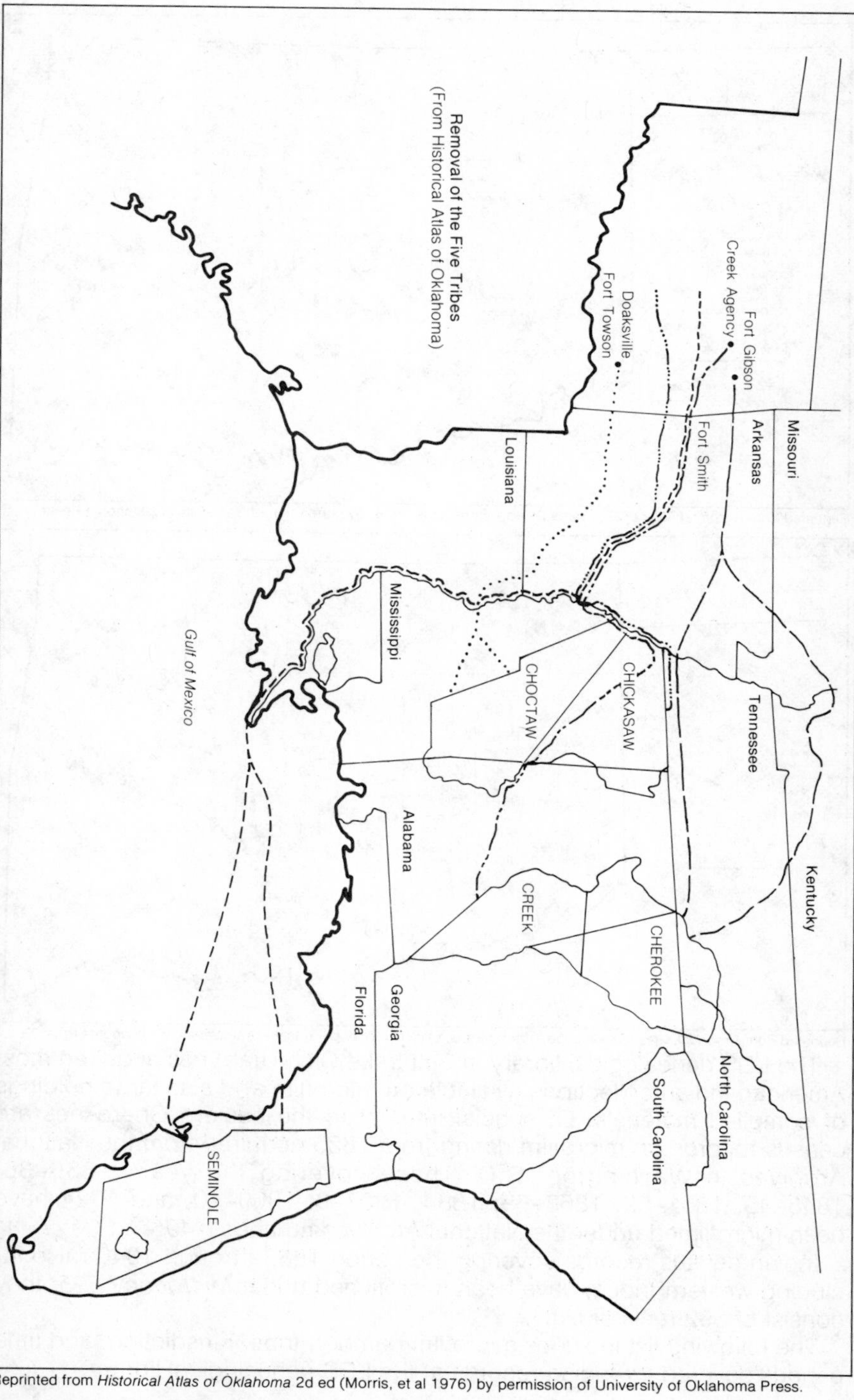

Reprinted from *Historical Atlas of Oklahoma* 2d ed (Morris, et al 1976) by permission of University of Oklahoma Press.

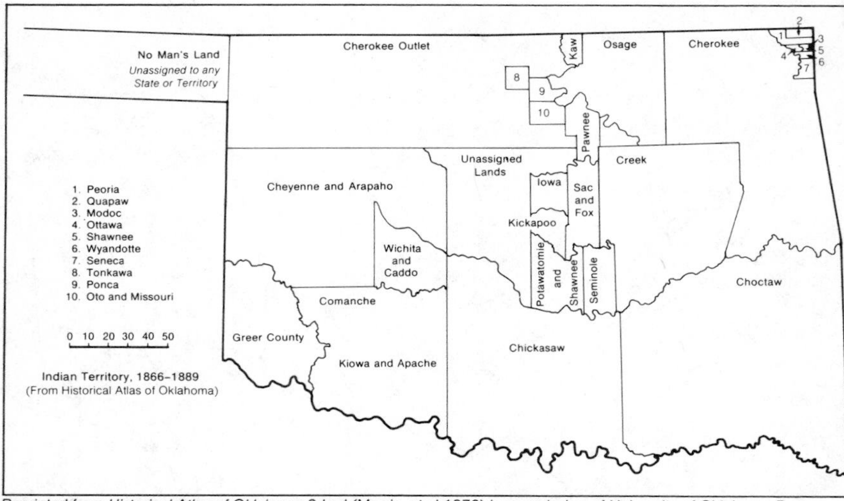

Reprinted from *Historical Atlas of Oklahoma* 2d ed (Morris, et al 1976) by permission of University of Oklahoma Press.

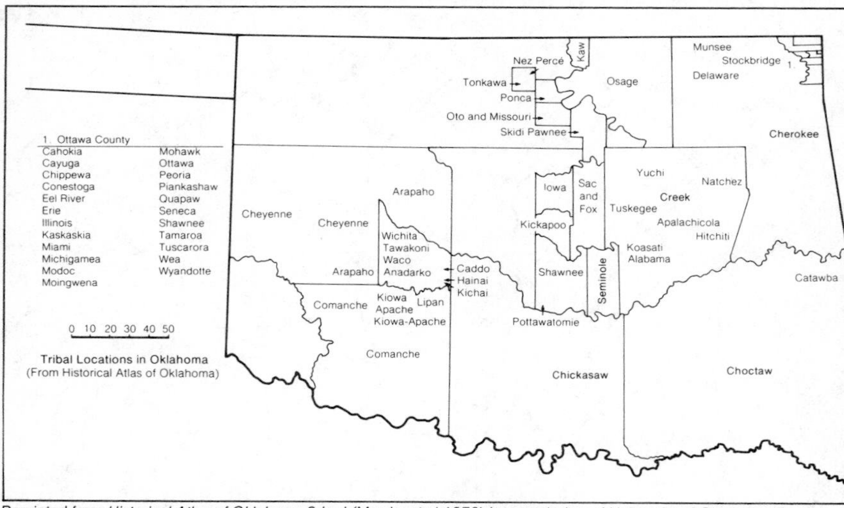

Reprinted from *Historical Atlas of Oklahoma* 2d ed (Morris, et al 1976) by permission of University of Oklahoma Press.

The LDS genealogical library in Salt Lake City, Utah, has acquired most American Indian collections available on microfilm and also large holdings of compiled materials. Of special interest to the eastern Cherokees are census records on microfilm dating from 1835 acquired from the National Archives in Washington, D.C. Those covering the years 1835–36, 1848–49, 1851–52, 1868–69, 1884, 1907–8, 1909–10, and 1924 have been microfilmed under the National Archives number *T-496*.

Indian census records covering the period 1885 through 1940 (also including western tribes) have been microfilmed under *Microcopy 595;* they consist of 692 reels of film.

The following list includes microfilm number, tribe, jurisdiction, and time periods covered for Indian records at the LDS genealogical library:

Census Films

Jurisdiction—Tribe

573847	Albuquerque School (Pueblo, Navajo)
573848	Chippewa, Sioux, Paiute, Other
573849	Blackfoot 1890–96
573850	Blackfoot 1897–1906
573851	Blackfoot 1907–13
573852	Blackfoot 1914–19
573853	Blackfoot 1920–25
573854	Blackfoot 1926–30
573855	Blackfoot 1931–32
573856	Blackfoot 1933–35
573857	Blackfoot 1936–39
573858	Bloomfield Seminole Calif. Spec. 1907–11
573859	California Special 1912–13
573860	California Special 1914–15
573861	Apache, Mojave, Cheyenne, Arapaho
573862	Cheyenne, Arapaho 1903–16
573863	Cheyenne, Arapaho 1917–27
573864	Paiute, Shoshoni, Washo 1909, 1925–30
573865	Paiute, Shoshoni, Washo 1931–32
573866	Paiute, Shoshoni, Washo 1933–36
573867	Paiute, Shoshoni, Washo 1937–39
573868	Potawatomi, Cherokee
573869	Potawatomi, Cherokee 1915–22
573870	Potawatomi, Cherokee 1923–29
573871	Potawatomi, Cherokee 1930–32
573872	Potawatomi, Cherokee 1933–39
573873	Cheyenne, Arapaho 1887–88, 1891–94
573874	Cheyenne, Arapaho 1895–1904
573875	Cheyenne, Arapaho 1905–20
573876	Cheyenne, Arapaho 1921–30
573877	Cheyenne, Arapaho 1934–39
574192	Sioux 1886–87, 1890–91
574193	Sioux 1892, 1894–1900
574194	Sioux 1901–7
574195	Sioux 1910–14
574196	Sioux 1915–20
574197	Sioux 1921–29
574198	Sioux 1930–32
574199	Sioux 1933–42
574200	Choctaw 1926–32
574201	Choctaw 1933–39
574202	Coeur d'Alene, Kalispel, Spokan
574203	Coeur d'Alene, Kalispel, Kutenai
574204	Coeur d'Alene, Kalispel, Nez Perce
574205	Mohave, Chemehuevi, Walapai 1885–93
574206	Mohave, Chemehuevi, Other 1906–29
574207	Mohave, Chemehuevi, Cocopa, Yuma
574208	Colville, Spokan, Lake, Nespelem

574209	Okanagon, Sanpoil, Nez Perce, Lake
574210	Colville, Spokan, Columbia, Nespel
574211	Sanpoil, Kalispel, Wenatchee, Lake
574212	Colville Reservation 1917–24
574213	Colville, Spokane 1925–29
574214	Colville, Spokane 1930–32
574215	Colville, Spokane 1933–39
574216	Consolidated Chippewa 1923
574217	Consolidated Chippewa 1924
574218	Consolidated Chippewa 1925
574219	Consolidated Chippewa 1926
574220	Consolidated Chippewa 1927
574221	Consolidated Chippewa 1928
574222	White Earth Subagency 1929
574223	Fond du Lac, Grand Portage, Nett Lake
574224	White Earth Reservation 1930
574225	Bois Forte, Winnibigoshish and Cass
574226	White Earth Reservation 1931
574227	Fond du Lac, Leech Lake, Boise Forte
574228	White Earth Reservation 1932
574229	White Oak Point, Nett Lake, Cass
574230	White Earth Reservation 1933
574231	Nonremoval Mille Lac, Leech Lake
575765	White Earth Reservation 1934
575766	Cass, Winnibigoshish 1934–36
575767	White Earth Reservation
575768	Cass, Winnibigoshish 1937–39
575769	Ute 1923–24, 1926–31
575770	Ute 1932–39
575771	Crow 1891–95, 1897–98
575772	Crow 1899–1905
575773	Crow 1906–8, 1912–16
575774	Crow 1917–24
575775	Crow 1925–30
575776	Crow 1931–33
575777	Crow 1934–37
575778	Crow 1938–40
575779	Yanktonai, Brule, Sioux 1886–92
575780	Yanktonai, Brule, Sioux 1893–1905
575781	Yanktonai, Sioux 1906–20
575782	Yanktonai, Brule, Sioux 1921–29
575783	Yanktonai, Brule, Sioux 1930–33
575784	Yanktonai, Brule, Sioux 1934–39, 1942
575785	Cushman, Skokomish, Clallam, Chehalis
575786	Sioux, Chippewa 1885–90
575787	Sioux, Chippewa 1892–97
575788	Sioux, Chippewa 1898–1902
575789	Sioux, Chippewa 1903–5
575790	Digger 1899; Eastern Navajo 1929
575791	Eastern Navajo 1930
575792	Eastern Navajo 1931
575793	Eastern Navajo 1932

575794	Eastern Navajo 1933
575795	Eastern Navajo 1934–35
575796	Fallon (Paiute Indians) 1909–24
575797	Flandreau 1892–1921
575798	Flandreau 1922–39
575799	Flathead 1886–93
575800	Flathead 1895–97, 1900–1905
576464	Flathead 1906–7, 1909–13
576465	Flathead 1914–18
576466	Flathead 1919–23
576467	Flathead 1924–28
576468	Flathead 1929–31
576469	Flathead 1932–34
576470	Flathead 1935–37
576471	Flathead 1938–39
576472	Fond du Lac 1910–20
576473	Apache 1898–1907
576474	Apache 1908–13
576475	Apache 1914–18
576476	Apache 1919–23
576477	Apache 1924–27
576478	Apache 1929–31
576479	Apache 1932–33
576480	Apache 1934–39
576481	Grosventre, Assiniboin 1885–95
576482	Grosventre, Assiniboin 1896–1908
576483	Grosventre, Assiniboin 1909–1911–20
576484	Grosventre, Assiniboin 1921–29
576485	Grosventre, Assiniboin 1930–35
576486	Grosventre, Assiniboin 1936–39
576487	Grosventre, Arikara, Mandan 1895–1902
576488	Grosventre, Arikara, Mandan 1903–15
576489	Grosventre, Arikara, Mandan 1916–29
576490	Grosventre, Arikara, Mandan 1930–35
576491	Grosventre, Arikara, Mandan 1936–39
576492	Paiute, Pit River, Digger 1915–30
576493	Shoshoni, Bannock 1885–87, 90–91
576494	Shoshoni, Bannock 1902–9
576495	Shoshoni, Bannock 1910–18
576496	Shoshoni, Bannock 1919–26
576497	Shoshoni, Bannock 1927–31
576498	Shoshoni, Bannock 1932–34
576499	Shoshoni, Bannock 1935–39
576834	Nez Perce 1902–10
576835	Nez Perce 1911–20
576836	Nez Perce 1921–29
576837	Nez Perce 1930–33
576838	Ute 1904–8; Paiute 1910–23
576839	Mohave, Chemehuevi, Hualapai, Walapai
576840	Sioux, Assiniboin 1885–96
576841	Sioux, Assiniboin 1897–1905
576842	Sioux, Assiniboin 1906–12

576843	Sioux, Assiniboin 1913–19
576844	Sioux, Assiniboin 1920–25
576845	Sioux, Assiniboin 1926–29
576846	Sioux, Assiniboin 1930–31
576847	Sioux, Assiniboin 1932–33
576848	Sioux, Assiniboin 1934–36
576849	Sioux, Assiniboin 1937–39
576850	Sioux, Chippewa 1906–9
576851	Sioux 1910–20
576852	Sioux 1922–29
576853	Sioux 1930–39
576854	Yuma, Cocopa(h) 1905, 1915–29
576855	Yuma, Cocopa(h) 1930–35
576856	Goshute, Shoshoni, Paiute 1917–23
576857	Winnebago 1916–17
576858	Grand Ronde 1885–92, 1894–1914
576859	Chippewa, Potawatomi 1936–37
576860	Chippewa, Potawatomi 1938–40
576861	Sioux 1892; Menominee, Oneida 1885
576862	Menominee, Oneida, Stockbridge 1895–99
576863	Menominee, Stockbridge 1900–1908
576864	Digger 1916–23
576865	Potawatomi, Kickapoo, Iowa 1927–31
576866	Potawatomi, Kickapoo, Iowa 1932–34
576867	Havasupai 1905–33
576868	Chippewa 1916–23
576869	Chippewa 1924–26, 1928–29
576870	Chippewa 1930–33
576871	Hoopa, Klamath 1885–97, 1899–1907
576872	Hoopa, Klamath 1915–22
576873	Hoopa, Klamath 1923–29
576874	Hoopa, Klamath 1930–32
576875	Hoopa, Klamath 1933–35
576876	Hoopa, Klamath 1936–39
576877	Hopi 1924–26
576878	Hopi 1927–29
576879	Hopi, Navajo 1930
576880	Hopi, Navajo 1931
576881	Hopi, Navajo 1932
576882	Hopi, Navajo 1933
576883	Hopi, Navajo 1934–36
576884	Hopi 1937–39
576885	Hualapai, Walapai, Havasupai
576886	Jicarilla 1916–29
576887	Jicarilla 1930–39
576888	Kaibab, Paiute, Goshute
576889	Keshena: Menominee, Stockbridge
576890	Menominee, Stockbridge 1915–19
576891	Menominee, Oneida 1920–24
576892	Menominee, Oneida 1925–29
576893	Menominee, Oneida 1930–31
576894	Menominee, Stockbridge 1932

576895	Menominee, Stockbridge 1933
576896	Menominee, Oneida 1934–35
576897	Keshena, Menominee 1936–37
576898	Keshena, Menominee 1938–42
576899	Kickapoo, Iowa, Sauk, Fox, Potawatomi
576900	Kiowa, Comanche, Apache, Caddo
576901	Kiowa, Comanche, Apache, Caddo 1900–1904
576902	Kiowa, Comanche, 1905–6, 1909–13
576903	Kiowa, Comanche, Apache 1914–17
576904	Kiowa, Comanche, Apache 1918–21
576905	Kiowa, Comanche, Apache 1922–25
576906	Kiowa, Comanche, Apache 1926–29
576907	Kiowa, Comanche, Apache 1930
576908	Kiowa, Comanche, Apache 1931
576909	Kiowa, Comanche, Apache 1932
576910	Kiowa, Comanche, Apache 1933
576911	Kiowa, Comanche, Apache 1934–36
576912	Kiowa, Comanche, Apache 1937–39
576913	Klamath, Modoc, Paiute 1885–1906
576914	Klamath, Modoc, Paiute 1907–20
576915	Klamath, Modoc, Paiute 1921–29
576916	Klamath, Modoc, Paiute 1930–33
576917	Klamath, Modoc, Paiute 1934–39
576918	Chippewa 1910–27
576919	Lac du Flambeau, Bad River 1928–30
576920	Lac du Flambeau 1931–1932
576921	Lac du Flambeau, Bad River 1933–35
576922	Laona, Potawatomi 1916–27
576923	La Pointe, Bad River 1886–89
576924	Bad River, Bois Fort 1890–92
576925	Bad River, Fond du Lac 1893–94
576926	Bad River, Fond du Lac 1895–97
576927	Bad River, Fond du Lac 1898–1902
576928	Bad River, Fond du Lac 1903–7
576929	Bad River, Fond du Lac 1908–15
576930	Bad River, Chippewa 1916–22
576931	Bad River, Red Cliff 1923–27
576932	Leech Lake, Chippewa 1899–1902
576933	Leech Lake, Chippewa 1903–5
576934	Leech Lake, Chippewa 1906–12
576935	Leech Lake, Chippewa 1913–17
576936	Leech Lake, Chippewa 1918–22
576937	Lemhi, Shoshoni 1885, 1887–1906
576938	Leupp 1915–17, 1920–25, 1927, 1929
576939	Leupp, Navajo 1930–32
576940	Leupp, Navajo 1933–35
576941	Lovelocks, Paiute 1910–12
579663	Machinac 1902–3, 1910, 1915–27
579664	Malki 1916–19
579665	Mescalero 1915–29
579666	Mescalero 1930–39
579667	Mexican Kickapoo 1899–1901

579668	Mission Tule River 1894–1901
579669	Mission Tule River 1898–1903
579670	Mission 1922–25
579671	Mission 1926–29
579672	Mission 1930–31
579673	Mission 1932
579674	Mission 1933
579675	Mission 1934–35
579676	Mission 1936
579677	Mission 1937–39
579678	Moapa River 1910–19, 1921, 1923–26
579679	Moqui 1915–16, 1918
579680	Moqui 1919–20
579681	Moqui 1921–23
579682	Navajo, Moqui Pueblo, Hopi 1885
579683	Navajo 1915
579684	Navajo 1936
579685	Eastern Navajo Reservation 1937
579686	Leupp Reservation 1937
579687	Northern Navajo 1937
579688	Southern Navajo 1937
579689	Southern Navajo 1937 (Arizona)
579690	Southern Navajo 1937 (New Mexico)
579691	Western Navajo 1937
579692	Navajo 1938–39
579693	Neah Bay, Makah, Ozette 1885–99
579694	Neah Bay, Makah, Ozette 1900–13
579695	Neah Bay, Makah, Ozette 1914–28
579696	Makah, Ozette, Hoh 1930–33
579697	Nett Lake, Bois Fort Band 1908–18
579698	Nevada, Paiute 1886–1905
579699	Nevada 1906–7, 1909–21
579700	New York 1885–87
579701	New York 1888–89, 1891–93
579702	New York 1894–97
579703	New York 1898–1901
579704	New York 1903–6
579705	New York 1907–9
579706	New York 1910–12
579707	New York 1913–15
579708	New York 1916–18
579709	New York 1919–21
579710	New York 1922–24
579711	Nez Perce 1890–1901
579712	Nisaually, Skokomish 1885–87
579713	Northern Navajo 1930
579714	Northern Navajo 1931
579715	Northern Navajo 1932
579716	Northern Navajo 1933
579717	Northern Navajo 1934–35
579718	Northern Pueblo 1920–24
579719	Northern Pueblo 1925–28

579720	Northern Pueblo 1929–30
579721	Omaha, Winnebago 1886–91
579722	Omaha, Winnebago 1892–98
579723	Omaha, Winnebago 1899–1905
579724	Omaha 1915–24
579725	Oneida 1900–10
579726	Oneida 1911–20
579727	Osage, Kansa 1887–88, 1890–96
579728	Osage, Kansa, Kaw 1897–1905
579729	Osage 1906–7, 1909–13
579730	Osage 1914–18
579731	Osage 1919–22
579732	Osage 1923–26
579733	Osage 1927–29
579734	Osage 1930–31
579735	Osage 1932
579736	Osage 1933
579737	Osage 1934–36
579738	Osage 1937–39
579739	Otoe, Missouri 1906–10, 1912, 1915–19
579740	Paiute, Goshute, Ute 1928–31
579741	Paiute, Goshute, Ute 1932–33
579742	Paiute, Goshute, Ute 1934–35
579743	Paiute, Goshute, Ute 1936–37
579744	Paiute, Goshute, Ute 1938–39
579745	Pala, Mission 1905–7, 1916–20
579746	Pawnee 1902–19
579747	Kansa, Kaw, Oto, Missouri 1920–27
579748	Kansa, Kaw, Oto, Pawnee 1928–30
579749	Kansa, Kaw, Oto, Pawnee 1931
579750	Kansa, Kaw, Oto, Pawnee, Ponca 1932
579751	Kansa, Kaw, Oto, Pawnee, Ponca 1933
579752	Kansa, Kaw, Oto, Pawnee, Ponca 1934–36
579753	Kansa, Kaw, Oto, Pawnee, Ponca 1937–39
579754	Phoenix, Pima, Apache 1928–31
579755	Phoenix, Pima, Apache 1932–33
579756	Apache 1934–37
579757	Pima, Papago 1887, 1890–91, 1894
579758	Pima, Papago 1895–96, 1899, 1901
579759	Pima, Papago, Maricopa 1919–21
579760	Pima, Papago, Maricopa 1922–24
579761	Pima, Papago, Maricopa 1925–26
579762	Pima, Papago, Maricopa 1927–28
579763	Pima, Papago, Maricopa 1929
579764	Pima, Papago, Maricopa 1930
579765	Pima, Papago, Maricopa 1931
579766	Pima, Papago, Maricopa 1932
579767	Pima, Papago, Maricopa 1933
579768	Pima, Papago, Maricopa 1934
579769	Pima, Papago, Maricopa 1935–36
579770	Pima, Papago, Maricopa 1937
580740	Pima, Papago, Maricopa 1938–39

580741	Sioux, Cheyenne 1886
580742	Sioux, Cheyenne 1887–88
580743	Sioux, Cheyenne 1890–91
580744	Sioux, Cheyenne 1893
580745	Sioux, Cheyenne 1894–95
580746	Sioux, Cheyenne 1896–99
580747	Pine Ridge 1900–1903
580748	Pine Ridge 1904–5, 1907
580749	Oglala Sioux 1913, 1915–17
580750	Oglala Sioux 1918–20
580751	Oglala Sioux 1921–23
580752	Oglala Sioux 1924–26
580753	Oglala Sioux 1927–28
580754	Oglala Sioux 1929
580755	Oglala Sioux 1930
580756	Oglala Sioux 1931
580757	Oglala Sioux 1932
580758	Oglala Sioux 1924–32
580759	Oglala Sioux 1933
580760	Oglala Sioux 1934
580761	Oglala Sioux 1934–36
580762	Oglala Sioux 1937
580763	Oglala Sioux 1937–39
580764	Pinestone 1914–15; 1918–19; 1923; 1924–39
580765	Ponca, Oto, Missouri, Pawnee, and Tonkawa 1886–90
580766	Ponca 1891–96
580767	Ponca 1897–1903
580768	Ponca, Tonkawa 1904–12
580769	Ponca, Tonkawa, Kansa, Kaw 1913–02
580770	Ponca, Tonkawa, Oto, Missouri 1913–27
580771	Potawatomi 1891–93, 1895–1902
580772	Potawatomi 1903–19
580773	Potawatomi, Iowa, Kickapoo, Sauk, Fox 1921–26
580774	Potawatomi 1935–40
580775	Pueblo 1885–86
581391	Pueblo 1887–88
581392	Pueblo 1889–90
581393	Pueblo 1891–92
581394	Pueblo 1898–99
581400	Pueblo Navajo 1917–19
581410	Shawnee, Miami, Ottawa, Peoria, Quapaw, Seneca, Wyandot 1936–39
581411	Quinaielt 1885–87
581412	Red Lake 1907–12
581413	Red Lake 1913–17, 1919
581414	Red Lake 1920–23
581415	Chippewa 1924–29
581416	Chippewa 1930–32
581418	Chippewa 1936–39
581419	Red Moon 1909–12, 1914–16
581420	Rocky Boy 1919–39
581421	Rosebud 1886–87, 1891

581424	Brule, Sioux 1901–05
581431	Sioux 1926
581434	Sioux 1930
581440	Roseburg 1915–17
581441	Round Valley 1885–1905, 1909
581444	Sac, Fox 1888–1910
581448	Sauk, Fox, Iowa, Citizen Potawatomi Absentee Shawnee Indians
581451	Sacramento 1934–39
581454	Salt Lake Paiute 1913, 1915
581458	San Carlos 1904–12
581459	Apache, Mohave 1914–15
581460	Apache, Mohave 1916–19
581461	Apache, Mohave 1920–24
581462	Apache, Mohave 1925–29
581479	Apache, Mohave 1930–33
581480	Apache 1934–39
581481	Mission 1904–6; Navajo 1916
581482	Santa Fe, 1904, 1906, 1910–14
581483	Santa Fe (Pueblo) 1931–32
581484	Santa Fe (Pueblo) 1933–35
581485	Santee, Flandreau Sioux 1885–98
581486	Santee Sioux, Ponca 1899–1907, 1909–10
581487	Santee Sioux, Ponca 1911–17
581488	San Xavier (Papago) 1904, 1910–17
581489	Seger (Cheyenne) 1903–12, 1914–17
581490	Sells (Papago) 1918–21
581491	Sells (Papago) 1922–24
581492	Sells (Papago) 1925–28
581493	Sells (Papago) 1929–30
581494	Sells (Papago) 1931–32
581495	Sells (Papago) 1933–34, 1937–39
581496	Seminole (Florida) 1913–29
581497	Seminole (Florida) 1930–40
581498	Quapaw, Seneca, Wyandot 1901–7
581499	Quapaw, Seneca, Wyandot 1910–21
581865	Shawnee 1904–6, 1915–19
581866	Shawnee, Mexican Kickapoo 1920–23
581867	Shawnee, Mexican Kickapoo 1924–29
581868	Shawnee, Mexican Kickapoo 1930–31
581869	Shawnee, Mexican Kickapoo 1932–33
581870	Shawnee, Mexican Kickapoo 1934–36
581871	Shawnee, Mexican Kickapoo 1937–39
581872	Shivwits 1910–17, 1919, 1921–22
581873	Shoshoni 1885, 1890–93, 1895–99
581874	Shoshoni, Arapaho 1900–11
581875	Shoshoni, Arapaho 1912–18
581876	Shoshoni, Arapaho 1919–25
581877	Shoshoni, Arapaho 1926–29
581878	Shoshoni, Arapaho 1930–32
581879	Shoshoni, Arapaho 1933–37
581880	Siletz 1885–1908
581881	Siletz 1909–25

581882	Sisseton 1886–91, 1893, 1895, 1897–98
581883	Sisseton, Wahpeton Sioux 1899–1907
581884	Sisseton, Wahpeton Sioux 1909–14
581885	Sisseton, Wahpeton Sioux 1915–18
581886	Sisseton, Wahpeton Sioux 1919–24
581887	Sisseton, Wahpeton Sioux 1925–27, '29
581888	Sioux 1930–31
581889	Sioux 1932–33
581890	Sioux 1934–36
581891	Sioux 1937–39
581892	Sioux 1916–20
581893	Southern Navajo 1929
581894	Southern Navajo 1930 (H–Z)
581895	Southern Navajo 1931 (A–G)
581896	Southern Navajo 1931 (H–Z)
581897	Southern Navajo 1932 (A–B)
581898	Southern Navajo 1932 (C–M)
581899	Southern Navajo 1932 (N–Z)
581900	Southern Navajo 1933 (Ariz., A–G)
581901	Southern Navajo 1933 (Ariz., H–Z)
581902	Southern Navajo 1933 (N. Mex.)
581903	Southern Navajo 1934 (Ariz., A–G)
581904	Southern Navajo 1934 (Ariz., H–Z)
581905	Southern Navajo 1934 (N. Mex.)
581906	Southern Navajo 1934–35
581907	Southern Pueblo 1920–21
581908	Southern Pueblo 1922–23
581909	Southern Pueblo 1924–25
581910	Southern Pueblo 1926–27
581911	Southern Pueblo 1928
581912	Southern Pueblo 1929
581913	Southern Pueblo 1930
581914	Southern Pueblo 1931
581915	Southern Pueblo 1932
583000	Southern Pueblo 1933
583001	Southern Pueblo 1934–35
583002	Southern Ute 1897–1905
583003	Southern Ute 1893–95, 1897–1908
583004	Southern Ute 1909–23
583005	Spokane 1913–24
583006	Standing Rock (Sioux) 1885–88
583007	Standing Rock (Sioux) 1889–93
583008	Standing Rock (Sioux) 1894–99
583009	Standing Rock (Sioux) 1900–4
583010	Standing Rock (Sioux) 1905–8
583011	Standing Rock (Sioux) 1909–11
583012	Standing Rock (Sioux) 1912–13, 1915–16
583013	Standing Rock (Sioux) 1917–20
583014	Standing Rock (Sioux) 1921–24
583015	Standing Rock (Sioux) 1925–29
583016	Standing Rock (Sioux) 1930–31
583017	Standing Rock (Sioux) 1932

583018	Standing Rock (Sioux) 1933
583019	Standing Rock (Sioux) 1934–35
583020	Standing Rock (Sioux) 1936
583021	Standing Rock (Sioux) 1937–38
583022	Standing Rock (Sioux) 1939
583023	Taholah, Quinaielt, Chehalis 1915–25
583024	Taholah, Chehalis, Nisqualli 1926–29
583025	Taholah, Chehalis, Nisqualli 1930–32
583026	Taholah, Chehalis, Nisqualli 1933
583027	Taholah, Chehalis, Makah 1934–36
583028	Taholah, Chehalis, Makah 1937–39
583029	Tomah, Winnebago 1911–15, 1916, 1927–29
583030	Tomah, Winnebago 1930–33
583031	Tomah, Winnebago, Oneida 1934–36
583032	Winnebago, Oneida 1937–39
583033	Tongue River 1886, 1888–1900
583034	Tongue River 1901–8
583035	Tongue River 1909–20
583036	Tongue River 1922–29
583037	Tongue River 1930–33
583038	Tongue River 1934–39
583039	Truxton Canon 1901–7, 1910–26, 1928–29
583040	Truxton Canon (Walapai) 1930–39
583041	Tulalip (Lummi) 1885–97
583042	Tulalip (Lummi) 1898–1910
583043	Tulalip (Lummi) 1911–15
583044	Tulalip (Lummi) 1916–20
583045	Tulalip (Clallam, Lummi) 1921–23
583046	Tulalip (Clallam, Lummi) 1924–26
583047	Tulalip, Snohomish, Clallam 1927–29
583048	Tulalip, Snohomish, Clallam 1930
583049	Tulalip, Snohomish, Clallam 1931
583050	Tulalip, Snohomish, Clallam 1932–33
583051	Tulalip, Snohomish, Clallam 1934–36
583052	Tulalip, Snohomish, Clallam 1937–39
583053	Tule River 1885–87, 1915–23
583054	Chippewa 1910–12
583055	Chippewa 1913–15
583056	Chippewa 1916–18
583057	Chippewa 1919–21
583058	Chippewa 1922–24
583059	Chippewa 1925–27
583060	Chippewa 1928–29
583061	Chippewa 1930
583062	Chippewa 1931
583063	Chippewa 1932
583064	Chippewa 1933
583065	Chippewa 1934–36
583066	Chippewa 1937–39
583067	Uintah, Ouray 1885–89, 1891–92, 1894–95
583068	Uintah, Ouray 1896–1902
583069	Uintah, Ouray 1903–11

583070	Uintah, Ouray 1912–20
583071	Uintah, Ouray 1921–29
583072	Ute 1930–33
583073	Ute 1934–39
583074	Paiute, Ute 1940, 1942–44
583075	Umatilla, Cayuse, Wallawalla 1886–94
583076	Umatilla, Cayuse, Wallawalla 1901–5
583077	Umatilla, Cayuse, Wallawalla 1913–17
583078	Umatilla, Cayuse, Wallawalla 1918–23
583079	Umatilla, Cayuse, Wallawalla 1924–29
583080	Umatilla, Cayuse, Wallawalla 1930–32
583081	Umatilla, Cayuse, Wallawalla 1933–39
583082	Choctaw 1885
583083	United Pueblos 1936
583084	United Pueblos 1937
583085	Laguna Pueblo 1938
583086	United Pueblos 1939
583087	Ute 1915–22; Chippewa 1907
583088	Paiute 1897–1912
583089	Paiute 1914–24
583090	Paiute, Monache, Shoshoni 1925–29
583091	Paiute 1930–31
583092	Paiute 1932–33
583093	Paiute 1934–35
583094	Warm Springs, John Day 1886–91, 1895
583095	Warm Springs 1909–11, 1913–21
583096	Warm Springs 1922–29
583097	Warm Springs, Paiute 1930–33
583098	Warm Springs, Paiute 1934–39
583099	Hopi, Navajo, Paiute 1905, 1923
583100	Navajo, Hopi, Paiute 1930
583101	Navajo, Hopi, Paiute 1931
583102	Navajo, Hopi, Paiute 1932
583103	Navajo, Hopi, Paiute 1933
583104	Navajo, Hopi, Paiute 1934–35
583105	Shoshone, Paiute 1885, 1887–90
583106	Shoshone, Paiute 1910–29
583107	Shoshone, Paiute 1930–39
583108	Chippewa 1885–88
583109	Chippewa 1890–92
583110	Chippewa 1894–95
583111	Chippewa 1896–97
583112	Chippewa 1898–1900
583113	Chippewa 1901–4
583114	Chippewa 1905–9
583115	Chippewa 1910–11
583116	Chippewa 1912–13
583117	Chippewa 1914–15
583118	Chippewa 1916–17
583119	Chippewa 1918–19
583120	Chippewa 1920–21
583121	Chippewa 1922

583122	Shoshoni, Arapaho 1938–39; Winnebago
583123	Omaha, Winnebago 1910–14
583124	Winnebago 1915–24
583125	Omaha, Winnebago 1925–29
583126	Omaha, Winnebago 1930–31
583127	Omaha, Winnebago 1932–33
583128	Omaha, Ponca, Santee 1934–36
583129	Omaha, Ponca, Santee 1937–39
583130	Winnebago, 1905; Yakima 1885, 1887–91
583131	Yakima 1898–1907
583132	Yakima 1910–16
583133	Yakima 1917–21
583134	Yakima 1922–25
583135	Yakima 1926–29
583136	Yakima 1930–31
583137	Yakima 1932–33
583138	Yakima 1934–39
583139	Yankton 1885–87, 1890, 1892–94
583140	Yankton 1895–1905
583141	Yankton 1906–7, 1909–11
583142	Yankton 1913–17
583143	Ponca, Santee, Yankton Sioux 1918–20
583144	Ponca, Santee, Yankton Sioux 1921–24
583145	Ponca, Santee, Yankton Sioux 1925–27
583146	Ponca, Santee, Yankton Sioux 1928–29
583147	Ponca, Santee, Yankton Sioux 1930–31
583148	Zuni 1904–5, 1907, 1915, 1916–20
583149	Zuni 1921–24, 1926–29
583150	Zuni 1930–32
583151	Zuni 1933–35

Genealogical instruction for the American Indian continues at Brigham Young University, and its record holdings relating to Indians continue to grow. Course instruction has been transferred to the Department of Indian Education at the university, and close cooperation exists with the Department of Family and Local History. A sharing of information and expertise between faculty members is also taking place, and the program continues to benefit students from all parts of the country.

An article recently published in the Salt Lake Deseret News serves as a fitting conclusion to this section on Indian genealogy:

> With the aid of special new classes on Indian genealogy, Lamanite students at Brigham Young University are discovering the joys and unique aspects of researching their ancestral lines.
>
> Even though American Indians may encounter peculiar problems as they search out their genealogy, finding their family history may not be any more difficult than it is for other peoples in the United States, said V. Robert Westover, assistant professor of Indian education at BYU.
>
> "There really are a lot more records on native American ancestral lines than we realize," he said.
>
> Professor Westover is finishing his Ph.D. degree at Arizona State University in counseling psychology and career exploration for native

Americans. Last year, he developed a course in Indian genealogical research that was taught for the first time last winter semester at BYU.

Thirty-one students from eleven different Indian tribes were enrolled in the course that the BYU professor believes was the first university class in the nation in Indian genealogy.

The class was also taught summer semester and has begun this fall as enthusiasm for genealogy among the more than five hundred Indian students at BYU increases.

Since the program began, the BYU Indian Education Department has received several letters from other Indian people asking for help with their genealogy.

"Contrary to what most people believe, there are many records available from which Indians may find genealogical information," Professor Westover said. "It is usually possible to trace American Indian lines back several generations."

There are, however, some unique problems encountered in American Indian records, he said.

"There is a scarcity of birth, death, and marriage records for Indians," he said. "Indian census was started about 1880. Records prior to that time are mostly from tribal rolls, land allotment records, church or mission records, and hospital records. Researchers must also be aware of tribal family structure—whether it is matriarchal or patriarchal."

He said most Indian families have kept word-of-mouth histories of their ancestors. But for students to record these histories, they must usually seek relatives on the reservations. "Some of the older Indians' religious beliefs forbid talking about the dead. This often makes them reluctant to tell researchers about their ancestors."

However, some of the students have been able to fill out four-generation forms just according to oral traditions.

Naming customs among Indians also cause some problems. "Generally, there are two classes of names—true, or personal, names; and titles or honorary names," Professor Westover said. "Naming customs may vary from tribe to tribe. Some tribes may have a clan system with a unique set of names for each clan."

He said names are sometimes applied in a definite order to boys and girls born to a couple among the Sioux, for example, or children may be named according to a dream of the father. "Names of children were announced at potlatches by the Haida and Tlingit Indians of the Northwest and western Canada, while the Navajo often used a nickname referring to a personal characteristic."

Personal names may have been given or changed at birth, adolescence, first war expedition, some notable feat, chieftainship, or retirement from active life. "But many of these problems can be overcome if the researchers become aware of changes of names as well as getting to the correct source of the native customs and methods of reckoning descent," Professor Westover added.

"Some Indians have found their ancestors so far back that they come up with only a single name—not a first and last name."

Another major difficulty is the variety of kinship systems found among Indian tribes. Kinship terms may vary among the different tribes. For instance, in the same generation, the term "father" may also apply to the uncle, stepfather or prospective father. "Sister" could mean sister, first cousin, stepsister, halfsister, daughter, or prospective stepdaughter.

There is also the problem of "paper Indians" and "nonpaper Indians," the instructor said. "Paper Indians" were those who lived under government supervision for whom records were created and kept. "Nonpaper Indians" were those who lived among the "paper Indians" but who did not accept or comply with the government programs. Therefore, no records were created for them."

He explained that Indians who want to find their roots should start with their area agencies of the Department of the Interior. "Individuals may find it necessary to obtain a letter from a tribal leader to get agency cooperation, but it is possible," he said.

"These agency or subagency offices of the BIA usually have good genealogical information. Since the Indian Reorganization Act of 1934, many tribes have created and preserved their own genealogical records."

The professor said that another important help for Indians seeking their roots is to be on the tribal rolls. "Students whose ancestors are on the tribal rolls may receive financial aid for going to college. Some tribes even have allotments coming from tribal businesses or from leasing oil, gas, or mineral rights."

He explained another problem in Indian research. "Most of the history of the tribes has been written by non-Indians because the tribes did not have a written language. Of the five so-called 'civilized' tribes—Cherokee, Choctaws, Chickasaw, Creek, and Seminole—only the Cherokees had a written language, and that was after 1800." Today, however, more than two hundred tribes have written languages.

He summarized the procedure for Indian ancestry investigation as follows:

1. Obtain as much information as possible from living relatives.
2. Determine tribal affiliation by using "Biographic and Historical Index of Americans and Persons Involved in Indian Affairs" or "Handbook of American Indians North of Mexico."
3. Search the Indian census rolls (1884–1940) available on microfilm.
4. Search records of the agency office in charge of the records of the particular area and tribe in question.
5. Search the records of the National Archives and the Federal Record Center(s) of the region in which the tribe in question is located.
6. Search the records of any churches that may have been active in missionary work among the tribal group in question.

[*Church News* 2 Dec. 1978]

Sources Relating to American Immigration

An important aspect of your American family history is determining essential facts about immigrant ancestors and their ancestral homes. Such information is essential in extending your pedigree and learning more about your family heritage. Actually you should be on the alert for such information from the outset of research, because any source might contain the desired information or clues to it. Any of the sources covered in previous chapters—or any combination of sources—might provide or lead to the desired facts.

Family and home sources. Important facts concerning the immigrant can sometimes be obtained in the home or from relatives and friends. Traditions may be known by the family concerning nativity, and associates may know of the family's previous places of residence. Certain national customs may persist in the family, or heirlooms might be identified with a particular time and country. Few families are without some idea of their national origin. Of course just knowing the country is not enough to extend a pedigree—knowing the town or village of origin is necessary to do much genealogically.

Family members may have various documents that give clues to a foreign place of birth or residence. Old letters, newspaper clippings, photographs, citizenship papers, land and estate papers—as well as Bibles, diaries, journals, and related books—should be considered.

One genealogy student located an article from the St. Louis Post-Dispatch that gave information about an ancestor. It also illustrated how the testimony of a family associate can provide important genealogical information.

> *Identified*—The Body of the Man Who Suicided Yesterday. The coroner held an inquest today on the body of the unknown man who was found yesterday afternoon lying on the ground in a small grove near the corner of Third and Welch streets. Peter D. Gramache testified that he lived at the corner of Third and Welch street, on the Carondelet road. Yesterday about twelve o'clock he started to walk through the grove, and as he entered a short distance into the woods he observed the body of a man lying with his face downwards. Going up to him he tried to arouse him, but in so doing he noticed a piece of rope tied around his neck. Upon further examination the witness found that the other end of the rope was tied to a limb of the tree under which the man was lying dead. The rope was small, and it appeared to the witness that the suicide had climbed into the tree, adjusted the rope, and jumped off. The rope broke but had accomplished its purposes the same. The witness could not tell how long the man had lain there. He notified the police, and the body was taken away to the morgue. The dead man's body has been exposed to the view of the curious who go to the morgue every day when the doors are thrown open and unknown bodies are laid upon the slab for identification. About twelve o'clock today a Bohemian named Mathias Boemisch, living at No. 1715 South Tenth street, called there and when he looked at the unknown suicide immediately recognized it as a fellow countryman of his own whom he had known during his life and whose name was Joseph Stetina. He was fifty years old and had a wife living in Europe, and a sister and two sons living in this city, but where Boemisch did not know. Deceased had lived somewhere in Frenchtown. He had been a laborer by occupation and was a morbid-minded sort of man. He had, however, never expressed an inclination to take his own life so far as the informant had known. The coroner rendered a verdict of death by suicide. Efforts will be made to find the relatives of the deceased.
> [18 November 1882, p. 4]

The above article might appear unpleasant in its implications—especially to family members—but it illustrates how an associate might have important family history information. Notice that the informant was able to give the deceased's age and details concerning his wife and sons; he probably could have given the name of the town of residence in Bohemia if he had been asked. Of course, by now Mr. Boemisch is also deceased, and testimony from him could no longer be obtained; however, research could be conducted on his place of birth and residence in Bohemia; it might turn out to be the same as that of Joseph Stetina.

Sometimes it is necessary to study the surnames and genealogy of several friends of the ancestor to get the needed information. Friends and family members often emigrated together and lived together, so the place of birth for an associate or friend might be the same as that of an ancestor. (This approach can also be used to trace families from one locality to another in America as well as from one country to another.)

The surname and locality. The surname itself might prove helpful in determining the country of origin, and the localities where the family has resided might also provide clues. A few years ago, a researcher at the Genealogical Society of Utah was able to establish a likely town of origin in Germany for a Kentucky "Zeigenfuz" family through his knowledge of German surname origins. Evidently the name "Zeigenfuz" (also spelled Zeigenfoot) was occupational in origin; it had its beginning with a family of clockmakers in a small German village. The "second hand" on the clock was the "Zeigenfuz" (swinging foot), and a particular family took that term as their surname. Of course this approach is not possible when the surname is common and cannot be used in all countries, but it might be helpful when the name is unusual. The anglicization of a foreign surname or other name changes might also confuse the issue. Is the surname "Black" the anglicized form of the German "Schwartz" or does it have an English origin? Is "Carpenter" from the German "Zimmerman" or is it English? The answers may not be readily apparent, and some other approach might have to be taken.

In early New England the name of the town where an ancestor settled might provide a clue to his origin; many early towns were named after the European home of the settlers—Braintree, Chelsea, or Malden in Massachusetts, or Londonderry in New Hampshire, for instance. It is also interesting to note that many towns and cities in the western part of America were named after their East Coast counterparts. From this it can be seen that a study of the early settlers and their places of settlement should be made, especially when the ancestor could have been one of the original settlers.

A careful study of the history and geography of foreign places of birth and residence must be made before successful searches can be conducted in the proper sources. Dr. Ottokar Israel emphasized this at the World Conference on Records.

> It occasionally happens that an American researcher comes to the city of Hannover with a request for help in his search for a particular ancestor who emigrated approximately 1850 to the United States from "Hannover." The result is that the ancestors cannot be found in today's capital of the state of Lower Saxony, because he did not come from the city of Hannover, but rather from the kingdom of the same name. This difference however was not known by his descendants in the New World. Similar mistakes are made with respect to the many ecclesiastical territories of the Holy Roman Empire of the German Nation, which were also named after their main cities. A person who came from Würzburg, Bamberg or Passau,

> Münster, Osnabrück or Hildesheim, might just as well come from the diocese of the same name. The origin is not always designated as it should be; "from the Hannoverschen" or "from the Würsburgishen." These examples indicate how important it is for a foreign researcher to become acquainted with the territorial development of Germany in order to have a general view of the many small German states and cities of the former Holy Roman Empire.
> [Israel 1969]

General archival collections. The Genealogical Society of Utah has created some general genealogical collections that can help in determining a foreign residence or place of birth; other libraries, societies, and archives have similar collections. Some have specialized in the history and genealogy of certain ethnic and national groups; biographies, genealogies, family histories, regional and local histories, genealogical indexes, genealogical dictionaries, periodicals, and miscellaneous manuscript collections are among their holdings. An effort should be made to investigate these special collections for emigration-immigration information.

The Temple Records Index Bureau and the Church Records Archives of the LDS genealogical library should be checked as soon as an ancestor has been identified as an immigrant. Information may be on file that refers to his place of birth in the old country, or you may find clues to his foreign residence by investigating records of others by the same surname.

When the immigrant is known to be from England and Wales, the International Genealogical Index (IGI) should be investigated. Birth and marriage information pertaining to individuals listed in early parish registers has been computerized and indexed in these collections. Boyd's Marriage Indexes also might prove helpful on certain English problems. They consist of several hundred volumes of English marriage records covering the period 1538–1837. The records are not complete and are arranged in three different series. Smith and Gardner's *Genealogical Research in England and Wales* (vol. 2, pp. 200–201) gives additional information on that collection.

The LDS genealogical library in Salt Lake City also has special collections of immigration records pertaining to members of The Church of Jesus Christ of Latter-day Saints who immigrated from Europe between 1849 and 1925. The records include good information on immigrants from Great Britain, Holland, and the Scandinavian countries.

Vital records and the obituary. Local and state vital records should always be investigated when there is a possibility the immigrant lived to a modern period or when his children did. Modern death records call for the place of birth of parents as well as of the deceased; many include the town or village of birth. Of course the information is no better than its source, but the facts might be correct and provide the very information needed to "cross the water." A child's birth record might also give the foreign place of birth or residence of parents, and records of other relatives also might provide the needed facts.

Vital records of foreign countries should also be considered, especially if the immigrant was born after national registration took place. As an example, if the immigrant was known to be from England or Wales and was born after national registration of vital statistics took place (1837), a copy of his birth record should be requested from Somerset House in London. National indexes exist, and copies are on file at the LDS genealogical library in Salt Lake City. A similar approach could be taken if the individual was born in Scotland after 1854 or Holland after 1811. Many countries did not have national registration until rather late, and in some countries the national approach is not possible. In Scandinavian countries, you must know the smaller locality and the year of birth. However, there are other excellent sources, including annual extracts of parish registers, police records, emigration papers, passport journals, and certain archival collections. These are explained in detail in Carl-Erik Johansson's *Cradled in Sweden* (1972).

Heinz F. Friederichs gives a brief but excellent account of sources that should be investigated for German immigrants in Germanic Research Problems (a paper read at the World Conference on Records in 1969). Dr. Ottokar Israel's paper on Germany, cited previously, is another excellent text on German emigration and gives bibliographic detail on source materials. Dr. W. H. Ruoff's paper, A Century of Emigration from the Palatinate to the USA—Switzerland, delivered at the same conference, also should be consulted. Copies are on file at the LDS genealogical library in Salt Lake City and at Brigham Young University in Provo. A few of the papers are available for purchase from the Genealogical Society at a reasonable price.

The obituaries or death notices from local newspapers are also good sources for emigration-immigration information, especially in a modern period. They sometimes list the foreign place of birth or residence, next of kin, and personal facts that might help determine the place of birth. The family might have kept copies of older newspaper clippings—in some cases they even may have copies of foreign newspapers that came from the "old home in Europe."

Church and cemetery records from the localities where the family resided should be investigated. Birth, christening, baptism, marriage, and death entries in those records might include the foreign birthplace or provide clues to it.

Census-population and mortality schedules. Federal and state population and mortality schedules also should be considered on immigrant problems. The 1850 and later federal schedules list the state or country of birth, and the 1880 and later records call for the state or country of birth for parents. The 1870 schedules include a special column that was marked when the parents were of foreign birth, though the actual place is not listed. The 1900 federal schedules also include statistics on naturalization and citizenship. These records are explained in detail in chapter 4.

When an immigrant lived into the 1850–80 period—and when he died in the twelve-month period preceding the census year—he could be listed in the federal mortality schedules. They list the state or country of birth and are explained in chapter 4.

Naturalization and citizenship records. This record group was explained in chapter 6, but also can be used to gain information about an immigrant ancestor—including his place of birth and residences in the Old World. Oaths of allegiance, declarations of intention to become citizens, petitions, and records of aliens are among the group. A few oaths of allegiance and declarations of intention to become citizens have been published, primarily for early immigrants, but most documents must be found with the family or in the courthouses.

British subjects were seldom included in such records prior to the Revolution because they were coming to a British colony; however, modern records often exist for them. Early volumes pertaining to naturalization and citizenship in Salt Lake and Utah counties often list only the country from which the immigrants came, not their village or town of birth in the old country. The same situation exists for many New York Irish immigrants in the 1840s; only the country is listed.

Laws and regulations pertaining to naturalization and citizenship have varied considerably over the years, and it was not until after 1900 that the United States Department of Immigration and Naturalization was established. Most records prior to that time, and some after, are found among local court records.

Immigration Laws of the United States by Helen Silving (1948) is a good reference pertaining to laws that have directly affected citizenship, and *Citizenship of the United States of America* by Sidney Kansas (1936) is excellent in its detail. Luella Getty's *The Law of Citizenship in the United States* (1934) is also good, and *A Collection of Nationality Laws of Various Countries,* edited by Richard W. Flourney (1929), is good for information concerning other countries.

Other court records and land records. Court records other than those relating to naturalization and citizenship also are helpful in determining the foreign place of birth or residence. Some individuals changed their names through court action; related documents and depositions often include reference to the Old Country. The basement vault of the Oneida County, New York, courthouse at Utica is half filled with Italian change-of-name records. Many immigrants who settled in Utica and Rome, New York, changed their names (usually to a shorter English version of the European form), and records on file in the courthouse often include their towns or villages of birth. This is probably true of other ethnic groups in other cities and counties of the United States.

An individual also may have given testimony in a civil or criminal court case; his deposition might include his age and place of birth. Reference may be given only to his place of residence in a foreign country, but that information could be used to learn the actual place of birth. The following entry was taken from Volume 1 of *Province and Court Records of Maine* (Maine Historical Society 1938, p. 72).

> *The declaration of John Winter and Johane his wife defendants* [plaintiffs] *against George Cleeve gent. plaint.* [defendant]
>
> Mr. John Winter cometh into this Courte, and declareth that this defendant aboute some six yeares past, within this Province did unjustly

> and wrongfully slander the said plaintiffe his wife in reporting that the said plaint. his wife (who then lived in the Town of Plymouth in old England) was the veriest drunkenest whore in all that towne, with divers other such like scandalous reports not only of the said plaint. his wife, but also of the said town in generall in saying that there was not foure honest women in all that towne, by which wrongfull and unjust accusation the plaintiffes hold themselves greately prejudiced in their reputation, for which the said plaintiffes bring their action of slander into this Courte against the said defendant as high as one hundred pound starling at the least, and humbly craveth a legall proceeding according to his Majesties lawes.

Probate court and guardianship records are of special importance in this regard and can refer to an immigrant in a number of different ways. The name and place of residence of the individual could be included in the will or petition or could be found written in other documents relating to the estate and its settlement. Many early Virginia testators left property to relatives in England, thus identifying their places of residence in the will. This undoubtedly happened in other colonies and was not limited to the colonial period of American history.

According to British researchers, when an individual left real or personal property to someone in America (or other countries, for that matter), administration of the estate was handled in a special court—the Prerogative Court of Canterbury—and records prior to 1859 have been microfilmed and are on file at the LDS genealogical library in Salt Lake City. These records contain excellent genealogical information to connect families from the two worlds.

Miscellaneous documents in probate files might also contain useful information. Petitions in New York records invariably contain the names and addresses of heirs to the estate, and letters from heirs living in foreign places are often included. This approach also can be used to trace persons from one locality to another in America.

Proprietors' records, land grants, deeds, mortgages, and other land or property records can also provide information about a foreign place of birth or residence. A few early Massachusetts proprietors' records include the English place of residence of early settlers, and land grants in some of the southern states include the previous place of residence in the Old World. Later documents of land title transfer include similar information.

Military records. Examples of documents found in service and pension files relating to the military were identified in chapter 8. These can also be a source for foreign place of birth or residence. The actual enlistment or induction notices may give the needed facts, or affidavits and depositions in the files may do the job. Some immigrants joined the military as a means of getting established in this country, then retired to a more peaceful life later.

Ship passenger lists. Prior to 1819 ships' captains or shipping companies were not required to preserve lists of passengers arriving at American ports, yet a surprising number are in existence for that period. Extensive lists pertaining to East and Gulf Coast ports are housed in the

National Archives for 1820–1945. Unfortunately, passenger lists for San Francisco were destroyed by fires in 1851 and 1940, and lists for other Pacific Coast ports, if they ever existed, were never transferred to the National Archives (Colket and Bridgers 1964, p. 22).

A majority of existing colonial lists have been published in periodicals and other compilations; *A Bibliography of Ship Passenger Lists 1538–1825,* compiled by Harold Lancour (1938), is an excellent guide to them. The book was revised and enlarged by Richard J. Wolfe and reprinted in 1963 by the Genealogical Book Company of Baltimore, Maryland. Almost two hundred and eighty published lists are identified in Lancour's work, with sources and annotations given. In addition, there are two appendexes. The first, "Published Lists of Ship Passengers and Immigrants after 1825," has nineteen lists entered; the second is Frank E. Bridgers' "Passenger Arrival Records in the National Archives." The book has one index by authors' names and a second by ships' names.

The following list includes some of the more popular published ship passenger lists on file at the LDS genealogical library in Salt Lake City, Utah:

Ames: *The Mayflower and Her Log: July 15, 1620–May 7, 1621.*
Banks: *The English Ancestry and Homes of the Pilgrim Fathers.*
The Planters of the Commonwealth.
Topographical Dictionary of 2,885 English Emigrants to New England.
The Winthrop Fleet of 1630.
Colket and Bridgers: *Guide to Genealogical Records in the National Archives.*
Egle: *Names of Foreigners Who Took the Oath of Allegiance to the Province and State of Pennsylvania, 1727–75, with the Foreign Arrivals 1786–1808.*
Farmer: *A Genealogical Register of the First Families of New England.*
Faust: *List of Swiss Emigrants in the Eighteenth Century to the American Colonies.*
Fothergill: *Emigrants from England, 1773–76.*
A List of Emigrant Ministers to America, 1690–1811.
French: *List of Emigrants to America from Liverpool, 1697–1707.*
Gerber: *Emigrants from Wuerttemberg: The Adolph Gerber Lists.*
Ghirelli: *List of Emigrants from England to America 1682–92.*
Greer: *Early Virginia Immigrants, 1623–66.*
Hansen: *The Atlantic Migration, 1607–1860.*
Hoffman: "Palatine Emigrants to America from the Principality of Nassau-Dillenburg."
Hotten: *The Original Lists of Persons of Quality, 1600–1700.*
Ireland: "Servants of Foreign Plantations from Bristol, England 1654–86."
Jewson: *Transcript of Three Registers of Passengers from Great Yarmouth to Holland and New England, 1637–39.*
Kaminkow: *A List of Emigrants from England to America, 1718–59.*
Knittle: *Early Eighteenth Century Palatine Emigration.*
Krebs: "Emigrants from Baden-Durlach to Pennsylvania, 1749–55."
"A List of German Immigrants to the American Colonies from Zweibruecken in the Palatinate, 1750–51."

Lancour: *A Bibliography of Ship Passenger Lists, 1538–1825.*
Landis: *Mayflower Descendants and Their Marriages for Two Generations After Landing.*
Myers: *Quaker Arrivals at Philadelphia, 1682–1750.*
Nicholson: *Some Early Emigrants to America.*
Putnam: *Two Early Passenger Lists, 1635–37.*
Revill: *A Compilation of the Original Lists of Protestant Immigrants to South Carolina, 1763–73.*
Robinson: *Early Voyages to America.*
Rupp: *A Collection of Upwards of Thirty Thousand Names of German, Swiss, Dutch, French, and Other Immigrants into Pennsylvania from 1727 to 1776.*
Sherwood: *American Colonists in English Records.*
Stanard: *Some Emigrants to Virginia.*
Steinemann: "A List of Eighteenth Century Emigrants from the Canton of Schaffhausen to the American Colonies, 1734–52."
Strassburger and Hinke: *Pennsylvania German Pioneers: A Publication of the Original Lists of Arrivals in the Port of Philadelphia from 1727 to 1808.*
Virginia Historical Society: *Documents Relating to the Huguenot Emigration to Virginia.*
Virkus: *Immigrant Ancestors: A List of 2,500 Immigrants to America Before 1750.*
Westcott: *Names of Persons Who Took the Oath of Allegiance to the State of Pennsylvania Between the Years 1777 and 1789.*

Passenger shipping lists are on file in the National Archives for the following ports covering the listed time periods:

Alexandria, Virginia: 1820–52
Annapolis, Maryland: 1849
Apalachicola, Florida: 1918
Baltimore, Maryland: 1820–1909
Bangor, Maine: 1848
Barnstable, Massachusetts: 1820–26
Bath, Maine: 1825–32, 1867
Beufort, North Carolina: 1865
Belfast, Maine: 1820–31, 1851
Boca Grande, Florida: 1912–35
Boston and Charlestown, Massachusetts: 1820–74; 1883–1943
Bridgeport, Connecticut: 1870
Bridgetown, New Jersey: 1828
Bristol and Warren, Rhode Island: 1820–28; 1843–71
Brunswick, Georgia: 1901–39
Cape May, New Jersey: 1828
Carabelle, Florida: 1915
Charleston, South Carolina: 1820–29; 1906–45
Darien, Georgia: 1823, 1825
Dighton, Massachusetts: 1820–36
East River, Virginia: 1830

Edenton, North Carolina: 1820
Edgartown, Massachusetts: 1820–70
Fairfield, Connecticut: 1820–21
Fall River, Massachusetts: 1837–65
Fernandina, Florida: 1904–32
Frenchman's Bay, Maine: 1821; 1822; 1825–27
Galveston, Texas: 1846–71
Georgetown, District of Columbia: 1820–21
Georgetown, South Carolina: 1923–39
Gloucester, Massachusetts: 1820; 1832–39; 1867–70; 1906–23; 1930–43
Gulfport, Mississippi: 1904–44
Hampton, Virginia: 1821
Hartford, Connecticut: 1832; 1929–43
Havre de Grace, Maryland: 1820
Hingham, Massachusetts: 1852
Jacksonville, Florida: 1904–45
Kennebunk, Maine: 1820–27; 1842
Key West, Florida: 1837–68; 1898–1945
Knights Key, Florida: 1908–12
Little Egg Harbor, New Jersey: 1831
Marblehead, Massachusetts: 1820–52
Mayport, Florida: 1907–16
Miami, Florida: 1899–1945
Millville, Florida: 1916
Mobile, Alabama: 1820–62; 1904–45
Nantucket, Massachusetts: 1820–62
New Bedford, Massachusetts: 1823–99; 1902–42
New Bern, North Carolina: 1820–45; 1865
New Haven, Connecticut: 1820–73
New London, Connecticut: 1820–47
New Orleans, Louisiana: 1820–1945
New York, New York: 1820–1942
Newark, New Jersey: 1836
Newburyport, Massachusetts: 1821–39
Newport, Rhode Island: 1820–75
Norfolk and Portsmouth, Virginia: 1820–57
Oswegatchie, New York: 1821–23
Panama City, Florida: 1927–39
Pascagoula, Mississippi: 1903–35
Passamaquoddy, Maine: 1820–59
Penobscot, Maine: 1851
Pensacola, Florida: 1900–45
Perth Amboy, New Jersey: 1820; 1829–32
Petersburg, Virginia: 1819–22
Philadelphia, Pennsylvania: 1820–1945
Plymouth, Massachusetts: 1821–43
Plymouth, North Carolina: 1820, 1823, 1825, 1840
Port Everglades, Florida: 1932–45
Port Inglis, Florida: 1912–13
Port Royal, South Carolina: 1865
Port St. Joe, Florida: 1923–39
Portland and Falmouth, Maine: 1820–68; 1873; 1893–1943

Portsmouth, New Hampshire: 1820–61
Providence, Rhode Island: 1820–67; 1911–43
Richmond, Virginia: 1820–44
Rochester, New York: 1866
Sag Harbor, New York: 1829–34
St. Andrews, Florida: 1916–26
St. Augustine, Florida: 1821–27; 1870
St. Johns, Florida: 1865
St. Petersburg, Florida: 1926–41
Salem and Beverly, Massachusetts: 1790–1800; 1865–66
Sandusky, Ohio: 1820
Savannah, Georgia: 1820–68; 1906–45
Saybrook, Connecticut: 1820
Tampa, Florida: 1898–1945
Waldoboro, Maine: 1820–33
Washington, North Carolina: 1820–48
West Palm Beach, Florida: 1920–45
Wilmington, Delaware: 1820–1848
Wiscasset, Maine: 1819; 1829
Yarmouth, Maine: 1820

Passenger shipping lists in the National Archives consist of customs passenger lists and immigration passenger lists. The records known as customs passenger lists were filed by the masters of ships with collectors of customs in compliance with congressional acts of 1819 and later. There are originals, copies, and abstracts, and State Department transcripts for the customs passenger lists. Few originals remain, but those that do are dated primarily 1820–1902 with copies and abstracts 1820–75 and transcripts 1819–32. The original lists were prepared on board ship, sworn to by the master of the ship, and filed with the collector of customs when the ship arrived at port.

There are two separate card indexes to the names on the copies and abstracts of passenger lists. One contains entries for passengers arriving at the port of New York 1820–46 and the other contains entries for passengers arriving at other Atlantic and Gulf Coast ports 1820–74; it includes a few entries for New York passengers. Both indexes are arranged alphabetically by passenger and include age and country of citizenship. The index to passengers arriving at Atlantic and Gulf Coast ports includes names for Baltimore, Mobile, New Bedford, New Orleans, and Philadelphia. The index to New York lists for 1820–46 is on microfilm at Brigham Young University and the Genealogical Society of Utah, but the second index has not been received by either institution at this time.

Original lists for Boston prior to 1883 were reportedly destroyed by fire in 1894, though some copies exist. The collection at the LDS genealogical library in Salt Lake City is a microfilm copy of cards arranged alphabetically and by date after 1883.

Copies and abstracts of passenger lists were made in the offices of the collectors of customs and were sent to the Secretary of State each quarter. Some collectors prepared copies of the individual lists while others prepared abstracts, which are consolidated lists of names of all passengers who arrived at a given port during the quarter.

Copies and abstracts include the name of the ship, the master, the tonnage, the ports of embarkation and debarkation, the names of the passengers, their ages, their sex, their occupation, the country to which they belong, the country they intend to inhabit, and whether they died on the voyage.

Customs collectors at New Orleans also prepared books containing abstracts covering the years 1845 through 1875, which they retained at the port. The National Archives has twenty-three volumes constituting that collection. There are also eight volumes of transcripts for various ports covering the period 1819 through 1832, which were prepared from copies or abstracts in the Department of State and then sent to the Secretary of State by the collectors of customs.

Volume 2 of the State Department Transcripts is missing, but some entries from it were printed in *Letter from the Secretary of State with a Transcript of the List of Passengers Who Arrived in the United States from the 1st October, 1819, to the 30th September, 1820* (16th Congress, 2nd Session, Senate Document 118, serial 45). The National Archives has a typescript index to the volume.

The Customs Lists of Aliens pertain to Salem and Beverly, Massachusetts, only and cover the period 1798 through 1800. The records include the name of the ship and its master, the name of the port and the date of arrival, the names of each passenger, their ages, their places of nativity, the country from whence they came, the nation which they owed allegiance, their occupation, and a description (including complexion and height). There are no indexes to the lists, but according to Colket, they were transcribed and printed in *The New England Historical and Genealogical Register,* volume 106 (July 1952): 203–209.

The National Archives also has negative microfilm copies of immigration passenger lists covering the period 1883 through 1945 that include not only the names of immigrants but also of visitors and American citizens returning from abroad.

The published colonial lists typically include the name of the ship and its captain, the port of embarkation and country of destination, the date, and the names and ages of the passengers. After 1820 they are much more inclusive, typically including the name of the ship and its captain, the ship's tonnage and passenger capacity, the port of embarkation and debarkation, the date, and personal information about each passenger. The personal information usually includes name, age, sex, color, occupation, marital status, place of birth or nativity, destination, and purpose for going there. Such other details are found in the later lists as amount paid for passage, type of accommodation, and amount of luggage.

An example of the value of these modern passenger lists can be demonstrated through my own family history. My great-grandfather Joseph Wright (born 1817 in Bubwith, Yorkshire, England) emigrated to America in 1849 arriving at the port of New Orleans in April. According to his journal he arrived with his family on the ship Zetland, then took a riverboat up the Mississippi to St. Louis, Missouri, where he bought wagons and came

AMERICAN LINE

Report or Manifest of all the Passengers taken on Board the S S Lord Gough whereof E. M. Hughes is Master, from Liverpool burthen 2370 Tons and owned by G. M. Papayannis of Liverpool and bound to Philadelphia

NAMES.	AGE.	SEX.	OCCUPATION.	To what Country belonging.	Country of which it is their intention to become Inhabitants.	Number and Names of Passengers who Died on the Voyage.
Cabin						
Mr W. J. B. Reeve		m	Gentleman	England	Philadelphia	Cabin Passenger
Mrs do		f	Lady	"	"	"
Steerage						
Syler Anderson	28	m	Lab	Norway	"	Steerage
John Allott	19	"	"	England	"	"
John Burgess	30	"	"	"	"	"
Milenda Buckle	22	f	Wife	"	"	"
Wm do	5	m	Child	"	"	"
Sidney do	3	m	"	"	"	"
Rose do	2	f	"	"	"	"
Thos do	Inft	m	"	"	"	"
Charles Bourne	20	m	Lab	"	"	"
Janos Bowan	40	m	"	Hungary	"	"

west. His wife, Hannah Mariah (Watson) Wright, and their children Eliza, William, and Martha constituted his family at that time.

For several years our family employed professional genealogists to learn more about Hannah's family in England, without success. We understood her father to be George Watson and her mother to be Ann (Rider) Watson, both of whom supposedly died in England. Imagine my surprise when I located the following family on ship passenger lists for the port of New Orleans:

Schedule A—ship Zetland, master, Brown; tons 1283; legal number ship can carry 333; bound to New Orleans; 276½ passengers authorized, 24 January 1849. Arrived 3 April 1849 at New Orleans.

Page 7

Joseph Wright	M 34	Mormon Laborer	Born: England
Anna Maria Wright	F 34		England
Eliza Wright	F 7		England
William Wright	M 5		England
George Watson	M 66		England
Ann Watson	F 65		England
Francis Ryder	M 52		England

No wonder the professionals could not find George and Ann in England; they were not there! From other information, we determined that Ann (Rider) Watson died of cholera on the Mississippi River, as did a small daughter Martha—but George Watson migrated to Michigan where he died in 1852.

10 Genealogical and Historical Repositories

We are very fortunate as a country to have so many valuable sources available for family and local history, and to have them in local, state, regional, and national repositories so convenient for our use. We owe a great deal to those who had the foresight to require that records be kept in the first place, and also to those who have preserved them and made them accessible. In spite of the many serious conflicts we have experienced as a nation, and the sometimes cataclysmic forces of nature, a remarkable amount of material still is available to help us understand our past.

Information has been gathered, classified, cataloged, and stored in libraries, archives, societies, and museums throughout the country. Thanks to modern microfilming techniques and expanding programs of records acquisition, many originals previously accessible to only a few researchers are now available to almost any interested person.

The Genealogical Society of Utah

Sooner or later every serious family historian will want to visit the LDS genealogical library in Salt Lake City, Utah—or will want to gain access to its microfilm holdings through one of its branch libraries scattered throughout Mexico, the United States, and Canada. This library is without doubt one of the finest repositories of genealogical and historical information in the world. Its current record holdings are in excess of one million reels of microfilm, one hundred seventy thousand volumes of family and local history, and twelve thousand manuscripts relating to genealogy and history. Records have been gathered from many parts of the world and cover a very wide time span. Moreover, the program for records acquisition and microfilming increases each year.

The Genealogical Society of Utah—an organization of the Church of Jesus Christ of Latter-day Saints—operates and maintains the main library in Salt Lake City and three hundred branch libraries throughout the United States, Canada, and Mexico. It also maintains the famous Granite Mountain vault located twenty miles southeast of Salt Lake City (used for microfilm processing and record storage) and administers a world-wide program for records microfilming and acquisition.

The Genealogical Society is a private, nonprofit organization funded through tithes and offerings of faithful church members; it spends considerable time, effort, and resources to make its records available for genealogical and historical research. The main library and its branches are open to the general public without charge and without regard to race or religious creed. The main library in Salt Lake City is open Monday through Saturday and maintains a staff of qualified personnel to help patrons. It does not conduct research in their behalf but guides and assists them in using the library facilities and responds to reasonable requests through correspondence. It also provides regular classroom instruction for beginners at no charge.

In addition to gathering and preserving source materials, the Genealogical Society has actively promoted genealogical and historical programs. It sponsored the first World Conference on Records and Genealogical Research at Salt Lake City in August 1969 and the second at the same place in August 1980. The theme of the first conference was "Records Preservation in an Uncertain World"; and the second "Preserving our Heritage." The Society also has sponsored twelve annual genealogical research seminars on the Brigham Young University campus at Provo, Utah, and has provided motivation, education, and instruction for genealogical seminars throughout the United States and Canada.

Perhaps one of its most important contributions to family history research is the establishment of branch genealogical libraries in various parts of the country so individuals can borrow microfilms from the Salt Lake City library to accomplish their research objectives. Because of contractual agreements made at the time the Society microfilmed certain record collections, restrictions were placed on the use of the films by other organizations. By establishing its own branch libraries, the Society has made its vast film collection available to researchers in outlying areas. Because of the effort to operate the program on a self-sustaining basis, there is a nominal fee to have microfilm copies sent on loan to branch libraries.

The Genealogical Society of Utah was formed primarily to help members of The Church of Jesus Christ of Latter-day Saints accomplish a religious goal—the identification and preservation of families as eternal units in the Kingdom of God through the performance of sacred ordinances.

These research and ordinance activities of Church members and the Genealogical Society have resulted in interesting and useful record collections. At this writing more than sixty million individual names have been identified and processed through the Society's facilities. Methods, procedures, and policies have changed in the 138 years since the work was initiated, but the basic result has been a unique identification of millions of families and individuals—an identification that has proved valuable in the genealogical and research efforts of nonmembers as well as members of the Church.

These unique collections should not be confused with the Society's original record holdings; rather they are special collections created through name-processing procedures. Most of the names were submitted by Church members or through special tabulation programs, but the entries represent people from many different countries, religions, and time periods.

Three collections of general interest to the researcher include the Temple Records Index Bureau (TIB), the Family Group Record Archives, and the International Genealogical Index (IGI). The first is a card file of almost forty million names, the second is a collection of more than six million family group records, and the third is a microfiche collection of more than 50 million names. The first two are not being expanded at the present time, but the third is growing by several million entries each year.

The Temple Records Index Bureau (TIB). The TIB was the first of the three record collections created. A file of three-by-five-inch cards, it consists of nearly forty million individual entries. Primarily it is an index to temple ordinances performed between 1842 and 1969. Cards are filed under a phonetic system by country of birth.

The quantity and quality of genealogical information listed on each card varies considerably; in short, the facts are no better than their sources. Some were given from personal knowledge or well-documented research while others were based on questionable sources or hearsay. The original source is not cited on the cards.

Because the file contains confidential information pertaining to living persons as well as dead, it is not open to the public for general searching. Access for information on your ancestral line (persons appearing on your pedigree chart and their children) is available upon request for a nominal fee or may be gained by employing an accredited genealogist to search the files for you. The library will supply a list of such genealogists at your request and provide search request forms without charge.

The TIB is of special value to those with Mormon ancestry but is sometimes helpful to researchers working on non-Mormon lines too. Often a pedigree can be traced several generations in these files, even to the immigrant ancestor or earlier. Even when this is not the case, facts can sometimes be ascertained that prove helpful in further research.

The Family Group Record Archives. In January 1942 Church members were asked to submit information for family ordinances on special family group record forms. Between January 1942 and October 1969 these forms were the primary means for name processing, and copies were filed for reference. These records constitute the main section of the Family Group Record Archives, but other family group record collections have been filed in the same area and are popularly referred to as patron section family group records.

Between six and eight million family group records are on file. Again, they vary considerably in quality and quantity of facts, but they do record the sources of information used to compile the form and the name and address of the person submitting the form. The records are filed in alphabetical sequence according to the name of the husband. They are open for general public inspection at the main library.

The main section of the archives has been microfilmed and is now available in that form. Records from the patrons' section also have been filmed and are available at the main library and most branches. Photocopy facilities are available at the main library at a reasonable cost, and requests through correspondence are honored for a nominal fee.

The International Genealogical Index (IGI). In October 1969 the Genealogical Society changed some of its procedures for submitting information and moved to a computer system for processing names (although regular family group record forms were still used for certain special entries). This action made the TIB and Family Group Record Archives secondary to the IGI in current indexing. The previous two files continue to exist, but information is not being added to them. The computer has become the primary means of processing names, and microfiche printouts are produced periodically to show processing results.

The IGI is available to the general public without charge at the main library and many of its branches. Several million names are included in the collection at this time and it continues to grow rapidly. Because of its nature and unusual content, this index is very important to the ordinary family historian.

The names on the microfiche printouts come from a wide range of genealogical sources. In addition to ancestral research submitted by Church members since 1969, an increasing number of names come from special extraction or tabulation programs administered by the Genealogical Society. Under these programs, Church members volunteer time and services to copy names from vital, church, cemetery, census, and other major records for computer processing. In many cases original parish registers or other original sources have been copied in their entirety, making the file an important index to primary genealogical information. Of course there is still a chance for error, and the collection should be used primarily as a lead to the original records.

Names in the file are arranged by regions—such as North America, England, Central Europe—then by country or province where the event occurred, then alphabetically by surname and given name (except in Iceland, Norway, Wales, and Monmouthshire, England, where patronymics are used). Reference can be made from each name on the microfiche cards to the original entries, which are available on microfilm at the main library.

Record holdings on microfilm. Microfilm holdings of genealogical and historical source materials are by far the most important of the Genealogical Society's collections. At the present time, there are more than one million reels of film cataloged, and they continue to be filed at the rate of fifty thousand per year.

It is neither possible nor appropriate to give an exhaustive listing of these microfilm holdings because of the size and changing nature of the collection, but a few statistics might give an idea of their scope.

COUNTRY: SWEDEN COUNTY: KRONOBERG AS OF AUG 1978 PAGE 10,118

SEX M MALE F FEMALE H HUSBAND W WIFE

JONSSON, SAMUEL

NAME	FATHER MOTHER OR SPOUSE	SEX	TYPE	EVENT DATE	PARISH, TOWN	B	E	S	SOURCE BATCH	SOURCE SERIAL SHEET
JONSSON, SAMUEL		M	C	10FEB1760	DADESJO	01MAR1977SL	24MAR1977SL	08AUG1977SL	7626646	21
	JONAS MATTISSON/ELISABETH ANDERSDR									
JONSSON, SAMUEL	KARIN PERSDOTTER	H	M	27JUN1762	URSHULT			10JAN1973OG	7223101	24
JONSSON, SAMUEL	INGEBORG PERSDOTTER	H	M	11JUN1769	LJUNGBY			14JUN1973AL	7226239	78
JONSSON, SAMUEL	BENGTA SVENSSON	H	M	11JUN1775	STENBROHULT			21NOV1958SL	A457383	0456
JONSSON, SAMUEL		M	B	25MAR1779	BLADINGE	08MAY1970LA	27JUN1970LA	11APR1972LA	6929351	61
	JONAS NILSSON/BRITTA JONSDOTTER									
JONSSON, SAMUEL		M	B	20JUL1791	SLATTHOG	06MAR1974LG	19APR1974LG	21MAY1974LG	7326924	91
	JOHANNES SAMUELSSON/MAJA ANDERSDR									
JONSSON, SAMUEL		M	C	27NOV1791	ALGUTSBODA	CLEARED	CLEARED	CLEARED	7800502	65
	JONAS MANSSON/BRITTA MANSDOTTER									
JONSSON, SAMUEL		M	C	20APR1794	ALGUTSBODA	INFANT	INFANT	27NOV1975SW	7508607	22
	JOHANNES NILSSON/MARIA MANSDOTTER									
JONSSON, SAMUEL		M	C	08MAR1797	VASTRA TORSAS	INFANT	INFANT	25FEB1974SL	7309928	45
	JONAS SAMUELSSON/MARTHA MANSDR									
JONSSON, SAMUEL	JON PERSSON/SARA PERSON	M	C	09JUN1798	ALGHULT	30JUN1971SL	06AUG1971SL	19JAN1972SL	7104016	88
JOHANSSON, SAMUEL		M	C	08DEC1799	FROARYD,URSHULT	21FEB1973PV	10APR1973PV	04MAY1973PV	7229827	6
	JOHAN PERSSON/BRITA NILSDOTTER									
JONASSON, SAMUEL	INGRID CHRISTINA NILSSON	H	M	30DEC1832	LINNERYD			12JAN1968SL	A537228	0409
JONSSON, SAMUEL		M	C	09DEC1838	VRA	CLEARED	CLEARED	CLEARED	7803802	21
	JOHANNES PERSSON/JOHANNA NILSDOTTER									
JONSSON, SAMUEL		M	C	20APR1842	ALGHULT	CLEARED	CLEARED	CLEARED	7812150	93
	JONAS PET JONSSON/LENA JOHANSDR									
JOHANSSON, SAMUEL	ANNA JONSSON	H	M	26DEC1844	GASHULT,TORPA			28JAN1943LG	A178086	3297
JOHANSSON, SAMUEL	BOTILD DAVIDSSON	H	M	30DEC1857	URSHULT			13DEC1955SL	A457010	1015
JONSDR, SARA	JONS ERICHSSON	W	M	1694	MOHEDA			06APR1977SG	M400971	0046
JONSSON, SARA	JONS/	F	C	31AUG1712	ANNERSTAD	04JAN1973PV	01MAR1973PV	31MAR1973PV	7221720	96
JONSSON, SARA	JOHAN NILSSON/INGRY MANSDR	F	B	12MAR1724	MOHEDA	25MAY1977PV	22JUL1977PV	11AUG1977PV	C400971	0689
JONSSON, SARA	MANS PERSSON	W	M	20JUN1724	ALGHULT			11MAR1965OK	A458745	0531
JONSSON, SARA	PER ARVIDSSON	W	M	11JUL1725	ANGELSTAD			31OCT1958IF	A459032	1895
JONSDOTTER, SARA		F	C	25SEP1726	SODRA LJUNGA	CLEARED	CLEARED	CLEARED	7731104	59
	JONS HAKANSSON/BENGTA JONSDOTTER									
JONSSON, SARA	JON/	F	B	1729	INGELSTROP,BERG SOCKEN	CLEARED	CLEARED	CLEARED	7708101	50
JONSSON, SARA	JOHAN SAMUELSSON/ELIN JONSDR	F	C	08MAR1730	MOHEDA	25MAY1977PV	22JUL1977PV	11AUG1977PV	C400971	0815
JONSSON, SARA	JONAS LARSSON/BRITTA NILSDR	F	C	30APR1730	MOHEDA	INFANT	INFANT	11AUG1977PV	C400971	0817
JONSSON, SARA	JONS BOSSON/SICILIA CARLSDR	F	C	16MAY1731	MOHEDA	21SEP1963	15JAN1964LA	14OCT1964LA	C400971	0844
JONSSON, SARA	JON SIMONSSON/INGRID JONSDR	F	C	12SEP1731	DADESJO	22JAN1977OK	24JAN1977OK	22MAR1977OK	7621609	19
JONSSON, SARA	JONAS LARSSON/BRITTA NILSDR	F	C	03OCT1731	MOHEDA	25MAY1977PV	22JUL1977PV	11AUG1977PV	C400971	0853
JONSSON, SARA	JOHAN MATTHSSON/ELIN NILSDR	F	C	18FEB1733	MOHEDA	25MAY1977PV	22JUL1977PV	11AUG1977PV	C400971	0881
JONSSON, SARA		F	B	15MAR1742	ALGHULT	17DEC1977OG	09FEB1978OG	16MAR1978OG	7719216	89
	JONAS ERIKSSON/SARA CARLSDOTTER									
JOHANSDR, SARA	SIGFRID HAKANSSON	W	M	07MAY1766	MOHEDA			06APR1977SG	M400971	0273
JONSDR, SARA	JON OGGESSON/SARA PERSDR	F	C	20SEP1747	ALGHULT	17DEC1977OG	09FEB1978OG	16MAR1978OG	7719217	2
JONSSON, SARA		F	C	19SEP1756	ALGUTSBODA	09JAN1976LG	29JAN1976LG	23APR1976LG	7526501	62
	JON YGGESSON/INGJERD CARLSDOTTER									
JONSDOTTER, SARA	OLOF STEPHANSSON	W	M	15NOV1767	ALGUTSBODA			21OCT1977OG	7701417	88
JONSSON, SARA	JONAS PERSSON/LAISA PERSDOTTER	F	C	27FEB1774	WRAEN,BERG SOCKEN	15MAR1974SW	13JUL1974SW	25JUL1974SW	7333301	87
JONSSON, SARA	JON CARLSSON/ELIN PETERSDOTTER	F	C	20AUG1775	URSHULT	06AUG1976MT	30SEP1976MT	18NOV1976MT	7603415	70
JONSSON, SARA		F	C	24JAN1779	LENHOVDA	23APR1977AL	18MAY1977AL	21JUN1977AL	7630808	49
	JONAS NILSSON/ANNICA PEHRSDOTTER									
JONSSON, SARA	JOHAN JOHANSSON/STINA JACOBSDR	F	C	06JAN1785	STENBROHULT	17JUN1974SL	27AUG1974SL	09SEP1974SL	7402401	59
JONSSON, SARA		F	C	27MAY1787	BOASTAD,HOTTEBACK	INFANT	INFANT	02JUN1977PV	7626709	4
	JOHANNES NILSSON/ELISABETH JOHANSDR									
JONASSON, SARA	JOHANNES PERSSON	W	M	03OCT1788	NYBYGGET,VAXJO			13OCT1959SG	A458209	0400

Σ = EVALUATED ENTRY

A = ADULT CHRISTENING B = BIRTH C = CHRISTENING D = DEATH OR BURIAL F = BIRTH OR CHRISTENING OF FIRST KNOWN CHILD M = MARRIAGE N = CENSUS W = WILL ALL OTHERS = MISCELLANEOUS

The one million reels of microfilm currently on file are the equivalent of about four million printed volumes of 350 pages each and represent records from the United States and fifty major countries of the world. Extensive collections are on file for the United States, Canada, Mexico, Great Britain, the Scandinavian countries, the Netherlands, Belgium, France, Germany, and certain Iron Curtain countries. Lesser collections are available for South America and other countries, but microfilming continues in most parts of the world. There are sixteen cameras operating in the United States at this time and almost one hundred operating in other countries.

The kinds of records and documents microfilmed for each country vary but are those considered most essential for genealogical and historical research. Public and official vital records are a prime source and have been filmed wherever possible, as have parish registers, other church records, and cemetery records. Census, court, land, military, emigration, and miscellaneous social/commercial records have also been included, as have compiled secondary sources. However, recent changes in the Genealogical Society's policies and procedures have resulted in more limited coverage, concentrating on public and official vital records, church records, and other sources that provide basic genealogical identification.

A few of the Society's filmed collections date prior to 1500, but most cover the late 1500s to the late 1800s. English-Welsh probate records date from 1200 to 1858; those for North Carolina date from 1670 to 1973 or later. Circumstances and policies in effect at the time of microfilming dictate the records copied and the time period covered.

Books and manuscripts. More than 170,200 printed volumes and almost 12,000 manuscripts relating to family and local history also have been cataloged by the library, and hundreds of volumes are added each month.

Compiled genealogies, biographies, family histories, and publications relating to local history constitute the major part of the collection, but periodicals and publications relating to source materials are also on file. From one to five county histories have been cataloged for each of the 3,050 counties of the United States. Similar collections relating to foreign countries are also available. Hundreds of volumes of records and record extracts have been acquired including cemetery inscriptions, parish registers, wills, deeds, court records, census indexes, tax lists, and numerous others.

The private manuscripts of many genealogists and historians have been acquired by the library, or microfilm copies have been made. For example, the Worth S. Ray collection of southern states genealogy, the Mamie M. McCubbins collection for North Carolina, the Benjamin Noyes collection for Maine, the Draper and Burton collections for the midwestern states, and the Anthony Tarbox-Briggs collection for Rhode Island are only a few.

The library also has acquired or created excellent reference materials to help the researcher, including guide books, manuals, registers, maps, atlases, gazetteers, and indexes—indispensible to competent research.

The LDS genealogical library uses the Dewey decimal system for classification and cataloging with some variations. It uses a dictionary type catalog and includes reference cards by author, title, subject, and locality. (The last item provides special emphasis to source holdings by geographical location.)

Even though the Genealogical Society of Utah has one of the most extensive collections of genealogical and historical material in the world, it does not have all records; research must be carried out in other repositories to extend some pedigrees.

The National Archives

The General Services Administration—through the National Archives and Records Service—is responsible for administering the permanent noncurrent records of the federal government. These archival holdings amount to more than one million cubic feet of records, dating from the days of the Continental Congress, and include basic records of the three branches of government (Colket 1968, p. iii).

Many of the records relate to ordinary citizens and are excellent family history sources. Federal population and mortality census schedules 1790–1890 are in its custody (except originals of the 1880 census, which were returned to the various states), as are special territorial and state enumerations for various years. Passenger arrival lists for East and Gulf Coast ports are available 1820–1945, but those for some West Coast ports are lost, having been destroyed by fires in 1851 and 1940.

The National Archives has a large collection of military records, dating primarily 1775 through 1917, with a few after that date. They include regular army enlistment registers and rosters 1785–1917; revolutionary war records 1775–1883; War of 1812 service files for volunteer organizations; Mexican War, Civil War, Spanish American War, and other records 1784–1902. Civil War draft records and burial records for soldiers and sailors are also preserved. Civilian birth, marriage, and death records at army posts 1884–1912 are on file, as are some records of the Confederacy. Some records of veterans' benefits 1775–1934 (exclusive of Confederacy and World War I veterans) are also on file.

Numerous land entry records pertaining to the public land states are also housed at the National Archives. They are dated chiefly 1800 through 1950, but some concern earlier transactions. The land entry records consist of documents relating to rights or claims to land before grants or patents were issued by the federal government. Genealogical data appearing in land records before 1862—with the exception of certain private land claims; donation entry files for Florida, Washington, and Oregon; and bounty-land script applications—are usually limited to the name of the entryman and the place of residence he gave at the time he made his purchase or entry.

The National Archives also has many records concerning North American Indians—mainly those who kept their tribal status or were removed to western lands by the federal government. They include annuity pay rolls, annual census rolls, special rolls relating to the Eastern Cherokees; estate files, and Carlisle Indian School files. In addition, there are some population census schedules and bounty-land warrant application files that relate in part to Indians. Many records relating to the Five Civilized Tribes in Oklahoma have been housed at the Federal Records Center at Fort Worth, Texas.

Other record collections at the National Archives include civilian personnel records to about 1910; the Revenue-Cutter Service and the Coast Guard records (1791–1915 and 1915–29); special claims records; passport applications received by the Department of State between 1791 and 1905; records concerning the deaths of Americans abroad (chiefly 1857–1922); and some records concerning merchant seamen.

Most of the records in the National Archives are originals, and microfilm copies of many record groups are available for purchase or for use at the Archives and other libraries. Copies of some collections are also at other federal record centers, such as the 1900 federal census and its soundex, recently made public.

Photo duplication facilities and services are available, and the Archives maintains a staff of specialists to assist you with research, both through correspondence or personal visits.

State Libraries and Archives

Great strides have been taken by state libraries and archives throughout the United States in locating, gathering, classifying, cataloging, preserving, and facilitating the use of important state and local records. Officials have initiated good programs in most instances, and legislatures have appropriated sufficient funds to accomplish realistic goals. At the same time library and archival personnel have been able to devote more time to assisting researchers, through guidebooks and aids as well as through personal help.

Nearly every state has done something toward better records preservation and use, and though present economic conditions are forcing austerity measures in government, most states continue to give this area attention and funds.

It is not possible to detail every state's records preservation and use program, but the following examples should illustrate the positive accomplishments of four states.

The North Carolina State Archives is the richest single source for genealogical material in the state of North Carolina. In its archives are original records of the governors and many other state officials, departments, and agencies; a variety of records from most of the one hundred counties; copies of federal census records; military records; collections of the private manuscripts of many important North Carolinians; records of many religious, patriotic, business, fraternal, and civic groups; and microfilm copies of North Carolina newspapers.

As early as 1914, the North Carolina State Archives began a program of receiving original official records from local county authorities for preservation. In 1959 the general assembly approved a local records program and appropriated funds for a staff to inventory all county and municipal records in the state; to microfilm permanently valuable local records for security purposes; and to provide for the repair, restoration, and rebinding of permanently valuable records remaining in local courthouses.

Local officials were encouraged to transfer to the state archives permanently valuable records no longer of current day-to-day use, and many availed themselves of the opportunity to free much needed space in local offices. As a result of the program, the local records branch completed records inventory and disposition schedules for all one hundred counties, supervised the restoration and rebinding of more than twenty-seven hundred volumes, produced more than forty-five thousand reels of microfilm, and encouraged the voluntary transfer of over fifty-eight hundred volumes and forty-eight hundred cubic feet of loose records to the archives.

State records on file in the archives include correspondence and appointments of the various governors; records of the secretary of state, treasurer, comptroller, adjutant general, and other state officials; original legislative bills and petitions; some early lists of taxables, justices, and militiamen; and the state census of 1784–87 (many counties are missing).

A wide variety of records from almost every county is among the material in the archives, but the quantity and quality varies. For many counties there are court minutes, tax lists, wills, deeds, inventories of estates, and marriage bonds to 1868. Most of the deeds, wills, and inventories are on microfilm and are copies of the recorded instruments retained at the county seat. Marriage bonds exist for about half the counties in the state, and a typed index—by county—is available. The register of deeds in each county is custodian for marriages after 1868. The period covered by the marriage bonds varies, but in some instances it extends from 1741 to 1868. A published *Guide to Research Materials in the North Carolina State Archives, Section B: County Records* is available for purchase from the archives.

The archives also has a good collection of military records, including revolutionary army accounts and vouchers; War of 1812 vouchers; a printed roster of North Carolina troops in the War with Mexico; an alphabetical card index to Moore's Roster of North Carolina Troops in the War Between the States; a printed roster of the North Carolina volunteers in the Spanish American War; and a few miscellaneous circulars and bulletins providing information on the location and use of military records.

Several miscellaneous record collections are also available in the search room of the archives. A few unpublished family genealogies are on file, but most of the printed genealogies of North Carolina families are in the state library section and not in the archives. The archives has a growing collection of church records on microfilm and a few church histories. Tombstone inscriptions for persons buried in many North Carolina cemeteries prior to 1914 are available, and an alphabetical card file for DAR burial listings is in the search room of the archives. The department is microfilming all early North Carolina newspapers, and positive copies are available for use. Nearly two thousand private genealogical and historical collections also are on file.

The primary functions of the state archives are collecting, preserving, and making available historical materials for public use. Records are made available only in the search room, and none may be loaned or taken out. The division is not in a position to do historical or genealogical research for an individual; normally a person seeking genealogical information from the records should arrange to visit the search room in person or engage a professional genealogist to do his work. Although the division does not recommend specific genealogists, it does supply interested persons with a list of those who offer their services to the public for a fee. Extensive genealogical research cannot be done by mail, and the archives suggests that research should be done in person whenever possible.

Facilities for producing photostatic and microfilm copies are available with some limitations. Typed, certified copies of certain types of records can be provided, but the staff of the archives cannot make long, typed transcripts of hard-to-read documents. Paper enlargements of microfilm records can be made, but since the condition of the microfilm often makes such copies dim and hard to read, it is recommended that patrons seek copies of the original records.

The research area of the North Carolina State Archives is located on the west end of the second floor of the Archives and History State Library in Raleigh. The mailing address is North Carolina State Archives, 109 East Jones Street, Raleigh, North Carolina 27611.

The state library comprises the west end of the first floor of the building, with reference services and personnel available. It has a dictionary card catalog and considerable published material relating to the state.

The South Carolina Department of Archives and History at Columbia, South Carolina, is another example of quality care for state and county records.

South Carolina has existed as a governmental entity for over three hundred years, but even before the first settlement in April 1670, records were being created and preserved concerning the area.

The South Carolina Department of Archives and History is the repository for noncurrent archives of the state. It evolved from two earlier agencies—the Public Record Commission of South Carolina, appointed in 1891 to obtain copies of South Carolina records in the British Public Record Office, and the South Carolina Historical Commission, created in 1894 to maintain the records obtained. The Archives Act of 1954 changed the commission's name to the South Carolina Archives Department and redefined its archival responsibilities. In 1968 the department became the South Carolina Department of Archives and History, with responsibilities for historic preservation, historical services, and records management.

The governing body is the South Carolina Archives and History Commission. By law it is composed of the heads of the history departments of The Citadel, the University of South Carolina, Clemson University, and Winthrop College. The department is under the immediate supervision of a director and deputy director appointed by the commission and assistant directors for each of the department's five sections. Public access to the records is provided by the reference and research division of the archives and publications section. That section is also responsible for documentary publications, inventory, arrangement, description, and indexing of the holdings; provision of photocopies; and document restoration. The historical programs section's responsibilities include the preservation and marking of historic sites and coordination of the activities of local historical societies.

The Department of Archives and History has acquired a variety of records relating to the state—some retrieved from England and other foreign countries—and maintains excellent facilities for their preservation and use. Important collections include legislative, executive, and treasury records; records of state agencies and departments; records of the Secretary of the Province and State; state land, court, and military records; and numerous county and local materials.

Records of the Secretary of the Province and State include wills, inventories of estates, marriage settlements, commission, mortgages, bills of sale, registers of trademarks, and charters of incorporation. Considering that there were no counties organized in South Carolina until after the Revolution, these early state records are critical. State land records include plats and grants (virtually complete from 1731); incomplete records of surveys and grants 1671–1730; memorials of land titles 1732–75; and a few miscellaneous records.

The department has over three thousand cubic feet of county records that date after 1783 and an ever-growing microfilm collection of public and semipublic records relating to South Carolina from the British Public Record Office, the National Archives, other state and national archives, and private manuscript repositories. It also has a good collection of published reference works, bibliographies, archival guides, and monographs on South Carolina history.

The South Carolina archives is located at 1430 Senate Street (corner of Senate and Bull Streets) in Columbia. It is two blocks from the state house and one block from the University of South Carolina campus. The South Carolina library, which houses a large collection of printed books and private manuscripts on South Carolina history, is within easy walking distance.

The reference and research division operates the search room and answers queries. The division will answer questions about the records or requests for specific information from the records that involve only a reasonable amount of research. The staff will check a few specified, easily searched indexes for a specific name and send a photocopy order for records in which that name appears. Extensive research cannot be undertaken, but recommendations for further research will be given. A list of persons willing to do genealogical research for a fee will be sent on request. In general, researchers with extensive or complicated projects will find it more profitable and enjoyable to do their own research on location.

Photocopies of records in the archives may be purchased at a reasonable fee, but the department will not reproduce published material. A limited microfilm copying service for scattered documents is available, but extensive filming cannot be done on demand. Microprints of records on microfilm can be furnished, subject to restrictions by the repositories holding the manuscripts. The department reserves the right to determine which process will be used and whether copying of particular documents will be feasible. A photocopy price list will be furnished on request.

Extensive microfilming of South Carolina records has been done by the Genealogical Society of Utah, and the South Carolina Archives has prepared a "Temporary Summary Guide" to its holdings (second edition, 1976). The guide lists the provincial, state, and local governmental records in the custody of the South Carolina Archives and History Commission on 1 January 1976. Virtually all extant historically significant records created by South Carolina state government from 1671 to 1940 are included. All pre-1900 documents of permanent value have been brought to Columbia, either in original form or on microfilm, from the courthouses of eight of South Carolina's forty-six counties, and the local records section will continue its work until records of the other counties have been taken care of.

Records during the colonial period of South Carolina history were kept on a provincial basis or at Charleston; destructive forces have taken their toll. Districts were established as early as 1769 and a few court records were kept in those jurisdictions, but it was not until 1783 that counties were established and began to keep records. The Genealogical Society of Utah has microfilmed existing county records from their organization to 1860, and copies are at Columbia. County records after 1860, except those for the eight counties mentioned above, must be investigated at their respective county courthouses.

The State Library at Richmond, Virginia, has implemented programs similar to those of the South Carolina Department of Archives and History. It has identified, gathered, published, and microfilmed many early county and state records of historical importance.

The Virginia State Library is located at Eleventh and Capitol Streets in downtown Richmond, directly across from Capitol Square. It is open to the general public between 8:15 a.m. and 5:00 p.m. Monday through Saturday, excluding legal holidays. It has a comprehensive collection of printed and manuscript materials relating to the state and an excellent facility for their preservation and use.

Printed materials may be consulted in the general library reading room, including a variety of reference works such as guides, manuals, maps, and other handbooks essential to research. It has a good collection of histories relating to Virginia and the South and has many biographies and genealogies pertaining to Virginia people. Special indexes—such as those by Swem, Stewart, and Wise—are available, and many genealogical periodicals are on file.

One of the most useful reference works in the library is Earl G. Swem's *Virginia Historical Index,* in 2 volumes. It is a detailed guide to references of Virginia and Virginians found in the following publications:

Statutes at Large: Being a Collection of all the Laws of Virginia, 1619–1792. William W. Hening, editor. Thirteen volumes. Reprinted in 1969 by the University Press of Virginia.

The Lower Norfolk County Virginia Antiquary. 1895–1906. Five volumes.

Calendar of Virginia State Papers and Other Manuscripts, 1652–1869. Eleven volumes. Reprinted in 1968 by Kraus Reprint Corporation.

Virginia Historical Register and Literary Advertiser, 1848–53. Six volumes.

The Virginia Magazine of History and Biography, 1893–1930. Thirty-eight volumes.

William and Mary College Quarterly. Series 1, 1892–1919. Twenty-seven volumes. Series 2, 1921–30. Ten volumes.

The following important compilations were not included in Swem's index:

> *The Statutes at Large of Virginia: Being a Continuation of Hening, 1792–1806,* by Samuel Shepherd. Three volumes. Reprinted in 1968 by AMS Press.
>
> *The Laws of Virginia: Being a Supplement to Hening's Statutes at Large, 1700–50.* Compiled by Waverly K. Winfree, Virginia State Library, 1971.

The library compiled cards for many individual family genealogies and filed them in the catalog under surname following author entries. Other items are identified according to author, title, and subject. A special key to manuscript holdings by county is available for consultation at the main reference counter.

The state library is the major repository for Virginia's historically valuable records, and the archives branch—located at the west end of the library—is responsible for their care and use. Among its holdings are records of the state government; copies of extant county court records (such as wills, deeds, orders, and marriage records) to 1865; a small number of church records; some personal papers; unpublished genealogical notes; and miscellaneous Bible records.

The county records are perhaps most important to the family historian; most of those prior to 1865 have been brought to the library and microfilmed. Records after 1865 must be searched in the respective counties. The Genealogical Society of Utah did most of the microfilming of Virginia's records; copies of those from approximately 1865 are on file in Salt Lake City, Utah.

The primary local county records include wills and inventories, deeds, marriage records, court order books, and miscellaneous loose records and documents. The records vary greatly in makeup and completeness. The wills, deeds, and marriage records generally are indexed, but most court records are not. Some court order books are individually indexed, but no general indexes exist. The county clerks were responsible for the records but were not always consistent in their recording practices. Wills are sometimes found in deed books and vice versa, and marriage records might be found in both will and deed books. Almost any event or circumstance might be found recorded in the court order books.

Marriage records were the earliest vital records kept, and date from about 1730. Marriage was authorized by license and banns, but bonds can be found after an early marriage act of 1660–61—though few have survived for that early date. Prior to 1780 marriages were performed only by ministers of the established church (Church of England or Anglican); banns fell into disuse during the revolutionary war in the Tidewater region. By 1780 minister's returns were popular; they constitute many of the county marriage records that have been preserved. Quaker marriages were not recorded in the county records during the colonial period, and many were not recorded after that period. The library's collection of marriage records date primarily from 1730 to 1865.

By an act passed in 1853, the state required the recording of vital statistics on a county basis, which continued until 1896. Microfilm copies of these early records are in the library and also on file in Salt Lake City. State registration was mandatory by June 1912; vital records from that date to the present are available for a fee from the Bureau of Vital Statistics, 109 Governor Street, Richmond, Virginia 23219.

Fire and other destructive forces have taken their toll of Virginia county records; the following counties are known to have suffered record losses in the years listed: Appomatox 1845 and 1892; Buchanan 1885 and 1977; Buckingham 1869; Caroline 1836; Charles City 1865; Dinwiddie 1864; Elizabeth City 1864; Gloucester 1821 and 1865; Hanover 1865; Henrico 1677; James City 1865; King William 1885; King and Queen 1828 and 1865; Mathews 1865; Nansemond 1866; New Kent 1787 and 1865; Prince George 1865; Prince William 1865; Strafford 1865; and Warwick 1865. There remain, however, some records to work with for each county.

The state library has federal and state census records both in book form and on microfilm for various years. The 1790 and 1800 federal census returns for Virginia were destroyed by fire during the War of 1812. A substitute 1790 census was compiled in 1908 from the 1782–85 state tax enumerations of thirty-nine of Virginia's eighty counties. These enumerations were published by the U.S. Bureau of the Census: *Heads of Families at the First Census of the United States Taken in the Year 1790—Records of the State Enumerations (Virginia) 1782–85*. Those counties not included in this publication are covered in Augusta B. Fothergill's *Virginia Tax Payers, 1782–87* (1967).

Federal census returns for Virginia from 1810 through 1880 and the indexes to the 1810 and 1880 schedules are available on microfilm in the archives reading room. They are arranged by county but are not alphabetized within each county.

Most of the church records in the library's collection are administrative in nature and contain very few references to births, deaths, or marriages. Records of Baptist, Episcopal, Lutheran, German Reformed, Methodist, and Presbyterian denominations date from the colonial period to approximately 1865. No master index exists for the records, but they are identified by locality. Records for a small number of Virginia churches have been published and are on file in the archives reading room.

The Church of England or Anglican (later known as Episcopal) Church was the established religion in Virginia until 1786 and was charged with keeping a record of births, deaths, and marriages within each parish. Comparatively few of these registers have been preserved. Other denominations were not required by law to record births, deaths, or marriages, and their records vary considerably. The library has very few of these denominational records on file; many still remain in the respective churches.

Some of the earliest records available for research are those of the Virginia Land Office filed at the state library. They begin as early as 1623 and include patents, grants, and records relating to the head-right system in effect to 1720. Some bounty land records for Virginia, West Virginia, and the Virginia military districts of Ohio and Kentucky are also on file. Tithable lists, or tax lists, as they are more popularly known, date from as early as 1702. Quit rents, poll tax lists, and rental lists also are available. In 1782 the state established a source of permanent revenue by requiring the annual collection of taxes on land and certain personal property. The library has lists of the returns for most counties from 1782.

The archives also has manuscript or photographic copies of documents attesting to the military service of Virginians during the colonial period, the revolutionary war, the War of 1812, the war with Mexico, and the Civil War. Military records of Virginians who served in the armed forces after 1865 may be obtained from the Department of Military Affairs, State Adjutant General, Ninth Street Office Building, Richmond, Virginia 23219.

A few muster rolls of colonial militia units prior to 1754 are on file; those that have survived are printed in such secondary sources as William A. Crozier's *Virginia Colonial Militia, 1651–1776* (1954), local county histories, and various volumes of the *Virginia Magazine of History and Biography.* Some of the muster rolls of units participating in the French and Indian War (1754–63) and Dunmore's War (1774) have also survived and are at the library. Most notable among these are the militia muster rolls in the Washington Manuscripts, Library of Congress (photocopies are available). In addition, volumes 7 and 8 of Hening's *Statutes at Large* contain individual references to the names of many noncombatants and to commanding officers of militia units, but not to members.

Affidavits of French and Indian War military service presented before a county court, accepted, then returned to the land office entitled a man to a bounty of land within Virginia, usually in the western and southwestern area of the state. These abstracts are on file among land office records, and though they are not military records in the strictest sense, they satisfy proof of service. A comprehensive index to these sources is Eckenrode's *List of Colonial Soldiers of Virginia.* County court order books and executive journals of the colonial council can also be used as military records, for they occasionally reveal the commissioning of an officer.

Account books, muster rolls, and affidavits testifying to service in the Revolution are also on file. They are available in original and photocopy form and are indexed in Eckenrode's *List of the Revolutionary Soldiers of Virginia* and in Gwathmey's *Historical Register of Virginians in the Revolution 1775–83.*

Other revolutionary war records on file include land office, state pension, and public service claim records. Only those men who served for three or more years in the state or Continental line unit and heirs of men who died in service were entitled to bounty land. The amount of land was dependent upon the individual's rank and length of service. Lands awarded for such service were located in the Virginia military districts of Kentucky and Ohio. Virginia kept no record of bounty land grants after issuing the warrant that entitled the individual to the grant. The number of a warrant issued to a specific individual can be found in an unpublished index to the land office military certificates, available in the archives. To determine the disposition made of a particular warrant, write to the Secretary of State (Attention: Land Office), Commonwealth of Kentucky, New State Capitol, Frankfort, Kentucky 40601; or the Ohio Historical Society, Archives and Manuscript Division, I-17 and Eleventh Avenue, Columbus, Ohio 43211.

Virginia did not pass a general pension act applying to veterans of the revolutionary war. Each individual case was brought before the legislature for action. Approximately six hundred acts for the relief of special persons were passed by the legislature.

War of 1812 muster and pay rolls, totaling twenty-six volumes, are in the archives collection. However, proof of an individual's military service during the War of 1812 is based on two printed volumes: *Pay Rolls of the Virginia Militia Entitled to Land Bounty Under the Act of Congress of September 28, 1850* and *Muster Rolls of the Virginia Militia in the War of 1812, Being a Supplement to the Pay Rolls.* Both were compiled by the state from official state records.

At the close of the Civil War, most Confederate war department records were confiscated by the federal armies. Those records pertaining to service in Confederate military units were abstracted by the War Department and are available at the National Archives (Consolidated Index to Confederate Veterans). The state library has a microfilm copy of the records of the Virginia Confederate and Union military organizations.

In 1888 the Virginia General Assembly passed the first of several acts providing pensions to Confederate veterans. This initial act included only those soldiers, sailors, and marines disabled in action and the widows of those killed in action. Subsequent acts broadened the coverage to include all veterans, widows, daughters, and sisters. The applications for pensions are available in the library, and microfilm copies are at Salt Lake City.

The Hall of Records, an agency of the Department of General Services, is the historical agency for the State of Maryland, serving as the central depository for government records of permanent value. Preserving records for posterity has long been a tradition in Maryland.

As early as 1729, a repository for old records was erected on the State House Circle, a brick structure measuring twelve by sixteen feet. When the new state house was erected in 1772, four rooms were set aside for an archives. In 1859 a new fire-proof record depository was completed. It was much larger than either of the first two archives, but its builders were overly optimistic when they predicted that it would "serve for ages as a depository of the archives of the state."

The present Hall of Records was constructed in 1934–35 as part of the Tercentenary Celebration of the landing of the Ark and Dove. Built on land deeded to the state by the Visitors and Governors of St. John's College, the Hall of Records is divided into two parts: a central stack area of concrete and steel completely cut off from the rest of the building, and the outer area devoted to the public search room, microfilm reading room, manuscript restoration lab, photo duplication facilities, and staff offices.

The Hall of Records has in its custody an invaluable collection of records for historians and genealogists, particularly probate, land, and court materials, and the state land and court records formerly maintained in the land office. The public search room of the Hall of Records is open from 8:30 a.m. to 4:30 p.m. Mondays through Saturdays, except on designated state holidays. Archivists are on duty to assist visitors and introduce new researchers to the many unpublished finding aids that are maintained. *A Guide to the Index Holdings at the Hall of Records* is available for purchase, giving detailed holdings of the archives. Send orders to: Bulletin No. 17, Hall of Records, Post Office Box 828, Annapolis, Maryland 21404. (Current cost is $1.00)

Personnel at the Hall of Records will respond to mail inquiries, but unless exact references are provided a charge is made, payable in advance. Because of limited staff, only one hour is devoted to each search. A fee is charged for photocopying and there is also a nominal handling fee for each order. A list of genealogists who have registered with the Maryland Historical Society will be provided on request, but the Hall of Records neither endorses nor guarantees their work.

Existing noncurrent government records, some as late as 1965, have been collected and filed at the Hall of Records. Many dating before 1865 have been microfilmed by the Genealogical Society of Utah, with film copies available for public search at both Annapolis and Salt Lake City. The primary records of genealogical and historical importance include marriage records, probates, land records, military records, and special card indexes.

County marriage license records and a card index—beginning as early as 1777 and extending to the late 1880s and 1900s—is available, as well as a statewide marriage collection and card index for 1865–67. Marriages on file with the Maryland Bureau of Vital Statistics 1914–30 are in book form at the archives, and Hodges Marriage References are card indexed for the period 1637–1851. Births, deaths, and burials found in land and court records have also been published and card indexed, beginning as early as 1649 and extending to 1880. Only a few church records are on file, and most are not indexed.

A card index to oaths of fidelity to the state of Maryland in 1778; a census for three counties in 1778; probate records for most counties to 1850 (and for some counties to 1960 or later); probate records of the prerogative court 1635–1777; land records for most counties through 1949; and military records dating from the Revolution through the Civil War are on file, with selected card indexes available. Originals are carefully preserved, and microfilm copies of the records may be consulted at both the Hall of Records and at the LDS genealogical library. The special card indexes have not been filmed at this writing and must be searched at the Hall of Records.

North and South Carolina, Virginia, and Maryland are good examples of states with excellent programs for records preservation and use, but they are by no means the only good examples. Other repositories I personally have visited where equivalent programs are in effect are Montgomery, Alabama; Atlanta, Georgia; Nashville, Tennessee; Indianapolis, Indiana; Topeka, Kansas; Trenton, New Jersey; Albany, New York; and Hartford, Connecticut, to name a few.

Historical Societies

State archives and libraries generally are committed to the preservation and care of official government records, not other types of records and documents. State historical societies have involved themselves in locating, preserving, and restoring many different types of records, documents, artifacts, buildings, memorabilia, and other items of historical interest. They also promote studies in local history and contribute much to family history.

The Virginia Historical Society at Richmond has acquired thousands of items pertaining to Virginia's history, including guns, rifles, and muskets from the Revolution; similar items from the Civil War; and uniforms, flags, maps, and other documents—both public and private—that relate in any way to the state. Photographs, paintings, etchings, letters, Bible records, newspapers, and other kinds of historical materials are being collected and preserved. Special projects for the restoration of historical buildings, monuments, and statues, and the marking of historical trails and landmarks have also been undertaken.

Other states have done similar work, and the state historical societies are gaining greater influence with government officials and legislatures in accomplishing historical objectives. In the past most of their funding was from private endowments and individual contributions, which also influenced their direction to some extent. For this reason, often it is necessary to gain membership in the organization to effectively utilize their facilities and holdings. Membership usually is reasonable in cost and provides such other benefits as subscription to a bulletin, newsletter, or other publication.

Private historical, genealogical, and patriotic societies also are doing great work in preserving our American heritage. Many have libraries or museums where research can be conducted, or they publish periodicals that benefit family history. Their members gather oral history, copy tombstone inscriptions, publish family Bible records, index records, and complete other worthwhile historical and genealogical projects.

The National Society of the Daughters of the American Revolution has done a monumental work in historical records location and preservation. Members have retrieved valuable records from apparent destruction, gathered family Bible records, copied tombstones, placed headstones on the graves of soldiers, and compiled countless volumes of genealogical and historical material. Their national headquarters is a credit to America's heritage, and their library is second to none in its specialized nature. Microfilm copies of their compilations are available at the LDS genealogical library in Salt Lake City, Utah, and typescript or published copies also are widely circulated.

County Courthouses and Town Halls

Even though several states have gathered, microfilmed, and deposited some local records in state libraries, archives, and historical societies, many remain in respective county courthouses and town halls and must be investigated at those locations. When the originals have been copied or microfilmed, research can be done elsewhere, but otherwise it must be carried out in place. Even though some work can be accomplished through correspondence or through agents, local records officials should not be expected to conduct extensive research; they have neither the time nor inclination for such work and are usually too busy with the routine business of their offices to help.

Most records covered in the previous chapters originate at the town or county level, and they constitute an important source for family and local history. All types of public and official records are found at courthouses and town halls, including vital, census, court, land, military, and government department records. Official birth, marriage, and death records usually are on file, as are civil, criminal, and probate court records. Records relating to the acquisition and use, title transfer, and taxation of real estate also are there. In addition, there are a great many records relating to the licensing of business and commercial establishments, and the operation of police departments, fire departments, public waterworks, other public utilities, and public-operated health-care facilities. The list is unending.

Where vital records exist, they should be investigated first, because they provide the foundation material. Then research should move to probate court and land records. Some birth and death records are confidential, but very often marriage records are open for public inspection. Marriage records can also provide additional surnames to work with in the probate and land records. Sometimes the maiden surname of the wife will lead to wills and inventories that contain useful family information or give in-law relationships that may lead to other records.

Tax lists also can provide kinship information, but usually probate and land records are the most productive in that respect. Check the probates first, then move on to deeds, mortgages, and leases. They take more time and in many instances yield less return. Where town or county census records exist, you should research them next, leaving civil and criminal court records until last. Usually they are not indexed, and they are voluminous.

After a few hours in the courthouse or town hall, you will learn the procedures and enjoy the work. Do not be afraid to ask questions about the location of records or about their use; staff personnel usually are quite helpful and often will go out of their way to assist you in family history research. Sometimes early records have been retired to a basement storage vault or some other location, and you must exercise determination and persistence in locating them. Be courteous to county or town officials and to others using the records, and help protect the records from mutilation or destruction. Express your appreciation for help received.

If you plan your vacations and business trips to take advantage of field research, you will accomplish a lot and will grow in both knowledge and satisfaction. Good luck!

References

Abraham, H. J. 1959. *Courts and judges: an introduction to the judicial process.* New York: Oxford University Press.
Adams, J. T. 1943. *Atlas of American history.* New York: Charles Scribner's Sons.
———. 1949. *The founding of New England.* Boston: Little, Brown and Co.
Adams, J. T., et al. 1961. *Dictionary of American history.* 6 vols. New York: Charles Scribner's Sons.
American Association for State and Local History. 1969. *Genealogical research: a basic guide.* Technical Leaflet # 14. Nashville, Tenn.: American Association for State and Local History.
American Genealogical Research Institute Staff. 1975. *How to trace your family tree.* New York: Doubleday and Co.
Ames, Azel. 1901. *The Mayflower and her log, July 15, 1620, to May 6, 1621; chiefly from original sources.* Boston: Houghton, Mifflin and Co.
Andrews, C. M. 1964. *The colonial period of American history.* 3 vols. New Haven: Yale University Press.
Armstrong, Z. 1918–33. *Notable southern families.* 6 vols. Chattanooga: Lookout Publishing Co.
Ashby, R. L., ed. 1955. *Ashby and Badger ancestry.* American Fork, Utah: R. L. Ashby.
Ayer, N. W., and sons. 1880 to present. *Directory of newspapers and periodicals.* Philadelphia: N. W. Ayer and Sons.
Bailey, R. F. 1954. *Guide to genealogical and biographical sources for New York City (Manhattan) 1783–1898.* New York: R. F. Bailey.
Baird, C. W. 1885. *History of the Huguenot emigration to America.* 2 vols. New York: Dodd, Mead and Co.
Baird, R. 1834. *The emigrants and travelers guide to the West.* 2d ed. Philadelphia: R. Baird.
Banks, C. H. 1963. *Topographical dictionary of 2885 English emigrants to*

New England 1620–50. Reprint. Baltimore: Genealogical Publishing Co.

______. 1967. *Bristol and America: a record of the first settlers in the colonies of North America 1654–85.* Reprint. Baltimore: Genealogical Publishing Co.

______. 1967. *Planters of the commonwealth: a study of the emigrants and emigration in colonial times.* Reprint. Baltimore Publishing Co.

______. 1968. *The Winthrop Fleet of 1630: an account of the vessels, the voyage, the passengers and their English homes.* Reprint. Baltimore: Genealogical Publishing Co.

______. 1976. *The English ancestry and homes of the Pilgrim Fathers who came to Plymouth on the Mayflower in 1620, the Fortune in 1621, and the Anne and the Little James in 1623.* Reprint. Baltimore: Genealogical Publishing Co.

Barck, O. T., Jr., and Lefler, H. T. 1958. *Colonial America.* New York: Macmillan Co.

Bayless, E. H. 1949. Genealogical research in Kentucky. *The National Genealogical Society Quarterly* (Sept.) 37:65.

Beers, H. P. 1968. *Guide to the archives of the government of the Confederate States of America.* Washington, D.C.: National Archives and Records Service, General Services Administration.

Bennett, A. F. 1957. *Family exaltation.* Salt Lake City: Deseret Book Co.

______. 1957. *Finding your forefathers in America.* Salt Lake City: Bookcraft.

______. 1959. *Advanced genealogical research.* Salt Lake City: Bookcraft.

______. 1960. *A guide for genealogical research.* 2d ed. Salt Lake City: Deseret News Press.

______. 1962. *Searching with success.* Salt Lake City: Deseret Book Co.

Bennion, H. W. 1964. *Genealogical research: a practical mission.* Salt Lake City: Deseret News Press.

Bidlack, R. E. 1962. *First steps in climbing the family tree.* Detroit: Detroit Society for Genealogical Research.

Billington, R. A. 1974. *Westward expansion: a history of the American frontier.* 4th ed. New York: Macmillan Co.

Boddie, J. B. 1957–80. *Historical southern families.* 23 vols. Redwood City, Calif.: Pacific Coast Publishers.

Bodge, G. M. 1967. *Soldiers in King Philip's War.* Reprint. Baltimore: Genealogical Publishing Co.

Bolton, E. S. 1967. *Immigrants to New England 1700–75.* Reprint. Baltimore: Genealogical Publishing Co.

Boykin, P. M., and Porter, D. J. 1967. *The welding link: a training course in genealogy.* Denver: P. M. Boykin and D. J. Porter.

Brigham, C. S. 1947. *History and bibliography of American newspapers 1690–1820.* 2 vols. Worcester, Mass.: American Antiquarian Society.

Brigham Young University, Family and Local History Studies. 1978. *Family history and genealogical research seminar course syllabus.* Syllabus for the First Annual Family History and Genealogical Research Seminar, held on the Brigham Young University Campus, Provo, Utah.

______. 1979. *Family history and genealogical research seminar course syllabus.* Syllabus for the Second Annual Family History and Genealogical Research Seminar, held on the Brigham Young University Campus, Provo, Utah.

Brock, R. A. ed. 1886. *Documents, chiefly unpublished relating to the Huguenot emigration to Virginia and to the settlement at Mankintown, with an appendix of genealogies, presenting data of the Fontaine, Maury, Dupuy, Trabue, Marye, Chastain, Cocke, and other families.* Richmond, Va.: Virginia Historical Society.

Brown, A. 1964. *The genesis of the United States.* 2 vols. New York: Russell and Russell.

Brown, J. 1896. *The Pilgrim Fathers of New England and their Puritan successors.* New York: Fleming H. Revell Co.

Brown, N. 1978. *The trace your own roots workbook.* New York: Grosset and Dunlap.

Brown, R. H. 1948. *Historical geography of the United States.* New York: Harcourt, Brace and World.

Brown, S. E. 1967. *Virginia genealogies: a trial list of printed books and pamphlets.* Berryville, Va.: Berryville Virginia Book Co.

Browning, C. H. 1969. *Americans of royal descent.* Reprint. Baltimore: Genealogical Publishing Co.

Bullinger's Guides. 1897 to present. *Bullinger's postal and shippers guide for the United States and Canada.* Westwood, N.J.: Bullinger's Guides.

Byington, E. H. 1899. *The Puritan as a colonist and reformer.* Boston: Little, Brown and Co.

Callins, S. R. 1830. *The emigrant guide to the United States of America; including several authors and highly important letters from English emigrants now in America to their friends in England.* 4th ed. London: Joseph Noble.

Cameron, V. R. ed. 1976. *Emigrants from Scotland to America 1774–75; copied from a loose bundle of Treasury papers in the Public Record Office in London, England.* Reprint. Baltimore: Genealogical Publishing Co.

Canada Public Archives. 1972. *Tracing your ancestors in Canada.* Ottowa: Dominion Archives.

Cantor, N. R., and Schneider, R. I. 1967. *How to study history.* Arlington Heights, Ill.: AHM Publishing Corp.

Cappon, L. J. 1957. Genealogy: handmaid of history. *National Genealogical Society Quarterly* (March) 45:1–9.

______. 1964. *American genealogical periodicals: a bibliography with a chronological finding list.* New York: New York Public Library.

Case, P. A. 1977. *How to write your autobiography.* Santa Barbara, Calif.: Woodbridge Press.

Casner, M. E., and Gabriel, R. H. 1931. *Exploring American history.* New Haven: Yale University Press.

Cattell, J. ed. 1960. *American men of science: a biographical directory.* 10th ed. Tempe, Ariz.: Arizona State University, the Jaques Cattell Press.

Chaddock, R. E. 1908. *Ohio before 1850.* New York: Columbia University

Press.
Chandler, A. N. 1945. *Land title origins: a table of force and fraud.* New York: Robert Schalkenbach Foundation.
Chandler, M. C., and Wade, E. W. eds. 1976. *The South Carolina archives: a temporary summary guide.* 2d ed. Columbia: South Carolina Department of Archives and History.
Child, S. B., and Holmes, D. P. 1969. *Check list of historical records survey publications.* Baltimore: Genealogical Publishing Co.
Chitwood, O. P. 1948. *A history of colonial America.* New York: Harper and Brothers.
Clark, J. R. 1969. The cultural and historical background of the Indian people; a vital part of the genealogical research problem. Paper read at the World Conference on Records, Salt Lake City, Utah.
Coddington, J. I. 1969. Migration from New England to New York and New Jersey. Paper read at the World Conference on Records, Salt Lake City, Utah.
Colket, M. B. Jr. 1968. Creating a worthwhile family genealogy. *National Genealogical Society Quarterly* (Dec.) 56:244–62.
Colket, M. B., Jr., and Bridgers, F. E. 1964. *Guide to genealogical records in the National Archives.* Washington, D.C.: Government Printing Office.
Consumer Guide. 1977. *Tracing your roots.* New York: Bell Publishing Co.
Cowan, H. I. 1961. *British emigration to British North America.* Toronto: University of Toronto Press.
Cowley, J., and Cowley, M. 1965. *Along the Old York Road.* New Brunswick: Rutgers University Press.
Craven, A. and Johnson, W. 1952. *The United States experiment in democracy.* Boston: Ginn and Co.
Crozier, W. A. ed. 1953. *A key to southern pedigrees.* 2d ed. Baltimore: Southern Book Co.
_______. 1954. *Virginia colonial militia 1651–1776.* Baltimore: Southern Book Co.
Cullum, G. W. 1891. *Biographical register of the officers and graduates of the United States Military Academy at West Point, New York.* 3rd ed. 9 vols. Boston: Houghton, Mifflin and Co.
Cumming, J. 1974. *A guide for the writing of local history.* Lansing: Michigan Department of State, History Division.
Danky, J. P. ed. 1979. *Genealogical research: an introduction to the resources of the State Historical Society of Wisconsin.* Madison: State Historical Society.
Daughters of the American Revolution, National Society. 1958. *Is that lineage right: a training manual.* Washington, D.C.: National Society of the Daughters of the American Revolution.
Davis, W. T. ed. 1952. *Bradford's history of Plymouth plantation 1606–46.* New York: Barnes and Noble.
Debo, A. 1967. *The road to disappearance.* Norman, Okla.: University of Oklahoma Press.
Doane, G. H. 1960. *Searching for your ancestors.* Minneapolis, Minn.:

University Press.
Draughon, W. R., and Johnson, W. P. 1966. *North Carolina genealogical reference: a research guide for all genealogists, both amateur and professional.* Durham: The Seeman Printery.
Dubester, H. J. 1948. *An annotated bibliography of censuses of population taken after the year 1790 by states and territories of the United States.* Washington, D.C.: Government Printing Office.
Duffus, R. L. 1930. *The Santa Fe Trail.* London: Longmans Green.
Eaton, A. W. H. 1910. *The history of Kings County, Nova Scotia, heart of the Acadian land, giving a sketch of the French and their expulsion; and a history of the New England planters who came in their stead, with many genealogies, 1604–1910.* Salem, Mass.: The Salem Press.
Echenrode, H. J. 1916. *List of colonial soldiers of Virginia.* Virginia State Library Report, 1915–16. Richmond: Virginia State Library.
Edwards, A. 1920. *The Old Coast Road from Boston to Plymouth.* Cambridge, Mass.: Riverside Press.
Egle, W. H. 1967. *Names of foreigners who took the oath of allegiance to the province and state of Pennsylvania 1727–75, with the foreign arrivals 1786–1808.* Baltimore: Genealogical Publishing Co.
Emigrants from England 1773–76. 1913. Boston: New England Historic Genealogical Society.
Esshom, F. 1913. *Pioneers and prominent men of Utah.* Salt Lake City: Utah Pioneers Book Publishing Co.
Everton, G. B. Sr. ed. 1971. *Handybook for genealogists.* 6th ed. Logan, Utah: Everton Publishers.
Falley, M. D. 1962. *Irish and Scotch-Irish ancestral research: a guide to the genealogical records, methods, and sources in Ireland.* 2 vols. Evanston, Ill.: M. D. Falley.
Farmer, J. 1829. *A genealogical register of the first settlers of New England.* Lancaster, Mass.: Carter, Andrews and Co.
Faust, A. B. 1920. *Lists of Swiss emigrants in the eighteenth century to the American colonies, volume I, Zurich, 1734–44.* Washington, D.C.: The National Genealogical Society.
Felt, T. E. 1976. *Researching, writing, and publishing local history.* Nashville, Tenn.: American Association for State and Local History.
Filby, P. W. ed. 1970. *American and British genealogy and heraldry: a selected list of books.* Chicago: American Library Association.
Finberg, H. P. R., and Skipp, V. H. T. 1973. *Local history: objective and pursuit.* Devon, Eng.: David and Charles.
Flourney, R. W. ed. 1929. *A collection of nationality laws of various countries. New York: Oxford University Press.*
Foreman, G. 1966. *The Five Civilized Tribes.* Norman, Okla.: University of Oklahoma Press.
Fothergill, A. B., and Naugle, J. M. eds. 1940. *Virginia tax payers 1782–87.* Reprint. Baltimore: Genealogical Publishing Co.
Fothergill, G. 1964. *Emigrants from England 1773–76.* Baltimore: Genealogical Publishing Co.
———. 1965. *A list of emigrant ministers to America 1690–1811.* Baltimore: Genealogical Publishing Co.

French, E. 1962. *List of emigrants to America from Liverpool 1697–1707.* Baltimore: Genealogical Publishing Co.

Friederichs, H. F. 1969. Germanic research problems. Paper read at the World Conference on Records, Salt Lake City, Utah.

Gandy, W. ed. 1922. *The association oath rolls of the British plantations 1696.* London: W. Gandy.

Gardner, C. K. 1853. *A dictionary of the Army of the United States.* New York: G. P. Putnam and Co.

Gardner, D. E., and Smith, F. 1959–64. *Genealogical research in England and Wales.* 3 vols. Salt Lake City: Bookcraft.

Genealogical Forum of Portland, Oregon. 1957–62. *Genealogical material in Oregon donation land claims.* 3 vols. Portland: Genealogical Forum.

Genealogical Index of the Newberry Library, Chicago. 1960. 4 vols. Boston: G. K. Hall and Co.

Genealogical Periodical Annual Index. 1962–65. Ellen Stanley Rogers, ed. Bladensburg, Md.: Genealogical Recorders.

______. 1966–69. George Ely Russell, ed. Bowie, Md.: Genealogical Recorders.

______. 1970–78. Laird C. Towle, ed. Bowie, Md.: Genealogical Recorders.

Getty, L. 1934. *The law of citizenship in the United States.* Chicago: University of Chicago Press.

Ghirelli, M. 1968. *List of emigrants from England to America 1682–92.* Baltimore: Magna Carta Book Co.

Gibbon, J. M. 1941. *The new Canadian Loyalists.* Toronto: The Macmillan Co. of Canada.

Gilroy, M. 1937. *Loyalists and land settlement in Nova Scotia.* Halifax: The Public Archives of Nova Scotia.

Giuseppi, M. S. 1969. *Naturalizations of foreign Protestants in the American and West Indian colonies.* Baltimore: Genealogical Publishing Co.

Glasson, W. H. 1918. *Federal military pensions in the United States.* New York: Oxford University Press.

Glenn, T. A. 1897. *A list of some American genealogies which have been printed in book form.* Philadelphia: T. A. Glenn.

Greenwood, V. D. 1973. The researcher's guide to American genealogy. Baltimore: Genealogical Publishing Co.

Greer, G. C. 1960. *Early Virginia immigrants 1623–66.* Baltimore: Genealogical Publishing Co.

Gregory, W. ed. 1937. *American newspapers 1821–1936: a union list of files available in the United States and Canada.* New York: H. W. Wilson Co.

Guillet, E. C. 1963. *The great migration: the Atlantic crossing by sailing ship since 1770.* 2d ed. Toronto: University of Toronto Press.

Hamersly, T. H. W. 1880. *Complete Regular Army register of the United States for one hundred years.* Washington, D.C.: T. H. W. Hamersley.

Hancock, H. B. 1940. *The Delaware Loyalists.* Wilmington: Historical Society of Delaware.

Handlin, O. 1959. *Immigration as a factor in American history.* Englewood Cliffs, N.J.: Prentice-Hall.

Hansen, M. L. 1940. *The immigrant in American history.* New York: Harper and Row.

Hansen, M. L. 1961. *The Atlantic migration 1607–1860: a history of the continuing settlement of the United States.* New York: Harper and Row.

Haley, A. 1976. *Roots.* New York: Doubleday and Co.

Hardon, J. A. 1956. *The Protestant churches of America.* Westminster, Md.: The Newman Press.

Hardy, S. P. 1974. *Colonial families of the southern states of America.* Baltimore: Genealogical Publishing Co.

Hargreaves-Mawdsley, R. ed. 1978. *Bristol and America: a record of the first settlers in the colonies of North America 1654–85.* Reprint. Baltimore: Genealogical Publishing Co.

Harland, D. 1963. *Genealogical research standards.* Salt Lake City: Bookcraft.

Havighurst, W. 1956. *The heartland: Ohio, Indiana, Illinois.* New York: Harper and Row.

Heitman, F. B. 1903. *Historical register and dictionary of the United States Army from its organization September 29, 1783, to March 2, 1903.* Washington, D.C.: Government Printing Office.

———. 1967. *Historical register of officers of the Continental Army.* 2d ed. Baltimore: Genealogical Publishing Co.

Helmbold, F. W. 1976. *Tracing your ancestry.* Birmingham, Ala.: Oxmoor House.

Hemenway, A. M. ed. 1868–1923. *The Vermont historical gazeteer: a magazine embracing a history of each town, civil and ecclesiastical, biographical and military.* 6 vols. Burlington, Vt.: A. M. Hemenway.

Heslop, J. M., and Van Orden, D. 1976. *How to write your personal history.* Salt Lake City: Bookcraft.

———. 1977. *How to make your book of remembrance.* Salt Lake City: Bookcraft.

———. 1978. *How to compile your family history.* Salt Lake City: Bookcraft.

Hill, E. E. ed. 1965. *Preliminary inventories: No. 163. Records of the Bureau of Indian Affairs.* Washington, D.C.: The National Archives and Records Service, General Services Administration.

Hilts, L. 1977. *How to find your own roots.* New York: Greatlakes Living Press.

Hoenstine, F. G. 1972. *Guide to genealogical and historical research in Pennsylvania.* 3rd ed. Hollidaysburg, Pa.: Hoenstine Rental Library.

Hoffman, W. J. 1941. Palatine emigrants to America from the principality of Nassau-Dillenburg. *The National Genealogical Society Quarterly* (June) 29:41–44.

———. 1941. Early Dutch emigration to America. *The National Genealogical Society Quarterly* (Sept.) 29:81–89.

Hofstadter, R.; Miller, W.; and Aaron, D. 1959. *The American Republic to 1865, vol. 1.* Englewood Cliffs, N.J.: Prentice-Hall.

Holben, R. E. 1968. *Researching the family history for beginners.* Albuquerque, N.M.: Family History Press.

Holbrook, S. H. 1950. *The Yankee exodus: an account of migration from*

New England. New York: Macmillan Co.

Hopkins, G. E. 1949. *Your family tree:* a hobby handbook. Richmond, Va.: Deits Press.

Hotten, J. C. ed. 1968. *The original lists of persons of quality: emigrants; religious exiles; political rebels; serving men sold for a term of years; apprentices; children stolen; maidens pressed; and others who went from Great Britain to the American plantations 1600–1700.* 2d ed. Reprint. Baltimore: Genealogical Publishing Co.

Hoyt, M. E. 1943–66. Index to Revolutionary War pension applications and bounty land files. *The National Genealogical Society Quarterly.*

Ireland, D. 1970. *Your family tree: a handbook on tracing your ancestors and compiling one's own pedigree.* Herts, Eng.: Shire Publications.

Ireland, G. 1948. Servants of foreign plantations from Bristol, England 1654–86. *New York Genealogical and Biographical Record* 79:65–75.

Israel, O. 1969. Bridging the Atlantic. Paper read at the World Conference on Records, Salt Lake City, Utah.

Jacobus, D. L. 1932. Probate law and custom. *The American Genealogist* (July) 9:4–9.

———. 1932–58. *Index to genealogical periodicals.* 3 vols. New Haven: D. L. Jacobus.

———. 1964. The value of searching original records. *The American Genealogist* (July) 40:171.

———. 1968. *Genealogy as pastime and profession.* 2d ed. Baltimore: Genealogical Publishing Co.

Jahoda, G. 1975. *The trail of tears.* New York: Holt, Rinehard and Winston.

Jaussi, L. R., and Chaston, G. D. 1968. *Register of LDS church records.* Salt Lake City: Deseret Book Co.

———. 1974. *Genealogical records of Utah.* Salt Lake City: Deseret Book Co.

———. 1977. *Fundamentals of genealogical research.* Salt Lake City: Deseret Book Co.

Jenkins, S. 1913. *The Old Boston Post Road.* New York: G. P. Putnam's Sons.

Jenson, A. 1920. *Latter-day Saint biographical encyclopedia: a compilation of biographical sketches of prominent men and women in the Church of Jesus Christ of Latter-day Saints.* 4 vols. Salt Lake City: Arrow Press.

———. 1941. *Encyclopedic history of the Church of Jesus Christ of Latter-day Saints.* Salt Lake City: Deseret News Publishing Co.

Jenson, L. O. 1978. *A genealogical handbook of German research.* Pleasant Grove, Utah: L. O. Jenson.

Jewson, C. B. 1964. *Transcript of three registers of passengers from Great Yarmouth to Holland and New England 1637–39.* Baltimore: Genealogical Publishing Co.

Johansson, C. E. 1972. *Cradled in Sweden: a practical help to genealogical research in Swedish records.* Logan, Utah: Everton Publishers.

Johnson, A. ed. 1927–36. *Dictionary of American biography.* 10 vols. New York: Charles Scribner's Sons.

Johnson, S. C. 1966. *A history of emigration from the United Kingdom to North America 1763–1912.* New York: A. M. Kelley.

Jonasson, E. 1978. *The Canadian genealogical handbook.* Winnipeg: Wheatfield Press.

Jones, E. A. 1930. *The Loyalists of Massachusetts, their memorials, petitions and claims with sixty-three portraits in photogravure.* London: Saint Catherine Press.

Jones, V. L., et al. 1972. *Genealogical research: a jurisdictional approach.* Rev. ed. Salt Lake City: Publishers Press.

Kaminkow, M. J. ed. 1972. *Genealogies in the Library of Congress: a bibliography.* 2 vols. Baltimore: Magna Carta Book Co.

_______. 1975. *United States local histories in the Library of Congress: a bibliography.* 5 vols. Baltimore: Magna Carta Book Co.

_______. 1977. *Supplement 1972–76 to genealogies in the Library of Congress: a bibliography.* Baltimore: Magna Carta Book Co.

Kansas, S. 1936. *Citizenship of the United States of America.* New York: Washington Publishing Co.

Kirkham, E. K. 1956. *Research in American genealogy.* Salt Lake City: Deseret Book Co.

_______. 1960. *A survey of American church records. Vol. 2.* Salt Lake City: Deseret Book Co.

_______. 1964a. *How to read the handwriting and records of early America.* Salt Lake City: Deseret Book Co.

_______. 1964b. *The land records of America.* Salt Lake City: Deseret Book Co.

_______. 1964c. *Military records of America.* Salt Lake City: Deseret Book Co.

_______. 1965. *The counties of the United States and their genealogical value: a verified and corrected listing that shows parent county, county seat, and census information for each county with miscellaneous information.* Salt Lake City: Deseret Book Co.

_______. 1968. *Simplified genealogy for Americans.* Salt Lake City: Deseret Book Co.

_______. 1971. *A survey of American church records.* Vol. 1. 3rd ed. Logan, Utah: Everton Publishers.

Knittle, W. A. 1965. *Early eighteenth century Palatine emigration: a British government redeptioner project to manufacture naval stores.* Baltimore: Genealogical Publishing Co.

Komaiko, J., and Rosenthal, K. 1963. *Your family tree.* New York: Parents Magazine Press.

Krebs, F. 1951. A list of German immigrants to American colonies from Zweibruecken in the Palatinate, 1750–71. *Pennsylvania German Folklore Society* 16:171–83.

_______. 1957. Emigrants from Baden-Durlach to Pennsylvania, 1749–55. *The National Genealogical Society Quarterly* (March) 45:30–32.

Kyvig, D. E., and Marty, M. A. 1978. *Your family history: a handbook for research and writing.* Arlington Heights, Ill.: AHM Publishing Corp.

Lancour, H. 1963. *A bibliography of ship passenger lists 1538–1825: being a guide to published lists of early immigrants to North America.*

3rd ed. Revised and enlarged by R. J. Wolfe, with a list of passenger arrival records in the National Archives by Frank E. Bridgers. New York: The New York Public Library.

Landis, B. Y. 1965. *Religion in the United States.* New York: Barnes and Noble.

Landis, J. T. 1964. *Mayflower descendants and their marriages for two generations after landing.* Baltimore: Genealogical Publishing Co.

LDS Genealogical Society. 1965. *A general index to a census of pensioners for Revolutionary or military service in 1840.* Baltimore: Genealogical Publishing Co.

Lewis, M. W. 1962. *The development of early emigrant trails in the United States east of the Mississippi.* Washington, D.C.: The National Genealogical Society.

Library of Congress. 1906. *Records of the Virginia Company of London.* 4 vols. Washington, D.C.: Government Printing Office.

Lichtman, A. J. 1978. *Your family history: how to use oral history, personal family archives, and public documents to discover your heritage.* New York: Vintage Books.

Lichtman, A. J., and French, V. 1978. *Historians and the living past: the theory and practice of historical study.* Arlington Heights, Ill.: AHM Publishing Co.

Linder, B. R. 1976. *How to trace your family history. New York: Everest House.*

List of emigrants to America from Liverpool 1697–1707. Boston: New England Historic Genealogical Society. (Reprinted from the *New England Historical and Genealogical Register,* vols. 64–65.)

Livingston, V. P. 1969. Some peculiarities of genealogical research in Virginia. Paper read at the World Conference on Records, Salt Lake City, Utah.

Ljungstedt, M. ed. 1972. *The county court notebook and ancestral proofs and probabilities.* Baltimore: Genealogical Publishing Co.

MacKenzie, G. N. 1907–20. *Colonial families of the United States of America.* 7 vols. Baltimore: Seaforth Press.

McAuslan, W. A. 1932. *Mayflower index.* 2 vols. Boston: The General Society of Mayflower Descendants.

McMullin, P. W. ed. 1972. *Grassroots of America: computerized index to the American state papers; land grants and claims 1789–1837.* Salt Lake City: Gendex Corp.

Maine Historical Society. 1928. *Province and court records of Maine.* Vol. 1. Portland: Maine Historical Society.

Martyn, W. C. 1867. *The Pilgrim Fathers of New England: a history.* New York: The American Tract Society.

Maryland Department of General Services. 1972. *Bulletin No. 17: a guide to the index holdings at the Hall of Records.* Annapolis: State of Maryland Department of General Services.

Merk, F. 1978. *History of the westward movement.* New York: Alfred A. Knopf.

Miller, J. C. 1966. *The first frontier: life in colonial America.* New York: Dell Publishing Co.

Miller, O. K. 1974. *Migration, emigration, immigration: principally to the United States and in the United States.* Logan, Utah: Everton Publishers.

______. 1978. *Genealogical research for Czech and Slovak Americans.* Detroit: Gale Research Co.

Moore, R. F. 1961. *The family history book: a genealogical record.* New York: Simmons-Boardman Publishing Corp.

Morris, J. W., et al. 1976. *Historical atlas of Oklahoma.* 2d ed. Norman: University of Oklahoma Press.

Morris, L. E. B. 1965. *Primer in genealogical research.* Dallas, Tex.: B. and W. Printing and Letter Service.

Munden, J. W., and Beers, H. P. 1962. *Guide to Federal Archives relating to the Civil War.* Washington, D.C.: National Archives and Records Service, General Services Administration.

Munsell's Sons. 1895. *Index to American genealogies and to genealogical material contained in all works, such as town histories, county histories, local histories, historical society publications, biographies, historical periodicals, and kindred works.* 4th ed. Albany: Joel Munsell's Sons.

______. 1899. *List of titles of genealogical articles in American periodicals and kindred works.* Albany: Joel Munsell's Sons.

______. 1900. *Index to American genealogies: and to genealogical material contained in all works such as town histories, county histories, local histories, historical society publications, biographies, historical periodicals and kindred works.* 5th ed. Albany: Joel Munsell's Sons.

______. 1900. *The American genealogist, being a catalogue of family histories: a bibliography of American genealogy or a list of the title pages of books and pamphlets on family history, published in America from 1771 to date.* 5th ed. Albany: Joel Munsell's Sons.

______. 1908. *Supplement 1900–08 to the index to genealogies published in 1900.* Albany: Joel Munsell's Sons.

______. 1968. *American ancestry.* 12 vols. Baltimore: Genealogical Publishing Co.

Myers, A. C. 1969. *Quaker arrivals at Philadelphia 1682–1750.* Baltimore: Genealogical Publishing Co.

National Cyclopaedia of American Biography. Being the history of the United States as illustrated in the lives of the founders, builders, and defenders of the republic, and of the men and women who are doing the work and moulding the thought of the present time. 1898–1979. 58 vols. New York: James T. White and Co.

New Jersey Department of Education, State Library, Archives and History Bureau. 1966. *Genealogical research: a guide to source materials in the Archives and History Bureau.* Trenton: New Jersey State Library.

Nichols, E. L. 1979. Statewide civil vital registration in the United States. *Utah Genealogical Journal* (Sept.) 8:135–58.

Nicholson, C. 1965. *Some early emigrants to America.* Baltimore: Genealogical Publishing Co.

North Carolina Department of Cultural Resources, Division of Archives and History, Archives and Records Section. 1978. *Guide to research materials in the North Carolina State Archives: Section B: County records.* 6th rev. ed. Raleigh: Department of Cultural Resources.

Norton, J. S. 1973. *New Jersey in 1793: an abstract and index to the 1793 militia census of the state of New Jersey.* Salt Lake City: J. S. Norton.

Noyes, S.; Libby, C. T.; and Davis, W. G. 1928–39. *Genealogical dictionary of Maine and New Hampshire.* Portland, Me.: The Southworth-Anthoensen Press.

Nugent, N. M. 1963. *Cavaliers and pioneers: abstracts of Virginia land patents and grants 1623–66.* Introduction by Robert Armistead Stewart. Reprint. Baltimore: Genealogical Publishing Co.

———. 1977. *Cavaliers and pioneers: abstracts of Virginia land patents and grants, vol 2: 1666–95.* Indexed by Claudia B. Grundman. Richmond: Virginia State Library.

Olmstead, C. E. 1961. *Religion in America, past and present.* Englewood Cliffs, N.J.: Prentice-Hall.

Palmer, S. J. ed. 1972. *Studies in Asian genealogy.* Provo, Utah: Brigham Young University Press.

Paquette, P. 1915a. Letter dated 30 June 1915 from Navajo Indian Agency, Ft. Defiance, Arizona, to the Commissioner of Indian Affairs, Washington, D.C.

———. 1915b. Report dated 26 December 1915 from Navajo Indian Agency, Ft. Defiance, Arizona, to the Commissioner of Indian Affairs, Washington, D.C.

Parker, D. D. 1944. *Local history: how to gather it, write it, and publish it.* Revised and edited by Bertha E. Josephson for the Committee on Guide for Study of Local History of the Social Science Research Council. New York: Social Science Research Council.

Passano, E. P. 1967. *An index of the source records of Maryland: genealogical, biographical, historical.* Reprint. Baltimore: Genealogical Publishing Co.

Peskett, H. 1978. *Discover your ancestors.* New York: Arco Publishing Co.

Peterson, C. S. 1963. *Consolidated bibliography of county histories in fifty states in 1961.* 2d ed. Baltimore: Genealogical Publishing Co.

Pine, L. G. 1967. *American origins.* Baltimore: Genealogical Publishing Co.

———. 1969. *The genealogist's encyclopedia.* Newton-Abbot: David and Charles.

Potter, G. 1960. *The golden door: the story of the Irish in Ireland and America.* Westport, Conn.: Greenwood Press.

Powell, S. C. 1965. *Puritan village: the formation of a New England town.* Garden City, New York: Doubleday and Co.

Powell, W. H. 1967. *List of officers of the Army of the United States from 1779–1900.* Detroit: Gale Research Co.

Putnam, E. 1964. *Two early passenger lists, 1635–37.* Baltimore: Genealogical Publishing Co.

Ray, W. S. 1950. *Tennessee cousins: a history of Tennessee people.* Austin, Tex.: W. S. Ray.

_______. 1956. *Index and digest to Hathaway's North Carolina historical and genealogical register, with genealogical notes and notations.* Baltimore: Genealogical Publishing Co.

_______. 1962. *The Mecklenburg signers and their neighbors.* Reprint. Baltimore: Genealogical Publishing Co.

Reed, E. L. 1947. *Ways and means of identifying ancestors.* Chicago: Ancestral Publishing and Supply Co.

Revill, J. 1968. *A compilation of the original lists of Protestant immigrants to South Carolina, 1763–73.* Baltimore: Genealogical Publishing Co.

Rhodes, J. A. 1960. *A short history of Ohio land grants.* Columbus: F. J. Heer Co.

Rider, F. ed. 1952–53. *American genealogical index.* 48 vols. Middletown, Conn.: The Godfrey Memorial Library.

_______. 1952–80. *American genealogical-biographical index to American genealogical, biographical and local history materials.* 113 volumes in 1980 ("A through McDavel"). Middletown, Conn.: Godfrey Memorial Library.

Robinson, C. 1848. *Early voyages to America.* Richmond: Sheperd and Colin.

Robinson, F. 1848. *An account of the organization of the United States Army.* 2 vols. Philadelphia: E. H. Butler and Co.

Rollings, V. H. 1975. *Instruction to help beginners in genealogical research.* Rev. ed. Hampton, Va.: Thomas Nelson Community College.

Rosenberry, L. K. M. 1909. *The expansion of New England: the spread of New England settlements and institutions to the Mississippi River 1620–1865.* Boston: Houghton, Mifflin Co.

Rottenberg, D. 1977. *Finding our fathers.* New York: Random House.

Rouse, P. 1973. *The Great Wagon Road from Philadelphia to the South.* New York: McGraw-Hill Book Co.

Rubincam, M. ed. 1960. *Genealogical research methods and sources.* Washington, D.C.: American Society of Genealogists.

Ruoff, W. H. 1969. A century of emigration from the Palatinate to the United States of America-Switzerland. Paper read at the World Conference on Records, Salt Lake City, Utah.

Rupp, I. D. 1965. *A collection of upwards of thirty thousand names of German, Swiss, Dutch, French, and other immigrants into Pennsylvania from 1727 to 1776.* 2d ed. Baltimore: Genealogical Publishing Co.

Ryerson, A. E. 1880. *The Loyalists of America and their times from 1720 to 1816.* 2d ed. Toronto: W. Griggs.

Sabine, L. 1964. *Biographical sketches of Loyalists of the American Revolution, with an historical essay.* 2 vols. Boston: Little, Brown and Co.

Savage, J. 1965. *Genealogical dictionary of the first settlers of New England, showing three generations of those who came before May, 1692, on the basis of Farmer's register.* 4 vols. Reprint. Baltimore: Genealogical Publishing Co.

Schlegel, M. W. 1949. Writing local history articles. *Bulletin of the American Association for State and Local History* (May) 2:47–74.

Scott, F. D. ed. 1968. *World migration in modern times.* Englewood Cliffs, N.J.: Prentice-Hall.

Shepherd, S. 1968. *The statutes at large of Virginia: being a continuation of Hening's Statutes 1792–1806.* 3 vols. New York: AMS Press.

Sherman, C. E. 1925. *Original Ohio land subdivision, vol. 3.* Columbus: Ohio State Reformatory Press.

Sherwood, G. 1978. *American colonists in English records.* Baltimore: Genealogical Publishing Co.

Silving, H. 1948. *Immigration laws of the United States.* New York: Oceana Publication.

Simons, G. F. 1975. *Journal for life: discovering faith and values through journal keeping.* Chicago: Foundation for Adult Catechetical Teaching Aids.

Sirmans, M. E. 1966. *Colonial South Carolina: a political history 1663–1763.* Chapel Hill: University of North Carolina Press.

Slauson, A. B. 1901. *A check list of American newspapers in the Library of Congress.* Washington, D.C.: Government Printing Office.

Smallwood, G. T., Jr. 1969. Meet the genealogical societies; hereditary and lineage societies; introduction, general description, and brief history, American Revolution to the present. Paper read at the World Conference on Records, Salt Lake City, Utah.

Sperry, K. ed. 1978. *A survey of American genealogical periodicals and periodical indexes.* Detroit: Gale Research Co.

Standard, W. G. 1964. *Some emigrants to Virginia.* 2d ed. Baltimore: Genealogical Publishing Co.

Steel, D. J., and Taylor, L. 1973. *Family history in schools.* London: Phillimore and Co.

Stemmons, J. D. 1973. *The United States census compendium.* Logan, Utah: Everton Publishers.

Stephens, W. B. 1973. *Sources for English local history.* Manchester: Manchester University Press.

_______. 1977. *Teaching local history.* Manchester: Manchester University Press.

Stetina, J. 1884. Death notice. *St. Louis Post Dispatch* for 18 Nov. 1884.

Stevenson, N. C. 1958. *The genealogical reader.* Salt Lake City: Deseret Book Co.

_______. 1977. *Search and research.* Salt Lake City: Deseret Book Co.

_______. 1979. *Genealogical evidence: guide to the standard of proof relating to pedigrees, ancestry, heirship and family history.* Laguna Hills, Calif.: Aegean Press.

Stewart, R. A. 1970. *Index to printed Virginia genealogies.* Reprint. Baltimore: Genealogical Publishing Co.

Strassburger, R. B., and Hinke, W. J. eds. 1966. *Pennsylvania German pioneers: a publication of the original lists of arrivals in the port of Philadelphia from 1727 to 1808.* 2 vols. Baltimore: Genealogical Publishing Co.

Stryker-Rodda, H. 1977. *How to climb your family tree: genealogy for beginners.* Philadelphia: J. B. Lipincott Co.

Stryker-Rodda, K. ed. 1971. *Genealogical research, vol. 2.* Washington, D.C.: American Society of Genealogists.

Swem, E. G. 1965. *Virginia historical index.* 2 vols. Reprint. Gloucester,

Mass.: Peter Smith.

Toedteberg, E. 1935. *Catalogue of American genealogies in the library of the Long Island Historical Society.* Brooklyn: The Long Island Historical Society.

U.S. Department of Commerce, Bureau of the Census. 1841. *A census of pensioners for Revolutionary or military services: with their names, ages, and places of residence, as returned by the marshals of the several judicial districts, under the act for taking the sixth census.* Washington, D.C.: Printed by Blair and Rives.

———. 1908. *Heads of families at the first census of the United States taken in the year 1790: records of the state enumerations (Virginia) 1782–85.* Washington, D.C.: Government Printing Office.

———. 1909. *A century of population growth.* Washington, D.C.: Government Printing Office.

U.S. Government Printing Office. 1961. *Biographical directory of the American Congress 1774–1961: the Continental Congress September 5, 1774, to October 21, 1788, and the Congress of the United States from the First to the Eighty-sixth Congress March 4, 1789, to January 3, 1961, inclusive.* Washington, D.C.: Government Printing Office.

U.S. National Archives and Records Service, General Services Administration. 1953. *General pension index file 1861–1934.* Washington, D.C.: National Archives Microfilm Publications. RG 15 T288 pts. 1–544.

———. 1957. *Consolidated index to compiled service records of Confederate soldiers.* Washington, D.C.: National Archives Microfilm Publications. RG 94 M253 pts. 1–535.

———. 1959. *Mexican War index to pension files, 1887–1926.* Washington, D.C.: National Archives Microfilm Publications. RG 15 T317 pts. 1–14.

———. 1959. *Old Wars index to pension files, 1815–1926.* Washington, D.C.: National Archives Microfilm Publication. RG 15 T316 pts. 1–7.

———. 1960. *Index to War of 1812 pension application files.* Washington, D.C.: National Archives Microfilm Publications. RG 15 M313 pts. 1–102.

———. 1963. *Registers of enlistments in the United States Army 1798–1877.* Washington, D.C.: National Archives Microfilm Publications. (LDS Genealogical Library film numbers 350307 through 350350)

———. 1964. *Indian census rolls 1885–1940.* Washington, D.C.: National Archives Microfilm Publications. RG 75 M595 pts. 1–692. (LDS Genealogical Library film numbers 573847 through 583089)

———. 1970. *Pension files, service records, land warrants, 1775–1913.* Washington, D.C.: National Archives Microfilm Publications. (LDS Genealogical Library film numbers 833170 through 833175 and 833308 through 833313)

———. 1971. *Indian Wars index to pension files, 1892–1926.* Washington, D.C.: National Archives Microfilm Publications. RG 15 T318 pts. 1–12. (LDS Genealogical Library film numbers 821610 through 821621)

______. 1975. *Revolutionary war and bounty land warrant files microfilmed at the National Archives for the Bicentennial Celebration, 1976.* Washington, D.C.: National Archives Microfilm Publications. (LDS Genealogical Library film numbers 970001 through 972669 "A–Z")

______. 1977. *Information Leaflet No. 7.* Washington, D.C.: Government Printing Office.

U.S. Public Land Commission. 1880. *The public domain: its history with statistics.* Washington, D.C.: Government Printing Office.

U.S. War Department. 1865. *Official army register of the volunteer force of the United States Army for the years 1861–65.* 8 vols. Washington, D.C.: Government Printing Office.

______. 1868. *Alphabetical index to places of interment of deceased Union soldiers.* Washington, D.C.: Memorial Division, Quartermaster General's Office.

______. 1871. *Roll of Honor 1865–71.* Washington, D.C.: The Quartermaster General's Office.

______. 1880. *The War of the Rebellion: a compilation of the official records of the Union and Confederate armies.* 68 vols. Washington, D.C.: Government Printing Office.

______. 1900. *Official register of officers of volunteers 1899–1900 in the service of the United States.* Washington, D.C.: Government Printing Office.

______. 1942. *Army list and directory.* Washington, D.C.: Government Printing Office.

Vallentine, J. F. 1963. *Handbook for genealogical correspondence.* Salt Lake City: Bookcraft.

Virginia Historical Society. 1936. *Documents relating to the Huguenot emigration to Virginia.* Richmond: The Virginia Historical Society.

Virginia, State of. 1852. *Muster rolls of the Virginia militia in the War of 1812: being a supplement to pay rolls.* Richmond: The State of Virginia.

______. 1852. *Pay rolls of the Virginia militia entitled to land bounty under the Act of Congress of September 28, 1850.* Richmond: The State of Virginia.

Virginia State Library. 1973. *Genealogical research in the Virginia State Library.* Richmond: Virginia State Library.

Virkus, F. A. 1925–43. *The abridged compendium of American genealogy; first families of America: a genealogical encyclopedia of the United States.* 7 vols. Chicago: A. N. Marquis and Co.

______. 1963. *Immigrant ancestors: a list of 2500 immigrants to America before 1750.* Baltimore: Genealogical Publishing Co.

Wagner, A. 1961. *English ancestry.* London: Oxford University Press.

Walker, J. D. 1969. U.S. military service and pension records housed at the National Archives. Paper read at the World Conference on Records, Salt Lake City, Utah.

Wallace, W. S. 1920. *The United Empire Loyalists: a chronicle of the great migration.* Toronto: Brook and Co.

Watts, J., and Davis, A. F. 1974. *Generations: your family in modern American history.* New York: Alfred A. Knopf.

Weis, F. L. 1936. *The colonial clergy and the colonial churches of New*

England. Lancaster, Mass.: Society of the Descendants of the Colonial Clergy.

Weitzman, D. 1976. *Underfoot: an everyday guide to exploring the American past.* New York: Charles Scribner's Sons.

Westcott, T. 1965. *Names of persons who took the oath of allegiance to the State of Pennsylvania between the years 1777 and 1789, with a history of the test laws of Pennsylvania.* Baltimore: Genealogical Publishing Co.

Westin, J. E. 1977. *Finding your roots: how every American can trace his ancestors, at home and abroad.* New ed. Los Angeles: J. P. Tarcher Co.

White, J. T., and Lesser, C. H. eds. 1977. *Fighters for independence: a guide to sources of biographical information on soldiers and sailors of the American Revolution.* Chicago: University of Chicago Press.

Whittemore, H. 1967. *Genealogical guide to the early settlers of America, with a brief history of those of the first generation, and reference to the various local histories and other sources of information where additional data may be found.* Reprint. Baltimore: Genealogical Publishing Co.

Who's Who in America: a biographical dictionary of notable living men and women. 1899 to present. Revised and reissued biennially. Chicago: A. N. Marquis Co.

Williams, E. W. 1960. *Know your ancestors: a guide to genealogical research.* Rutland, Vt.: Charles E. Tuttle Co.

Wilson, J. G., and Fiske, J. eds. 1887–97. *Appletons' cyclopaedia of American biography.* 11 vols. New York: D. Appleton and Co.

Wilson, S. M. 1924. *Catalogue of Revolutionary soldiers and sailors of the Commonwealth of Virginia to whom land bounty warrants were granted by Virginia for military service in the War for Independence.* Frankfort: Kentucky State Land Office.

Winfree, W. K. 1971. *The laws of Virginia: being a supplement to Hening's Statutes at Large 1700–1750.* Richmond: Virginia State Library.

Wright, N. E. 1968. *Genealogy in America: Massachusetts, Connecticut, and Maine, vol. 1.* Salt Lake City: Deseret Book Co.

_______. 1968a. *North American genealogical sources: Middle Atlantic States and Canada.* Provo, Utah: Brigham Young University Press.

_______. 1968b. *North American genealogical sources: Midwestern States.* Provo, Utah: Brigham Young University Press.

_______. 1968c. *North American genealogical sources: Southern States.* Provo, Utah: Brigham Young University Press.

_______. 1968d. *North American genealogical sources: Southwestern States.* Provo, Utah: Brigham Young University Press.

_______. 1969. *Pioneers on the move: the migrations within North America.* Paper read at the World Conference on Records, Salt Lake City, Utah.

_______. 1973. *Genealogical reader, Northeastern United States and Canada: supplement to Independent Study Course 311x.* Provo, Utah: Brigham Young University, Department of Home Study, Division of Continuing Education.

_______. 1974. *Building an American pedigree.* Provo, Utah: Brigham

Young University Press.
Wright, N. E., and Pratt, D. H. 1967a. *Genealogical research essentials.* Salt Lake City: Bookcraft.
———. 1967b. *Key to migration sources, Great Britain and North America: a manual for students attending the second annual Priesthood Genealogical Research Seminar.* Provo, Utah: Brigham Young University Press.
Younkin, C. G. 1969. Historical and genealogical records of the Five Civilized Tribes and other Indian records. Paper read at the World Conference on Records, Salt Lake City, Utah.
Zabriskie, G. O. 1969. *Climbing our family tree systematically.* Salt Lake City: Parliament Press.

Index